Women, International Development, and Politics

In the series

Women in the Political Economy,

edited by Ronnie J. Steinberg

Women, International Development, and Politics

The Bureaucratic Mire

Updated and Expanded Edition

Edited by
Kathleen Staudt

Temple University Press
Philadelphia

To Asha

Temple University Press, Philadelphia 19122
Copyright © 1990,1997 by Temple University. All rights reserved
Published 1997
Printed in the United States of America

∞ The paper used in the publication meets the requirements
of the American National Standard for Information
Sciences—Permanence of Paper for Printed Library Materials,
ANSI Z39.48—1984

Library of Congress Cataloging-in-Publication Data
Women, international development, and politics : the bureaucratic mire : updated
and expanded edition / edited by Kathleen Staudt.
        p.   cm.—(Women in the political economy)
     ISBN 1-56639-546-1 (paper)
     1. Women in development.   2. Women—Government policy.   3. Women
in politics.   I. Staudt, Kathleen A.   II. Series
HQ1240.W662   1997   97-3227
305.42—dc21   CIP

Contents

Preface to the 1997 Edition

Seven years have passed since the first edition of this book was published. Women's organizations continue to blossom, amid the heavy burdens of structural adjustment and the so-called *transitions to democracy* that leave little space for women and notions of democracy that expand into homes and workplaces. Yet non-governmental organizations (NGOs) continue to expand the public policy agenda, both confronting and nudging at governments, international development organizations, and the people that staff bureaucracies in those institutions.

Why have NGOs flourished and policy agendas expanded? The Fourth World Conference on Women, under United Nations auspices, is one important reason among many. Actually several United Nations-affiliated international meetings in the early 1990s established strong connections to women and gender-fair agendas, including those on the environment (1992), human rights (1993), social development (1995), and most importantly, population and development, held in Cairo (1994). Beijing, however, was a threshold. The *UN Chronicle* of December 1995 estimates that 50,000 people attended, one of the largest U.N. conferences ever. Among attendees, one could count government representatives, NGO members, and ordinary people. And despite impressions left among those limited to the U.S. media, far more action occurred than Hillary Clinton's speech on human rights abuses in China.

Beijing elevated and deepened the global women's agenda, mobilizing organizations and bureaucratic institutions to prepare for and, subsequently, to act at levels heretofore unknown. The updated and expanded edition of this book acknowledges and celebrates this new reality with its contributions.

The contributions in this volume offer continuing, timely, and classic analyses and insights about transformative gender struggles both inside and outside bureaucracies. Institutions and those who staff or lead them have changed, altering the context somewhat. Let us consider just a few of the

vii

chapters in the first and second editions of this volume. The official space that women occupied in Nicaragua (Chapter 11, "Tough Row to How") and Brazil (Chapter 3, "Contradictions of a 'Women's Space'") narrowed in some particular forms, but widened in others. Amazingly, staff from the women's project in Nicaragua's CIERA continued working a year after anti-Sandinista conservative Violeta Chamorro became President (but the project functioned for only a year more—not all women prioritize equality.) By law in Brazil women must now occupy a fifth of local government councils, opening new space for dialogue and struggle. The Women's Center leader's tragic death in northern Mexico (Chapter 4, "Hierarchy and Class") has not ended NGO work for women; her daughter continues, complemented by health, community development, and other self-proclaimed feminist organizations.

Despite the depth of NGO activity and the breadth of policy agendas, bureaucratic obstacles are still with us. However, in two new chapters and elaborations in a new co-authored closing chapter, analysts reveal how the post-Beijing era radiates new hopes for emerging from a mire sooner rather than later in the twenty-first century. In fact, the closing chapter addresses not a post-Beijing bureaucratic *mire,* but a post-Beijing bureaucratic *roadmap* out of the mire.

The new closing chapter features analyses of some of the new research and political action that has emerged since 1990. Comparative research grows in both the academic and the institutional-practitioner worlds, each pursuing venues that only occasionally overlap. *Bridging* that gap should be part of the global agenda. It is therefore fitting that Sally Baden and Anne Marie Goetz, who co-author the new lead chapter following the introduction, should be affiliated with BRIDGE, housed at the Institute for Development Studies. They take on the language issues so contested at Beijing: sex and gender. In the Draft Platform of Action, over a third of the words were in brackets, denoting the need for further negotiation among governments. Gender brackets figured prominently in these struggles. We are grateful to *Feminist Review* for their permission to reprint the Baden and Goetz article from issue 56, June 1997.

In another new chapter Rounaq Jahan compares four bureaucratic institutions and traces their rhetoric and procedures to action and responsiveness to women's movements. Jahan documents how forward-looking bilateral agencies, themselves embedded in publicly accountable democracies, have allocated as much as a fifth of spending on women. This is still far from balance. Her chapter offers a roadmap for thinking about strategies to foster and to deepen institutional transformation.

The post-Beijing hope rests on several active political commitments. One commitment is to engage governments and bureaucracies in more fundamental ways. Another commitment is to sustain partnerships with ever-expanding allies who use policy to connect gender to virtually every principle and issue discussed in international and national arenas. This volume represents yet another commitment to sustain some important bridges of engagement and partnership, connecting academia and classrooms with the entire global process.

Preface to the 1990 Edition

We live in a world of obscene inequalities and looming crises associated with international development strategies. Yet enormous possibilities also exist for transforming inequalities and responding to people's needs. In this volume, we examine problems of development ideology and institutions, particularly their gendered quality and the bureaucratic mire in which seemingly progressive programs and policies become stuck.

Policy rhetoric may not be real, for policies are routinely ignored, contradicted, and distorted in bureaucracies. Bureaucratic politics can make or break programs, and analysts and activists who ignore the bureaucracy do so at their peril. What is amazing about the growing literature on women and politics is the lingering silence on bureaucratic politics. While analyses of legislatures, parties, movements, and policies are crucial, the picture is incomplete without attention to bureaucratic politics and implementation.

Bureaucracies—relatively closed institutions, but complex and fascinating—are Orwellian bastions in more ways than one. The language of bureaucracy is dense, sometimes deceptive. Often, only insiders have detailed knowledge of the discourse and strategy therein. Insiders who reveal the process to outsiders pose risks to themselves and their issues; exposure also explodes the myth of neutrality that pervades bureaucracy.

I am grateful to the contributors in this volume for their foresight in choosing to analyze gender in bureaucratic process. They bring expertise, keen analytic minds, and commitment to this transformative project, both in intellectual and applied senses. Not unimportant to an editor, they followed up on queries and responded to deadlines in a timely, substantive way. Insiders, particularly, used precious time, something that always seems to be in short supply to those working on gender issues in chronically understaffed and underfunded efforts. I also give thanks for permission to use versions of previously published work in this volume to the Institute for Food and Development Policy, also known as Food First; to the African Studies Association's *Issue: A Journal of Opinion;* to the Michigan State University

Women in International Development paper series; and to *International Family Planning Perspectives*.

Most contributors to this volume look to the day when public institutions, spending, and staff will be accountable to women as well as to men. They analyze bureaucratic institutions in which such accountability is present in different degrees. Thus, they examine institutions *in transition*. How can accountability to women begin? Through what political processes can it move beyond symbolism into some real redistribution of values and resources? What conditions facilitate the transformation of organizational culture and of gender relations in the larger society?

I have long been interested in the politics of development institutions, aiming to combine the analytic skills of a social scientist with the eye of an anthropologist. Fifteen years ago, I studied the inequitable distribution of agricultural services and credit to men and women farmers in western Kenya. After teaching several years, I was "exchanged" under the Intergovernmental Personnel Act to work inside the U.S. Agency for International Development for a year. Then and now, I participate in the fortune and fate of women's studies in university politics. The parallel to women's programs in government agencies, women's studies programs have been far better documented.

I am grateful to various people who helped my thinking in these different intellectual journeys. Norman Uphoff, Lenny Markovitz, and Jane Parpart encouraged comparative analysis beyond Kenya. At AID's Office of Women in Development, Coordinator Arvonne Fraser and Deputy Coordinators Elsa Chaney and Paula Goddard were inspiring and gifted leaders in the complex world of AID's internal and external constituency politics. Throughout all, my friends and intellectual collaborators, Jane Jaquette, Sandy McGee-Deutsch, and Gay Young, have sustained and supported me.

Beyond colleagues and friends, my husband, Robert Dane'el, son, Mosi, and daughter, Asha, enrich my life. Together we work on another important transformative project: the family.

Introduction

1/Gender Politics in Bureaucracy: Theoretical Issues in Comparative Perspective

Kathleen Staudt

Over the international decade for women, 1975–1985, there were many dialogues, lobbying activities, legislative and policy mandates, yet barely a dent was made in the redistribution of resources and values from men to women. The oft-quoted statement from the 1980 Copenhagen Programme of Action starkly summarizes how one-half the world's population performs two-thirds of the world's work, receives one-tenth of world income, and owns less than 1 percent of world property.[1] At least at the aggregate level, little progress has been made in dismantling institutionalized male privilege. Such institutionalized privilege is deeply embedded in the state[2] and grounded in a western cultural heritage[3] that has spread throughout the world in different degrees. Prospects for redistributive change look grim.

At the same time, changes over the past century would appear to set the stage for gradual redistribution. First, states seek to legitimize themselves through public policy and participation-based accountability. State policies intrude, for better or worse, into a so-called private sphere in which women are located. Participation expands to include women as voters, group advocates, and decision makers.[4]

Second, a veritable explosion of women's organizational activity and political agenda setting transpired over the women's decade. Many activists hope to take a concrete feminist agenda into the bureaucracy and thereby broaden state accountability to women. Over the decade, what the United Nations terms "national machineries" for the advancement of women have

For reading and commenting on this chapter, I thank Judith Bruce, Jane Jaquette, Bonnie Shepard, Gay Young, and the reviewers associated with Temple University Press.

been promoted, such that 120 were counted by 1980[5] and 90 percent of governments were covered by 1985.[6] If the aim is to get a female foot in the door and work from within, a better understanding is needed of what approaches work best in which settings. More than one-half of the resolutions of *Forward Looking Strategies,* from the 1985 end-of-the-decade conference in Nairobi, call for action from governments, ranging from equalizing access to education and removing stereotypes from the media to providing credit and land ownership to women farmers.[7] Yet these are the very same governments that have heretofore perpetuated the kind of gendered policies that disempower women within gendered bureaucratic organizations. Should women work in, with, or against the state? Can state bureaucracies empower women?

States respond to calls for gender redistribution in varying ways; comparisons of institutions, their cultural, political, and economic contexts, and their inhabitants' prevailing ideologies should tell us why. Contributors in this book explore women's politics and programs in the bureaucracy, as well as the implementation processes. At minimum, this exploration leads to a focus on both attitudes and structures: the bureaucrats and their ideologies of gender and of household relations, and their interactions with the institutional settings in which they work. We need to know more about men who dominate decision making in the bureaucracy and how they vary in diverse institutional settings.

At the same time, we need to ask whether women will infuse a new sort of politics into male-oriented bureaucracy. Women have entered the realms of bureaucratic politics, and women's organizations increasingly form part of bureaucratic constituencies. Will women's very presence on the inside help women on the outside? Will women encourage bureaucracy to operate according to its Weberian "ideal" fashion, that is, in a neutral or gender-neutral fashion? (And is that a "good"?) Or does the hierarchical ordering of dominant-subordinate relationships in bureaucracy mire any prospects for gender redistribution? Some feminist theorists have argued that bureaucratic means are incompatible with feminist ends[8] and that the male-oriented state cannot accommodate or respond to women.[9]

This book takes the first step toward comparative analysis of gender redistributive policy by looking at its practices in international, governmental, and nongovernmental institutions in a wide variety of national and cultural contexts. This introductory essay examines the existing literature on bureaucratic movement toward gender redistribution, which suggests a grim scenario for upcoming decades. A discussion of "gendered bureaucracy" is then put forward to frame and explain the phenomenon in political terms. After that, the chapter explores possibilities for change. The closing contains an overview of the papers in the book, though discussion of their contents is woven into the body of this essay as well. First, however, the connections between gender, development, and the state are laid out.

Women, Development Crisis, and State Bureaucracy

Women had little or no hand in the process of state formation and consolidation. Yet male control over women—specifically, their labor, sexuality, and reproduction—was central to laws and policies that governed the gender realm. In some cases male household authority was reproduced in collective male authority, whereas in others the structure of that collective male authority was transferred through colonialism. These legacies of male preference prompt a corresponding need for gender redistribution: in the allocation of public resources, in civic and participation rights, in positions of power and authority, in the value of men's and women's work. Such legacies transcend both the capitalist and socialist economic systems in which people work.[10] The historical foundations of state formation should forewarn that affirmative action or gender staff-balancing approaches are limited solutions. Bureaucrats act in institutional and political contexts that are more often reproduced than transformed. Such historical legacies also forewarn the likely contradictions that arise in the transitional process toward transformation.

Bureaucrats are responsible for an enormous number of tasks associated with this loose and loaded term *development,* ranging from education, family planning, and health to agricultural surplus generation, industrialization, and capital accumulation. Whether by choice or by default, states assume a lead role in aggregating the resources and hiring the technical expertise to help plan, regulate, or manage the development process—to the extent state capacity and popular acceptability permit. In many parts of Latin America, Asia, and Africa, states are the key employers. Yet capital and technical resources are often in short supply, so states look to official bilateral and multilateral agencies such as the World Bank and the International Monetary Fund (IMF), and to private voluntary organizations (PVOs) and banks. In so doing, they incur various costs or conditions, ranging from, most obviously, interest on loans to policy reform, expatriate personnel, external agency or PVO priorities, and other ideological baggage.

In the eyes of many, major state investments in economic and social development are necessary: to ensure political stability; to provide access to food, health, and education; and to sustain the kind of economic growth that supplies people with means to assure their livelihoods. Yet such investments are made in ways that allocate neither opportunities nor resources in an even manner. Urban bias has long been documented by development studies, and some of the newly industrializing countries contain the widest gaps between rich and poor. Inequitable patterns within nations are overlaid by the contrasts among states in food/caloric availability, the wastage of life (expressed in life expectancy and infant mortality figures), per capita income, and vulnerable dependence associated with commodities offered in the world market.[11]

The gender dimensions of these stark contrasts can and must be illuminated further, for as the DAWN (Development Alternatives with Women for a New Era) international network concludes, women constitute "the majority of the poor, the underemployed, and the economically and socially disadvantaged in most societies."[12] Numerous academic studies, U.N. reports, and even official documents demonstrate the many inequitable gaps between men and women: in wages and job opportunities; in literacy and education; in adequate health care as evidenced by high maternal and infant mortality rates and intrusive family planning efforts; in extensive and arduous unpaid work in water and firewood collection and agricultural production; in control over land; and in political voice.[13]

In much of the early literature on women and development, analysts outlined the negative effects of development on women: it displaces their labor, strips them of past rights, and entrenches legal male control over women both in the family and the state. Such generalizations have now been modified with greater recognition of and attention to national historical specificity, mixed gains for women (such as *absolute* increases in life expectancy and literacy), indigenous cultural sources of subordination, and contradictory patterns. As an example of the last, Susan Joekes concludes that women's participation in the industrial labor force has expanded—to the extent that they constitute a majority of the manufacturing labor force in high export-oriented industrializing economies—but in the context of the vagaries of international trade and of the insecure but "feminized" garments and electronics industries.[14] Women and men experience the development process in different ways, ways that hardly empower women. Obviously, female subordination has not disappeared in the advanced or postindustrial economies. As the geographers Joni Seager and Ann Olson remark, "In the world of women there are few 'developed' nations."[15]

Whatever the nation-state, such gender gaps aggravate bureaucrats' efforts to develop economies and supply human services. According to U.N. reports, women are the majority of farmers in Africa, providing well over half the labor; in Asia and Latin America their contributions are also extensive. In many parts of the world women haul water and firewood to homes. Women labor in both the informal and formal economic sectors as traders, vendors, and factory laborers. Their income is crucial to household maintenance even in households other than the sizable number headed by females.[16] Whatever the development sector, women are central. Were bureaucracies to "integrate" women, an overall effect would be that by permitting them to better realize bureaucratic goals, women would empower bureaucrats rather than vice versa. Key, therefore, is the kind of voice women have—collectively or individually—in determining development or program strategies that meet their needs.

How would women fare under a supposed "free" market, avoiding bureaucracy altogether? The feminist critique of women in the modernization process actually emerged under capitalist market conditions, without bureaucratic attention to women's programs. Women's work in agriculture, informal trade, and reproduction is often unpaid and invisible. Women's responsibilities limit their "freedom" to seize opportunities, and gender ideologies color the supposed neutral hand of the market. Women generally figure prominently at the lower ends of market-generated class inequalities.[17] Thus, even their self-help efforts would draw on limited resources. The decade of the 1980s has seen an assault on state bureaucracy from academic, popular, and policy quarters. Even market-oriented development strategies occur in political and bureaucratic contexts. Rarely do gender researchers make specific policy recommendations.[18] Some radical theorists are reluctant to taint solutions within the existing political-economic establishment; instead, the obligatory call for revolutionary transformation is sounded for this or future lifetimes.

Are socialist economies any different? The dislocating effects of revolution along with the emancipatory proclamations of official ideology would appear to provide the kind of conditions under which gender redistribution could occur and occur quickly. Yet socialist societies, in pursuing the widened political agenda associated with wealth redistribution and social program expansion, usually enlarge the bureaucracy. Often, too, they rely on some of the very same personnel that "manned" the bureaucracy before revolution. In short, the questions posed about gendered bureaucracy and women's possible empowerment are perhaps even more relevant under socialism.

For better or worse, bureaucracies are with us for our lifetimes and probably for many generations to follow. Feminist strategies to avoid bureaucracy and mainstream policies have not long sustained themselves, and the absence of feminist voice may prolong a public status quo that is antithetical to female empowerment. Those opting to work in the mainstream, however, encounter deep resistance and face troubling ethical questions about where they invest their energies and the ends they thereby serve.

A Grim Scenario?

Great resistance has been faced by those working with women's programs in national and international agencies. Despite mandates—both internal to the agencies and from legislative authority—bureaucrats, operating in long-gendered bureaucracies, are reluctant to respond to women's work in its rich productive and reproductive dimensions. It is becoming increasingly clear that a key source of this problem is to be located in bureaucratic institutions and in the ideologies officials use as they act on gender issues.

The United Nations has long advocated that "machinery" be established to eliminate discrimination and to integrate women into the economic development process. Such machinery is of many types, including bureaus, ministries, commissions, committees or councils, political organs (such as a women's wing of the dominant political party), and nongovernmental organizations. Their tasks often involve data collection, project sponsorship, policy or program monitoring of other government agencies, and political mobilization.[19]

Despite great hope, this female machinery has accomplished little thus far. In an assessment of seventy-nine countries, machineries were found to be limited by small budgets and staff, by attitudes that legitimize female subordination, and by mandates that focus on welfare. Separate women's projects, a controversial mark of the decade that seemed to offer the beginnings of a compensatory approach to long years of male preference, rarely empowered women politically or economically. They were funded at miniscule levels, even as their importance was magnified in detractors' minds. Separate women's divisions and ministries are hard pressed to influence *all* of government. The obverse may occur as other agencies shift their responsibility for women onto the women's unit.[20] Such irresponsibility is also reproduced within agencies with a women's unit. Several contributors to this volume provide greater insight into the powerlessness of these units, for example, David Hirchmann on Malawi, or they elaborate further on the dynamics of women's bureaus: Nüket Kardam on the World Bank, where a women's unit operates uneasily amid technical units, and Barbara Lewis on the Cameroonian women's ministry's distance from its alleged constituents.

Also problematic, separate women's projects often contain a traditional social welfare focus that threatens no redistribution of economic resources and opportunities from men to women and, importantly, no conflict or confrontation in gender terms.[21] Perhaps even more troublesome politically, women's programs and projects create an appearance of activity, even if starved for funding and behind the closed doors of bureaucracy. Nice appearances placate constituents and incur political quiescence.[22] "Women's desks" in some countries are literally a desk and person charged with the responsibility to initiate women's projects and monitor the whole of government for responsiveness and accountability to women.

Many international development agencies have policies to "integrate" women ᴜs participants in their programs and projects. Yet progress here has been meager. For U.N. agencies, 3.5 percent of projects benefit women, representing 0.2 percent of budget allocations; less than 1 percent of FAO projects contain strategies to reach women. The $5 million budget of UNIFEM (formerly the U.N. Voluntary Fund for Women) is a drop in the bucket of its host, the U.N. Development Program, at $700 million. Barbara Rogers argues that agencies have actually damaged women by promoting female "domestication."[23] The U.S. Agency for International Development (AID), the chief U.S. bilateral assistance organization responsible for approximately $4 billion worth of annual transfers, moved little toward integrating women over the course of the decade. With a mandate from Congress in 1973, U.S. AID established an Office of Women in Development (WID) with an annual budget of one-third of a million dollars; at its high point it reached nearly $3 million. WID office advocates pursued internal bureaucratic politics to encourage the agency to include men and women equitably in development projects around the world but could document little concrete progress: no more than 4 percent of development funding went to women and development; one-tenth or less of the agricultural projects, a key sectorial emphasis, specified a women's component; and fewer than one-fifth of all international trainees were female.[24] In the less hierarchical, grassroots-oriented U.S. Peace Corps, with two-fifths of its volunteers female, women constituted about one-third of the recipients of volunteers' activity. Still, females—whether volunteers or recipients—were concentrated in programs that did not transfer marketable skills and resources.[25] The seemingly progressive Inter-American Foundation (IAF), which Sally W. Yudelman analyzes in her chapter, distributed a surprisingly limited amount of resources to women.

Given the overwhelming distribution of resources to men, the international infusion of new benefits may actually increase the gaps between men and women. Despite an impressive array of research generated over the decade, it would appear that most bureaucracies perpetuate programs based on conventional ideals of men as breadwinners and women as domestics rather than on a full appreciation that includes women's economic activities or potentials. Heavily bureaucratized societies sometimes appreciate women's economic potential with a kind of vengeance. Women in China seem weary of the productive and reproductive demands made of them.[26] We have few historic models for development policies that empower women.

Gendered Bureaucracy: Its Layers

Gender is a social construct that differentiates men and women in ways that become embedded and institutionalized in the political and bureaucratic authority of the state.[27] Women rarely have voice in conceptualizing such institutional forms. Although gender constructs change over time, the legacies of past constructs have been to direct property, income, public representation, and state benefits into the hands of husbands or fathers as household heads and to relate directly to women, if that is done at all, as reproducers and mothers. As socially defined biological beings, women are governed by the public framework but are not official actors in that framework or direct beneficiaries therefrom. With the extension of female political rights, dents were made in the institutionalized barriers, though the basic biological model was still functioning throughout the world. Men gained from these arrangements, both individually and collectively.

The prospect of female empowerment threatens male privilege, along with those women who have a stake in existing male privilege. That these *are* threats is manifested in reactions to women's programs, in decisions about budgets and staff, in decisions about priorities over public spending, and in processes by which decisions are made. Gender redistributive politics are as conflict-laden as any other redistributive issue but are subtle in the personalized resistance they incur and complex in their confusion with cross-sex interpersonal relations.[28] For redistribution to occur, advocates will probably need to ally with men who are either unthreatened by power sharing or supportive for ideological, professional, or technical reasons. Perhaps even more lethal for the prospects of women's program success in redistribution, though, are the historical foundations of institutionalized preference embedded in policy assumptions and standard operating procedures, which tend to change only incrementally. How do bureaucratic insurgents confront such "normal" operations?

Jill Conway, Susan Bourque, and Joan Scott remind us how recent it was in the social sciences that gender was not only assumed to be biological but also modern. Talcott Parsons, one of the chief adherents of this approach, believed that modernization had "brought about a rationalization in role allocation," that is, in "economic and sexual function" that "transcended class and national cultures."[29]

The absorption of this peculiar gender ideology into bilateral and multilateral assistance agencies, coupled with the invisibility of women's productive work that economic development disciplinary discourse entails, makes it appear professionally rational to direct resources and opportunities to men. This continues to occur, despite the elaborate detail of research on women's production, such as that cited by contributors Katherine Jensen for Egypt and Alice Carloni for cross-regional cases. The many interviews Kardam conducted with economists at the World Bank underline the intransigence of a discourse that renders women's work irrelevant to their mission. Moreover, the gendered states and bureaucracies worldwide make it convenient to use resources and opportunities according to these constructs. The result appears to be gendered bureaucratic resistance to women's programs.

This gendered reality is relevant at several different levels. The first, on which this collection is grounded, is that *bureaucratic outcomes*—the substance of what bureaucracies produce, provide, or control in the way of projects, programs, and policies—will tend to be gendered, but gendered according to the constructs that privilege men and subordinate women. Can a gendered bureaucratic approach, or as Sonia E. Alvarez terms it in her chapter, "gendered bureaucratic subversion," produce changes that lead toward outcomes that empower women? Most contributors to this volume share misgivings about the prospects for a gender-neutral bureaucratic approach amid the extensive and continuing gendered distribution of rewards, burdens, and opportunities in all societies.

Second, *institutions,* or the means by which gendered outcomes have heretofore been produced, are a key locus of the problems and their solutions. Are institutional hierarchies flat or steep? As Yudelman analyzes in her chapter, IAF's relatively flat, decentralized operation may actually increase women's invisibility to staff. Do structures provide for open, shared decision making with their clients and constituencies, or are decisions secret, made behind closed doors? Brazil's women's commission had healthy, if sometimes volatile, relationships with feminist constituencies, as Alvarez discusses in her chapter. Do they use, even generate, data that are relevant to problem solving? Do they learn from their mistakes, and are they held accountable for those mistakes? Many contributions suggest that mere tinkering with bureaucracy is no match to overhauling it to assure that technical units have incentives to include women. If women's programs exist within institutions, where are those programs located and what authority and resources do they control? Do women's programs pursue separate initiatives or aim to infuse their agendas into institutional operations? With what strategies?

Third are the *bureaucrats* who bring life to these institutions, their gender balance or lack of it, their ideologies, professional demeanor and discourse, their elitism or egalitarianism. Will more women inside bureaucracy empower women outside of it? More feminists, male or female? (And what sort of feminism is this?) Several chapters give reason for optimism that feminists, as staff and constituents, can make a difference, particularly when they coalesce their own with other activists' agendas. For example, Karin Himmelstrand's analysis of the Swedish International Development Authority (SIDA) shows how feminists in international donor agencies align with women who have strong interests in safe water in places like Kenya and Ethiopia. More grassroots developmentalists who seek to respond to the needs of people in their reproductive and productive dimensions? In their chapter, Judith Helzner and Bonnie Shepard discuss the merits of PVOs, usually characterized as operating at the grassroots. More responsive political appointees or protected civil servants? Women appointees, as contributors Lewis and Yudelman chillingly note in the cases of Cameroon and the IAF, do not necessarily serve women's interests.

Lurking over all is the troubling argument that bureaucratic forms, indeed hierarchies themselves, are so deadly a means that progressive ends become impossible. And bureaucratic hierarchies may be matched with constituency (even women's constituency) hierarchy. Are we to avoid action altogether, amid these murky conditions? What follows is an elaboration of these thoughts, drawing on analyses of statist institutions, the gender composition of staff, and bureaucratic political constituencies.

STATIST INSTITUTIONS

Rather than assume that bureaucratic officials and politicians respond to society—whether the dominant class, pressure groups, or individuals—statist approaches[30] focus our attention on public officials: Who are they? What are their values and ideologies? To what extent do those ideologies provide the bases for their behavior, bureaucratic policies, standard operating procedures, program operations, and new initiatives?

In a bureaucratic setting, ideally, inhabitants make decisions based on rational or principled grounds. Clearly, though, many decisions are personalistic and political. From many studies in political science and public administration, we know that diverse personality types inhabit the bureaucracy, with varying motivations and not predictably rational consequences for decision making.[31]

But people alone do not make up the state. Institutions are "political actors in their own right."[32] Whether, or how, bureaucrats translate their concerns into institutional practice depends on the amount of discretion they are accorded, the degree of autonomy of their bureaucratic home, and the nature of the state in which those bureaucracies form a part. Preliminary efforts to categorize states based on their degree of autonomy and amount of societal support have only just begun. Eric Nordlinger's typology consists of "strong," "independent," "responsive," and "weak" states.[33] A transcendent feature of states, so obvious that mainstream statist theorists analytically dismiss it, is men's overwhelming preponderance among state sustainers. Feminist theorists have now begun to grapple with the insights of a gendered analysis of state development and action.[34] Although men are overwhelmingly predominant in states built on gender constructs that institutionalize their interests, such conditions are neither inevitable nor without their internal contradictions. A basic question in this collection asks: under what conditions will women have voice in using the state and its bureaucracies to serve women's productive and reproductive interests?

Statist perspectives tend to reify state action, diverting attention from people's efforts to either embrace or disengage from the state or from indigenous ideologies.[35] State efforts to infuse new ideologies, whether benevolent or self-serving, confront indigenous forces to which they usually accommodate. Examples include polygyny and child marriage, ritual ceremonies that make women "beautiful" or "adults," and material transactions over women, such as bridewealth and dowry. In her discussion of the Chinese communists' retreat from promoting women's rights and family reform, Kay Johnson makes perhaps the case most strongly when she argues that the party accommodated itself to the male peasant constituency, "whose aspirations and sense of manhood were shaped by and tied to traditional patriarchal, patrilineal, familial-religious institutions and ideals." Local cadre (often recruited from among male kinship leaders) were complicit in punishing those who defied indigenous norms; the Ministry of Justice itself reported as many as 80,000 annual deaths, women "murdered or forced into suicide." Gender equality became an issue only when it related to other priorities, and party inaction came to haunt it with population control efforts of the last decade.[36] In Nicaragua, as the chapter by the Rural Women's Research Team indicates, the locus of gender struggle was within cooperatives themselves, though the law entitled women to inclusion. State officials merely facilitated or hindered attitude change and technical resource allocations. In her chapter Cathy Small argues that planning and bureaucracy are simply irrelevant, given long, sturdy patterns of gendered class accumulation in Tonga.

GENDER BALANCE IN GENDERED INSTITUTIONS

What's the likelihood that larger numbers of women in bureaucracy will make a difference? Are those women feminist, not only in terms of the *process* by which they interact with colleagues and constituents, but also in terms of the *substance* of their actions? Limited evidence indicates that a clinician's being female makes some difference in the delivery of family planning, though the hierarchical medical-patient mode can cloud that pattern.[37] In the view of the authors in this book, feminist work, to be substantive, would aim toward the redistribution of resources and values among men and women.

We know very little about the numbers of women in bureaucracy worldwide, much less the possibility that they hold some sort of feminist values. Elise Boulding estimates that women hold 6 percent of policy-making positions.[38] Although the United States and Europe represent a small fraction of the world's population, their state models, historically, were transplanted over far reaches of the globe through colonialism. In a comparison of six European countries, women were found to constitute less than 1 percent of all senior civil servants, a figure prompting the authors to remark that "being male is little short of a necessary condition for obtaining power."[39] In the United States, women hold 6 percent of moderately high and high posts; their proportions grow as the level of the hierarchy decreases.[40] Specialized agencies of the United Nations are similarly imbalanced, save the specialized commissions addressed to women and children and more recently the U.N. Development Program (UNDP).[41]

Of course, significant bureaucratic behavior and program operations are to be found not merely at the top of the hierarchy. Day-to-day bureaucratic operations do not necessarily mesh with official policy, and information about agency operations may be thereby sufficiently distorted that top officials, much less outsiders or constituents, know little of what is going on. At various times, World Bank presidents, including Barber Conable and Robert McNamara, FAO's Director-General Edouard Saouma, and U.S. AID administrators (who undergo considerable turnover, as political appointees) have publicly and strongly supported institutional resource allocations to women.[42] Though such assertions may sometimes be sops to appease institutional constituencies, they are often backed up in official internal policy and procedures. If agency staff members did the bidding of their directors, analyses like those in this book would be unnecessary.

As important as top-level policy are the significant on-the-spot "policy" decisions made at the middle and "street" levels by field personnel who often operate with considerable discretion—discretion that permits prejudices and ideologies to affect action. Such prejudices operate against the interests of ostensible clients in U.S. urban police and poverty programs and in U.S. AID field operations outside the United States.[43]

With women positioned in larger numbers at middle or lower levels in a bureaucratic environment who are receptive to or supportive of women's empowerment, we can envision for bureaucracy the possibilities of Carol Gilligan's analysis of women's "difference" from men—a difference perhaps born in the gender division of labor or in gendered socialization. Women seem to show a greater ethic of care, responsibility, and relatedness, in contrast to men's abstract disconnectedness and individualism.[44] Studies of U.S. women politicians in state and local government bear out some of this difference.[45] Women politicians are more likely to articulate a "women's agenda." But can analysts "Gilliganize" women throughout the world? Are women different in a way that can build or sustain both a difference in process and in outcome?

Rosabeth Kanter presents the provocative hypothesis that increasingly higher proportions of the "different"—whether women or ethnic minorities—will affect *process:* cross-group perceptions and relationships, prospects for group-relevant differences to emerge among the "different", and likelihoods of coalition building therefrom. A key question is whether such change results in different substance *and* outcome, or, to use the language of this chapter, a redistribution of resources and values between men and women in what bureaucracy produces, provides, and performs for the larger population. For Kanter, men and women are not intrinsically different, nor is gender socialization particularly relevant for job performance. What *does* differ is an opportunity structure that privileges white men. Once this opportunity structure is made open and fair, differences in work-related aspirations of men and women should disappear. A female bureaucrat will be free to aspire, compete, and perform in the way that is standard in the bureaucracy that engulfs her. "Normal" operations can thus continue, without confronting, touching, or disturbing the historically based institutionalization of male interests in these "men's institutions." In fact, studies of women who "make it" into management often show few gender differences in motivation and performance.[46] But how representative are these rare women of other women? They are far from reaching a critical numerical mass in management.

In the same way, can we universalize men's predispositions toward women? Nancy Chodorow locates men's negative attitudes and behaviors toward women in the separation-individualization period of preschool boys, behaviors that then become rigidified in their gender training. "A boy represses those qualities he takes to be feminine inside himself, and rejects and devalues women and whatever he considers to be feminine in the social world."[47] Chodorow's analysis is grounded in western industrial society—specifically, twentieth-century capitalism in the United States. Given the exaggerated role that the United States plays in international development decision making, both in its own assistance agencies and in training of decision makers from outside the United States, this analysis might provide insight into the psychoanalytic depths of male resistance to gender redistribution. Comparative management theorists like Geert Hofstede have operationalized differing degrees of "masculine culture," with the United States in the middle, and countries like Japan, Austria, Venezuela, and Italy labeled "high masculine."[48] Men's studies analysts stress themes to which boys and men are constantly subject, such as the need for men to be in control, to control others, to be aggressive, and to be breadwinners; men depend on women to make them feel powerful. Yet the majority of men are unable to be in control in a heavily bureaucratized, class-based society where their subordinate status "feminizes" them, says Kathy Ferguson.[49] Potentially confrontational politics about gender redistribution in bureaucracy would eliminate this pseudo-power for women. In studies from various countries, alterations in cross-sex behavioral patterns that upset male authority and female subordinate status—even if only symbolically or in artificial research settings—have been found to be profoundly troubling to men.[50]

To further complicate matters, how might women's potentially shared values be warped by other differences among them? A class agenda separating privileged women in government from others has been documented in numerous studies, worldwide.[51] David Hirschmann's chapter, on the gender divide in Malawian bureaucracy, predicts an impending class divide among women. Class divisions are problematic for women's agendas and women's organizations, as Gay Young analyzes conceptually and in the Mexico case. Overlapping that is the hierarchical and technical relationship between "expert" and "client."[52] Finally, nationality differentiates women, and it conditions their living standards and forms of feminism. In the world of development, interorganizational relations are *cross-national* relationships, with individuals exerting their own culturally distinct forms of bureaucratic support, resistance, or neglect. Such complexity makes for challenging work in U.N. organizations with their "geographic" (national) quotas. Jensen analyzes numerous interorganizational relationships both within the United States and between the United States and Egypt, relationships that complicate gendered agendas in exponential ways.

Would the presence of more feminists change such patterns? Institutional context constrains or enhances a bureaucrat's position. To illustrate, studies of "representative bureaucracy" in the United States conclude that bureaucratic transformation or increased group representation cannot be expected with the integration of the underrepresented, be they working class, female, or minorities.[53]

Perhaps a key question is: how many feminists? Rarely is there a "critical mass," to challenge or transform the whole institution, for only a handful of staff are responsible for women's programs. Kanter also analyzed the effects of skewed representation on the quality of the work climate for the minority of female representatives. Dominant group members usually view or treat minorities in stereotyped or distorted fashion, creating "performance pressures." Minorities are watched and judged not just (or even) for the merits of their work but for validation of the watchers' assumptions.[54]

What might this mean for feminists working in gendered bureaucracy that nevertheless prides itself as being neutral or fair? Feminists may be wary of showing their feminism. At AID, for example, WID advocates assiduously avoided the terminology for the scoffs and laughs it would bring and the resultant lower credibility and capability to make even minor changes. IAF staffers, in Yudelman's chapter, moaned about "women's libbers." UNIFEM, which supported women's projects over the decade, aims to reach global and national planners, but its "representatives are often 'brushed aside' as 'feminists'." To cope with hostile audiences, Ruth Engo argues that technicians need to emphasize development and not feminist issues.[55] As former head of AID's WID office, Arvonne Fraser stated succinctly: "If I am too much of a feminist, I lose credibility as a policymaker and manager. If I am not enough of a feminist, I lose credibility in my job, which is to help women overseas. I lose credibility with those outside, whom I need to do my job effectively."[56]

Feminists may bend so far backward to avoid conflict or even avoid criticism for being feminist that their efforts are ineffective or perpetuate female subordination. The Umoja Ya Wanawake Ya Tanzania (UWT, the women's wing of the political party) sponsored home economics, child care, and income-generating activities but never really confronted the core issue of gender subordination that grassroots women themselves articulated. Men control women's and household income, women do a disproportionate share of the work in subsistence agricultural production, and fundamental gender inequalities prevail. Both UWT and WID activists were aware of the "derogatory impressions" of western feminism, so refrained from creating any appearance or taking actions that called it to mind.[57]

The real difference relevant to transformation in redistributive bureaucratic outcomes will depend on the possession of an ideology or professionalism blind to narrowly biological gender contructs *and* the wherewithal, authority, and discretion to act on that ideology. But that necessary authority will probably derive from a *political context* supportive of female empowerment. So once again, the state within which bureaucratic institutions are embedded, but also its political constituencies, loom as centrally important.

BUREAUCRATIC CONSTITUENCIES

If we rely too much on internal bureaucratic politics and the few women, feminists, or women's program personnel who populate them, we invest a dangerous faith in hierarchical institutions staffed with experts. Unless directed or held accountable to outside political forces, bureaucracies begin to pursue their own agenda—what organizational theorists term "goal displacement"—and that agenda is often reduced to maintaining and enhancing their own authority, resources, and staff.

Bureaucratic agencies and program offices within these rarely monolithic organizations interact with constituencies to which they respond or which they serve or regulate. To what extent do women's programs draw on or respond to women's constituencies, and which ones do they hear? Outsiders can provide a base of support for insiders. To what extent, even, is the state structured to listen or respond to outside political forces? Some authoritarian systems are not so structured, whereas in others, the bureaucratic implementation process is virtually the only vehicle that is responsive to mass voice. Brazil's democratic transition provided an opening for women's constituencies to insert their voices in the state, as Alvarez outlines in her chapter. At quite the opposite extreme, the personalized authoritarian system of Malawi articulates President Hastings Kamuzu Banda's agenda for "his women", as Hirschmann discusses. Leaning toward authoritarianism, the competitive opportunism of Cameroonian politics, as Lewis analyzes, tinges women's politics with more of the same.

The so-called people-oriented development literature advocates that bureaucrats use a "learning process," rather than a top-down approach, drawing on the grassroots for ideas, resources, and direction on programs and projects. Such an approach has the potential to empower people politically. Yet one is hard-pressed to find any indication that these writers see other than men at the grassroots.[58] In people's organizations with men at the helm or in numerical dominance, women's voices may go unheard and their issues may remain at the bottom of priorities. Gender struggle occurs as much *in* these organizations as between such organizations and bureaucracy or within bureaucracy itself. The chapter on Nicaragua provides an excellent example of the struggles to end women's silence, a silence to which men have become accustomed and women have learned well. If their "voice" cannot be heard, women may "exit" rather than continue in "loyalty" to the organization. With such exit comes the possibility for women's organizations to articulate, share in, or guide their development, thereby empowering themselves in the process. Separate women's cooperatives in Nicaragua, as the chapter in this collection outlines, are both economically and psychologically productive. Paradoxically, some case studies indicate the necessity of top-down approaches to empower women in community (men's) organizations and of efforts to reinforce the gender division of labor.[59]

International development agencies add a peculiar twist to external constituency force, for the clientele ostensibly "served" is outside the political process in bilateral aid or inside a complicated, expert-laden, obscure, and distantly linked national representation in the United Nations. In U.S. AID, the WID office drew support from outside U.S. women's constituencies in its battles with recalcitrant bureaucracy to allocate more resources to women in AID-assisted countries. These U.S. constituents made their interests in the WID office known to other AID bureaucrats and to Congress. Though a political thorn in the side of AID, they also represented general supporters of development assistance for this perennially unpopular issue and agency; AID depends on a great many organizations for political support, as do many of those PVOs who depend in turn on AID for some or most of their budgets. Women constituents, however, were caught in the dilemma of criticizing yet supporting an agency that continued to direct resources to men at the overwhelming rate of 96 percent of program funds. Sometimes fighting for its very survival, AID's WID office sought, even nurtured, outside interaction for ideas, support, and legitimacy. Such efforts were all too successful, producing a differentiation and hybridization among its U.S. clientele to the extent that competition existed about appropriate direction of and grant support for their proposals. Such competition inheres in the wider political process; that feminist constituents reproduced it should not be surprising.[60] Helzner and Shepard offer insight on the mixed blessings of public funding in their chapter on population PVOs. Some PVOs—such as Food First—opt to avoid public funding connections altogether for the independence and freedom (though not necessarily monies) that brings.

Women's constituencies for women's programs may also be affected by class considerations. Such was the problem in the first few decades of the Women's Bureau in the U.S. Department of Labor. Amid reforms of the "progressive era," the Women's Trade Union League and other middle-class organizations pushed for a unit in the labor bureaucracy. Though headed for some time by an immigrant, working-class woman, its college-educated professionals had no such experience, and it depended greatly on middle-class women's groups for its survival in a bureaucracy that treated it as an enclave. Its long-standing support for protective legislation alienated equal-rights women's groups (similarly middle class and distant from working-class women's needs). Coupled with its "insider" status, the bureau never acted on the larger structural and organizational critique.[61]

A potentially even more devastating characteristic of women's organizations involves their own hierarchy; in effect, they are miniature bureaucracies, which Ferguson finds antithetical to feminism. Yet the degree to which women's organizational hierarchy can coexist with effective outcome is not crystal clear. Some hierarchy, and with it, accountability and effectiveness, may be healthy.[62] Young's chapter is a case in point. Is an end to hierarchy possible or desirable?

A gendered understanding of bureaucratic resistance to women's programs must consider the many reactions activists will encounter. The prospects that women's politics will infuse a new kind of politics in bureaucracies committed to redistribution initially appear dim; such an outcome seems achievable only with supportive people in specific institutional circumstances.

A Scenario of Possibilities

Although studies done thus far suggest little chance for quick movement toward state-supported gender redistribution, tentative generalizations about existing strategies provide a basis by which to consider chapters in this collection. The cases below began within institutions that embodied male privilege, but they were able to utilize supporters as leverage to initiate the redistributive process. All, however, are short-lived or ongoing; the redistribution of resources and values between men and women has only just begun. The chapters in this book take this slim, but important, literature much further, provoking still more questions in the virtually unexplored territory of women's politics in bureaucracy. The French, Soviet, and Zimbabwean cases described here began amid seemingly transformed ideological conditions that sparked women's structural representation inside of government or the dominant party, while the U.S. and Canadian cases emerged from persistent women's constituencies in reformist political settings. Himmelstrand's Swedish case, in this volume, illustrates the combined effects of ideology, structure, and feminist vigilance.

With the victory of the left in France in 1981, feminist party activist Yvette Roudy was appointed to head the first Ministry of Women's Rights.[63] Its budget of 100 million francs was impressive and its staff of one hundred, substantial. Initially, the ministry worked toward advancing women's ability to exercise their reproductive rights and toward greater trade union involvement in workplace equality. By 1983 the ministry mobilized a full 136 administrative organizations throughout France, linked to regional prefects and designed to disseminate information about women's rights and conditions. It published as many as 1.7 million guides, distributed by trained and paid *animatrices* who facilitated contact between women and the agencies that enforce their rights. This network created a clientele that was to protect the ministry against threat in the same way clientelist connections did for other French ministries. Roudy's antisexism legislation, which would permit charges to be leveled against public advertisers who used degrading images of women (physically abusive rather than sexually explicit), was modeled on the antiracist law of a decade earlier. Although support existed among the French public, it was fought by the media and advertisers (Roudy was even called the "Madame Ayatollah") and defeated in the National Assembly. The ministry was later replaced with a less visible Delegate for Women's Status. What happened? Jane Jenson theorized that when feminist activities both coincided with traditional left ideological emphases (including women's economic independence) and utilized traditional bureaucratic practices, the issues moved forward.[64] Others pointed to economic decline and socialists' decreased popularity under economic austerity. In the meantime, "the grassroots women's movement has weakened, having been replaced in large part by the new ministry which is itself dependent upon the broader future (both economic and political) of the Mitterand government."[65]

As far back as the 1920s Soviet researchers generated data on unpaid work in the home and its impact on women's outside employment and the economy. Soviets pursued a veritable compensatory, "affirmative-action"—

like policy in education and employment for many decades, resulting in significant proportions of women in what many western countries view as traditional men's fields. Such policies were congruent with larger Soviet industrial goals, rather than squarely related to gender.[66] Indeed, women's political participation has been limited and their independent organizational impact on the state, totally absent. The relatively short-lived official Zhenotdal, a women's unit within the Communist party that sought radical transformation in women's lives during the 1920s (at sometimes great cost to Soviet Central Asian women)[67] waxed and waned with prevailing political winds. How are we to understand the Zhenotdal's demise? It is difficult to sort out the reactions to the possible gender threats it posed from the Stalinism that engulfed Russian society at the time.

After more than a decade of guerrilla warfare in Zimbabwe's nationalist struggle, when women were estimated to have been a quarter of those fighting in the Patriotic Front, party leaders accumulated an obvious debt to women.[68] Moreover, the Zimbabwe African National Union (ZANU) party promised before independence to end the *lobola* (bridewealth payment), seen as symbolic of male domination and of capitalist transactions. An ex-commander minister of women's affairs and her Ph.D. deputy minister headed a staff of disproportionately female civil servants, many field workers among whom specialized in "domestic science." The ministry sponsored education and income-generating programs and articulated women's needs to other parts of government; female ex-combatants were taught to read, type, and sew. When *lobola* was challenged, its supporters claimed this was western feminism, a "cultural imperialism" that would damage the national heritage. Women respondents of a ministry-supported survey articulated a bitter and thorough critique of gender subordination, in women's "double load of domestic and productive labor," polygamy, and the "irresponsible behavior of some men towards their families, children and wives." The report was not released publicly. Gay Seidman concluded that the leaders serve "at the behest of the party," back off from opposition, and rarely call for changes among men, though she acknowledged women's weak structural and budgetary position representing 1 percent of the national budget. Elsewhere, the minister indicated that she faces greater obstacles in government than during her years as a guerrilla fighter but that she values her membership in Zimbabwe's Politburo, where she can infuse women's issues into planning and policy making.[69] The bureaucratic puzzle is analytically painful; seemingly, ideologically progressive and revolutionary origins should have been ideal conditions under which the *public* sphere and bureaucratic accountability to women were heightened.

Other cases emerged under reformist conditions, and practitioners utilized traditional bureaucratic practices. In 1918 the Women's Bureau was established in the U.S. Department of Labor in response to women's labor force participation, increased political power, and its key constituency, the Women's Trade Union League. Mandated to investigate and improve working women's status, it produced research bulletins, disseminated data, and conducted field visits to advise on women's work. An historical study of the bureau from 1920 to 1950 found its staff size to average sixty and its budget, $167,300; its percentage of departmental funding declined, however, from 1 percent in 1920 to 0.15 percent in 1950. Its impact on the department was limited, owing to insular status, a lack of authority, threats to survival, unsupportive secretaries, and difficulties making reform from within such circumstances. Women's Bureau advocates were classic "outsiders on the inside," accused of being politically subversive, yet they operated without great challenge to mainstream thinking, according to Judith Sealander.[70] At the same time, bureau survival legitimized official interest in employment, supplied timely data on gender wage gaps, and served to facilitate networking among state commissions with similar or broadened mandates during the 1960s and 1970s.[71]

Second only in the United States, perhaps, to the bureau is the aforementioned WID office of AID. The WID office exemplifies the extent to which women's programs can survive and thrive when utilizing traditional bureaucratic practices.[72] A small office staff worked with WID officers in four internal regional bureaus and in some sixty field offices in developing countries. The structure of representation was not optimal, though; the dispersed WID officers did not necessarily have interest or expertise in the issue, nor did the WID office have a hand in their selection. The WID office made alliances with other offices that shared similar concerns, such as Social Analysis, Forestry, and Education, where enough data had been generated to convince staff that gendered approaches were legitimate and contributed to the success of projects. However, staff in other offices were steeped in conventional gender ideology such that WID training programs and top-level support did little to budge the traditional approach. A good example was agriculture. Home economics, with its more domestic orientation to women, was so institutionalized in the agricultural universities about which staff were familiar, that it seemed only transformations in that discipline could change AID's approach. Still, the WID office sponsored training with top-level staff, with case studies prepared in conjunction with the Harvard Institute of International Development. WID materials were integrated into agency short courses, ranging in length from a week to three months. WID requirements infiltrated document procedures, elaborating on a weak and meaningless "woman-impact statement" to require gender-disaggregated data. The existence of written procedures was by no means evidence that procedures were followed, however.

The key to this *relative* bureaucratic success was a visible external political constituency that reminded congressional members and many AID offices of its concern. Internally, the office circulated a policy paper in 1982 making a forceful case for women in development as an economic and efficiency issue as opposed to its earlier unpopular emphasis on equity (despite equity's grounding in a variety of congressional mandates to AID). Some WID constituents wondered if the case had been made all too well, with detrimental consequences for women. Would women's hard work, motivated from sheer desperate circumstances and a lack of choice, be used to further bureaucrats' economic goals? Suppose women's unpaid reproductive work (childbearing and rearing, domestic labor) left little productive energy for remunerative work. Was it legitimate to exclude their participation on economic grounds?

Other WID units of national assistance agencies learned of the early trials and tribulations inside AID. Their leaders periodically interact within the Development Assistance Committee of the Organization of Economic Cooperation and Development. The WID Directorate in the Canadian International Development Agency (CIDA) illustrates a thriving operation that has begun to transform its host. CIDA is an historically centralized organization, concerned in the 1980s with fiscal management, as is common in many agencies and states. The directorate uses economic *and* equity discourse and justifies a gender-sensitive approach with "equality of result" language. With these conditions, the directorate mandate has permeated planning and operations through the use of a "corporate strategy," in which its able past and current leaders establish accountability from a steering committee of vice-presidents, personnel, evaluations containing WID goals, and internal training programs. Also present is a supportive woman president reporting to a woman minister for external relations. No figures are available, however, on the extent to which women benefit from CIDA resources.[73]

Women's programs in these ordinary or revolutionary times played usually by public bureaucratic rules, or they did not play at all. Private institutions have greater potential for flexibility and innovation than do public institutions, as Helzner and Shepard show. Cornelia Butler Flora analyzed how the women's "bureaucratic insurgency" in the Ford Foundation achieved partial redistribution of resources from men to women in that private institution.[74] Female staff used internal strategies appropriate for that bureaucratic context to secure 3.5 percent of international funding for women's programming, plus the use of sizable sums from general reserves thereafter from President Franklin Thomas, who publicly stated that "sexism is a fundamental obstacle keeping the powerless from realizing their potential." That visibility was ultimately transformed into a sensitivity sustained with supportive staff but without a separate program and special funding. Yet once merged in the organization and lacking a gender strategy, women's programs can disappear, and few would notice their disappearance.

Why, with so much seemingly politically savvy activity, are results for all these cases undramatic? And by whose and what standards do we define success and failure?[75] Perhaps insiders, from their vantage point, have a higher tolerance for the slow, painstaking increments in all the nooks and crannies of an agency that are part of change: procedural changes, new allies and respectability for the issue, former foes who become true believers. For outsiders, perhaps, this may be much ado about nothing—spinning wheels and wasting precious energy on hopeless or hopelessly tainted organizations. With hindsight, British women's organizational lobbying for women to enter line positions in the Colonial Service (beyond their only authorized employment as "Lady Education Officers" and "Nursing Sisters") so as to provide a "woman's point of view" seems naïve.[76] Similar analogies can be made about development assistance under neocolonial conditions. We perhaps need to remind ourselves of the chilling—though hardly representative—example of what was probably the world's largest-ever Women's Bureau in Nazi Germany. The Frahenwerk at its height employed 25,000 women who in turn supervised 8 million volunteers, many of whom belonged to religious women's organizations. The bureau existed solely to serve Nazi dictates but operated in a separate somewhat autonomous fashion.[77]

Shall we throw up hands in despair at the limited progress toward gender redistribution? Looking at change—or the lack of it—through the lens of gendered bureaucracy, we can understand the threats that feminist bureaucratic strategies pose to individual and collective male privilege, long institutionalized in government. Possibilities exist for building on widespread official policy support and its still weak institutional levers for change. Among the many conditions that facilitate moves toward the redistribution of resources from men to women include a congruence with political, ideological, and professional agendas; feminist constituencies that engage the bureaucratic political process; alliance building; internal structures that legitimize feminist agendas; feminist bureaucratic insiders; and fastidious attention to implementation details, among others. Still other conditions can waylay or undermine redistributive agendas: examples are political opportunism and bureaucratic instrumentalism in the absence of feminist constituencies, class privilege among women, and sheer bureaucratic inertia. The contributors to this volume focus on these and other factors as they analytically "take on" rather than "write off" bureaucracy.

Overview of Selections

Contributors to this volume come from a variety of work experiences and countries, from Africa, Europe, Latin America, the Middle East, and North America. Many of them have participated in or along the sidelines of bureaucracies about which they write; they include a former vice-president of an international assistance agency and participant-observers in women's organizations; others are scholar-activists, in the sense that they have been involved with research that is explicitly tied to practice. The chapters themselves provide analysis of many parts of the world, from Brazil, Cameroon, and Malawi to Mexico and Tonga in the Pacific region and to international assistance agencies, complex cultural entities in and of themselves.

This volume is divided into four sections, focusing first on women's politics outside and with public bureaucracy over women's programs. The next sections illustrate the importance of institutional and political context, first for international and then national agencies. The final section addresses specifically internal bureaucratic issues, ranging from procedural reform to interorganizational relations, but finally questions the efficacy of bureaucracy to create change. Development sectors and issues, such as agriculture and family planning, cut across the sections, given the institutional focus of this collection. Following the four sections is a conclusion. Kristen Timothy and I draw together both insider and outsider perspectives to answer some of the many questions raised in the collection. We also discuss a post-Beijing bureaucratic roadmap that builds on recent research/practice and posits new research directions.

In the lead contribution, political scientist Sonia E. Alvarez sets the tone for the volume in her analysis of women's politics within the Brazilian state. Specifically, she focuses on Councils on the Status of Women, established as women participated in the transition from authoritarian to democratic politics. The feminist politicization of policy issues and the interaction of feminists inside and outside government provide a useful model with which to compare efforts elsewhere. Alvarez argues that Brazilian feminists have "developed successful strategies for what might be termed 'gendered bureaucratic subversion.' "

In the next chapter sociologist Gay Young examines hierarchy and class relations in women's organizations, looking at optimal structure and at feminist leadership. Her analysis culminates in a case study of a women's development organization in Mexico, outside the official state bureaucracy but home of hierarchical contradictions.

The second section of this volume focuses on structural and contextual issues in international development assistance institutions, both bilateral and multilateral bodies. In the first selection, Karin Himmelstrand, who builds on long years of development experience in Africa and with SIDA, traces changes in SIDA's responsiveness to women to determine whether evidence of female empowerment can be found. As is common in many international agencies, the WID office experimented with a variety of strategies to tie women's development activities to the mainstream of SIDA's planning, country and sectorial efforts. Himmelstrand concludes that women empower themselves through their organizations, a process that sometimes meshes with donor agency missions to emphasize people's participation in projects.

If there is any institution that is unlikely to have women central to its mission, it is the World Bank. It is an organization of economists whose discipline, data, and approaches tend to render women invisible. Political scientist Nüket Kardam, after interviews with fifty staff members, discusses the bank's response to its WID policy. Although resistant on the whole, the bank has responded inconsistently and on ad hoc bases, only if women's instrumental "economic viability" can be demonstrated in a controlled manner. Receptivity is conditioned, too, by the governments with which the bank deals.

In the third selection, Sally W. Yudelman analyzes the U.S. IAF, long known for its innovative, grassroots-oriented approaches. If there is any institution that *should* have had female empowerment central to its mission, it would be the IAF for some of the following reasons: its participatory, non-hierarchical style; its large number of female staff, including a woman president more recently; and its mandate to address structural oppression. Yudelman, who brings many years of experience in IAF to her chapter, analyzes the many reasons why the IAF has not seized the opportunity that its structures would seem to predict. Her interviews with twenty current and former staff members add richness to the chapter.

Judith Helzner and Bonnie Shepard examine private international family planning organizations. They focus on the Pathfinder Fund, which has supported innovative programming with and without a women's unit. They analyze some of the practical and ethical dilemmas of different degrees of dependency on public institutions. Helzner and Shepard consider feminist programming, its obstacles, and actual practices in this distinctive development sector.

The third section contains chapters set in national context, beginning with the chilling case of Malawi, in southern Africa, which has an authoritarian ruler who plays symbolically to his female constituency. Political scientist David Hirschmann analyzes policies and programs for women in an undemocratic bureaucratic state, based on his interviews with administrators, reviews of documents, and long residence in the area. Just as women began to get an ever-so-minor place on the development agenda in this resistant setting, class divisions among women began to loom large on the horizon, portending ill for the way government serves women. Thus, women's constituency differentiation adds important dimensions to the analysis. Whether the very recent changes in gender data collection and job redefinitions that Anita Spring documents in Malawi's Ministry of Agriculture actually stick in this state with its firmly established male-orientation will bear close watching.[78]

In her study of a less authoritarian political system, that of Cameroon, political scientist Barbara Lewis details a ministry mired in the opportunist politics and bureaucratic competition so prevalent in this west African nation—not uncommon politics in many parts of the world. Women farmers, a constituency served by the ministry, sought individual gain for the labor they contributed to agricultural projects, but politicians preferred collective agricultural plots, from which the fruits of women's labor could be siphoned. In the absence of large numbers of political women and feminist organizations, will women's programs merely serve elite interests?

The Nicaraguan case, as the Rural Women's Research Team documents in the next chapter, illustrates efforts of a revolutionary, participatory socialist society to integrate women into agricultural cooperatives. With progressive law and policy in place, women still struggle with state officials, but most importantly, with people's attitudes about the traditional gender division of labor and the values placed on that labor.

The fourth section looks specifically at internal issues, such as changes in procedure, data generation, and use. Yet how effective can such changes be in light of interagency, constituency, and contextual conditions? The U.N. FAO presumably has the kind of mission and professionals for whom gender would be central in this world of many women farmers. Alice Carloni, long familiar with FAO field projects, compares cases of actual development projects from three world regions. Her detailed analysis of project design and implementation shows the complexity of turning bureaucracy around to better serve women. Progressive policy often has little bearing on the day-to-day realities of projects.

Sociologist Katherine Jensen traces the struggle with hierarchy and gendered resistance in cross-national inter-organizational relations from U.S. universities to the AID mission to Egypt, where U.S. officials had little interest in increasing responsiveness to the well-documented participation of Egyptian women in agriculture. Relevant gender data were neither utilized nor absorbed in these uncertain, politically charged bureaucratic relationships.

Finally, anthropologist Cathy Small questions the relevance of bureaucracy and planning altogether in her analysis of a seemingly successful Tongan women's development organization. Whatever the good intentions of program activists, indigenous social structure and historical patterns of class accumulation determined the waxing and waning of a women's organization.

A policy analyst and a political scientist, Kristen Timothy and I, respond to the chapters in the concluding essay. With vantage points in both academia and international organizations, and with both of us also engaged with non-government organizations, we draw on issues raised in each chapter about internal and external bureaucratic politics, the connection between them, and the engulfing state and international contexts in which they are located.

Notes

1. Programme of Action, Copenhagen Conference, *Report of the World Conference of the United Nations Decade for Women*, A/CONF.94/35 (Copenhagen, 1980).

2. Sue Ellen Charlton, Jana Everett, and Kathleen Staudt, eds., *Women, the State, and Development* (Albany, N.Y.: State University of New York Press, 1989).

3. Gerda Lerner, *The Creation of Patriarchy* (New York: Oxford University Press, 1986).

4. Sue Ellen Charlton, "Female Welfare and Political Exclusion in the Western European State," in Charlton et al., *Women, the State, and Development*, pp. 20–43.

5. U.N. International Research and Training Institute for the Advancement of Women (INSTRAW), *National Machineries for the Advancement of Women: Selected Case Studies* (New York: United Nations, 1980).

6. *The State of the World's Women*, World Conference to Review and Appraise the Achievements of the United Nations Decade for Women, Nairobi, Kenya, July 15–26, 1985, as reprinted in U.S. Congress, House of Representatives, *U.N. Conference to Review and Appraise the U.N. Decade for Women: Report of the Congressional Staff Advisors to the Nairobi Conference to the Committee on Foreign Affairs*, 99th Cong., 2nd Sess., H.R. 55-25690, January, 1986, p. 80.

7. Kathleen Staudt and Jane Jaquette, "Women's Programs, Bureaucratic Resistance, and Feminist Organizations: The End of the Decade," *Women, Power and Policy*, ed. Ellen Boneparth and Emily Stoper, 2nd ed. (New York: Pergamon, 1987), 263–81.

8. Kathy Ferguson, *The Feminist Case Against Bureaucracy* (Philadelphia: Temple University Press, 1984).

9. Catherine MacKinnon, "Feminism, Marxism, Method, and the State: Toward Feminist Jurisprudence," *Signs* 8, no. 4 (1983): 635–58. Even with such absolutist language, attorney MacKinnon tries to influence the state and substate governments with ordinances against pornography.

10. Kathleen Staudt, "Women, Development and the State: On the Theoretical Impasse," *Development and Change* 17 (1986): 325–33.

11. See, e.g., the World Bank's appendices in its annual *World Development Report;* Michael Kideron and Ronald Segal, *The New State of the World Atlas* (New York: Simon and Schuster, 1987); Ruth Sivard, *World Military and Social Expenditures*, 12th ed. (Leesburg, Va.: World Priorities, 1987).

12. Gita Sen and Caren Grown (for DAWN), *Development, Crises, and Alternative Visions: Third World Women's Perspectives* (New York: Monthly Review, 1987), p. 23.

13. See sources cited in nn. 1, 12; also, Sue Ellen Charlton, *Women in Third World Development* (Boulder, Colo.: Westview Press, 1984).

14. Susan Joekes, *Women in the World Economy: An INSTRAW Study* (New York: Oxford University Press, 1987), chap. 8.

15. Joni Seager and Ann Olson, *Women in the World: An International Atlas* (New York: Simon and Schuster, 1986), p. 8.

16. On female-headed households, see Mayra Buvinic and Nadia Youssef, *Women-Headed Households* (Washington, D.C.: U.S. Agency for International Development/Office of Women in Development, 1978). United Nations, Report of the Secretary General, "Effective Mobilization of Women in Development," UN/A/33/238 (New York: United Nations, 1978).

17. Ester Boserup, *Woman's Role in Economic Development* (New York: St. Martin's Press, 1970), is the classic reference. Also see Staudt and Jaquette, "Women's Programs," on capitalism. Kathryn Ward, *Women in the World-System: Its Impact on Fertility* (New York: Praeger, 1984), is one of the first to document women's deteriorating situation, with quantitative indicators, under dependent capitalist development.

18. For example, Joekes, *Women in the World Economy*, p. 145, says women need to consolidate gains and reverse harmful effects; she supports calls in the Nairobi conference's *Forward Looking Strategies* (reprinted in source cited in n. 6) to use public resources and enforcement powers as means.

19. U.N. INSTRAW, *National Machineries for the Advancement of Women*.

20. Oki Ooko-Ombaka, "An Assessment of National Machinery for Women," *Assignment Children* 49/50 (1980): 45–61; Kathleen Staudt, *Women, Foreign Assistance and Advocacy Administration* (New York: Praeger, 1985), p. 98.

21. Mayra Buvinic, "Projects for Women in the Third World: Explaining Their Misbehavior," *World Development* 14, no. 5 (1986), 653–64.

22. Murray Edelman, *The Symbolic Uses of Politics* (Urbana: University of Illinois Press, 1964); Staudt, *Women, Foreign Assistance and Advocacy Administration*, chap. 1.

23. Barbara Rogers, *The Domestication of Women: Discrimination in Developing Societies* (New York: St. Martin's Press, 1979).

On the overall track record of progress, see Nüket Kardam, "Social Theory and Women in Development Policy," *Women and Politics* 7, no. 4 (Winter, 1987): 67–82. On the FAO, "Women in Agriculture and Rural Development: FAO's Programme Directions," 24th Session, Conference, Food and Agricultural Organization of the United Nations, Rome, November 7–26, 1987, reports 40 field projects, totaling $15 million, specifically targeted to women in agricultural extension, marketing, credit, training, and support services, and 150 large-scale projects in nutrition, statistics, forestry, fisheries, irrigation, and other agricultural sectors (p. 7) and 20 percent women among all trainees (p. 12). Although the years do not coincide, FAO reports involvement in more than 2,500 projects in 1985 in *FAO: What It Is, What It Does* (Rome: FAO, 1986). DAWN cites an FAO report indicating that .05 percent of all U.N. agricultural sectors in 1982 were to rural women's programs (Sen and Grown, *Development*, p. 44).

24. Staudt, *Women, Foreign Assistance and Advocacy Administration*, chap. 6.

25. Steven Cohn, Robert Wood, and Richard Haag, "U.S. Aid and Third World

Women: The Impact of Peace Corps Programs," *Economic Development and Cultural Change* 29, no. 4 (1981): 795–811.

26. Margery Wolf, *Revolution Postponed* (Stanford, Calif.: Stanford University Press, 1985).

27. Jill Conway, Susan C. Bourque, and Joan W. Scott, "The Concept of Gender," in the "Learning About Women: Gender, Politics, and Power" issue of *Daedalus* 116, no. 4 (1987): xxi–xxix. They say, "The production of culturally appropriate forms of male and female behavior is a central function of social authority and is mediated by the complex interactions of a wide range of economic, social, political and religious institutions" (p. xxii) and indicate that "gender boundaries, movable and negotiable, are drawn to serve political, economic and social interests" (p. xxiii).

Theorizing about prehistory, however dangerous for its limited empirical base, is suggestive as well. Drawing partly from Mary O'Brien, who argues that men "need to compensate for their inability to bear children through the construction of institutions of dominance," Gerda Lerner elaborates that men's fear and awe must have led them "to create social institutions to bolster their egos, strengthen their self-confidence, and validate their sense of worth" (*Creation of Patriarchy*, pp. 45–46). For related ideas, see Azizah al-Hibri, "Reproduction, Mothering, and the Origins of Patriarchy," and Eva Feder Kittay, "Womb Envy: An Explanatory Concept," in *Mothering: Essays in Feminist Theory*, ed. Joyce Trebilcot (Totowa, N.J.: Rowman and Allanhead, 1983), pp. 81–128.

28. The late Erving Goffman stated that gender is one of the most profound social divisions for understanding our ultimate nature. *Gender Advertisements* (New York: Harper Colophon, 1976), p. 8. An early form of "gendered bureaucracy" was first developed in Staudt, *Women, Foreign Assistance and Advocacy Administration*, chap. 1.

29. Conway et al., "Concept of Gender," p. xxi.

30. Theda Skocpol, "Bringing the State Back In: Strategies of Analysis in Current Research," in Peter Evans, Dietrich Rueschemeyer, and Theda Skocpol, eds., *Bringing the State Back In* (Cambridge: Harvard University Press, 1985), pp. 3–37; Eric Nordlinger, "Taking the State Seriously," *Understanding Political Development*, ed. Samuel Huntington and Myron Weiner (Boston: Little Brown, 1986), pp. 353–90; Nicos Poulantzas, *Political Power and Social Classes* (London: New Left Books, 1978); Stephen Krasner, "Approaches to the State: Alternative Conceptions and Historical Dynamics," *Comparative Politics* 16, no. 2 (1984): 223–46.

31. Anthony Downs, *Inside Bureaucracy* (Boston: Little Brown, 1966); Robert Presthus, *The Organizational Society* (New York: St. Martin's Press, 1978).

32. James G. March and John P. Olsen, "The New Institutionalism: Organizational Factors in Political Life," *American Political Science Review* 78 (1984): 738.

33. Nordlinger, "Taking the State Seriously," p. 370.

34. Charlton, et al., *Women, the State, and Development;* MacKinnon, "Feminism, Marxism, Method"; Zillah Eisenstein, *The Radical Future of Liberal Feminism* (New York: Longman, 1981); Jane Parpart and Kathleen Staudt, eds., *Women and the State in Africa* (Boulder, Colo.: Lynne Rienner Publishers, 1988).

35. For exceptions, see Jana Everett, "Incorporation v. Conflict: Lower Class Women's Collective Action and the State in India," in Charlton, et al., *Women, the State, and Development,* pp. 152–76; Donald Rothchild and Naomi Chazan, eds., *The Precarious Balance: State and Society in Africa* (Boulder, Colo.: Westview, 1988).

36. Kay Johnson, "Women's Rights, Family Reform, and Population Control in the People's Republic of China," *Women in the World,* ed. Lynne Iglitzin and Ruth Ross (Santa Barbara, Calif.: ABC Clio, 1985), pp. 439–62. Also see Sen and Grown, *Development,* and Joel Migdal, "Strong States, Weak States: Power and Accommodation," in Huntington and Weiner, *Understanding Political Development,* pp. 391–434.

37. Judith Bruce, "Users' Perspectives on Contraceptive Technology and Delivery Systems: Highlighting Some Feminist Issues," *Technology in Society* 9 (1987): 376. On hierarchical modes, see Kathleen Staudt and Jane Jaquette, "Women as 'At Risk' Reproducers: Biology, Science and Population in U.S. Foreign Policy," *Women, Biology, and Public Policy,* ed. Virginia Sapiro (Beverly Hills, Calif.: Sage, 1985), 235–68.

38. Elise Boulding made the 6 percent estimate in *Handbook of International Data on Women* (Beverly Hills, Calif.: Sage, 1976), p. 36.

39. Joel Aberbach, Robert D. Putnam, and Bert P. Rochman, *Bureaucrats and Politicians in Western Democracies* (Cambridge: Harvard University Press, 1981), p. 47.

40. U.S. Office of Personnel Management, cited in James Q. Wilson, *American Government* (Lexington, Mass.: D. C. Heath, 1987), p. 249.

41. Rogers, *Domestication of Women,* chap. 3; in *Women in the United Nations (1945–1988)* (Vienna: Commission on the Status of Women, 1988), women are reported to have occupied 4.8 percent of the top two levels of geographic posts (totaling one woman) in 1977 and 16.8 percent in 1987 (totaling four women), p. 137. According to the Association for Women in Development (AWID), *Gender Issues in Development Cooperation,* Colloquium Report, Jane S. Jaquette, Conference Coordinator, April 11–12, 1988 (Washington, D.C., 1988) women make up 22 percent of the UNDP staff.

42. Barber B. Conable to the Joint World Bank IMF Meetings, September 1986, as cited in *CARE Briefs on Development Issues* 6, n.d., p. 6; Edouard Saouma at the 13th Regional Conference, Africa, Zimbabwe, 1986, as cited in *Ceres: The FAO Review* 113 (vol. 19, 5), 1986, p. 15; on AID, see Staudt, *Women, Foreign Assistance and Advocacy Administration,* p. 136, though also see pp. 65–66.

43. Michael Lipsky, *Street-Level Bureaucracy: Dilemmas of the Individual in Public Services* (New York: Russell Sage, 1980); Staudt, *Women, Foreign Assistance and Advocacy Administration,* chap. 6.

44. Carol Gilligan, *In a Different Voice* (Cambridge: Harvard University Press, 1982), has stimulated much interest in the heretofore male-oriented "moral development" field. Yet a computer search I did of 139 moral development studies in 1986 revealed that the interpersonal 3 level (where women were supposedly "stuck," in pre-Gilligan interpretation), was common for males sampled in Algeria and Tunisia and that less than a quarter of a U.S. male-female sample exhibited principled

reasoning at the 5–6 levels. A significant number of studies found no support for sex-differentiated reasoning. Moreover, Virginia Sapiro, "Reflections on Reflections: Personal Ruminations," *Women and Politics* 7, no. 4 (Winter 1987), reports that later meta-analyses of the literature found no Gilligan-like gender differences (p. 22). Also see Ferguson, *The Feminist Case,* chap. 5, on gender difference.

45. Denise Antoli, "Women in Local Government: An Overview," *Political Women,* ed. Janet Flamming (Beverly Hills, Calif.: Sage, 1984). The generalization applies to women whose sole task outside the home is as politician, as opposed to a combined task with another occupation.

46. Rosabeth Kanter, *Men and Women of the Corporation* (New York: Basic, 1977), chaps. 6, 8. Diane Franklin and Joan L. Sweeney, "Women and Corporate Power," *Women, Power and Policy,* ed. Ellen Boneparth and Emily Stoper (New York: Pergamon, 1988), pp. 52–53. Franklin and Sweeney, as well as Ferguson, provide good though different critiques of Kanter.

47. Nancy Chodorow, *The Reproduction of Mothering: Psychoanalysis and the Sociology of Gender* (Berkeley: University of California Press, 1978), pp. 180–81. Also see Dorothy Dinnerstein, *The Mermaid and the Minotaur: Sexual Arrangements and the Human Malaise* (New York: Harper and Row, 1977).

48. Geert Hofstede, *Culture's Consequences: International Differences in Work-Related Values* (Beverly Hills, Calif.: Sage, 1980).

49. Ferguson, *The Feminist Case,* chap. 3. On men's studies, see Joseph H. Pleck, *The Myth of Masculinity* (Cambridge: MIT Press, 1981); James M. O'Neil, *Male Sex-Role Conflicts, Sexism and Masculinity* (Lawrence: University Press of Kansas, 1980); Clyde W. Franklin II, *The Changing Definition of Masculinity* (New York: Plenum Press, 1984).

50. Sharon Mayes, "Women in Positions of Authority: A Case Study of Changing Sex Roles," *Signs* 4 (1979): 556–68; Anthony Astrachan, *How Men Feel: Their Responses to Women's Demands for Equality and Power* (New York: Anchor/ Doubleday, 1986), chap. 3; Susan J. Pharr, "Tea and Power: The Anatomy of a Conflict," *Perspectives on Power: Women in Africa, Asia, and Latin America,* ed. Jean F. O'Barr (Durham, N.C.: Duke University Press, 1982), on Japan.

51. Kathleen Staudt, "Women's Politics, the State, and Capitalist Transformation in Africa," *Studies in Power and Class in Africa,* ed. Irving L. Markovitz (New York: Oxford University Press, 1987), 193–204; Helen Safa and June Nash, eds., *Sex and Class in Latin America* (New York: Praeger, 1976); Patricia Caplan and Janet M. Bujra, eds., *Women United, Women Divided* (Bloomington: Indiana University Press, 1978).

52. Ferguson, *The Feminist Case;* Staudt and Jaquette, "Women's Programs."

53. Samuel Krislov, *Representative Bureaucracy* (Englewood Cliffs, N.J.: Prentice-Hall, 1974), and David Rosenblom, *Federal Equal Employment Opportunity* (New York: Praeger, 1977).

54. Kanter, *Men and Women of the Corporation,* pp. 221–37.

55. In AWID, *Gender Issues,* pp. 10–11.

56. In Staudt, *Women, Foreign Assistance, and Advocacy Administration,* p. 74.

57. Susan G. Rogers, "Efforts Toward Women's Development in Tanzania:

Gender Rhetoric vs. Gender Realities," *Women in Developing Countries: A Policy Focus,* ed. Kathleen Staudt and Jane Jaquette (New York: Haworth Press, 1983), pp. 23–42.

58. David C. Korten, "Community Organization and Rural Development: A Learning Process Approach," *Public Administration Review* 40 (September–October 1980): 480–510; also selections in Korten and Rudi Klauss, *People-Centered Development* (West Hartford, Conn.: Kumarian Press, 1984). Judith Helzner, "Bringing Women into People-Centered Development," unpublished manuscript, 1984.

59. Sen and Grown, *Development,* chap. 3. On the paradoxes, Marina Fernando, "New Skills for Women: A Community Development Project in Colombo, Sri Lanka," *Women, Human Settlements, and Housing,* ed. Caroline O. N. Moser and Linda Peake (London: Tavistock, 1987), and Cornelia Butler Flora, "Income Generation Projects for Rural Women" and Elsa Chaney, "Women's Components in Integrated Rural Development Projects," both in *Rural Women and State Policy,* ed. Carmen Diana Deere and Magdalena Leon (Boulder, Colo.: Westview, 1987); Albert O. Hirschman, *Exit, Voice and Loyalty: Responses to Decline in Firms* (Cambridge: Harvard University Press, 1970).

60. Staudt, *Women, Foreign Assistance and Advocacy Administration,* chap. 5.

61. Judith Sealander, *As Minority Becomes Majority: Federal Reaction to the Phenomenon of Women in the Work Force 1920–1963* (Westport, Conn.: Greenwood Press, 1983).

62. Ferguson, *The Feminist Case;* Jo Freeman, *The Politics of Women's Liberation* (New York: David McKay, 1975), on structural determinants of organizational effectiveness.

63. The details in this paragraph come from Jane Jenson, "The Work of the Ministere Des Droits de la Femme," *Conference Group on French Politics and Society* 4 (1983): 3–9. The change is highlighted in *Women of Europe* 45 (Commission of the European Communities) (May 1986), p. 16.

64. Jenson, "The Ministere Des Droits de la Femme," p. 9.

65. Wayne Northcutt and Jeffra Flaitz, "Women, Politics and the French Socialist Government," *Women and Politics in Western Europe,* ed. Sylvia Bashevkin (London: Frank Cass, 1985), pp. 51ff., quoted on p. 67.

66. Gail Lapidus, *Women in Soviet Society* (Berkeley: University of California Press, 1978).

67. Gregory Massell, *The Surrogate Proletariat: Moslem Women and Strategies in Soviet Central Asia, 1919–1929* (Princeton, N.J.: Princeton University Press, 1974).

68. The information here is from Gay Seidman, "Women in Zimbabwe: Post-Independence Struggles," *Feminist Studies* 10, no. 3 (Fall 1984): 419–40.

69. Kathy Koch, "Ex-Guerrilla Finds Fight for Women's Rights Her Toughest Battle," *Christian Science Monitor International,* March 3, 1988.

70. Judith Anne Sealander, "The Women's Bureau, 1920–1950: Federal Reaction to Female Wage Earning" (Ph.D. diss., Duke University, 1977); also see Sealander, *As Minority Becomes Majority.*

71. Ester Petersen, "The Kennedy Commission," *Women in Washington: Ad-*

vocates for Public Policy, ed. Irene Tinker (Beverly Hills, Calif.: Sage, 1983), pp. 21–34, who, when director of the Women's Bureau, headed the President's Commission on the Status of Women.

72. Staudt, *Women, Foreign Assistance and Advocacy Administration.*

73. I am grateful to Marnie Girvan, director of the CIDA/WID Directorate, and to former director Elizabeth McAllister, for sharing several internal unpublished reports with me. Also see AWID, *Gender Issues.*

74. Cornelia Butler Flora, "Incorporating Women into International Development Programs: The Political Phenomenology of a Private Foundation," in *Women in Developing Countries: A Policy Focus,* ed. Staudt and Jaquette, pp. 89–106.

75. I am grateful to Bonnie Shepard for clarifying my thinking on this point.

76. Helen Callaway, *Gender, Culture and Empire: European Women in Colonial Nigeria* (Urbana: University of Illinois Press, 1987), p. 140. Once in, however, women did not deal with women's issues; besides, a totally "masculine ethos" still prevailed (pp. 160–62).

77. Claudia Koonz, *Mothers in the Fatherland: Women, the Family and Nazi Politics* (New York: St. Martin's Press, 1987), pp. 217, 392.

78. Anita Spring, *Agricultural Development in Malawi: A Project for Women in Development* (Boulder, Colo.: Westview, 1988).

I

Women's Political Organizations: Links with Bureaucracy

2/Who Needs [Sex] When You Can Have [Gender]? Conflicting Discourses on Gender at Beijing

Sally Baden and Anne Marie Goetz

For academics working in the gender and development (GAD) field, the concept of "gender" is everyday currency. In the U.K., at least, social relations of gender analysis, with its roots in socialist feminism, is a major foundation for GAD thinking.[1] Understanding the concept of "gender" in the context of social relations analysis remains a touchstone of gender and development research, teaching, and training in many institutions in the U.K. and elsewhere. However, outside of academia, within policy and activist arenas, the utility and relevance of "gender" has been highly contested. Indeed, in some policy applications, "gender" has come to lose its feminist political content. This chapter explores conflicting discourses on the relevance and meaning of gender in policy and activist contexts. We draw on debates over "gender" aired at the NGO (non-government organization) Forum of the United Nations (U.N.) Fourth World Conference on Women in September 1995.[2] This conference provided an extraordinary opportunity to investigate a vast range of contemporary policy and activist discourses, given the very broad spectrum of interest groups represented there.

The first section of this chapter is inspired by the challenge to GAD from grassroots development workers and women activists in the South. This challenge is linked to the current debate over the institutionalization of gender in development policy and practice, and relates to the perceived depoliticization of the concept of gender. The second part explores a completely different critique of "gender" from conservative groups, who attacked "gender" during the official Conference on the grounds that it is an over-radical and unrepresentative approach to thinking about social relations.

This essay first appeared in *Feminist Review*, issue 56, 1997.

We consider the ways the conservative critique illuminates contradictions and lacunae in feminist theorizing about gender. Underlying both sections are questions about what happens to feminist concepts in activist and policy arenas and about our own role in this process, as gender and development researchers.

The Mainstreaming Agenda

The Beijing Conference reflected the extent to which gender issues have entered the "mainstream," at least at the level of rhetoric. The entire range of bilateral and multilateral development agencies and institutions vied to display their gender-sensitivity with a range of policy documents and promotional literature and well as presence at workshops and on panels at both official and NGO events. For example, the World Bank launched its analytical framework, "Toward Gender Equality: The Role of Public Policy," while the United Nations Development Programme (UNDP) proferred the *1995 Human Development Report* focusing on gender.

In the 1990s, "mainstreaming" has become a dominant theme in gender and development policy circles. Mainstreaming evolved from the earlier call for the "integration" of women in development, dating back to the 1970s. It arose following the Nairobi U.N. Women's Conference in 1985, in part reflecting the perceived failure of national women's machineries, many set up in the 1970s and early 1980s, to achieve significant results or influence over government policy. Mainstreaming signifies a push towards systematic procedures and mechanisms within organizations—particularly government and public institutions—for explicitly taking account of gender issues at all stages of policy making and program design and implementation. It also represents a call for the diffusion of responsibility for gender issues beyond small and underfunded women's units to the range of sectoral and technical departments within institutions.[3]

Mainstreaming has been heavily promoted within international development circles by gender policy advocates in a relatively small group of bilateral agencies, sometimes leading to accusations of a donor-driven agenda. It has also been argued that the mainstreaming agenda focuses on process and means rather than ends, leading to a preoccupation with the minutiae of procedures at all levels, rather than clarity or direction about goals.[4] Feminist (or radical and Marxist) critiques of bureaucracies and their potential for promoting women's interests—or indeed those of any other disempowered social group—are not new although they have only relatively recently filtered into the GAD field.[5] Echoing these critiques, disquiet about the mainstreaming agenda and the way in which the GAD discourse is evolving was in evidence at the NGO Forum, from both the left and the right.

The Platform for Action of the official Beijing Conference had comprehensively adopted the language of gender and, specifically, of gender mainstreaming. In the final chapter on Institutional Arrangements, a commitment was made to "promote an active and visible policy of mainstreaming a gender perspective . . . in the monitoring and evaluation of all policies and programmes."[6] The pre-occupation with institutionalization was also evident in the number of workshops at the Huairou Forum (and panels at the official Conference in Beijing) that focused on the issue from a variety of perspectives.

One of these, convened early on in the Forum by the Applied Socioeconomic Research (ASR) organization of Pakistan, was entitled "Feminism: From Movement to Establishment." Nighat Khan, director of ASR and a panelist at this workshop, argued that gender analysis had become a technocratic discourse, in spite of its roots in socialist feminism, dominated by researchers, policy makers, and consultants, which no longer addressed issues of power central to women's subordination. She identified factors underlying this shift as the professionalization and "NGOization" of the women's movement and the consequent lack of accountability of "gender experts" to a grassroots constituency. A more radical perspective on the Beijing process and associated discourse on gender came from the Revolutionary Women of the Philippines, whose pamphlet, "The Gender Trap: An Imperialist Scheme for Coopting the World's Women," attacked gender mainstreaming as a scheme to buy off once-committed activists.[7]

Nighat Khan asserted that the focus on gender, rather than women, had become counterproductive in that it had allowed the discussion to shift from a focus on women, to women and men, and, finally, back to men. This latter point was echoed by others at the NGO Forum. Eudine Barriteau, presenting on a panel for Development Alternatives with Women in a New Era (DAWN), described how in Jamaica the shift in discourse from women to gender had resulted, in policy circles, in a focus away from women, to "men at risk," reflecting concern about men's failure in education and in securing employment, while women perform much better educationally and many support families alone.

This view is also reflected in other accounts. A Bangladeshi development worker is quoted by Kabeer as saying: "Do you think we are ready for gender in development in Bangladesh when we have not yet addressed the problems of women in development?" It transpired that "the new vocabulary of gender was being used in her organisation to deny the very existence of women-specific disadvantage and hence the need for specific measures which might address this disadvantage."[8] According to Razavi and Miller in their recent review of conceptual shifts in the women and development discourse: "Although the gender discourse has filtered through to policy making institutions, in the process actors have re-interpreted the concept of gender to suit their institutional needs. In some instances, 'gender' has been used to side-step a focus on 'women' and on the radical policy implications of overcoming their disprivilege."[9]

Mainstreaming in Research: From Subordination to Disaggregation

The contradictions generated by mainstreaming resonate closer to home. As gender has become a more mainstream and therefore more respectable and fundable field of research, new players who bear no allegiance to feminist research are entering the field, and they may not even have any familiarity with its basic texts, concepts, and methodologies. Economists, statisticians, and econometricians (many, though not all of them, men), responding to the growth in demand from major development bureaucracies for research and analysis to inform their new "gender-aware" policy directions, have taken up research into gender issues. This recent body of research has tended to look at gender as an interesting statistical variable although certainly not a defining or universally relevant one.[10] Elson refers to this as "the gender-disaggregation approach."[11] Drawing heavily on the neoclassical economic paradigm, it tends to a static and reductionist definition of gender as (woman/man)—stripping away consideration of the relational aspects of gender, of power and ideology, and of how patterns of subordination are reproduced. To the extent that such approaches do consider the factors underlying gender disadvantage or inequality, they tend to look to information problems (for example, women's tendency to follow female role models) or to "culture" (defined as outside the purview of mainstream economics) as explanatory factors.[12] While such research may be of great interest and can provide invaluable insights and empirical evidence, it can under-specify the power relations maintaining gender inequalities, and in the process, de-links the investigation of gender issues from a feminist transformatory project.

Bureaucratic requirements for information tend to strip away the political content of information on women's interests and reduce it to a set of needs or gaps, amenable to administrative decisions about the allocation of resources. This distillation of information about women's experiences is unable to accommodate or validate issues of gender and power. Women are separated out as the central problem and isolated from the context of social and gender relations. Furthermore, bureaucracies tend to privilege certain kinds of information perceived as relevant to dominant development paradigms and attribute significance to information in proportion to the perceived social and political status of the informer. Thus the information provided by Western feminists has tended to get a better hearing than the perspectives of Southern women.[13] It now appears that the quantitative expertise of male economists on gender is gaining increasing weight as the discourse becomes more technocratic, with the danger that in-depth, qualitative, feminist research may be devalued.

The Beijing Conference itself saw the production of several compendia of gender-disaggregated data, including a new edition of *The World's Women* produced by the U.N. Statistical Office [14] and UNDP's *1995 Human Development Report*. [15] This latter featured two new indices—the Gender Disparity Index (GDI) and the Gender Empowerment Measure (GEM). The GEM is an interesting departure in that it attempts to establish a universal index by which "empowerment" (a highly culturally loaded concept) can be measured and compared between countries, based on a composite of measures of income, participation in professional and managerial jobs, and formal political participation. [16] It is especially ironic that the rhetoric of grassroots, collective, bottom-up development ("empowerment") is invoked to name a topdown and universalizing statistic.

This is not to say that quantitative data or analysis of gender issues is not valuable. One key victory at Beijing was the successful campaign for the Platform of Action to include a commitment to the valuation of women's unpaid labor in satellite national accounts, making concrete a long-standing feminist rallying cry. In this case, an organized feminist campaign was able to exploit the increasing sophistication of gender-disaggregated statistics and of statistical method in general.

Advocacy and Accuracy: Lies, Damned Lies, and Gender Statistics

As feminist researchers we felt it important in the build-up to Beijing to forge alliances with activists and campaigners within NGOs and women's organizations, who are attempting to change the policies of public institutions. This proved challenging in a number of ways. Specifically, it highlighted our distance from the language used in the lobbying process, in both its conceptual underpinnings and style: our proclivity for academic rigor, complexity, and critique seemed at times to be in direct opposition to the demands of consensus building, political utility, and direct campaigning messages.

A couple of examples illustrate the point. We are all familiar with the claim that "Women [account] for two-thirds of all working hours, receive only one-tenth of the world income, and own less than one percent of world property." [17] It has recently come to light that the figure was made up by someone working in the U.N. because it seemed to her to represent the scale of gender-based inequality at the time. [18] It has since been taken up and repeated endlessly, to the point of becoming a cliché, as a justification for attention to gender inequality in access to resources. The point is that, while highly effective as an advocacy slogan (still in circulation 15 years on!), the claim had no empirical basis and thus had the potential to backfire and discredit feminist research. In the context of "mainstreaming," such slogans may have little credibility.[19]

Nevertheless, similarly dubious statistical claims continue to be made by activists and gender advocates in order to justify attention to women. DAWN's position paper for the Beijing Conference asserts that "Women world-wide produce half of the world's food, constitute 70 percent of the world's 1.3 billion absolute poor and own only 1 percent of the world's land."[20] Throughout the conference, the "feminization of poverty" featured prominently as a topic of discussion and as a justification for channeling resources to poor women. The Platform of Action features a chapter on the "persistent and increasing burden of poverty on women" that specifically refers to the "feminization of poverty" and identifies female-headed households as a particularly vulnerable group in this context.[21]

At the Conference we distributed a briefing paper on gender and poverty reduction strategies, which, drawing on recent work in the GAD field,[22] questioned the growing orthodoxy on the feminization of poverty and, specifically, the claim that rising female headship is responsible for this.[23] But other critics of the "feminization of poverty" at Beijing tended to be those on the religious right who viewed the association with female headship and the resulting demands for resources to be channeled to lone women as a threat to family values. Thus, we found ourselves going against the tide of the advocacy effort in rather unwholesome company.

Instrumentalism and Opportunism

Activists, lobbyists, and gender policy advocates working within institutions have adopted a variety of strategies to influence institutional agendas and bring about "mainstreaming," often resorting to instrumental arguments to convince hardened bureaucrats of the need to address gender issues. Common instrumental arguments used are the need to invest in female education to serve population control and child welfare goals or the importance of women's participation in community organizations to improve service provision and assist anti-poverty efforts. Such arguments appear justified to get gender issues on the table in organizations whose mandate and goals do not embrace social justice or equity. The World Bank's recent policy document for Beijing, for example, makes the case for gender almost entirely on efficiency grounds, constructing a convergence between the interests of women and the promotion of economic liberalization: "Sound economic policies and well functioning markets are essential for growth, employment and the creation of an environment in which the returns to investing in women and girls can be fully realised."[24]

Instrumental arguments, while they may prove successful in raising gender issues, are problematic in that attention to women or gender is often simply a means to other ends. Further, they run the risk of being discredited. Tenuous evidence on the relationships between female education and fertility decline, or female education and productivity, can be easily challenged, weakening the justification for addressing gender issues and posing a danger that resources will be withdrawn. Finally, the use of instrumental arguments fails to recognize the gendered nature of institutions themselves: information or the right arguments will not in themselves produce change. Institutional structures, rules, and cultures, including the ways in which information is collected, processed, and prioritized, reflect dominant gender interests, so that the pursuit of gender equity must include demands for organizational change.

Mainstreaming: The Depoliticization of Gender?

The ambivalence about—or even hostility towards—the GAD discourse expressed by some Southern women activists at Beijing perhaps reflects deeper anxieties about the imposition of what is perceived as an external agenda and about whose interests are served by the mainstreaming project. This is underlined by the lack of accountability of Northern development agencies to the Southern women in whose interests they claim to be acting. While Northern feminist groups can lobby their governments, albeit to limited effect, the responses of Southern women to policy decisions taken in Washington or London have not until recently formed part of the "feedback loop" characteristic of pluralist politics.[25]

The variety of ways in which "gender" has come to be institutionalized and operationalized in the development arena presents a contradictory and ironic picture. There is a disjuncture between the feminist intent behind the term and the ways in which it is employed such as to minimize the political and contested character of relations between women and men. A problem with the concept of "gender" is that it can be used in a very descriptive way and the question of power easily removed. In order to bring the power back into gender, feminists need to move away from the idea of simple oppression and bring a gender critique into new theorizing about power.[26] More practically, we also need to challenge the privileging of certain kinds of information on women and, as a consequence, particular kinds of expertise within development bureaucracies.

It is ironic that a concept that was engineered to carry a political message can be so depoliticized in its use as to be rejected by some of the people most committed to gender-redistributive change, such as feminist development activists. This speaks not to a need to reject the concept of "gender," but rather, to the need for much greater, and perhaps much more pragmatic and applied, dialogue between researchers and practitioners to ensure that concepts developed for activist arenas are not developed in the isolation of theory. Theorists can never, of course, control what happens to concepts when they are taken up by activists, nor would that be desirable. But given that much of feminist academic research grounds its legitimacy on a claim to relevance to the struggles of contemporary women, the ways in which feminist concepts can be distorted, even by well-meaning newcomers and potential allies, deserves careful monitoring.

The second half of this chapter now turns to a virulent challenge to the concept of "gender" that came from a very different direction in Beijing: conservative backlash politics. While the first set of challenges related to concerns about the depoliticization of gender relations, this contrasting challenge, ironically, related to a view that ideas behind the concept of "gender" tend to over-politicize the relations between women and men. This backlash challenge demonized "gender" as a code for the disruption of cherished certainties about human relations.

The Bracketing of Gender in the Platform for Action

"We have to try to neutralize the tremendous amount of gender, gender perspectives, which are going to go directly against our families and against our children."—speaker on a panel of conservative women at the Fourth U.N. Conference on Women, Beijing, fringe meeting, September 1995

The Platform for Action agreed in September 1995 at the Beijing Conference was a more highly contested text than any of the other international statements agreed at recent international conferences—at one point two paragraphs of text alone had generated 31 pages of amendments. Unlike any of these other agreements, debate over the Platform for Action was unique in calling into question the conceptual foundation and subject matter of the Conference itself—the concept of gender, and with it, notions of the injustice, and mutability, of gender relations. Was the Conference to be about "sex" or "gender"? At the final Preparatory Committee meeting in March 1995 in New York, divergent views on this question emerged as country delegations took their last opportunity to signal their reservations over parts of the text prior to the Beijing meeting. Most dramatically, the representative from Honduras, backed by representatives from other Catholic countries, proposed the bracketing of the word "gender" throughout the text. A working group eventually compromised on an acceptably broad definition of the term, but the tremendous anxieties over the meaning and implications of the "gender perspective" illuminate an unexpected politicization of the concept of "gender," which expressed, in part, aspects of backlash reactions to contemporary feminism. The debates over the word also shine light on some contradictions and inconsistencies in feminist theoretical and political distinctions between sex and gender.

It may be that the conservative opposition to the concept expressed a second-wind reaction after the failure to prevent agreement at the International Conference on Population and Development in Cairo in 1994 on a broad definition of women's reproductive health rights. Other factors explaining the conservative fixation on gender may include the perceived greater influence and presence of feminist NGOs, the greater visibility of lesbians in NGOs, and the inclusion, for the first time in the U.N. series of Conferences on Women, of very open language on sexual and reproductive rights.

The issue of the perceived influence of feminist NGOs became a particularly important target for conservative concern. The U.N. Conferences on Women over the last twenty years have set in place mechanisms for collaboration between feminist non-governmental groups and multilaterals that are of a much more sophisticated nature than is conventional in these forums. In part, the growing importance of these NGOs in the U.N. Conferences on Women is a reflection of their relative weakness at the national level; international forums have become arenas where they can "leap frog" past the boundaries of state sovereignty to propose visions of women's liberation that national governments might not countenance—and for which there is often insufficient domestic support, even from among women. As a consequence, there is a high degree of discursive familiarity between NGOs and multilaterals such as the U.N. on issues such as women's rights, or the meaning of "gender," sometimes leaving individual states in the dark. This appears to have fanned conservative suspicions of a conspiracy by a minority of unrepresentative women in these NGOs to undermine national sovereignty and cultural self-determination.

The Trouble with Gender

The conservative challenge to the use of the concept of "gender" raises issues central to feminist epistemology and politics. How is the body constituted in gendered identity formation? What is the relation between gender identities and political subjectivities? Does sensitivity to gender reveal a concern for equality or for a celebration of difference? Does a concern with equity risk assimilating women to the masculine mean? Would a celebration of difference play into the hands of a tradition that has used notions of "biology is destiny" to explain and justify inequality?

The trouble with gender is that it allows for considerable variation in the ways feminists interpret identity formation and the relationship between anatomy and culture. This variation has been seen as part of the richness and flexibility of feminism, but it has also meant the production of ambiguities, inconsistencies, and contradictions that conservative groups exposed in attacks on feminism. On the one hand, the lingering essentialism or "biological foundationalism"[27] in feminist thought encourages romanticism about women's shared experiences and interests, and supports policy solutions that assume a relationship between female embodiment and representation of women's interests—such as the assumption that more women in decision making will result in feminist decisions. This is incompatible with, on the other hand, the postmodern exposure of "women" as a product of a masculine dominative logic, and the degendering of ontology, which so fundamentally denies a determinate meaning to both "woman" and "women" that it hardly makes sense to have a conference on "women" at all.

Problems of universalism, essentialism, relativism, and nihilism are not new to critical feminist theory or feminist practice. What is argued here is that the conservative reaction to "gender" highlighted inconsistencies and areas of neglect in contemporary feminist approaches to the constitution of gender identity and political subjectivity, and that these are problems that stand in particularly stark relief in an internationalist context like the Beijing Conference, which puts feminist claims to represent the meaning of women's experiences in all their heterogeneity to their starkest test. To develop this argument, a conservative polemic attacking feminist conceptions of gender that was circulated at the Huairou NGO Forum is analyzed here, with a particular focus on its implications for feminist conceptions of the sex/gender relationship, and for conceptions of desire, motherhood, relationships to men, and the equality/difference tension.

"Gender: The Deconstruction of Women"

"Gender, The Deconstruction of Women" is a 29-page essay by Dale O'Leary, which was widely circulated at the NGO Forum.[28] O'Leary is a writer for the U.S. conservative Catholic publication: *Hearth—Journal of the Authentic Catholic Woman*. It is not assumed here that her paper is representative of all conservative views or of fundamentalist religious perspectives in general. The paper does deserve some attention, however, in that of all the conservative documents available at the NGO Forum, it is the only one we are aware of that engages directly with feminist theory, and thus directly outlines some ways in which conservatives are politicizing gender in reaction to feminism. The paper will not be analyzed in terms of what it shows of a conservative position but, rather, in terms of the issues it raises for the coherence of feminist approaches to gender.

To emphasize the problem of gender, though at the cost of any subtlety, O'Leary lumps together virtually all feminisms under the general title "Gender Feminism." The agenda of "gender feminists" is presented through a translation of their "code words" in the Platform for Action (this heightens the sense of conspiracy): "free choice in reproduction" is explained to be a code for abortion on demand, "lifestyle" a code for homosexuality.[29]

The argument of O'Leary's paper runs as follows. If gender is defined as the social construction of roles and relationships between women and men, then sexuality can be fluid, the centrality of the family can be challenged, role assignments such as motherhood and male breadwinner are revealed as social constructs, and indeed the fixity or irreducibility of anatomical sex itself can be questioned. All of this of course has always been central to a feminist logic, though there has been less certainty about the last point, as will be suggested shortly.

O'Leary's reaction to the feminist argument on social construction is to point out that there is no scientific proof for any of it, nor is there evidence that women do not freely choose traditional roles. On the contrary, science is showing that sexed behavioral characteristics and social choices are programmed genetically,[30] and surveys of women show that they do freely chose their roles and are not victims of "false consciousness," and that even if they want equal opportunities, they do not necessarily desire a sex/gender revolution—they value their womanliness.

These views might be considered fairly typical of conservative reactions to feminism. The key reason for the panic in relation to the term gender, however, appears to be its implications for sexuality and reproduction, reflecting two major conservative bogeys—homosexuality and abortion. Interestingly, conservative positions on the naturalness of restricting women to mothering roles, or to secondary economic positions, and so on, are not particularly stressed in O'Leary's document nor, by and large, in other conservative pamphlets available at the Forum. This reflects perhaps changes in the economic roles of women in conservative countries worldwide. Poverty and male unemployment globally has pushed more women into work and enhanced their role in supporting families, and few conservatives would suggest women withdraw from work in the context of poverty (though they might defend men's privileged access to favored labor market positions). Nor is any disapprobation expressed for women in public decision making roles and, indeed, many conservative delegations, including the one from the Vatican, were led by women. This may reflect pressure from conservative women for more participation in decision making and a secular increase in women's education levels and participation in government in many developing countries.

Declaring War on Women's Natures?

Although the predominant concern with sexuality and reproduction reflects perennial conservative anxieties, it is also a direct reflection upon the implications of the gender argument for the way we think of the body. Implicit in O'Leary's document is an understanding that taken to its logical extreme, the argument about social construction must eventually deconstruct the body. As Linda Nicholson points out, this understanding of the implications of gender thinking has come unevenly to feminists. She shows that there have been two trends in the ways feminists currently think of gender. First, there is the more familiar use of the term to stress the social construct in contrast to the biological given. Second, gender is increasingly used to refer to any social construction having to do with the male/female, as opposed to the masculine/feminine distinction.[31] Nicholson quotes Scott to show how sex is subsumable under gender: "gender is the knowledge that establishes meanings for bodily differences . . . We cannot see differences except as a function of our knowledge about the body, and that knowledge is not 'pure,' cannot be isolated from its implication in a broad range of discursive contexts."[32]

Nicholson argues that the problem with the first definition is that it is self-contradictory and risks biological essentialism, because biological sex has to be invoked at the very moment that the influence of the biological is being challenged—in other words, "woman" remains a given upon which characteristics are imposed through social reactions to the body.[33] This first understanding of gender has grounded feminist cross-cultural work on women's status in the sense that sufficient physiological givens are assumed to be shared by all women to generate a common range of social constructions. The changeability of these social reactions across culture, the important exceptions, rescues this approach from complete biological essentialism in stressing the mutability of sex identities. The cost of this approach has been a central dilemma and political schism within feminism, stemming from the underplaying of differences between women, across culture and race in particular, in the interests of maintaining a notion of universality in the cross-cultural feminine, a universality, moreover, that disguised its roots in the experiences of white Western women.[34]

O'Leary's discussion of this first understanding of sex and gender illuminates familiar problems it poses for the ways we think about equality and difference. The notion of social construction can be interpreted as suggesting a fundamental equality and sameness between the sexes, and O'Leary touches on a problem with this. Bringing up the liberal feminist concern to see parity for women and men in all forms of employment, she argues that this will inevitably force women to conform to the male standard. She explains this, however, rather differently from feminists who point to structural pressures on women to become sociological males when they cross the public/private divide. Instead, she argues, the problem inheres in men's incapacity to become biological females: "Trying to pretend that all the obvious differences are socially constructed and can therefore be changed, or that men and women can and should be the same, makes maleness the standard for women, because while women can enter the world of work, men cannot give birth."[35] This ignores, of course, the wide range of reproductive activities which men are perfectly capable of performing, but it does touch on a widely shared disappointment among women about the difficulty in winning social value for women's work rather than struggling for success in the public sphere, only to be found wanting by a male standard. O'Leary links this problem with the obsession with generating gender-disaggregated statistics on women's representation of women in all public forms of employment or politics. Though she does not intend the point in this way, she is identifying a problem with the unreflective pursuit of formal equity. Not all statistical differences reflect discrimination. Nor does fifty-fifty statistical equality reflect genuine equality and a cultural change to value women's interests—male/female equity in enrollment levels, for instance, tells us little about gender bias in the curriculum.

The second account of gender, in which "sex, by definition, will be shown to have been gender all along,"[36] is so sensitive to problems of essentialism that it rejects any account of sexual difference that invokes what is unique in female sexuality because this would re-cement the boundaries of gender identities. All associations with the term "woman" are exposed as arbitrary meanings, and biology, rather than being something that women in all countries share, is instead a culturally specific set of ideas with little translatability across cultures. Now, the extreme postmodern unraveling of both "woman" and "women" is disconcerting enough to many feminists, whether academics or activists—it has often been pointed out that it may lead to a nihilistic conception of women.[37] As Nicholson observes: "If those who call themselves feminists cannot even decide upon who women are, how can political demands be enacted in the name of women?"[38] To those espousing a conservative interpretation of women's roles[39] this is not the issue, as they have never made the politically motivated assumption that women are socially constructed. Instead, the anxiety is over the challenge to the notion that "biology is reality."[40]

This second approach to understanding gender appears to have been identified more clearly by conservative groups than it has been, perhaps, by feminist activists—for instance, in the gender and development field it does not appear to have much currency. One strategy to bring out the implications of these notions of the fluidity of the body in an alarmist and trivializing way prior to the Beijing Conference was the mock horror expressed by conservatives in the U.S. over a scientific paper about genital abnormalities. Anne Fausto Sterling's discussion, "The Five Sexes: Why Male and Female Are Not Enough," showed that genital abnormalities produce "herms" (hermaphrodites), "ferms" (female hermaphrodites), and "merms" (male pseudo hermaphrodites). Conservatives used this as a springboard for insisting on clarifying the status of "sex" in the Platform for Action, demanding "assurance that only two sexes would be recognized."[41]

While these kinds of reactions and strategies can be and often are dismissed by feminists as distracting irritations, it is worth noting that feminists have not been consistent in the way notions of sex and gender, of biology and culture, ground their tactics. There is a tendency to use social constructivist arguments when convenient, and biologically essentialist ones at other times. At the Beijing Conference there were examples of policy arguments made on the basis of either sex or gender. Some lesbians invoked both in contradictory ways—for instance, it was widely maintained that the brackets around "gender" in the Platform for Action directly signified homophobia, in that they expressed an attack on the notion of fluidity in the construction of the sexed body and of desire. Yet at the same time, a lesbian was reported as announcing, at one of the human rights tribunals, that she had been "born a lesbian," insisting on a biologically grounded notion of her identity.[42]

The Straw Man of Patriarchy—and Other Feminist Universals

"Everyone has a right to be listened [to] . . . and atheists and lesbians do not have the right to impose their views on the rest of us"—speaker from the floor at a meeting of conservative women at the Beijing conference.

O'Leary presents a crude version of feminism that bears little resemblance to the complexity of feminist thought. It is hard to imagine feminists today who would accuse happy mothers of suffering from false consciousness or dismiss women's subjective interpretations of meaning in their lives. However, her interpretation of feminism is probably not so different at a general level from popular understandings of feminism, and as such it points to certain "sore points"—or neglected issues—within feminism that have alienated women and men, perhaps more than necessary. Not all feminists are "atheists and lesbians," but if this is the popular perception of feminism, this suggests that feminists have undertheorized, or been dismissive of, a range of important aspects of women's lives. These include the role of women in many parts of the world in maintaining tradition and the centrality of religion to their lives, women's joy in mothering and nurturing, and women's individual choices to make "bargains with patriarchy."[43] Another neglected area is the great range of masculinities. This list may seem a reactionary set of concerns to some. Others may argue, and rightly, that feminists do deal with each of these areas, with masculinity perhaps more neglected than other areas because of the political imperative of addressing women's concerns first. Though feminists do deal with religion, motherhood, and so on, their analytical proclivities have been oriented primarily to critiquing not the subjective experience of motherhood or worship or partnership with men, but rather the conditions that are felt to strip freedom from women's choices in these situations—feminists critique the conditions of motherhood, not the value of parenting; they critique the gendered constraints of religion, not the value of spirituality. These subtleties are lost, however, on most people, and unfortunately the negative language that is sometimes used—such as speaking of women's "burden" of child care or of the "reproductive tax"[44]—does not convince people that positive value in women's choices and identities is being recognized. Nowhere is this more so than in popular perceptions of the way feminists think about men and their relationship with women.

O'Leary brings this out rather wittily, charging feminists with creating a "straw man of patriarchy": "the proto-typical male chauvinist, patriarchal sexist oppressor who believes biology is destiny and wants women confined to the house, barefoot and pregnant, inferior, subordinate, [a] second-class citizen." She points out that if this person actually existed he would "probably be confined to a maximum security facility as a sociopath."[45] Feminists have always had trouble theorizing patriarchy with enough subtlety to embrace historical and cultural variation,[46] let alone individual male subjectivities. Though they have not been quite as crude as O'Leary suggests, there is room for much more work in understanding masculinity and male domination. More critical, perhaps, is the need to move beyond the sharply dualistic confrontational categories in which Western feminists have tended to place the relations between the sexes. Feminists from the South have pointed out that this male/female opposition may be more central to the constitution of gender identity of white middle class Western women than women elsewhere.[47] Postmodern feminists have pointed out that the very sharpness of this male/female dualism informing the concept of "woman" actually undermines any meaning that "woman" might have. Crowded "with the overdeterminations of male supremacy, invoking in every formulation the limit, contrasting Other, or mediated self-reflection of a culture built on the control of females,"[48] "woman" is emptied of any meaning of its own and is less useful for feminist politics. Feminists have argued for the need for a more plural interpretation of "woman" that refuses to "brace woman's mobility against the fixity of a petrified man,"[49] but more plural interpretations of "man" are needed also.

In the Name of Women

Given that feminists are indeed, as conservatives charge, a minority of women, and given that they are not in a position to legitimize their claims to represent the concerns of most women on the basis of democratic processes in social and political institutions that produce feminist representation, challenges to the relevance of feminist claims to women must be taken seriously. What is at stake is very clear in O'Leary's text—the relevance of feminism to women in developing countries:

The success or failure of the Beijing conference depends on the delegates from developing countries. . . . one senses their frustration with the Gender Perspective. Most are pro-family, pro-religion, and basically pro-life. They know instinctively that Gender Perspective is not the perspective of women in their countries. On the other hand, they strongly support the advancement of women. . . . They are grateful for Gender Feminists' willingness to join with them in the battle against economic neocolonialism. They do not want to appear to be opposing the equality of women.[50]

As O'Leary implies, feminism has an edge in the developing country context because of its tendency to take a structural approach to problems of women's poverty and oppression.[51] But to return to the subject of this paper, a broader concern for feminists working in coalition the world over relates to the place of gender in theorizing women's political subjectivity in cross-cultural contexts. Postmodernists argue that the only way to avoid generalizing from an essentialized Western version of the feminine is to refuse to seek shared sex or gender characteristics and to deny them political status. Cultural feminists propose instead a celebration of a multiplicity of feminine identities, but this can lead to a politically paralyzed relativism.[52] The risk is that the reality of women's oppression can fall between the many stools of feminist anxieties over identity.

It seems possible to construct a feminist politics without insisting that the category of "woman" or "women" has a determinate meaning. The key, as Mohanty suggests, is to refuse to make an elision between "women" as a socially constructed group and "women" as material subjects of their own history so that the material and ideological specificity of women's positions is appreciated and generalization about gender relations is avoided.[53] According to Nicholson, this also means refusing to assume sisterhood on the basis of gender or sex, but to seek instead to construct coalitions that acknowledge difference.[54] The creation of coalitions between groups with very different interests certainly seemed to be taking place in Beijing, with for example, a broad alliance on reproductive rights between North and South women, which allowed for rather different interpretations of these rights— abortion rights concerns predominating among Northern women and concerns for freedom from coerced abortions and contraception among Southern women. Similarly, coalitions concerned with economic crisis were formed between Southern women affected by structural adjustment, Western women dealing with social service cuts, and women in transitional economies dealing with high unemployment.[55] As Agarwal notes, this was the expression of the emergence of a "strategic sisterhood" to replace the "romantic sisterhood" of the past.[56]

At some level, however, the appeal to coalitional politics as a replacement for appreciating the relevance of sex, or even gender, to feminist politics is unsatisfactory. Why then organize together as women at all? It is hard to find space in contemporary feminist theory for the genuine sense of connection that so many women spoke of in Huairou and Beijing. In spite of great differences, it seems dishonest not to bear testimony to that palpable sense of commonality. It seems important not to confuse discursive constructions of "woman" with the living, talking, real person who engaged with other women in the Forum and the Conference. If we still find meaning in shared biology only because the world continues to behave and treat women as though this were their primary defining characteristic, this does not erase its meaningfulness as a point of connection between women. Acting as women in the name of women, we will inevitably infuse "sex" with meaning, but attention to the various paths by which we each come to be "sexed" should help ensure that we avoid sinking back to reductive essentialisms. What seems critical, however, is that we are consistent in applying to feminist activism and policy work the politically motivated assumption that woman is a socially constructed category. This will protect us from the dead end of essentialism, the cultural brutality of universalism, and will also allow us to broaden our base of allies beyond the boundaries of "sex."

Conclusion

Departing from Huairou clutching somewhat battered gender concepts and wondering how to reclaim their feminist content without alienating potential allies, particularly among Southern researchers and activists, where does this leave us?

As Northern feminist researchers in gender and development, one role we can play is to track the redefinition of concepts as discourses become institutionalized and to help identify opportunities for advancing feminist ideas within this process, being aware that we are often complicit in it. An example is the current debate in donor circles about good governance and participation, which provides considerable scope for questioning the nature of participation, and indeed politics, from a feminist perspective and, concretely, the opportunity to push for greater accountability of donor agencies and wider institutions to women and their organizations.

It is also important that we engage in dialogue with colleagues who work on gender issues from outside a feminist perspective, to attempt to broaden the scope of their studies and to see how their findings can inform our own work and campaigns. Training workshops in feminist research methods might be one vehicle for such a dialogue. We also need to ensure that the pioneering contribution of feminist theorists and researchers are recognized as gender and development work moves into the mainstream, and thus to convince funding agencies of the value of supporting non-quantitative, innovative, and challenging research.

Finally, and perhaps most importantly, we need to look at whether and how GAD research serves those attempting to promote women's interests either in grassroots development work or by influencing policy. Some might claim that as academics it is not our business to determine how our research is used, but this view is increasingly redundant in a world where much research is commissioned precisely to inform policy. At the very least, we need to maintain an open dialogue with feminist researchers and activists in the South, to listen to their critiques of current gender and development thinking, policy, and practice, including our own, and to take on board their perspectives and priorities.

Notes

1. K. Young et al., *Of Marriage and the Market: Women's Subordination in International Perspective* (London: CSE Books, 1981); S. Razavi and C. Miller, "Gender Mainstreaming: A Study of Efforts by the UNDP, the World Bank and the ILO to Institutionalise Gender Issues," UNRISD Occasional Paper for the Fourth

World Conference on Women, Beijing 1995, OP 4 (Geneva: UNRISD/UNDP, August, 1995), 27–32.

2. We were part of a team from several U.K. universities comprising, apart from ourselves, Bridget Byrne, Lyla Mehta, Kirsty Milward, and Sheelagh Stewart (IDS, University of Sussex), Cecile Jackson and Ruth Pearson of the University of East Anglia, Tina Wallace of the University of Birmingham, and Inez Smyth, formerly of the London School of Economics, now based at Oxfam. Tahera Yasmin Huque, who works for the Canadian International Development Agency in Bangladesh, was also involved in the UEA/IDS workshop, "Breaking In; Speaking Out: Making Development Organisations Work for Women."

3. Razavi and Miller, "Gender Mainstreaming," 1995.

4. Ibid.

5. K. Staudt, "Gender Politics in Bureaucracy: Theoretical Issues in Comparative Perspective," in K. Staudt, ed., *Women, International Development, and Politics: The Bureaucratic Mire* (Philadelphia: Temple University Press, 1990); Razavi and Miller, "Gender Mainstreaming," 1995; A. M. Goetz, "The Politics of Integrating Gender to State Development Processes: Trends, Opportunities and Constraints in Bangladesh, Chile, Jamaica, Mali, Morocco and Uganda," UNRISD Occasional Paper for the Fourth World Conference on Women Beijing 1995, OP 2 (Geneva: UNRISD/UNDP, 1995, May).

6. United Nations, *Draft Platform for Action, Fourth World Conference on Women, Beijing, China, 4–15 September 1995*, A/CONF.177/L.1, May 24 (New York: United Nations, 1995), 134.

7. Makibaka, "The Gender Trap: An Imperialist Scheme for Co-opting the World's Women: A Critique by the Revolutionary Women of the Philippines of the U.N. Draft Platform of Action, Beijing 1995" (Luzon, Philippines: Makibaka, 1995), 5.

8. N. Kabeer, *Reversed Realities: Gender Hierarchies in Development Thought* (London: Zed Press, 1994).

9. Razavi and Miller, "Gender Mainstreaming," 1995.

10. S. Appleton et al., "Gender, Education and Employment in Cote d'Ivoire," Social Dimensions of Adjustment Working Paper, No. 8 (Washington: World Bank, 1990); L. Haddad, "Gender and Adjustment: Theory and Evidence to Date," paper presented at the workshop on the Effects of Policies and Programmes on Women, 16 January 1992 (International Food Policy Research Institute: 1991).

11. D. Elson, "Introduction," in N. Çagatay et al., *World Development*, vol. 23, no. 11, Special Issue—Gender, Adjustment and Macroeconomics (Pergamon Press, 1995, November).

12. See M. Lockwood, "Engendering Adjustment or Adjusting Gender: Some New Approaches to Women and Development in Africa," IDS Discussion Paper No. 315 (Brighton: Institute of Development Studies, 1992), on Collier, for example.

13. A. M. Goetz, "From Feminist Knowledge to Data for Development: The Bureaucratic Management of Information on Women and Development," *IDS Bulletin*, vol. 25, no. 4 (Brighton: Institute of Development Studies, 1994).

14. United Nations, *The World's Women: Trends and Statistics* (New York: United Nations Statistical Office, 1995).

15. UNDP, *Human Development Report 1995* (New York: UNDP, 1995).

16. This is not the place for a detailed critique of this index; suffice to say that numerous questions could be raised about the validity of the measures chosen as indicators of "empowerment."

17. U.N., *Women 1980*, Conference Booklet for the World Conference of the United Nations Decade for Women, Copenhagen, 14–30 July, 1980 (U.N. Division for Social and Economic Information, 1980), cited in M. I. Duley and M. I. Edwards, eds., *The Cross Cultural Study of Women: A Comprehensive Guide* (Feminist Press: New York, 1986), 48.

18. The figure for the proportion of work done by women is variously reported at 60 percent, 67 percent (P. Maguire, *Women in Development: An Alternative Analysis* [Center for International Education: University of Massachusetts, 1984], 1, citing *World Bank, 1980*, U.N., 1979), and "nearly two thirds" (U.N., *World Bank, 1980*).

19. A few weeks before the conference, a senior policy advisor in a bilateral agency rang the Institute of Development Studies to enquire whether there was any evidence to support the "two thirds" figure, since male colleagues had challenged her use of it. In a similar vein, a recent evaluation of the gender activities of the Canadian International Development Authority (CIDA) found that CIDA had not been able convincingly to back up its claim that failure to take on board gender will hinder the development process, such that this claim was now met with considerable skepticism (CIDA, "Gender and a Cross-cutting Theme in Development Assistance: An Evaluation of CIDA's WID Policy and Activities, 1984–1992: Final Report," CIDA project no. 851/11109/S22564/139025/15/0103 (1993).

20. DAWN, "Securing Our Gains and Moving Forward to the 21st Century: A Position Paper by DAWN for the Fourth World Conference on Women, Beijing, September" (Barbados: University of the West Indies, 1995), 6.

21. United Nations, *Draft Platform for Action*, 21.

22. C. Jackson, "Rescuing Gender from the Poverty Trap," in *World Development*, vol. 24, no. 3 (1995).

23. This questioning arises partly from the lack of conceptual clarity over what feminization means, partly from the limitations of empirical evidence and partly from the implication that poor women should be the focus of our attention, rather than broader processes of gender discrimination.

24. World Bank, "Toward Gender Equality: The Role of Public Policy," *Development in Practice* (Washington: World Bank, 1995), 5.

25. J. Jaquette and K. Staudt, "Politics, Population and Gender: A Feminist Analysis of US Population Policy in the Third World," in K. Jones and A. G. Jonasdottir, eds., *The Political Interests of Gender* (London: Sage, 1988). Beijing provided an opportunity for strategic alliances between Northern and Southern activists to coalesce, notably the Women's Eyes on the World Bank campaign. Since Beijing, the World Bank has also set up a hand-picked External Consultative Group composed of prominent Southern women activists as a step forward to a greater accountability and increased legitimacy for its position on gender issues. The degree of influence, modality, and representativeness of this group, still in its early days, is not yet clear.

26. J. Oldersma and K. Davis, "Introduction," in K. Davis, M. Leijenaar, and J. Oldersma, eds., *The Gender of Power* (London: Sage, 1991).

27. L. Nicholson, "Interpreting Gender," in *Signs,* 29/1 (1994), 82.

28. Dale O'Leary, "Gender, the Deconstruction of Women," mimeo, distributed at the NGO Forum of the Fourth World Conference on Women in China, September 1995.

29. Ibid, 19.

30. Interestingly, in the months following the Beijing conference, many U.K. newspapers carried stories reviving socio-biological arguments and presenting new scientific evidence for gendered genetic programming.

31. Nicholson, "Interpreting Gender," 79.

32. J. Scott, *Gender and the Politics of History* (New York: Columbia University Press, 1988), 2.

33. Nicholson, "Interpreting Gender," 80–81.

34. Nalini Persram, "Politicising the *Feminine,* Globalising the Feminist," *Alternatives,* vol. 19 (1994); C. T. Mohanty, "Under Western Eyes: Feminist Scholarship and Colonial Discourses," in Mohanty et al., eds., *Third World Women and the Politics of Feminism* (Bloomingdale Indiana: University Press, 1991).

35. O'Leary, "Gender," 14.

36. J. Butler, *Gender Trouble: Feminism and the Subversion of Identity* (London: Routledge, 1990), 8.

37. Persram, "Politicising the Feminine," 287.

38. Nicholson, "Interpreting Gender," 102.

39. Or, as O'Leary puts it, women's "vocations," "Gender," 12.

40. O'Leary, "Gender," 14.

41. Ibid, 6.

42. I am grateful to Cecile Jackson for this example.

43. D. Kandiyoti, "Bargaining with Patriarchy," *Gender and Society,* vol. 2, no. 3 (1988).

44. I. Palmer, "Gender and Population in the Adjustment of African Economies," ILO Working Paper: Women, Work and Development, no. 19 (1991).

45. O'Leary, "Gender," 17.

46. Nicholson, "Interpreting Gender," 91–92.

47. T. M-H. Trinh, "Difference, Identity and Racism," *Feminist Review,* vol. 25 (1987), 18.

48. L. Alcoff, "Cultural Feminism vs. Post-structuralism: The Identity Crisis in Feminist Theory," *Signs,* 13/3 (1988), 504.

49. E. Berg, "The Third Woman," *Diacritics,* 12/2 (1992); Persram, "Politicising the Feminine" 286.

50. O'Leary, "Gender," 28.

51. Interestingly, O'Leary's text refuses structural explanations for a whole range of oppressions women experience—like inner city poverty, domestic violence, lack of employment opportunities. However, she makes one exception, referring to women's poverty, lack of social rights, and poor labor market options when explaining why some women become prostitutes (1995), 23.

52. Persram, "Politicising the Feminine"; A. M. Goetz, "Feminism and the

Claim to Know: Contradictions in Feminist Approaches to Women in Development," in R. Grant and K. Newland, eds., *Gender and International Relations* (Milton Keynes: Open University Press, 1991).

53. Mohanty, *Third World Women.*
54. Nicholson, "Interpreting Gender," 103.
55. B. Agarwal, "From Mexico to Beijing," *Indian Express,* October 6 (1995).
56. Ibid.

3/Contradictions of a "Women's Space" in a Male-Dominant State: The Political Role of the Commissions on the Status of Women in Postauthoritarian Brazil

Sonia E. Alvarez

Whether the state and the bureaucracy can be viable arenas for promoting improvements in the condition of women's lives is an especially pressing question for Latin American feminism today. Until recent years, feminists in the region completely dismissed state-centered political strategies and pressure-group tactics. Indeed, during the two decades when military authoritarianism reigned supreme in South America, the state was most often viewed as women's worst enemy.

At the rhetorical level authoritarian rulers extolled the virtues of motherhood and traditional womanhood. Yet in reality their policies brought about dramatic changes in women's social, economic, and political roles and, ultimately, in their consciousness as women. Regressive economic policies pushed millions of women into low-paying, low-status jobs in the least progressive, most exploitive sectors of the economy. Authoritarian development policies undermined working-class survival strategies, propelling hundreds of thousands of women to seek solutions to their families' needs by participating in the community self-help organizations and grassroots social movements that blossomed throughout Latin America in the 1970s. And the repressive social policies and exclusionary politics characteristic of bureaucratic-authoritarian regimes also drew women of all social classes in unprecedented numbers into the swelling ranks of the political opposition to military rule.[1]

These rapid changes in women's roles helped spark a second wave of the women's movement in South America. Working-class feminine groups and middle-class feminist organizations could be found throughout the region by the late 1970s.[2] And by the early 1980s women's groups had mobilized hundreds of thousands of women in protest of the detrimental effects of authoritarian development on women's lives and lives of all politically excluded social groups and classes.

Originally, most women's groups, like other opposition organizations in civil society, engaged exclusively in the politics of protest and in promoting grassroots survival efforts. But as authoritarianism began to crumble in the late 1970s and the military ushered in "political liberalization" schemes of various types and durations, women's movement activists began making gender-based claims on the state and political society. The return of civilian rule and political efforts to consolidate precarious democracies in South America in the 1980s now pose new challenges for feminist theory and practice in the region.[3]

The opposition political parties who courted the female electorate and appealed to organized female constituencies during the final stages of the transition to democracy are now in power. As newly established democratic regimes "seek to legitimize themselves through public policy and participation-based accountability" (Staudt, in Chapter 1), feminist claims have perilously made their way into male-dominant policy-making arenas. In some countries, such as Brazil, the new civilian regimes have endorsed such historic feminist demands as safe, accessible, noncoercive family planning, publicly financed day care, and equal pay for equal work and have established new government "machineries" for the promotion of gender equity. Brazilian feminists are confronted with a new conjuncture in gender politics.[4] The state, heretofore widely perceived to be women's worst enemy, is suddenly portraying itself as women's best friend.

The Brazilian Case

An examination of gender politics in Brazil during the 1970s and 1980s sheds light on a number of theoretical questions posed by Staudt in the introduction to this volume. Brazilian feminists have indeed gotten a "female foot in the door" and are developing new strategies for working "from within" (Staudt, in Chapter 1) the new civilian state and federal governments. Feminists gained political leverage during the ten years of "political liberation" as women made their presence felt among the ranks of the opposition to military rule and added their specific demands for gender equity, reproductive and sexual freedom, and the democratization of daily life to the opposition's demands for social, economic, and political democracy.

Since the early 1970s women's movement organizations have flourished throughout urban Brazil. Under the Catholic church's institutional shield, poor and working-class women organized movements for improved public services such as public education, running water, health care, and day care and thus joined other community organizations in challenging the foundations of the military's social and economic policies. By the late 1970s women of the popular classes, mobilized through thousands of neighborhood-based mothers' clubs and housewives' associations, had launched citywide, and even nationwide, movements for day care (such as the Struggle for Day Care Movement in São Paulo) and against the rising cost of living.[5]

Feminist groups, composed mostly of middle-class women, have built fairly successful cross-class alliances with these popular women's organizations since the mid 1970s. Feminism, like the gay, Black, and ecology movements, seized upon the military's post-1974 political liberalization policies to articulate new democratic goals within the larger opposition. Feminists organized debates, circulated petitions, staged numerous protest actions denouncing violence against women and unequal and exploitive conditions of women's work and education, demanding changes in the realm of family and civil law, and calling for reproductive freedom. Emerging from within the student movement, militant political organizations, and politicized professional associations in the early 1970s, Brazilian feminists protested the patriarchal foundations of authoritarian rule and struggled to gain a voice in the only opposition party, the Brazilian Democratic Movement (MDB).[6]

When the MDB gained electoral strength after 1974, women's movement participants lobbied the party to include gender-related issues in its platforms and programs. After the regime forcibly divided the opposition into several parties in the later 1970s, the women's movement was also split over new partisan options. But there was hidden strength in these new divisions. Feminists now took their demands into a variety of institutional and noninstitutional arenas. They remained active in community women's groups, student and militant organizations, and other grassroots movements, though to a lesser extent. But in 1981–1982 they also successfully lobbied all opposition parties to address feminist issues in campaigns for municipal, state, and federal office.[7]

The opposition gained control of eleven state governments in 1983—including those of the most industrialized and populous states of the south and southeast. Since that time women working within opposition-controlled state and local governments have introduced a number of innovative public

policies that have enhanced the status of Brazilian women and have generated new access points through which the autonomous women's movement
can influence decision making and monitor policy implementation. Under
the first opposition government in the state of São Paulo, ruled by the Partido do Movimento Democrático Brasileiro (PMDB), the direct successor of
the MDB, women pioneered a number of progressive gender policies that
have subsequently been implemented in other Brazilian states. After the return of civilian rule at the federal level in 1985, some of these policies have
been extended to the nation as a whole.[8]

This essay examines feminist activism and state response in two areas
of gender policy in postauthoritarian Brazil: family planning and day care.
Much of the analysis centers on 1983–1985 policy developments in the state
of São Paulo. Since 1983 São Paulo has been ruled by the PMDB—the party
that now presides over the New Brazilian Republic, inaugurated in 1985—
and therefore represents a test case for what the New Brazilian Republic
may hold in store for women as women. Attention is focused on the role of
recently created municipal, state, and federal councils on the status of women
in "infusing a new politics into male-oriented bureaucracy" and public policy (Staudt, Chapter 1). I will argue that, in the period under consideration,
Brazilian feminists developed successful strategies for what might be termed
"gendered bureaucratic subversion"—the feminist counterpoint to Staudt's
"gendered bureaucratic resistance" model—strategies that might be adopted
by activists in other comparable national contexts at similar political conjunctures.[9]

The Creation of a Council on the Status of Women in São Paulo

One of the most controversial policy initiatives of the post-1983 PMDB
regime in São Paulo may yet prove to be the most significant for promoting
concrete improvements in the status of women through public policy. The
creation of a council on the status of women heralded the beginning of a
new relationship between women's movements and the state in postauthoritarian Brazil.[10]

The creation of the council can be traced to the efforts of feminist
activists within opposition political parties since the early 1970s. Feminists
were especially active in the 1982 electoral campaign, which brought the
opposition to power in eleven states during the final stages of military rule.

Dozens of feminists worked on the PMDB campaign in São Paulo during 1982, forming a special Study Group on the Situation of Women within
the party's women's division. In consultation with women party members

throughout the state, the study group identified gender policy priorities and proposed the creation of a special government council or commission to formulate and oversee the implementation of those policies.

Following the overwhelming victory of the PMDB in São Paulo (gubernatorial candidate Franco Montoro received more than 5 million votes and the PMDB won the majority of seats in the municipal, state, and national legislatures in 1982), the study group and other PMDB women militants began to push for the creation of the Conselho Estadual da Condição Femenina (literally, the State Council on the Feminine Condition, hereafter referred to as the CECF), which would implement a State Program in Defense of Women's Rights. And the autonomous women's movement, divided and temporarily demobilized by the electoral conjuncture, began a process of reconciliation and remobilization, the symbolic expression of which was the planning of the 1983 International Women's Day celebration.[11]

Discussions of how the CECF would in fact be constituted, whether a separate women's department would be preferable to a council, and which areas of government policy toward women would have high priority under the new administration remained a closed partisan discussion within the PMDB. The fact was that some sectors of the women's movement (those that had supported the PMDB during the campaign) were now in "power," and the "opposition" women (members or sympathizers of the more left-leaning PT or Workers' Party) and nonpartisan women's movement activists saw themselves as marginalized from the decision-making process that was to define the new administration's policy toward women.

The result was that even before the PMDB had officially announced its plan of action vis-à-vis women, strong opposition to the CECF was already emerging among the ranks of the more grassroots-based feminist groups, the more politicized neighborhood women's groups, and the day care movement. This incipient opposition viewed the plan for the CECF as a possible instance of "institutionalization" of the women's movement by the state and saw the sectors of the movement involved in policy planning as "unrepresentative" of the women's movement as a whole.

The Women's Study Group presented a proposal for an executive decree creating the CECF to the governor-elect on March 8, International Women's Day, without previous consultation with local women's movement organizations as to its content, requesting that it be Montoro's first executive decree when he took office on March 15. Created by decree on April 4, 1983, the São Paulo Council on Women's Condition was granted broad "advisory" powers but no executive or implementation powers of its own, nor was it allowed an independent budget, being totally dependent on the governor's civilian cabinet for financial and technical assistance. The decree made no mention of the State Program in Defense of Women's Rights developed and proposed by PMDB feminists. Instead, the CECF was granted the power to:

"propose measures and activities which aim at the defense of the rights of women, the elimination of discrimination which affects women, and the full insertion of women into socio-economic, political and cultural life . . ."; it will "incorporate preoccupations and suggestions manifested by society and *opine* about denunciations which are brought before it . . . *support* projects developed by organs, governmental or not, concerning women, and *promote* agreements with similar organizations and institutions." [12]

The avowed purpose of this council, according to both the governor and the PMDB women who proposed it, was to give women influence over several areas of the state administration rather than isolate women in a separate women's "department." The structure of the CECF is fairly innovative in this regard, as its members include "representatives of civil society," ostensibly linked to women's movement organizations of various types, and official representatives of several state-level executive departments. The idea was to create direct access points to those departments, which would then enable the CECF and, through it, the women's movement, to influence the formulation of gender-specific or gender-related public policies and to monitor their implementation. However, since the CECF was given *no* executive power, its influence on policy is necessarily somewhat limited—though its very creation unquestionably represented an advance for women in comparison with their position under the previous administration (controlled by the military-government party, the Partido Democrático Social, or PDS).

Since the CECF's official tenure began in September of 1983, many of the women's movements' original fears of "institutionalization" and "cooptation" have proven partially unfounded. The CECF openly admits to its "partisan" composition, stating that "the criterion for supra-partisan representation [within the council] is still a dream, unviable at the time of the Council's creation." [13] Futhermore, the women who made up the original CECF seemed to be aware of the problematic nature of the council's relationship both to the male-dominated state apparatus and the autonomous women's movements. In one of its earliest official publications, Eva Blay, then president of the CECF, addressed the precariousness of the council's position within the regime:

Another question to be profoundly considered refers to the political-administrative form chosen [to represent women's interests within the new government]; a Council. Social movements, and among them, women's movements, desire and should guarantee their autonomy vis-a-vis the State. To be part of the State apparatus in order to be able to utilize it from within but at the same time maintain the freedom to criticize it is an extremely complex question. Nevertheless, this difficulty must not constitute an obstacle which paralyzes the participatory process. The [political-administrative] form devised to avoid the reproduction of vices typical of the traditional [political] structure is the creation of a Council which has a majority representation of sectors of civil society. The mechanisms of selection [of said representatives], have yet to be defined as it is hoped that organized groups or independent feminists will pronounce their opinions on the subject. . . . Created within an opposition party, due to the initiative of a study group, the Council on the Status of Women now belongs to all women, who can and should manifest themselves as to its future direction.[14]

But the problem posed by the CECF itself as to which women's organizations were to be represented within the council and which women were to represent them immediately generated a great deal of conflict between the Paulista women's movement and the new regime. The July 1983 appointment to the council of fifteen PMDB party women,[15] predominantly from the more liberal, professionally based feminist organizations in São Paulo,[16] led some PT-linked women and independent women's groups, under the leadership of Workers' Party municipal councilwoman Irede Cardoso, to accuse the CECF of being "undemocratic" and "unrepresentative" of the women's movement as a whole. These women argued that the council was an entirely partisan organism, that the regime was trying to coopt and institutionalize the women's movement through the creation of the council, and that the PMDB women who composed the CECF had failed to consult the broader women's movement in the establishment of its political priorities and its organizational structure and composition. The CECF in turn argued that its political strength and effectiveness depended on the strength and effectiveness of women's movement organizations, that it needed the support and collaboration of those organizations in order to gain clout within the state administration. Some autonomous women's organizations indeed recognized the council as a legitimate political conquest of the women's movement (and particularly of organized women within the PMDB) and chose to approach the new institution in a cautious but supportive manner.

The creation of the CECF in and of itself remobilized and strengthened the women's movement in São Paulo. Confronted with a new "women's institution" created by a regime theoretically sympathetic to women's claims, São Paulo feminist and feminine movement organizations had to concretize and redefine their political priorities so that they could be effectively channeled through the CECF or else risk having those priorities manipulated by the new regime for its own political gain.

A few autonomous women's groups called a public forum in May of 1983 to discuss the movement's potential relationship to the CECF, and this forum was established as a monthly event to discuss relevant political developments within the new regime and to plan unified movement strategies in response to those developments. These monthly forums were the first instance of ongoing, unified feminist and feminine political action since the 1981 International Women's Day celebrations.

The State Council on Women's Condition itself acknowledges the importance of sustained political pressure on gender-specific issues from outside the regime and "hopes to serve as an instrument for the dynamization and reinvigoration of the autonomous women's movement."[17] And, in spite of the considerable demobilization of the remaining autonomous women's movement organizations in São Paulo in the aftermath of the 1982 election, the CECF advanced a number of innovative public policies during the first two years of its tenure.

Day Care Policy in Metropolitan São Paulo: State Initiatives, Council Intervention and Movement Response

Since the early 1970s neighborhood women's groups had been pressuring the municipal Department of the Family and Social Welfare to install public day care facilities in São Paulo's urban periphery. And during the First Women's Congress in São Paulo in March of 1979, those previously isolated groups of neighborhood women and their middle-class feminist allies launched a united effort to attain state funds for community-based day care.[18]

In a May 1979 manifesto signed by forty-six São Paulo feminine and feminist groups, the newly founded Struggle for Day Care Movement (Movimento de Luta pela Creche or MLC), unmasked women's role in the domestic or "personal" sphere as politically and economically determined, demanding that the state and private capital assume increased responsibility for the reproduction of the labor force:

We are workers who are a little different than other workers . . . we are different, in the first place, because we are not recognized as workers when we work at home 24 hours a day to create the conditions for everyone to rest and to work. This is not recognized, but our work creates more profit that goes directly into the pocket of the boss.

We are different because when we also work outside the home, we accumulate two jobs—at home and in the factory. . . . We want *creches* that function full-time, *entirely* financed by the State and by the companies, close to workplaces and places of residence, with our participation in the orientation given to children and with good conditions for their development—we will not accept mere depositories for our children.[19]

This manifesto was followed by dozens others like it, demanding that "personal" childcare become "public day care," pushing the state to assume responsibility for women's domestic burden. The day care movement quickly expanded throughout São Paulo's working-class suburbs as women organized in neighborhood women's groups and church-linked mother's clubs created day care groups or commissions. The movement's political strategies focused on directly pressuring the municipal government and on popular mobilization in support of public day care through rallies, assemblies, neighborhood petitions and surveys, and direct actions.

In late 1979 the day care movement took its demands to newly appointed São Paulo mayor Reynaldo de Barros. The recently inaugurated PDS administration had adopted a legitimacy formula based on neopopulist concessions to the demands of increasingly active popular organizations—a formula inspired by the need to seek electoral support for the PDS in opposition-controlled metropolitan São Paulo. With the "economic miracle" long over and the first gubernatorial elections since 1965 scheduled for 1982, the government party in São Paulo sought a new social basis of support among São Paulo's poor through the provision of meager social services to peripheral, economically depressed neighborhoods.

And day care centers or *creches* were the social service that featured most prominently in de Barros' neopopulist formula. Despite the fiscal crisis already faced by the county of São Paulo in 1979, de Barros promised a commission of representatives from thirty women's groups from the city's Southern Zone that he would build 830 day care centers during his administration and that these *creches* would be administered by community councils selected and trained by local neighborhood organizations. At the time of his announcement São Paulo had 123 *creches* serving 17,055 children, but only three of them were publicly funded.[20]

By 1981 his 1979 promise of 830 *creches* had dwindled to 330. And by the end of de Barros' administration, only 141 day care centers, the so-called *creches diretas* entirely financed by the municipal government, had been constructed in the county of São Paulo. De Barros, who became the PDS gubernatorial candidate for São Paulo, made *creches* a rallying cry of his political campaign, stating in numerous campaign materials that "when Reynaldo de Barros came into office São Paulo only had three day care centers. Now São Paulo has 333!" The 333 were in the planning stages, at best, though de Barros had further served his political aspirations by appointing ahead of time the directors of all unconstructed day care centers.

The centers that had been constructed but had not been put into operation during the PDS regime became the primary focus of conflict between the day care movement and the 1983 PMDB regime. In April of 1983 leaders of the day care movement met with Governor Franco Montoro, who promised to call on all the state's mayors to give the construction of day care centers special attention.

During the first two months of the PMDB administration the *creche* movement expressed its confidence that the "new, democratic government of São Paulo would support the people's demand for free, community-administered day care." However, the movement's political posture soon changed as the PMDB regime appeared to place more emphasis on the cost of day care, in light of the present economic crisis, than on the political benefits of meeting day care movement demands. Arguing that municipal coffers had been virtually ransacked by the corruption of the previous regime and that the 1982–1983 debt crisis had only emptied them further, the PMDB administration ignored movement demands and decided to make the sixty-eight *creches* built under the de Barros administration indirect rather than direct ones. Indirect *creches* have been rejected by the day care movement as inefficient and pedagogically unsound. Partially financed by the municipal government but administered by private entities (usually charities), indirect *creches* preclude community participation in the administration of community-based day care—participation that has been a fundamental demand of the movement since its inception.

The result was open conflict between the new "democratic" regime and the day care movement after June of 1983—generating protest actions of the sort that had not characterized the movement since the early days of the de Barros administration. PMDB resistance to the further construction of day care facilities and to community administration of existing day care facilities generated the massive remobilization of the day care movement in São Paulo. In interviews I conducted at the time, a number of movement activists pointed to the irony of the situation—under authoritarian rule *creches* had been conceded by the state; under democratic rule they were being denied.

Throughout 1984 day care movement participants argued about what the MLC's political strategy should be vis-à-vis the new PMDB municipal government. Underlying partisan conflicts, subsumed during 1982 because of the endorsement of movement demands by both the PT and the PMDB electoral platforms, assumed much sharper lines within the city wide movement during 1983 and 1984. The PMDB sympathizers within the MLC argued for a new political strategy, one that would be sensitive to the new democratic situation and attempt to negotiate with the PMDB regime in spite of its seeming resistance to fundamental movement demands. The PT supporters within the MLC, on the other hand, insisted that the movement had to assume an oppositional or adversarial posture vis-à-vis the local administration and mobilize movement groups throughout the city to delegitimize the new regime's day care policy by proclaiming it to be "unrepresentative of the popular will."

The movement's citywide and regional coordinations were unable to reach consensus on the most appropriate strategy to confront the local government's policy initiatives on the day care issue. By late 1984 the MLC's citywide and regional organization had been totally dismembered. All that remained of the previously massive united grassroots movement were a few dispersed neighborhood-based day care groups.[21]

In 1984 the São Paulo Council on Women's Condition stepped in as the major day care advocate. Early on, the CECF established day care policy as one of its four principal areas of political action. It elaborated the following position on day care under the PMDB administration:

1. The right to day care should be considered an extension of the universal right to education.
2. Official policy on day care should integrate existing initiatives, guarantee minimal coherence in the actions of the various organs involved [in policy implementation], avoid the dispersion of resources to innumerable programs and organs, and be open to new proposals.
3. In this integrational effort, it is necessary to be clear that the State and society must assume responsibility for the child, guaranteeing it care, protection, and education, principally for the children of working women who constitute that portion of the population most in need of places where they can safely leave their children during working hours.
4. The popular movements, and especially the women's movement, have revindicated day care as a right of working mothers and have already accomplished, through their struggles, the recognition of that right through the installation of "direct *creches*" in several cities.
5. Day care policies to be elaborated should integrate the community, parents and professionals, in the process of implementation of the day care center and in the guarantee of popular participation in its functioning.
6. The day care centers should function during periods that correspond to the working hours of mothers.[22]

This statement illustrates the council's need to juggle the policy constraints imposed by the local regime, which clearly favors "indirect *creches*," and the demands of the popular-based day care movement, which is an important segment of the CECF's constituency within civil society.

After considerable deliberation the council decided to support the regime's contention that the present economic crisis precludes the creation of

additional direct *creches,* which necessitate greater state investment in the
"means of reproduction" than do indirect or privately administered day care
centers. At the same time, the CECF sided with the day care movement in
supporting its claim that those *creches* that were designated as direct by the
previous PDS Paulista regime should be maintained as such, as these represented a "right of working mothers" legitimately acquired through "popular struggle."

The CECF also participated in the preparation, supervision, and coordination of the Special Inquiry Commission on Day Care created in the São
Paulo municipal legislature in October of 1984. The commission, presided
over by PMDB councilwoman Ida María Jancsó, was created partially as a
response to the conflicts that had emerged between the local PMDB administration and the day care movement since 1983.[23] The CECF refined its
position on day care in its testimony before this commission:

The municipal chain of direct *creches* constitutes a conquest of the popular movements and the women's movement and as such should be *discussed.* An effort in the
sense of *discussion* and adopting a *creche* policy which perfects the existing chain
of direct *creches* is urgent, as [the present system] aside from its high cost (due to
inefficiencies and excessive centralization) offers low quality care.[24]

This statement reflects the precarious *structural* position within the state
apparatus of a "women's space" that simultaneously claims to "represent"
the interests of women *outside* the state. On the issue of day care the CECF,
as part of the state apparatus, supported the regime yet appears also to have
pushed the local administration to acknowledge the legitimate claims of the
popular-based day care movement.

For 1985 the council opted to redefine its day care policy—focusing
now on the private provision of day care by enterprises employing more
than thirty women, an aspect of the 1943 labor laws (the Consolidation of
Brazilian Labor Legislation, or CLT) that has never been enforced by the
state.[25] The CECF encouraged unions and government agencies to increase
their enforcement of this CLT provision, thus resolving the conflict between
the day care movement and the state by deflecting the revindications for,
and the costs of, day care onto the private sector.[26] The CECF also pressured the Ministry of Labor to revise the CLT's current provisions for day
care in the workplace. At the state level it also hoped to promote closer
Department of Labor monitoring of commercial and industrial establishments in order to ensure that they are providing pedagogically sound and
conveniently located day care services for their female employees.

Interestingly, the day care issue has to a certain extent been depoliticized in a gendered sense by the CECF. Whereas day care movement organ-

izations had insisted that day care was a "woman's right" or a "mother's right," given women's socially ascribed responsibility for domestic labor and childrearing, the council now argues that "the *creche* is a right of children, of workers . . . the right to day care should be seen as an extension of the universal right to education."[27] This political "renaming" of the day care issue seems to have been strategically warranted given the clear resistance of some sectors of the state and local administration to the idea and feasibility of direct *creches*. At the local level, resistance emanated primarily from municipal secretary of the family and social welfare Marta Godinho and São Paulo mayor Mario Covas. At the state level the governor's wife, Lucy Montoro—and, some argue that by extension, Governor Montoro himself—also pushed for alternative approaches to the "problem" of day care. Since 1983 Dona Lucy Montoro in particular has been promoting the idea of *mães crecheiras* or day care mothers—neighborhood women who would be employed and trained by the state to care for the children of other working women and who would provide these children with a "familial environment"—as an alternative to more expensive "impersonal" and "inefficient" public day care centers.

Opponents to this alternative, both within the day care movement and the state apparatus, argue that given the precarious conditions of life in urban working-class neighborhoods, *mães crecheiras* could not possibly adequately meet children's pedagogical, recreational, and nutritional needs. Just as importantly, they suggest, transferring the responsibility for childcare from one low-income woman to another and paying the second substandard wages and granting her no worker's benefits (as supporters of the alternative have proposed) is glaringly exploitive. Moreover, opponents argue, a *mãe crecheira* policy would reinforce existing patterns of gender inequality be creating *more* low-paying, low-status jobs for women, jobs that merely commodify women's socially ascribed mothering roles.

But the sectors within the PMDB ruling coalition that support the *mãe crecheira* alternative do not necessarily see these contradictions as problematic. They come from the centrist Christian democratic wing of the PMDB and espouse fairly conservative generic and reproductive ideologies.[28]

The São Paulo Council on Women's Condition, then, had to combat this traditionalist tendency within the local and state administrations. Thus, the council increasingly argued for day care in "broader" terms, appealing to "universal rights" rather than "women's rights" in order to widen political support for council day care proposals within the ruling coalition. The CECF's "generic" discourse on day care, however, has also had the indirect effect of depoliticizing the *genderic* content of the Struggle for Day Care Movement's historic political claims.

Significantly, there has been little gender-conscious political pressure for day care from without the PMDB ruling coalition since mid-1984. By late 1984 the repercussions of partisan conflict within political society upon the MLC had totally divided the previously unified citywide movement. And in the absence of such a movement, day care policy is at present being determined primarily by intrastate conflicts rather than by movement-state interaction.

State Population Control Policy: Movement Mobilization, Council Intervention, and State Response

Reproductive rights and women's health have been the most successful items on the CECF's policy agenda. When the federal government, still under military control, began formulating a population control program in 1983, the council and the autonomous women's movement worked to ensure that, at the state level, the would-be population control program would provide Paulista women with safe, accessible, and noncoercive family planning, made available to them through the state's public health network.[29]

Until the early 1980s the military-authoritarian regime had been overwhelmingly pronatalist, or, at best, ambivalent in terms of population politics. Subimperialist, expansionist ideology led the military regime to resist the implementation of a nationwide family planning program in the 1960s and 1970s when most other Catholic Latin American nations were doing so. The regime argued that Brazil's vastness of unpopulated territory and the richness of its untapped resources could accommodate unlimited population growth.

Coupled with this expansionist component of the regime's reproductive ideology in its early stages was a firm ideological commitment to the family. Indeed, bourgeois civilian supporters of the 1964 military coup that installed the regime had mobilized thousands (primarily women) against João Goulart, who allegedly threatened the very moral fabric of the Brazilian family through his "communist" social welfare policies. The political right organized marches throughout Brazil in the name of "Family, God, and Liberty" (the now infamous Marchas da Familia, com Deus, pela Liberdade) in the months preceding the coup.[30] The Family, writ large and abstractly, thus became one of the backbones of the new authoritarian regime in Brazil, just as it has often functioned as the bulwark of conservatism elsewhere in Latin America.[31] This gender-based component of the Brazilian regime's ideological support of the family therefore must also be considered a significant factor shaping the pronatalist policies of the regime in the 1960s and early 1970s.[32]

But by the late 1970s the military government had begun to reverse its position on population control. As the economy experienced a downturn after 1978–1979, the federal government and the São Paulo state government formulated new programs for curbing population growth.

The women's movement in São Paulo and other major cities mobilized in response to state initiatives in population control. The first statewide meeting of São Paulo feminist groups, held in Valinhos in June of 1980, created a special movement commission to study the government's past and present population control and family planning policies and to propose a feminist alternative "which would express the real interests and needs of Brazilian women." The commission released an extensive document for internal discussion within the movement in late 1980, a pamphlet-length version of which was widely distributed during the 1981 International Women's Day celebrations throughout the state of São Paulo. Proclaiming that "women's right to control their own bodies has long been one of the great banners of feminism" and that "both natalist and anti-natalist politics have utilized sexuality, the body of woman, as a social patrimony, denying her rights and her individuality," the documents vehemently opposed the "ambiguous official proposal for intervention in the 'regulation of fertility' of women" and argued for the "right to have the necessary conditions to opt freely for maternity." [33]

The feminist position differed markedly from that of the male-dominant opposition parties. Agreeing with the progressive opposition that "it is not the demographic explosion which is causing hunger, misery, and the *aggravation* of our historical situation of oppression but rather the unjust distribution of national wealth and the lack of democratic freedoms which are there to preserve the privileges of a minority, to the detriment of the overwhelming misery of the majority," [34] the women's movement further argued that the state *did* have the responsibility to provide women with safe, accessible, noncoercive methods of birth control:

Today we struggle to have the conditions with which to exercise the right to opt freely to have or not have children, how many to have, and the spacing between one pregnancy and another. This is for us a legitimate and democratic revindication because it contains a series of aspects which are essential to the advance of the liberation of women such as: the strict respect for the free exercise of our sexuality; the demand that motherhood and domestic work be assumed as social functions; the battle against any and all forms of utilization of our bodies as a social patrimony, above our individual right to choose. [35]

Feminists also denounced the government's proposed programs for isolating women's reproductive function from the general conditions of women's health. By introducing the notion of reproductive choice as an essential condition for women's liberation, the women's movement introduced a new gender-specific element in the Brazilian pronatalist versus antinatalist debate—proclaiming that the heretofore "personal" control of fertility *was* an issue for public, political debate and state action, not to be dismissed solely as an "imperialist plot" to "kill *guerrilheiros* in the womb."

Facing the 1982–1983 debt crisis and consequent renewed negotiations with the International Monetary Fund and other international lenders, the authoritarian regime made population control one of its political priorities in 1983. Population control policies in the Third World have often gone hand in hand with strict monetarist policies imposed on national governments by the international aid community.[36]

During the extended period of negotiation of Brazil's debt, population control found new advocates in the federal government. In March of 1983 President João Batista Figueredo called for a national debate on the subject, and the government party-controlled Senate established a Parliamentary Inquiry Commission on Population Growth. "Responsible paternity" became the catchword of antinatalist arguments in 1983. Senator Eunice Michiles, the only woman in the national Senate and president of the Movimento de Mulheres Democráticas Sociais (MMDS), the feminine branch of the ruling party, made it her primary political banner. In a speech before the Senate on April 28, 1983, the "women's Senator" combined neo-Malthusian arguments with women's rights arguments to propose the creation of an Interministerial Department for Family Planning (Departamento Interministerial de Planejamento Familiar) to be directly linked to the presidency and to be directed by a woman "because of her natural affinity with the program." After blaming a score of national ills on the "population problem," Michiles added:

The important fact is that women have been systematically omitted from the discussion of family planning; one cannot omit the fact that it is woman who is the principal agent of human reproduction, the one who spends nine months carrying a child, protecting it with her own body, the one who gives birth with all the joy and suffering that involves. . . . the understanding of contraceptive methods opens the doors to feminine independence, in the sense that a woman can decide *how many* children she will have, *when* she will have them, giving her the sensation of control over her destiny, allowing her a greater utilization of opportunities for education, and employment.[37]

The executive branch of the federal government also began its own plans for the institution of a national family planning program, independently of the deliberations of the National Congress. The Ministry of Health elaborated a new program called the Program for Integral Assistance to Women's Health (Programa de Assistencia Integral a Saúde da Mulher, or PAISM), which, like Michiles' proposal, also appropriated the "reproductive rights" discourse developed by the Brazilian women's movement, an ideological emphasis notably absent from the pre-1983 state population policies. Elaborated by two feminist doctors in the Ministry of Health, the program called for a holistic approach to women's health in contrast to the status quo: "traditionally a woman has been attended by the health system almost exclusively during the period in which she crosses the cycle of pregnancy and childbirth, leaving other aspects or phases situated outside that cycle on a secondary plane."[38] Though the program's emphasis remained on the female reproductive role, the ministry's recommendations were explicitly anti-*controlista* in rhetoric, denouncing "isolated vertical actions of family planning" that would interfere directly in "women's right choose" maternity or that would be preoccupied with the "reproductive aspects of women and not with their general health."[39]

In June of 1983 the Ministry of Health directed all state health departments to begin to discuss state-level implementation of the program. But in São Paulo the discussion of a possible family planning program had already been initiated within the opposition-controlled PMDB state government. At the urging of feminists active in the 1982 electoral campaign that brought the PMDB to power in São Paulo and ten other Brazilian states in 1983, the Department of Health, under the leadership of left-leaning Secretary Jose Yunes, had initiated a discussion of a comprehensive health program that was to respond to demands of organized women in São Paulo. Written with input from a special working group of leading PMDB feminists, representatives of the São Paulo Council on Women's Condition, and health and demographic specialists, the *Programa da Saúde da Mulher* (Women's Health Program) was even more in tune with women's movement demands than the federal program.

Ideologically, the program reflected the links established between certain sectors of the women's movement and the São Paulo opposition regime. Openly feminist in its discourse, this unprecedented document addressed issues of women's equality, women's sexuality, sex education, reproductive rights, and other issues that were first raised as political claims by the Paulista women's movement:

Facing, in a general sense, adverse conditions in the workplace (where the worst paid and least gratifying functions are customarily reserved for them), women accumulate domestic obligations in a toilsome double shift which consumes their physical and mental health. As housewives who dedicate themselves integrally to unpaid domestic labor, they also suffer the consequences of carrying out uninterrupted, repetitive, isolated and socially-devalued activities.

Besides the specific conditions of women's work, the role of women in reproduction requires special attention, since pregnancy, childbirth, and lactation are processes that demand their biological, psychological, and social involvement. Women's psycho-social involvement with maternity assumes larger proportions in our society, where the sexual division of the labor of childcare determines that this responsibility fall exclusively on the shoulders of women, without the participation of their companions and without the provision of nurseries, day care centers, or other services by the State.[40]

The program hoped to contribute to the "demystification of anti-natalist and natalist fallacies . . . and clearly disassociates itself with a demographic policy, that is, does not seek to interfere in fertility, either to reduce it, maintain it, or increase it."[41]

But even these seemingly "women-centered" federal and state family planning programs elicited distrust on the part of Brazilian women's movement organizations, left-wing opposition parties, the progressive church, and some sectors of the state apparatus and of the official government party, the PDS. No clear federal or state population guidelines were established, and the implementation stage awaited some sort of consensus within the governing coalition at both the national and state levels.

While key sectors of the federal government endorsed a national family planning program, opposition to such a program emerged elsewhere within the state apparatus and among the ranks of the governing party. Key political figures such as Minister of Social Welfare Helio Beltrão, Minister of Education Ester Figueredo, Minister Jarbas Passarinho, and some sectors of the Superior War College and of the armed forces, for example, continued to espouse natalist opposition to family planning or advocated a more balanced approach to population control—arguing that increased state outlays in education and health care would lead to a natural reduction of the national birth rate.

The traditional left and sectors of the progressive church denounced both federal and state family planning as genocidal and imperialist-imposed. The Workers' Party in São Paulo, for example, publicly proclaimed its wariness of even the state health department's feminist-inspired Women's Health Program as potentially *controlista*.

Many individual women's movement activists and autonomous women's organizations in São Paulo outside the ruling PMDB coalition shared in this wariness. They argued that the scarce funds likely to be allocated to these programs (estimated at only CR$11 million, less than US$20,000, for the federal program in 1983) would lead to the arbitrary distribution of birth control pills (and not other, more expensive, but safer methods) and to sterilization abuse among low-income populations, rather than in comprehensive health care for women.

Autonomous women's groups were caught in a bind in confronting state initiatives in reproductive politics. Suddenly the state—heretofore perceived as their primary adversary—was espousing a politic that approximated their own. And women's movement activists expressed an urgent need to distinguish their own proposals for reproductive freedom from state attempts to intervene in the control of fertility—a difficult task given that the women's movement had been the first to introduce the notion of state responsibility for the provision of birth control to all women.

Reproductive politics headed the agenda at the III National Feminist Meeting held in Brasília in July of 1983. Attended by women from more than twenty women's groups from São Paulo, Rio de Janeiro, Belo Horizonte, Salvador, Recife, Fortaleza, Goiania, Curitiba, and Florianópolis, the meeting resolved to elaborate a document specifying a national feminist position on birth control, abortion, and family planning to be widely distributed to the press and among opposition leaders. Participants also agreed to form state-based movement commissions to monitor the implementation of state and federal programs to prevent contraceptive abuses such as indiscriminate distribution of pills and forced sterilization.

Rio feminists also brought their proposal for a national pro-choice campaign to be initiated on September 22, 1983, throughout Brazil. The result of a national meeting on Women's Health, Sexuality, Contraception, and Abortion, held in Rio on March 4–6, 1983, and financed by the Pathfinder Fund, the campaign was not endorsed by many of the women present as they feared that a stress on abortion would be problematic at a time when the government had antinatalist intentions that could compromise this demand politically. Some participants asked, "Did the feminist movement want abortion to be legalized as a further State measure to control population size?"

Throughout 1984 sectors of the national women's movement and of the above-mentioned political opposition consistently pressured the Ministry of Health and other policy-making arenas within which the PAISM was being developed in order to assure that the regime was true to its anti-*controlista* political discourse, a discourse that was made more vulnerable to such organized pressure because it had incorporated or coopted so many of the concrete gender-specific demands raised by women's movement organizations during the past decade.

At the federal level some state fractions continued to push for the immediate establishment of a "National Council on Population" that would implement a national population control policy. Coopting the most prevalent opposition slogans during the 1984 direct elections campaign, which centered on the immediate end to military rule ("Direct Elections Now!" "Tancredo Neves Now!" "Constitutent Assembly Now!"), *controlista* segments within the ruling party and the state began advocating "Family Planning Now!" *(Planejamento Familiar Ja!).*[42] The chief of the Military High

Command, General del Aire Waldir de Vasconcelos, made population control his principal political concern during most of 1984—he traveled extensively throughout Brazil, meeting with prominent politicians, industrialists, and community leaders, and arguing that curbing population growth was essential to Brazilian economic growth and prosperity and therefore was a crucial component of "national security." Micheles' MMDS also engaged in a massive nationwide propaganda campaign to promote its own neo-Malthusian brand of "feminist" family planning.[43]

The Brazilian women's movement, acutely aware of the cooptative potential of these antinatalist offensives, launched a counteroffensive of its own. In July of 1984 the IV National Feminist Meeting, held in São Paulo and attended by ninety-seven women from thirty-three feminist organizations, focused on the issues of women's health and family planning in an attempt to further develop a feminist position on reproductive rights with which to contest *controlista* policy proposals at the state and national levels. And such a position began to take definitive shape during the remaining months of 1984:

It would occur to no one to suggest that the federal Program of Integral Assistance to Women's Health is what women aspire to in terms of a public health policy. This program, created by the military regime in recent times, however, contains some of the demands that feminists have been making. In spite of this, we believe that the bureaucratic manipulation of this program could result in few advances [for women] and for this reason, we have decided to participate more actively in its implementation, monitoring it, demanding forums and debates with institutional organisms, participating in conferences and other activities proposed by these organisms.[44]

In September and October of 1984 follow-up regional meetings were organized in Rio and in São Paulo. And in November of that year several feminine and feminist groups in São Paulo organized the First National Meeting on Women's Health, held in the city of Itapecirica and attended by more than 400 women from nineteen Brazilian states. The resulting document, *Carta de Itapecirica,* called for "the participation of women's groups in the elaboration, execution and monitoring of women's health programs, sex education for all the population, the reclaiming of popular and feminist wisdom against the excessive medicalization [of women's health] and a revalorization of natural forms of life and health."[45]

In contrast to the day care movement, the feminist movement reformulated its historically "anti-state" posture in the face of a new political conjuncture and exacerbated the contradictions inherent in state family planning initiatives. In this sense, then, the Brazilian women's movement and the organized opposition to any attempt at state population control successfully mobilized against those state factions that promoted *controlista* solutions and "beat" the outgoing authoritarian regime "at its own game." Organized sectors of civil society, spearheaded by women's movement organizations, and of opposition political parties, led by their respective women's divisions, pushed the regime to confront its own internal contradictions regarding the formulation and implementation of population policies.

The organized opposition to state factions that advocated *controlista* or neo-Malthusian formulations of family planning policy seems to have had an important impact on the regime's formulation of the PAISM. Such intervention by civil society in the regime's policy process was possible because of the variables then at play in the final stages of the Brazilian regime's transition to democracy. In its last attempts to consolidate political support for its "political project" in the face of widespread opposition, even from among its previous "allies" (sectors of the national bourgeoisie and the PDS that defected to the Liberal Front over the issue of direct elections), some factions within the regime, and apparently within the Ministry of Health in particular, appear to have become more receptive to political demands emanating from civil society.

In fact, the Ministry of Health proved to be an unusual "point of access" through which the Brazilian women's movement could influence the authoritarian state appartus.[46] The team to which the ministry's PAISM was initially entrusted was presided over by feminist, progressive health professionals who were exceptionally responsive to women's movement demands for reproductive rights and who actively combated the efforts of General Vasconcelos, the MMDS, and other sectors of the ruling coalition to wrest the state's would-be family planning program from the purview of the Ministry of Health. To counter Vasconcelos' pro–population control crusade, the ministry launched its own educational campaign in favor of noncoercive family planning—the women and men responsible for the PAISM within the ministry also toured Brazil, appearing in public debates, radio and television programs, and even directly debating General Vasconcelos on a few occasions.[47]

As noted, the CECF played a critical role in the formulation of family planning policy at the state level. But the danger of cooptation and manipulation of women's demands for reproductive freedom is greatest at the implementation phase. The historical tendency in Latin America and elsewhere in the Third World has been for state-sponsored "family planning" to consist of the arbitrary distribution of birth control pills and the encouragement of sterilization, especially among women of color and poor women. Thus, the existence of a gender-conscious mechanism, within the state apparatus, to supervise the implementation of state-sponsored family planning is critical in mediating this historical tendency.

While divergences with the PMDB regime and within civil society delayed the implementation of the state Women's Health Program, the Council on Women's Condition consistently supported the inclusion of "conception and contraception, with information about and access to all of the contraceptive methods" within the program. The CECF sponsored several public forums about this issue, and one of its subcommittees, the Women's Health Commission, worked closely with the state Department of Health in the further elaboration of the program.

The CECF had to contend with a rather different reproductive ideology in the case of family planning than it faced in the day care issue. The left or *auténtico* wing of the PMDB ruling coalition predominated within the state Department of Health, and, as we saw above, the left in Brazil as a whole has historically equated family planning policy with imperialist population-control initiatives. Though this position is certainly warranted given the neo-Malthusian content of "family planning" policies proposed by the right and the international aid community, the CECF has insisted that the *Programa da Saúde da Mulher* is also a legitimate need of Paulista women. The council's Commission on Women's Health argued that if the program was properly administered and accompanied by popular education, it would advance the status of women by enabling women of all social classes to make informed reproductive choices. In short, as Margaret Arilha put it, "the Council had to combat the ghosts of population control" among left-wing sectors of the PMDB adminstration and other progressive sectors of civil society.[48]

The CECF exerted constant pressure to get the Health Department to begin the implementation phase of the program. Its access to the department's policy process was facilitated by the fact that a representative from the Health Department sat on the council (whereas, for example, there was no such access to the municipal agencies in charge of day care policy). The CECF's structure and membership, combining representatives from both "civil society" and the state, proved especially effective in the area of family planning policy. Council members directly lobbied the secretary of health, the directors of the department's seventeen regional subdivisions, and other key policy planners throughout 1984 in order to convince them of the worthiness and the urgency of implementing the Program for Women's Health. It also launched an extensive propaganda campaign to dispel fears of population control among progressive sectors of civil society. As a direct consequence of the CECF's sustained efforts, the department made the Program for Women's Health one of its programmatic and budgetary priorities for 1985.

After months of discussion and deliberation within the CECF, it was agreed that family planning representatives, trained and supervised by the

Department of Health in conjunction with the council's Commission on Women's Health, would supervise the implementation of the Program for Women's Health in all seventeen subdivisions in the state of São Paulo. Pamphlets and other educational materials developed by women's movement organizations were employed in the training of health technicians involved in the PAISM. "Consciousness-raising" and sex education components were included in the orientation of the program's clients.

The CECF also facilitated the women's movements' access to the policy implementation process, urging the Department of Health to hold monthly public "Forums to Accompany the Implementation of the Program for Women's Health." These forums, held throughout 1985, brought state health policy planners, employees of the public health network, and movement participants active in grassroots sex education, health, and reproductive rights advocacy together to discuss the progress of the program.[49] The São Paulo council was also instrumental in generating new access points through which women's movement organizations could impact the federal PAISM, pressuring the Ministry of Health to create a "Commission on Reproductive Rights," which, like the state forums, brought policy makers, health professionals, and women's movement activists together to ensure a safe, accessible, and noncoercive federal family planning policy.

What differentiated the CECF's actions within the regime, then, from similar administrative organs created throughout Latin America (largely as a consequence of the U.N.-sponsored women's decade), was the pronounced *feminist* presence within the São Paulo Council on Women's Condition between 1983 and 1986. Though nonfeminist women and PMDB party militants were also members of the council, a feminist position on family planning, largely derived from the contributions of the Brazilian feminist movement to political discourse on population policy, emerged firmly within CECF policy.

In supervising the implementation of family planning policy at the state level, the CECF accomplished what the autonomous women's movement could never accomplish on its own because of its structural position "outside" the pact of domination. The women's movement, in turn, organized continual discussions on family planning and closely monitored the council's and the Department and Ministry of Health's deliberations and policy proposals on this issue. And unquestionably, such consistent gender-conscious political pressures from within civil society contributed to the regime's responsiveness to the CECF's proposals.

Politicization or Institutionalization? Concession or Cooptation? Contradictions of a "Women's Space" within a Male-Dominant State

Between 1983 and 1985 the CECF formulated and monitored the implementation of a number of innovative public policies that addressed the special needs and concerns of Paulista women. In addition to the policy initiatives discussed above, for example, the Commission on Violence against Women of the São Paulo Council on Women's Condition persuaded the mayor to create the Delegacia de Defesa da Mulher in August of 1985, a police precinct, staffed entirely by specially trained female police officers, that processes cases of rape, sexual abuse, and domestic violence.[50] The groundbreaking recognition of this gender-specific aspect of crime by the state is unprecedented in Brazil, and indeed the "women's precinct" structure is unparalleled elsewhere in the world. Again, on this issue, the CECF's effectiveness in promoting policies that directly address the concrete needs of Paulista women *as women* is partially derived from the São Paulo women's movements' constant protest actions and public education campaigns centering on the issue of violence against women.

But the danger of cooptation or institutionalization of the women's movements and the private issues they have politicized remains; the activities of the CECF may absorb or preempt such gender-conscious political pressure emanating from the autonomous women's movement. Since 1983 the São Paulo council has assumed many of the activities that were previously orchestrated by women's movement organizations. In 1984 and 1985 the International Women's Day celebrations in São Paulo, which had previously been peak mobilizational moments for the autonomous women's movements, were transformed into peak mobilizational strategies in support of the CECF's conception of "women's interests" and in support of the PMDB's local and national "political projects." In 1984 the theme of International Women's Day was *"Direitos, Diretas e Paz"* (Rights, Direct Elections, and Peace), a theme reflecting not only the concerns of the autonomous women's movement (couched in more acceptable rhetoric) but also the interests of the nationwide "political project" of the PMDB in promoting direct elections for 1984.

The danger in the CECF's strategy is that, however unintentionally, it has also to some extent preempted the mobilization of gender-conscious political pressure from outside the PMDB regime. The council's activities have at least temporarily absorbed or preempted the political initiatives of organized female constituencies within civil society. The CECF's mobilizational capacity as part of the state apparatus has often been used not only to promote the eradication of gender inequality, but also to support the "larger" interests of the PMDB coalition in power in the state of São Paulo. And this fact, in part, accounts for the continuing skepticism of sectors of the women's movement outside the ruling coalition as to where the CECF's primary loyalties lie.

A further source of concern among movement participants "outside" the state has been that the institutionalization of some of the women's movements' gender-specific demands within the new PMDB regime has threatened to "over-absorb" the dynamism of feminism, and women's mobilization in general, as forces for social change in civil society. After all, what distinguishes social movements from political parties is that movements have cultural and social, as well as political, goals. They seek normative as well as structural transformations of society more actively than do traditional political parties.

Our comparative analysis of day care and population policy developments during the first PMDB micro-regime in São Paulo suggests that continued political pressure from civil society has been crucial to the success of movement goals in male-dominant policy-making arenas. That is, Brazilian feminism's success in the area of reproductive health is attributable to organizing at the base, both within and without the state. The São Paulo state Council on Women's Condition provided new access points to the state apparatus that would otherwise not have been available to women's movement organizations.

However, the success of the original CECF was partially determined by a number of specific conjunctural variables that might not be characteristic of other such "women's spaces" in other local, regional, or national contexts. First, the council had a firm feminist majority during its first two years in operation, and this fact unquestionably influenced the nature and content of its fairly radical generic policy initiatives. Second, the PMDB administrations at both the state and local levels were new regimes, still invested in transforming their electoral support into solidly hegemonic social bases of support for the new "democratic" regimes within civil society. And third, the ruling PMDB remained essentially a coalition of political forces from the extreme left to the center-right of the political spectrum. As we saw in the discussion of day care and family planning policies, different and even competing reproductive ideologies were represented within different sectors of the state apparatus. Thus, some sectors of the state (such as the state Department of Health) proved more malleable or amenable to gender-specific political claims than other sectors (such as the municipal Department of the Family and Social Welfare).

In other states where the PMDB ruling coalition was politically narrower, as in Minas Gerais where center and center-right elements of the PMDB predominated, the range of generic policy initiatives and reproductive ideologies represented within the regime was far narrower as well. In

1983 Governor Tancredo Neves had also created a Council on the Status of Women, but unlike its São Paulo counterpart, the council in Minas was composed primarily of women party members with few, if any, links to or experience within autonomous women's movement organizations. The women's movement in Minas, in fact, has remained aloof from the council, viewing it merely as a "bureaucratic ornament," directly subservient to the PMDB's more conservative elements—"a place where deputies' wives can be appointed to the government."

In sum, in the case of São Paulo from 1983 to 1985, the institutionalization of genderic political claims did *not* for the most part result in the deradicalization or depoliticization of the more radical genderic content of those claims. As we have seen, the continued dynamism of autonomous women's movement organizations within civil society and the successful reorientation of movement strategies, in response to the new democratic political conjuncture, were key factors in preventing state family planning policy from becoming cooptative or coercive state population control initiatives.

The day care issue has to some extent been "depoliticized," in terms of its genderic content. The "blame" for this, however, cannot be placed solely on the precarious position of the state Council on Women's Condition within the local state apparatus nor on its subservience to the more traditional reproductive ideologies represented within the PMDB micro-regime. Rather, the responsibility for the partial depoliticization and manipulation of day care policy is shared by day care movement organizations that were unable to articulate a united position vis-à-vis the new political conjuncture. In failing to sustain gender-conscious political pressure within civil society, the day care movement indirectly weakened the bargaining position of the council within the local administration and failed to pressure either the CECF or the relevant government agencies to implement a day care policy that reflected the historic gender-specific demands of the Struggle for Day Care Movement.

A National Council on Women's Rights in the New Brazilian Republic

The lessons of the São Paulo case are particularly relevant to the present conjuncture in Brazilian gender politics. In 1985 the March 8 International Women's Day celebrations coincided with the nation's transition to civilian rule after twenty years of military dictatorship. The national women's branch of the PMDB and the state councils on the status of women in São Paulo and Minas Gerais (the home state of Tancredo Neves) marked the occasion of the "transition to democracy" by presenting the new administration with a proposal for the creation of a National Council on Women's Rights (Conselho Nacional dos Direitos da Mulher, or CNDM).

The PMDB feminists who mobilized women in support of Neves' candidacy also sought Tancredo's support for their gender-specific political claims. In June of 1984 São Paulo state assemblywoman Ruth Escobar, elected on a feminist platform in 1982, organized a "supra-partisan" commission of more than sixty women to present the candidate with a *carta das mulheres* specifying the generic issues that they felt must be included in the candidate's platform and asking that he consider the creation of a women's council or ministry at the federal level.

In November of 1984 Escobar organized a national conference, attended by more than 500 women from eighteen Brazilian states, to discuss the organizational form such a federal "women's institution" should take and the public policy goals it should pursue. And in January of 1985 Neves officially endorsed the creation of such an institution and appointed a multipartisan commission of women legislators, presided over by Escobar, to elaborate a legislative proposal for the creation of a National Council on Women's Rights.[51]

Existing state councils served as models for the proposed national council. PMDB women activists learned valuable lessons from the successes and failures of the councils established in Minas Gerais and São Paulo in 1983. The experience of these councils suggested that success in pursuing a feminist policy agenda *is* possible, *if* the following conditions are met: (1) a gender-conscious, feminist-identified majority must prevail within the council; (2) the council must facilitate movement access to the state apparatus and policy-making arenas; (3) council activities must not preempt autonomous women's movement activities; and (4) the autonomous women's movements must sustain gender-conscious political pressure from without the regime in order to prevent the deradicalization or depoliticization of the generic content of their political claims.

The CNDM was officially installed on September 11, 1985, thanks to the tireless lobbying of Escobar and other women legislators who pressured for rapid congressional approval of the executive proposal developed by the women's parliamentary commission earlier in 1985.[52] The original council was presided over by Escobar and was composed of women legislators from the PMDB, the Partido da Frente Liberal (PFL),[53] and the PT, "representatives of civil society" linked to autonomous women's movement organizatons, and intellectuals and academics who specialize in the field of women's studies.

Escobar secured an initial budget of CR$6 billion (close to US$1 million) for the CNDM's first three months of operation alone—an allocation greater than that of many of the smaller executive departments or ministries.

The CNDM does seem to have a fairly solid feminist majority, in spite of its need to accommodate the multitude of political tendencies within the ruling PMDB-PFL coalition and within the national women's movement itself.

In an interview conducted in late August of 1985, CNDM president Ruth Escobar outlined some of the principal political and organizational goals of the national council: "The Council will be a more dynamic organ than a Women's Ministry could possibly be. It will open new spaces, new channels . . . it will create new groups within the various ministries which will enable us to influence policy more broadly, more effectively." Escobar suggested that the council structure was a preliminary step toward the creation of a full-scale ministry on the status of women. She argued that women must first "conquer greater political space and strength" within the state apparatus and within policy-making arenas (hence the presence of women legislators on the council) and must prove its mobilizational capacity vis-à-vis organized female constituencies in civil society before such a ministry can be created—"without such a power base, the Ministry would be ineffective . . . like in Venezuela, where a Ministry on the Status of Women was created in the mid-70s and dissolved less than a year later."

Escobar was confident that partisan rivalries and ideological differences could be overcome within the CNDM; the multipartisan commission that planned the council had reconciled many partisan tensions, she argued, as she insisted that "women's issues supersede the parties even if they [the parties] don't want them to." However, the ruling coalition of the New Republic is extremely disparate and the ascension of center-right tendencies or the increased hegemony of President Jose Sarney's PFL, whose platform on women's issues is little more progressive than that of its "parent party," the PDS, might compromise the CNDM's ability to promote women's gender interests at the national level.

Mediating the Relationship between Women's Movements and the State? New Contradictions of Women's Institutions in Postauthoritarian Brazil

In the enthusiasm of reform that followed the installation of the first civilian federal administration in twenty-one years, it seemed as if these newly created "women's spaces" could ensure further progress toward the eradication of gender inequality. And since the mid-1980s Brazilian feminists have indeed consolidated some of the gains made during the *abertura* process. Since the installation of eleven opposition-led state governments in March of 1983, feminists have promoted several important and innovative public policies and have secured more "women's spaces" within the opposition-led government structures—state councils on the status of women were established not only in São Paulo but also in Minas Gerais in 1983 and subsequently in twenty-three other states and municipalities. On December 19, 1986, the São Paulo State Assembly voted to institutionalize the State Council on Women's Condition, making it a permanent organ of the state government.

In late 1985 and throughout much of 1986 the National Council on Women's Rights intervened in favor of women in federal agrarian reform deliberations, promoted a national day care policy, implemented antisexist educational reforms, expanded its outreach to women in civil society through its access to government-controlled media, and developed a "Women's Proposal" for the new Brazilian constitution (which was promulgated on October 5, 1988). The CNDM initially remained true to the goals of Brazilian feminism, calling for an expanded definition of democracy that encompasses the democratization of both public and private life:

> For us, women, the full exercise of citizenship means, yes, the right to representation, a voice and a role in public life, but at the same time, it also implies dignity in daily life, which the law can inspire and should ensure, the right to education, to health, to security, to a family life free of traumas. Women's vote brings with it a double exigency: an egalitarian political system and a non-authoritarian civilian life.
>
> We, women, are conscious of the fact that this country will only be truly democratic and its citizens truly free when, without prejudice of sex, race, color, class, sexual orientation, religious or political creed, physical condition or age, equal treatment and equal opportunity in the streets, podiums, workshops, factories, offices, assemblies, and palaces, are guaranteed.[54]

In sum, in 1985 and 1986 the National Council on Women's Rights and some state and municipal councils worked to strengthen the autonomous women's movement, providing direct and indirect subsidies to independent feminine and feminist organizations, coordinating national educational and mobilizational campaigns on women's issues, and providing the movement with new access points to state policy-making arenas. The National Council itself became the principal stage for the practice of a 1980s brand of Brazilian interest-group feminist politics. During this early post-transition period the CNDM advanced a fairly radical and successful policy agenda. The CNDM was also especially active in the areas of family planning, day care, and preventing violence against women.

At the National Council's recommendation, the Ministry of Labor has promised to enforce compliance with day care provisions included in national labor legislation since 1943, requiring that all establishments employing more than fifteen women provide day care facilities for female employees. In late 1986 the National Bank for Social Development approved a resolution requiring all projects and programs seeking bank loans to conform to these provisions. The CNDM has since been pressuring other national and state banks to adopt the same requirements.[55]

The CNDM also promoted ongoing debates, conferences, and educational and media campaigns around family planning and abortion rights. In October of 1986 the CNDM and the ministries of Health and of Social Welfare cosponsored the First National Conference on Women's Health and Women's Rights. Held in Brasilia and attended by more than 1,200 women representing state and municipal health departments, public hospitals and clinics, political parties, and autonomous women's groups, the conference reaffirmed the women's movement's staunch opposition to population control and its fervent support of women's reproductive freedom. Conference participants agreed to create local "Committees for the Defense of Women's Health" to "act effectively in the planning, implementation, and execution of health programs."[56] After protracted debate, participants also endorsed a more radical proposal—that abortion be legalized under the new Brazilian constitution. Arguing that "the conditions under which it occurs in the country, abortion constitutes a serious problem for women's physical and mental health," the conference's final recommendations call for a national plebiscite on abortion[57] and urged lawmakers to give serious consideration to legalization, or minimally, decriminalization.

A national campaign against violence against women headed new CNDM president Jacqueline Pitanguy's political agenda in 1986–1987. The council compiled a "national dossier on the impunity with which violence against women is cloaked"[58] and in mid-1986 launched a "Say No to Violence against Women" campaign, with television spots featuring renowned actors, transmitted on government air time.

Importantly, the National Council encouraged autonomous women's movement organizations to apply pressure on policy makers and bureaucrats in support of the CNDM's policy agenda. The legitimacy and ultimate success of that agenda, council members have argued, is predicated on the autonomous movement's continued mobilizational capacity. This is especially true in the case of reproductive rights, as the church hierarchy and conservative factions of the ruling party have mounted a nationwide campaign against reproductive choice and the women's health program since early 1987.

But the reformist euphoria of the first two years of the civilian regime has given way to widespread disillusionment in the late 1980s. New women's councils and forty-six women's police precincts have been created throughout Brazil. But these new institutions have been somewhat disappointing for Brazilian feminists, even for some of the "founding mothers" of the councils.

According to feminists who have served on or currently work in the CECF and CNDM, many of the new "women's institutions" are profoundly partisan.[59] Most have few if any links to autonomous women's movement organizations and instead were created as electoral gambits by mayors and governors, providing these with a new source of democratic legitimacy. To the dismay of the feminists who conceived of the councils as institutions that would channel women's demands into policy arenas and monitor policy implementation, many of the new councils have instead served as mechanisms for the top-down mobilization of women.

The São Paulo Municipal Council on the Status of Women, created by Janio Quadros in 1987, is one of the most disappointing examples of the political manipulation and distortion of some these women's institutions by opportunistic governments and antifeminist groups. Created at the behest of women active in the antifeminist Federação de Mulheres Paulistas, the municipal council has primarily served as a launching pad for that organization's sectarian mobilizational agenda. Conservative São Paulo mayor Janio Quadros served his neopopulist coalition in creating this local women's council, and its purpose, according to one staff member I spoke with, was quite different from that proposed by the feminists who conceived the councils: the new administration thought that women were "politically backward" and needed to be encouraged to "bring their special qualities" to politics; they have "special needs," defined by "unique role as mothers," which the council should advance.[60] Just how even these "special needs" were to be advanced was unclear. The municipal council has no independent budget, a minimal staff (only two part-time secretaries), no specific legislative or policy agenda, no apparent links to either the municipal legislature or other policy arenas, and no ties to any local women's groups except the Federação de Mulheres Paulistas, whose founding convention swallowed up most of the municipal council's limited 1988 budget. Indeed, most of the São Paulo women's movement activists I spoke to in 1988 had never even contacted the municipal council and believed it did not actually exist.

Of even greater concern to many of the feminists who originally supported the establishment of the São Paulo CECF and the National Council on the Status of Women, these too appear to have fallen prey to partisan manipulation or have lost much of their already limited political clout since 1987. There has been a critical change in the structure of political opportunities resulting in decreased leverage for both the CECF and CNDM, both of which, as we saw above, had played a crucial role in advancing a fairly radical feminist-inspired policy agenda.

The original "micro-regime" PMDB coalition in São Paulo has experienced serious rifts, and the national ruling coalition has shifted radically to the right since the end of 1986. In the state of São Paulo the center-left decentralizing, popular participation–oriented PMDB administration of Franco Montoro has been replaced by the center-right centralizing administration of Orestes Quercia, whose power is based on the allegiance of small-town mayors and which has dismantled or deactivated many of the participatory mechanisms established under Montoro.

Feminist PMDB activists scrambled to secure the "institutionalization" of the CECF in late 1986 for fear that Quercia would close the women's space created by Montoro. Their fears appear to have been well founded. Though Quercia did not try to dissolve the CECF, its clout within the new state administration has been significantly reduced. One CECF staff member summarized the governor's attitude as follows: "Leave the girls over there at the CECF to their little games but don't give them any resources or real power."

Since the original councilors' terms were to expire under Quercia, strategic discussions were held within the CECF during the final months of 1986 as to who should head the CECF under the new administration. It was ultimately decided that the president must come from Quercia's wing of the PMDB or else the council would lose its limited political clout within the state adminstration. The new governor did indeed serve his own power base in his new appointments to the CECF: feminists and women linked to the *movimento de mulheres* are now in the minority of the reconstituted state council. Of the twenty-three current councilors, according to one person I interviewed, only ten have any experience in the movement; the rest are dubbed *fisionómicas* (physiognomical, or women who appear to be representative of women's groups).[61] And though the National Council on Women's Rights retains a solid feminist-identified majority, a similar danger of "political or partisan appointments" looms large as the present councilors' terms expire. The new "women's institutions" appear to be becoming part of traditional patronage politics, spaces to be filled on the basis of favors owed to male politicians by the appointment of women from local patronage networks.

These developments are especially problematic for two reasons. First, much of original councils' legitimacy vis-à-vis the movement was based not on its "representativeness" but on the fact that the majority of council members were widely recognized to be longtime feminist activists, even if all were from the PMDB. Second, as argued above, successful institutional mediation of the relationship between women and the male-dominant state is possible only if a gender-conscious, feminist-identified majority prevails within the council, the council facilitates movement access to the state apparatus and policy-making arenas, and the council does not preempt autonomous women's movement activities.

As a consequence of the turn to the right at both the state and federal levels, both the CECF and the CNDM today exercise little clout either within the state or civil society. Whereas in 1985 the São Paulo council was a veritable hotbed of "feminist subversion," in mid-1988 it had only one active commission (the Black Women's Commission) and, as several staff members told me, "had to scramble for funding for paper clips, let alone women's programs."

The National Council's political effectiveness, some feminists argue, has also waned since early 1987. Though the CNDM retains a sizable budget and maintains a solidly feminist staff, several movement activists and council staff members I talked with believe that "it functions more as an educational institution, disseminating information on women's issues and women's programs" and now "exercises little influence in most government ministries." [62]

Many feminists today have begun rethinking the nature, structure, and purpose of these women's institutions in the New Brazilian Republic. One problem cited by several women interviewed was the "hybrid structure" of most councils, that is, the fact that councils are composed of "representatives" of civil society and of relevant municipal, state, or federal departments. This mixed structure is still praised by some, but others now argue that such a structure confounds feminist practice. The latter maintain that the women's movement should "call the state a state," that the movement must recognize the limitations inherent in working in a state institution, even a putatively feminist one, and that the mixed composition of the councils has confused some movement cadres, who are still asking "is this the State or is this feminist activism?" [63] I also witnessed another dimension of this confusion during heated discussions about the nature of the CECF and CNDM at a São Paulo PT women's meeting in late June of 1988. Though both institutions had been around for several years, many movement and PT activists were still uncertain as to the role these "women's spaces" played in Brazilian gender politics. Some argued that "the councils are completely harnessed to the state," while others retorted "but they *are* the state."

This same confusion plagues the movements' relationship to women's police precincts. Many feminists have been disappointed with the ways in which some of these precincts replicate the problems of regular precincts in dealing with the victims of violence. Though in some cases feminist scholars and activists were brought in to train female police personnel at these specialized precincts, feminists have been marginalized from most in recent years, as the selection and training of staff is entrusted to local police forces. Indeed, it seems especially hard for feminists to penetrate the repressive apparatus of the Brazilian state. In contrast to the United States, where grassroots feminists run rape-crisis centers and shelters for battered women and are brought in to advise victims and police, there has been little ongoing collaboration between feminists and the new *delegacias*. [64]

This situation is further complicated by the disappearance or deactivation of most feminist groups dedicated to combating violence against women by 1985. There has therefore been a marked decline of feminist pressure outside the state that might keep the *delegacias* more closely in line with feminist principles. The creation of new "women's spaces" within the repressive apparatus of the state, then, will not in itself resolve the problems of rape and domestic violence. As Raquel Moreno, one of the founding members of SOS-Mulher, the first feminist group to dedicate itself to combating violence against women in the early 1980s, compellingly argues:

Women continue to be beaten, and will continue to be beaten as long as machismo is not extirpated, as long as the structure and ideology that tolerates, permits it, and benefits from the atomization of power, so that the most impotent of men still feels aggrandized by the perception of the existence of someone—his woman—whom he has power over and even beats.[65]

This passage highlights the importance of continued feminist activism within civil society and the danger that the institutionalization of the feminist agenda might indirectly compromise feminist efforts to transform the politics of daily life.

Another troublesome aspect of the councils on the status of women according to many movement activists is that these institutions have drawn in many women who were key organizers in the women's movement, robbing the movement of its best cadres. Some claimed that former activists had been "transformed by the institutions," becoming bureaucrats in the service of the state, and not of the movement.

The issue of who serves on the councils has also posed another pressing question for Brazilian feminism. Are these new women's institutions to become mechanisms of "neo-corporatist representation?" Thus far, councilors have been appointed by the local, state and federal executives, with little or no input from the women's movement organizations they purportedly represent. Thus, many women now argue that the council structure is inherently nonrepresentative, and some suggest that the goal of representativeness should be abandoned altogether.

Several of the women interviewed in 1988 advocated the creation of nonpartisan "women's institutes" to replace the hybrid council structures. The idea would be to create permanent organs of state administration responsible for monitoring gender policy developments and compiling information on the status of Brazilian women where appointments would be civil service and merit-based and not designated by presidents, governors, or mayors. Such a structure, proponents of this alternative argued, would be less dependent on the correlation of political or partisan forces in power or the good will of changing administrations; it would make "women's spaces" part of the state, not part of local, state, or federal regimes, making them less susceptible to patronage politics or top-down manipulation.

"Gendered Bureaucratic Subversion" in Postauthoritarian Brazil? Implications for Feminist Theory and Practice

Our analysis of gender politics in postauthoritarian Brazil suggests an alternative to current feminist theories about the state and the bureaucracy. Western feminist theorists such as MacKinnon and Ferguson[66] have portrayed the state and the bureaucracy as immutably masculine. Indeed, for some feminists, the state—whether capitalist, socialist, or dependent capitalist—is inevitably women's worst enemy. In this view, the state is the ultimate mechanism of social control in women's lives, always acting to "empower men and depower women."[67] Other North American feminists, such as Piven and Ehrenreich, have enthusiastically embraced the state, especially the welfare state, as "women's best friend," viewing women's relationship to the state in the postdepression era as essentially an empowering one.[68]

Evidence from Brazil suggests a need for a more complex, less Manichaean perspective on gender and the state. First, our discussion of Brazilian gender politics points to the importance of political *regimes* and political *conjunctures*. State structures and policies that regulate and mediate gender, race, and class relations of power in society are hardly immutable, especially in the Third World. Changes in political regime—in the institutions that structure the relationship between state and society—may open up new opportunities for women to influence policy formulation and implementation. Clearly, the state, though still bourgeois and male-dominant, has been far "friendlier" to Brazilian women under civilian rule than under military authoritarianism. The difference for Brazilian feminists is hardly a trivial one.

Second, the Brazilian case highlights the fact that *the state is not monolithically masculine* or antifeminist. If we "unpack" the state and examine its multiple institutional and ideological instances, we may find points of access, points where concerted gender-conscious political pressure might make a difference. Even under authoritarian rule, Brazilian feminists secured new *access points* to state policy arenas, as is clear from our discussion of family planning and day care policy developments. This suggests the need for a selective feminist strategy, one that apprehends the full spectrum of gender ideologies represented within a given political regime, identifies points of gendered bureaucratic resistance, and attempts to impact those policy arenas that are most accessible and amenable to feminist influence at a specific political conjuncture.

Finally, the Brazilian experience points to the importance of a flexible, multidimensional feminist strategy—one that organizes gender-conscious political pressure *at the base,* both within and without the state.[69] When faced with democratizing conjunctures in state and national politics, Brazilian feminists modified and diversified their political strategies accordingly. Some seized the political space made available to women by parties and the post-1983 state governments and promoted innovative changes from within. Others continued organizing at the grassroots, fostering a critical, organizationally and ideologically autonomous feminist politics, and indirectly legitimating the actions of women active in male-dominant policy arenas. In spite of continuing conflicts amongst feminists "in" and "out" of "power," this two-pronged strategy, which might be termed "gendered bureaucratic subversion," proved surprisingly effective in the early post-transition period. In light of the ascendancy of center-right forces at the local, state, and federal levels since late 1986, feminists are today confronted with a less favorable political conjuncture and are again contemplating new political strategies.

In conclusion, the Brazilian case suggests that feminists should neither dismiss the state as the ultimate mechanism of male social control nor embrace it as the ultimate vehicle for gender-based social change. Rather, under different political regimes and at distinct historical conjunctures, the state is potentially a mechanism either for social change or social control in women's lives. An informed feminist political practice is principally concerned with discerning the difference, seizing available opportunity space, and avoiding excessive "institutionalization" or depoliticization of the feminist agenda. An engaged feminist political theory and political science would help chart the path toward change by examining the varied historical and cross-cultural experiences of feminist attempts to influence state policy "in the meantime," while patriarchal practices and assumptions remain embedded in the structures and policies of socialist and capitalist states.

Notes

1. For a comprehensive discussion of the dynamics of military authoritarian regimes in Latin America during the 1960s and 1970s, see David Collier, ed., *The New Authoritarianism in Latin America* (Princeton, N.J.: Princeton University Press, 1979); on the proliferation of urban social movements under authoritarian rule, see David Slater, ed., *New Social Movements and the State in Latin America* (Amsterdam: Centre for Latin American Research and Documentation, 1985); Alfred Stepan, "State Power and the Strength of Civil Society in the Southern Cone of Latin America," in *Bringing the State Back In,* pp. 317–46, ed. P. Evans, D. Rueschemeyer, and T. Skocpol (New York: Cambridge University Press, 1985); and Scott Main-

waring and Eduardo Viola, "New Social Movements, Political Culture, and Democracy: Brazil and Argentina in the 1980s," *Telos* 17 (Fall 984): 17–52.

2. A distinction between "feminine" and "feminist" women's movement organizations is commonly made by both movement participants and social scientists in Latin America. Paul Singer clarifies the usage of these concepts: "The struggles against *carestia* or for schools, day care centers, etc., as well as specific measures to protect women who work interest women closely and it is possible then to consider them *feminine* revindications. But they are not *feminist* to the extent that they do not question the way in which women are inserted into the social context." "O Feminino e O Femenismo," in *São Paulo: O Povo em Movimento*, ed. P. Singer and V. C. Brant (Petrópolis: Vozês, 1980), pp. 116–17.

3. For a comparative discussion of women's movements in regime transitions in Peru, Chile, Argentina, Uruguay, and Brazil, see Jane Jaquette, ed., *Women's Movements in Latin America: Feminism and Transitions to Democracy* (Boston: Unwin Hyman, 1989).

4. Political conjuncture, as conceptualized by French Marxists and Latin American social scientists, refers to the correlation and articulation of social and political forces, within a given social formation, at a specific historical moment.

5. For a general discussion of the "feminine" side of the Brazilian women's movement, see Marianne Schmink, "Women in Brazilian Abertura Politics," *Signs* 7, no. II (1981). See also Eva Alterman Blay, "Mulheres e Movimentos Sociais Urbanos: Anistia, Custo de Vida e Creches," *Encontros com a Civilização Brasileira—Mulher Hoje*, special issue (1980).

6. A more complete discussion of the emergence and development of the contemporary feminist movement in Brazil can be found in Sonia E. Alvarez, "A Latin American Feminist Success Story? Women's Movements and Gender Politics in the Brazilian Transition," in *Women's Movements in Latin America: Feminism and Transitions to Democracy*, ed. Jane Jaquette (Boston: Unwin Hyman, 1989). Much of the ensuing discussion is based on more than one hundred formal and informal interviews conducted with movement participants between 1981 and 1988 and on an analysis of movement documents and other primary sources. On the Brazilian feminist movement and the issues it has politicized, see María Lygia Quartim de Moraes, *Mulheres em Movimento* (São Paulo: Nobel and CECF, 1985); Anette Goldberg, "Feminismo em Regime Autoritário: A Experiência do Movimento de Mulheres no Rio de Janeiro (Paper presented at the XII Congress of the International Political Science Association, Rio de Janeiro, August 1982), and "Os Movimentos de Liberação da Mulher na França e na Itália (1970–1980): Primeiros Elementos para Um Estudo Comparativo do Novo Feminismo na Europa e no Brasil," in *O Lugar da Mulher*, ed. M. T. Luz (Rio de Janeiro: Graal, 1982); Ana Alice Costa Pinheiro, "Avances y Definiciones del Movimiento Femenista en el Brasil" (Master's thesis, Colégio de México, 1981); and Branca Moreira Alves and Jacqueline Pitanguy, *O Que e O Feminismo?* (São Paulo: Brasilense, 1981). For an overview of feminist initiatives in several areas of women's rights, see Comba Marques Porto e Leonor Nunes de Paiva, "Direito: Difernetes mas Não Desiguais," in *Mulheres em Movimento*, ed. Equipe Projeto—Mulher do Instituto de Ação Cultural (Rio de Janeiro: Marco Zero, 1983).

7. On the relationship between women's movements and political parties, see Iara María Ilgenfritz da Silva, "Movimentos de Mulheres e Partidos Políticos: Antagonismos e Contradições" (Paper presented at the V Encontro Anual da Associação e Pesquisa em Ciências Sociais, Nova Friburgo, Rio de Janeiro, 1981); Fanny Tabak and Silvia Sánchez, "Movimentos Feministas e Partidos Políticos" (Paper presented at the same Encontro, 1981); Sivia Pimentel, "A Necessária Participação Política da Mulher" (mimeo, n.d.); and María Teresa Miceli Kerbauy, "A Questão Femenina: Mulher, Partido, e Representação Política no Brasil" (Paper presented at the XII International Conference of the Latin American Studies Association, Albuquerque, N.M., April 1985).

8. For a discussion of authoritarian regime breakdown and transitions to democracy in South America, see Guillermo O'Donnell, Phillippe C. Schmitter, and Laurence Whitehead, eds., *Transitions from Authoritarian Rule: South America* (Baltimore: Johns Hopkins University Press, 1986); Paul W. Drake and Eduardo Silva, eds., *Elections and Democratization in Latin America* (San Diego: Center for Iberian and Latin American Studies, Center for U.S.-Mexican Studies, and Institute of the Americas, 1986). On the Brazilian transition, see María Helena Moreira Alves, *State and Opposition in Military Brazil* (Austin: University of Texas Press, 1985), and Alfred Stepan, ed., *Democratizing Brazil* (New York: Oxford University Press, 1989).

9. For an in-depth analysis of movement dynamics and policy developments since the return to civilian rule in 1985, see my *Engendering Democracy? Women's Movements and Gender Politics in Brazil's Transition from Authoritarian Rule* (Princeton, N.J.: Princeton University Press (forthcoming), chap. 9.

10. For a different treatment of this data, see Sonia E. Alvarez, "Politicizing Gender and En*gender*ing Democracy," in *Democratizing Brazil,* ed. Alfred Stepan (New York: Oxford University Press, 1989) 250–51.

11. International Women's Day has been a central rallying date for unified action for the Paulista women's movement since 1975. In 1979, 1980, and 1981 the various types of women's movement organizations coordinated their efforts to sponsor the I, II, and III Congress of São Paulo Women, which brought together approximately 800, 4,000, and 6,000 women militants, respectively.

12. Governo do Estado de São Paulo, Decree no. 20892, *Diario Oficial,* April 5, 1983, my emphasis.

13. Governo do Estado de São Paulo, Conselho da Condição Femenina, untitled newsletter, 1984. In an interview conducted in August of 1985, Council president Eva Blay reiterated the notion that a "nonpartisan" council was unviable given the pronounced and continuing conflicts between the ruling PMDB and the "opposition" PT or Workers' Party in São Paulo.

14. Governo do Estado de São Paulo, Conselho da Condição Femenina, untitled document, fall 1983.

15. Because of the lobbying efforts of the São Paulo Black Women's Collective and the Unified Black Movement, the CECF later added a Black woman to its group of "representatives" of civil society. It is important to note that people of color are extremely poorly represented in the New Republic and that race-specific political claims are among the most difficult to articulate within institutional arenas,

due in large part to the continuing myth of "racial democracy" upheld by even the most progressive white Brazilians. It should be stressed that Black women have been dissatisfied with the extent to which the predominantly white feminist movement has confronted race issues in the women's lives and have formed their own separate feminist organizations in recent years.

16. The representatives of civil society appointed to the council were mostly women who entered the feminist movement through academic or professional networks as opposed to women who came into feminism through experiences in the militant opposition or the student movement.

17. Governo do Estado de São Paulo, Conselho da Condição Femenina, untitled document, 1984.

18. For earlier and distinct examinations of this data, see my *Politics of Gender in Latin America: Comparative Perspectives on Women in the Brazilian Transition to Democracy* (Ph.D. diss., Yale University, 1986) and "Politicizing Gender."

19. Movimento de Luta pela Creches, "Manifesto," March 1979.

20. *Estado de São Paulo,* October 21, 1979.

21. Much of the foregoing discussion is based on interviews with María Amelia de Almeida Teles, coordinator of the Conselho Estadual da Condição Femenina's Day Care Commission and former member of the Executive Committee of the MLC, August 19, 1985; and, Isabel, the Director of the Jardim Miriam day care center and former member of the regional and citywide coordinations, August 23, 1985.

22. Governo do Estado de São Paulo, Conselho da Condição Femenina, *Mulher* 1(September 1984).

23. Interview with Ana María Wilheim, legislative staff of Vereadora Ida María Janscó, August 20, 1985. See also São Paulo, Camara Municipal, Commissão Especial de Inquérito sobre Creches, "Relatorio Final. Nossos Filhos, Nosso Futuro. Vamos Melhorar Nossas Creches" (1984).

24. São Paulo, Commissão Especial, "Relatorio Final," emphasis in the original.

25. Interview with María Amelia de Almeida Teles, São Paulo, August 19, 1985.

26. Governo do Estado de São Paulo, Conselho Estadual da Condição Femenina, Commissão de Creche, "Levantamento e Caraterísticas dos Bercarios / Creches no Local do Trabalho" (1985). This study found that virtually none of the establishments obligated by law (those that employ more than thirty women) to provide day care for infant children of their employees do so. In the entire state of São Paulo, only thirty-eight businesses maintain day care services for their employees.

27. Governo do Estado de São Paulo, Conselho da Condição Femenina, "Creche no Local de Trabalho" (1985, pamphlet).

28. Interview with Ana María Wilheim, São Paulo, August 20, 1985.

29. For a related discussion on these themes, see my "Politicizing Gender."

30. On the right-wing mobilization of women against the Goulart regime, see Solange de Deus Simões, *Deus, Patria e Familia: As Mulheres no Golpe de 1964* (Petrópolis: Vôzes, 1985).

31. For an analysis of the role of gender in right-wing mobilizations of women against Allende in Chile, for example, see María de los Angeles Crummett, "El

Poder Femenino: The Mobilization of Women against Socialism in Chile,'' *Latin American Perspectives* 4, no. 4 (1977):103–113; and Michele Mattelart, "Chile: The Feminine Side of the Coup d'Etat,'' in *Sex and Class in Latin America,* ed. J. Nash and H. I. Safa (New York: Praeger, 1976). See also Patricia Chuchryk, "Protest, Politics and Personal Life: The Emergence of Feminism in a Military Dictatorship, Chile 1973–1983 (Ph.D. diss., York University, Toronto, 1984).

32. María Inacia d'Avila Neto explores some of the psychosocial dimensions of the relationship between authoritarianism and the subordination of women in *O Autoritarismo e A Mulher: O Jogo da Dominação Macho-Fêmea no Brasil* (Rio de Janeiro: Achiame, 1980). For an analysis of gender ideology and policies of militaristic states in different national contexts, see Ximena Bunster-Burroto, "Surviving Beyond Fear: Women and Torture in Latin America," in *Women and Change in Latin America,* ed. June Nash and Helen Safa (Massachusetts: Bergin and Garvey, 1986); Cynthia H. Enloe, "Women Textile Workers in the Militarization of Southeast Asia," in *Women, Men, and the International Division of Labor,* ed. June Nash and María Patricia Fernandez-Kelly (Albany: State University of New York Press, 1983); and Chuchryk, "Protest, Politics, and Personal Life," especially chaps. 3 and 4.

33. Commissão de Estudos sobre Planejamento Familiar das Entidades Feministas de São Paulo, "Controle da Natalidade e Planejamento Familiar'' (São Paulo, 1980, mimeographed).

34. Ibid., p. 4.

35. Ibid., p. 8.

36. See Carmen Barroso, "UN Population Policies and Women'' (1984, mimeographed), for an excellent discussion of the relationship between U.N. population-control initiatives and its efforts to promote improvements in the status of women (as these are thought to reduce fertility). See also Carmen Barroso, "Innovations in Reproductive Health in Brazil'' (Paper presented at the 1987 Meeting of the Association for Women in Development, Washington, D.C., April 1987).

37. Brazil, Senado Federal, "Palestra da Senadora Eunice Michiles sobre Planejamento Familiar'' (April 28, 1983, mimeographed), emphasis in the original.

38. Brazil, Ministério da Saúde, "Assistência Integral á Saúde da Mulher. Subsídios para uma Ação Programática'' (June 1983, mimeographed), p. 4.

39. Ibid., p. 20.

40. Estado de São Paulo, Secretaría de Saúde, "Programa da Saúde da Mulher'' (1983, mimeographed), p. 5.

41. Ibid., p. 6.

42. Interview with Margaret Arilha, Coordinator of the São Paulo State Council on Women's Condition Commission on Women's Health and member of the council's Executive Committee, São Paulo, August 22, 1985.

43. Movimento de Mulheres Democráticas Sociais, "Planejamento Familiar Ja!'' (1984, mimeographed).

44. Coletivo Feminista Sexualidade e Saúde, "Brasil: Mujeres y Salud,'' in *La Salud de las Mujeres: La Experiencia de Brasil, Reflexiones y Acciones Internacionales,* ed. ISIS International (Santiago, Chile: ISIS, 1985), p. 11.

45. Ibid., p. 13.

46. I am indebted to Margit Mayer for having drawn my attention to differential "access points" within the state apparatus. See her "Urban Social Movements and Beyond: New Linkages between Movement Sectors and the State in West Germany and the United States" (Paper presented at the Fifth International Conference of Europeanists, Washington, D.C., October 18–20, 1985).

47. Interview with Margaret Arilha, São Paulo, August 22, 1985.

48. Ibid.

49. Informal interview with Ana María P. Pluciennik, coordinator of the Women's Health Program, Secretaria da Saúde, São Paulo, August 21, 1985.

50. Since its creation, the Delegacia has been reportedly receiving 200–300 complaints per day. Similar "women's precincts" have since been installed elsewhere in greater São Paulo and in more than twenty other Brazilian cities.

51. Interview with Ruth Escobar, president of the National Council on Women's Rights, São Paulo, August 26, 1985.

52. Informal interview with María Aparecida Schumacher, member of Ruth Escobar's legislative staff, August 25, 1985.

53. The PFL or Partido da Frente Liberal was created by the dissenting wing of the PDS, which left the ruling party in 1984 over the issue of direct elections and joined with the PMDB to create the Alliança Liberal, the political coalition which advanced the "indirect" candidacy of Tancredo Neves of the PMDB in 1984. With Tancredo's untimely death on the day before his inauguration as the first civilian president in twenty-two years, his running mate from the PFL, José Sarney, became president.

54. Conselho Nacional dos Direitos da Mulher, "Carta das Mulheres aos Constituintes de 1987" (December 1986, pamphlet).

55. *Informe Mulher* (bulletin of the National Council on Women's Rights) (Brasilia, 1986), p. 5.

56. Brasil, Ministério de Saúde, *Boletim Informativo da 8a Conferencia Nacional de Saúde* (December 1986), p. 4.

57. "Aborto descriminalizado," *Mulherio* 6, no. 26 (September/November 1986):18. Several studies have estimated the number of illegal abortions performed in Brazil each year to exceed 3 million.

58. *Informe Mulher* (1986), p. 2.

59. The ensuing discussion is based on a thorough review of 1985–1988 council documents, the feminist print media, formal interviews with María Amelia Telles de Almeida, former coordinator of the CECF day care and women and work commissions, June 22, 1988; Edna Roland, member of the CECF Black Women's Commission, June 24, 1988, Zuleika Alambert, former president of the CECF, June 27, 1988; Cristina Masagão, former vice-president of the CECF, June 27, 1988; Ida María Jancsó, current CECF president, July 14, 1988; and informal interviews with María Aparecida Schumacher, executive secretary, CNDM, July 16, 1988; Vera Lucia Soares, technical director, CNDM, June 28, 1988; and Ruth Cardoso, former CECF councilor, July 7, 1988.

60. Telephone interview with staff member of the São Paulo Municipal Council on the Status of Women, July 15, 1988.

61. Interview with María Amelia Telles de Almeida, São Paulo, June 22, 1988.

62. Interviews with Lia Zanotta Machado and Ana Vicentine, former members of the autonomous feminist group Brasilia-Mulher, who participated in discussions about the goals and structure of the CNDM with founding president Ruth Escobar and others prior to the installation of the council in late 1985. Brasilia, July 1, 1988.

63. Interviews with Edna Roland and Bia, São Paulo, June 24, 1988, and Vera Lucia Soares, Brasilia, June 28, 1988.

64. See Conselho Nacional dos Direitos da Mulher, *I Encontro Nacional de Delegadas Lotadas em Delegacias de Defesa da Mulher* (Brasilia, 1986).

65. Raquel Moreno, "De Feminismos, de Feministas, de Mulheres," in *A Condição Feminina,* ed. Nanci Valadares de Carvalho (São Paulo: Vertice, 1988), pp. 46–47.

66. Catherine A. MacKinnon, "Feminism, Marxism, Method and the State: Toward a Feminist Jurisprudence," *Signs,* 8 (Summer 1983); Kathy Ferguson, *The Feminist Case Against Bureaucracy* (Philadelphia: Temple Unversity Press, 1984).

67. Wendy Brown, "Prolegomena for a Feminist Theory of the State (Paper presented at the annual meeting of the Northeastern Political Science Association, Boston, November 1986), p. 3.

68. See especially Barbara Ehrenreich and Frances Fox Piven, "Women and the Welfare State," in *Alternatives: Proposals for America from the Democratic Left,* ed. I. Howe (New York: Pantheon, 1983); Frances Fox Piven, "Women and the State: Ideology, Power, and the Welfare State," *Socialist Revolution,* 14 (March/April 1984).

69. For a similar perspective on state power and social change, see Martin Carnoy, *The State and Political Theory* (Princeton: Princeton University Press, 1984).

4/Hierarchy and Class in Women's Organizations: A Case from Northern Mexico

Gay Young

The case against separate women's development organizations is widely known: women become further marginalized because separate is not equal, especially since such organizations focus more often on women's reproductive activities than on their contributions to production. Just as well known is the critique of "integrated" programs as not integrated but instead male-dominated, with women's interests either subsumed under men's or assumed to be the same as men's. However, even if women were integrated as equals into mainstream development projects, that would not eliminate the need for separate women's development organizations.[1]

Separate women's organizations "offer . . . the opportunity to develop self-confidence and skills within a supportive framework . . . and enable women to gain access to resources and . . . to take greater economic and political responsibility."[2] Moreover, women's rationale for such organizations—self-management and respect for their productive activities—challenges their "proper" roles.[3]

Given that women's organizations are a legitimate part of the development landscape, how they function becomes a key question for investigation. The analysis herein reveals how issues of internal structure (hierarchy) and the socioeconomic position of participants (class relations) in women's development organizations influence organizational functioning. Concepts from feminist organization theory and from development literature on women il-

An earlier version of this paper was presented at the Association for Women in Development meetings, April 17, 1987, Washington, D.C. The final work benefited greatly from Kathleen Staudt's ability to probe significant issues regarding women and organization.

luminate a case from northern Mexico. It is a case fraught with paradoxes—for example, a commitment to "democracy" in the midst of a *mystified* hierarchy—due, in part, to the lack of models for avoiding the reproduction of traditional (male) inequality in organizations.

A Feminist Theoretical Analysis of Social Organizations

Women's organizations in the United States have struggled with issues of both hierarchy and class. Four ideas or themes in feminist theory that developed in the context of the women's movement merit particular attention. Three of them address the phenomenon of hierarchy—bureaucratization, structurelessness, and leadership; the fourth comprises questions about the intersection of gender issues and class divisions. Some years ago Boulding summarized the antihierarchy position of feminists in the statement: women are nurturers, and nurturance is nonhierarchical.[4] This assertion undergirds the belief (as well as the wish, Boulding suggests) that women can develop organizational techniques that do not require the exercise of dominance. Yet, feminists still seek to elaborate nonhierarchical patterns for working in large-scale organizations. *Bureaucratization,* as the typical response to scale, has been recognized as antithetical to women's interests.[5] Simply staffing bureaucratic organizations with women will not alter them, for relations of hierarchical domination in bureaucracy serve to perpetuate social inequalities. Specifically, bureaucracy systematizes male preference and limits discussion of change in gender relations.[6]

One of Ferguson's central arguments is that embedded in women's traditional experience as caregivers is the outline of a nonbureaucratic vision of collective life.[7] Others assert that the anchoring effect of children has left women closer to and more aware of nurturance needs of their families as well as sensitized to such needs among their neighbors; thus, community redistribution systems became the business of women. These traditional networking skills present an alternative to hierarchical organizational patterns.[8] However, Ferguson suggests that the values coming out of the experience of mothering also lead women to avoid risk and conflict—that is, the "clash of will that authentic nonbureaucratic [organizational] politics requires."[9]

Ferguson's own analysis of organizational class structure—in which all but the elite undergo a process she identifies as "feminization" in order to function in a subordinate status in the bureaucracy—implies a more general source of these attributes. Within the context of male organizational patterns, the feminized are industrial and clerical workers, marginal workers in secondary labor market jobs, clients of service bureaucracies, and even the so-called new working class made up of white-collar professionals and technicians. That is, all embody traits that women have adopted to accommodate to the power of men.

It is noteworthy that a similar process (unlikely to be called feminization, however) appears to be working in Smith's discussion of the rationale for success in the Mexican political system since the 1940s.[10] He elaborates a set of "rules" (most obvious when they are broken) for surviving and achieving within the bureaucratic authoritarian state structure. Examples include: study the system and make lots of friends; don't make enemies but do demonstrate loyalty to your superior; don't rock the boat; avoid mistakes by staying in line, following orders, and keeping quiet; pass difficult decisions on to your superior. No provisions exist for "clashes of will." Rather, these are guidelines for subordinates, for only the president, an office few among the elite will achieve, is not in a subordinate relation to someone higher in the Mexican system of politics and government. Viewed another way, the rules provide an outline for socialization into the male dominance system.

Thus, bureaucracy contributes to social inequality, and doubts exist regarding its capacity to offer solutions to the problems created by social inequalities. Indeed, Ferguson asserts that organizations representing women's interests—even those that routinely work with bureaucracies—cannot themselves become bureaucratic or they cease to be representative of their constituents. In a study of women's international nongovernmental organizations (NGOs), Boulding concludes that these NGOs' activities have been limited because women have accepted male organizational patterns, bureaucratic hierarchy, in particular.[11] However, she also notes that that system of status gave the NGO women the little recognition they were getting.

If women's experience as caregivers leads to an identity of connection and an ethic of responsibility, women still must extract this experience from the many others in their daily lives that are linked to the survival of subordination.[12] Only in this way can they act on the integrity of those virtues and change society. Do women have rooted in their nurturing relations the capacity to solve the persistent problems facing egalitarian and participatory, nonbureaucratic organizations?

Hierarchical structure is an issue with which the contemporary women's movement in the United States has had to struggle. Freeman asserts that among the consequences of the movement idea that all hierarchy is bad ("because it gives some people power over other people and does not allow everyone's full talents to develop") have been problems created by *structurelessness*.[13] Although structurelessness is not a necessary result of horizontal leadership, in practice, antihierarchy has meant antileadership more often than shared leadership.[14] The consequence has been the limitation of task efficiency and political effectiveness because of the time devoted to group process rather than group ends, according to Freeman. In addition, there was loss of control of movement leadership (to the media, in part), and the performance of leadership functions by thousands of other women had to be "hidden," as Bunch puts it.

Although attention to process may have the potential to humanize bureaucracy, it does not necessarily lead to outcomes in women's interest.[15] Moreover, in the women's movement emphasis on process in the absence of any structural framework forced "leaders" to put extra energy into maintaining good personal relations and maintaining a personable environment. Besides its balance against instrumental action, Freeman contends, participation that is aimed at maintaining good interpersonal relations is not conducive to confronting and resolving conflict, which is part of the democratic process.

The structurelessness resulting from antihierarchical sentiments contains contradictory implications for *leadership* in women's organizations. For example, Bunch describes one double bind experienced through the 1970s: women identified as leaders in the women's rights sector, often working in hierarchical organizations, were judged in the movement by the collectivist norms of the liberation sector and condemned as elitist.[16] As another example, highly visible women were vilified as "media stars," but there was no mechanism to "remove" them. Nonetheless, even in situations that are antihierarchical, women have performed leadership functions. But they must then hide their leadership activities, and they cannot be supported—or held accountable.[17] Relations of leadership in the women's movement have produced persistent problems and thus generated theoretical analyses.

In a special collection of *Quest* on feminist theory, St. Joan presents an "ideal type" of feminist leadership.[18] She asserts that a leader's authority comes from the quality of her relationships with constituents; the group empowers the leader with certain responsibilities. Also critical to her typification is the notion of "shifting leadership." She sees in the empowering aspects of mothering a model or analog for feminist leadership: the relations of letting go of power, on the one hand, and of accepting responsibility, on the other. This is akin to Bunch's understanding of power identified with "energy, strength, and effective interaction, rather then with manipulation, domination, and control."[19] The feminist model of leadership, then, contains commitment to the empowerment of others rather than their subordination. In practice, empowerment means broad responsibilities for all and widely visible decision-making power. It is not the same as structurelessness—indeed, it requires clear delineation of participants' tasks.[20]

Freeman's account of experience in the women's movement reveals that the ironic result of the antihierarchy (antileadership) position was only a slight variation on the kind of discriminatory and exclusive system of leadership women historically have fought. The criteria used to select leaders were similar to those people use to select friends (background and personality), not those an organization uses to be politically effective (competence and potential contribution to the movement).[21] Moreover, with no structure in place to enhance participation, consensus was built through homogeneity, which, in turn, served to exclude women who did not match the white middle-class norm—for whatever reason—and deprived the movement of these women's leadership, energy, and strength.[22]

Yet another style (if one is willing to take antileadership as a style) of leadership, noteworthy because it has been observed in women's organizations, is charismatic leadership. Charisma stands against bureaucratic hierarchy in ways that are different from feminism's opposition to it.[23] People submit to charismatic leadership because of their belief in the extraordinary qualities of the specific person: the image of the leader verges on the divine. The charismatic leader derives her right not from selection by the people but rather from followers' conviction that it is their *duty* to recognize her as their leader by virtue of her mission. Duty to obey is implied; compliance with the leader's directives creates a particular hierarchical relationship between leader and followers.

Recognition and response to charismatic leadership are distinctive in yet other ways.[24] It is a nonformal style of leadership: relations between the followers and the leader are conducted on a personal basis that is not formalized in positions; thus followers respond to the leader by internalizing her ideas and definitions of reality. It is an inherently unstable style of leadership largely because of the intensity and quality of the emotional commitment by followers that involves devotion, awe, and reverence for the leader. Among the relations of charismatic leadership, there are no mechanisms for resolving conflict, which thus appears personal or "heretical."

In her study of five women's organizations in Latin America and the Caribbean, Yudelman reviews the pros and cons of charismatic leadership. Charismatic leaders represent their organizations effectively and they often have political clout. However, an organization can become identified with its charismatic leader, which impedes institutionalization. In addition to strong, emotional commitment on the part of organization members, charismatic leadership engenders informal management styles that lack "procedures for internal reporting, role definition, personnel evaluation and staff training." Such leadership also creates relationships within the organization that appear "personal rather than professional," and it unintentionally may give rise to "dependency, resentment, and internal conflict."[25]

In sum, Yudelman observes that women seem to have real difficulty creating and maintaining organizations that are "participatory, conflict-free *and* functional."[26] She suggests that underlying this problem is the high level of emotional commitment organization members feel toward charismatic leaders, making them demanding of themselves and critical of others. In contrast, Ferguson and Boulding root the apparent problem in obstacles to women's drawing on the relevant values arising from their caregiver relations, and Freeman identifies it as part of the so-called tyranny of structurelessness.

Feminists have begun to analyze the ways in which internal organizational structure, particularly the issue of hierarchy, can present obstacles to the pursuit of women's interests. Feminists have also struggled with the issue of how women's subordination connects to class inequalities.

In order to portray the complexity of women's lives and of social organization, feminist analysis must take fully into account the interplay of gender, race, and class. All women experience gender subordination, but gender relations have "race-specific" and "class-specific" dimensions as well.[27] The various inequalities interact to condition the particulars of women's lives. For example, a working-class, lesbian *mestiza* experiences female oppression in specific ways.

Although wide recognition exists of women's experience of oppression other than gender subordination, the relations among them have not been thoroughly elaborated. For example, feminists acknowledge class divisions, but, in Bunch's view, they have little understanding of the significance or the consequences of class for feminist activism.[28] As another example, it appears to be easier to reveal the exclusion of women of color from women's studies than to demonstrate how working-class women have been marginalized in the discipline.[29]

Class distinctions are in a mutually reinforcing relationship with male domination. Class relations structure the concrete meaning gender has for women, and male-female relations condition women's experience of productive activities. Moreover, the class system puts some women in positions of power relative to other women and thereby weakens all women in their struggle against domination.[30] How can feminists act on common interests as well as embrace a diversity of actors?

First, women do share interests that transcend class lines (and color lines) around which they can organize and which can inform the agenda of women's organizations. These include the gender-based division of labor, patriarchal authority, personal aspirations, and the need for self-respect.[31] Yet, in women's diverse experiences feminists gain a more complete understanding of complex systems of domination and of obstacles to be overcome for treatment as equals.[32] Historically, however, those people in the most privileged positions in society have presented difference as a threat to the situation—even survival—of the group. That is, they transformed diversity into a tool for maintaining domination.

Middle-class women clearly benefit from the class system. Through struggles against their own oppressive behavior as well as against oppression in society, they can relieve their responsibility for their class privilege. This can begin with the recognition that one does not need a college degree to "see political solutions to personally experienced problems." Class supremacy views working-class women as less personally "evolved" or politically "savvy" because they do not act and talk the way middle-class women do.[33]

A diverse and inclusive feminism that forgoes the security of familiarity will allow women to see how the individual's struggle links to a wider struggle shared with women who are different. Personal experience is political, and it is shaped by the sociocultural system. It alone does not suffice as a basis for feminist analysis and action, however. Pushing beyond the limits of personal experience and learning from the diversity of women's lives is crucial to the struggle against domination.[34]

The Women in Development (WID) literature adds the dimension of nation to relations of class and race when studying women's situation. Attending to inequalities other than female subordination illuminates the reality that women share various experiences based on gender. Analyses inspired by the U.N. Decade for Women, especially those by Third World women, illustrate both women's differences and the common interests among them.

Development Organizations and Development Strategy

Writing at the close of the women's decade, Sen assesses the beginnings of the process of empowering women in developing countries and empowering women's development organizations to oppose gender oppression as well as the oppression of class, race, and nationality.[35] She, as well as Staudt, argues that the nature of the task involves both an ongoing process of self-empowerment among women *and* their making demands collectively on governments and other bureaucracies for wider changes.[36] Thus, to create effective change organizations, women must tie together a process orientation and values from their daily experience with knowledge and skill development and leadership formation.

Sen outlines issues that continue to challenge women's development organizations: reluctance to propose development programs for society from women's perspective; an unrealized potential of allying with other grassroots organizations; the problematic nature of relations with bureaucratic structures (agencies and governments) that are vital to effecting gender redistribution; innovative ways of delegating authority and responsibility that do not perpetuate relations of dominance and subordination; developing styles of conflict management and resolution within a democratic process.[37]

The last point—conflict in women's organizations—remains a central challenge. However, in her analysis of what five women's development organizations do well, Yudelman illustrates how they are meeting some of the other challenges Sen presents.[38] That they organize and mobilize women and enhance their self-worth and capacity for self-help is clear. They are also attempting to connect with larger frames of reference—that is, to see the "big" picture. Indeed, women's organizations have used political clout to bring about policy changes and are beginning to network with other organizations.

Yet, women's organizations remain constrained in ways that hinder their responses to certain challenges. Two constraints Yudelman identifies are the sometimes hostile cultural climate in which women's development organizations operate, especially regarding women's proper role, as well as their pervasive need for funds. As these organizations have grown, their loose structures and informal management styles (once strengths) now present problems as well—among them difficulties in dealing with donor agencies.[39] Finally, relations of leadership and power remain ambiguous as women struggle to create new forms for organizing for change.

Against this backdrop I examine a women's development organization in northern Mexico in terms of the ways in which issues of class relations and hierarchical structures arose in the organization and influenced its functioning. A few comments about Mexico's development strategy provide the larger context for this analysis.

One troubling aspect of many Third World state development strategies has been the use of women's low-cost labor to transform the economy.[40] In a comparative analysis of development strategies and the status of women, Leahy concludes that, although Mexican women could offer an abundant source of cheap labor, "the political and economic costs of fully utilizing this labor would be great."[41] In Mexico's northern border region, tens of thousands of women have been drawn into the new international division of labor as low-cost assembly workers for transnational corporations. No thoroughgoing account of the consequences of this process yet exists.[42]

The *maquiladoras,* export-oriented assembly plants of Mexico's industrialization program, constitute a key element in the nation's development strategy.[43] Approximately 1,000 plants with close to 250,000 assembly workers (and about another 50,000 administrators and technicians) are currently operating.[44] For twenty years the *maquiladoras* have been employing predominantly female labor to work in factories assembling garments and electric or electronic components for subsidiaries of (mainly) U.S.-based corporations. The vast majority (90 percent) of these plants have been located in the northern border regions. By the mid-1980s the *maquiladora* industry had become Mexico's second most important producer of foreign exchange after oil, although still only about 5 percent of the total.

The organization that is the empirical case in this analysis emerged in response to perceived problems arising from the influx of women into the wage labor market created by the *maquiladoras*. The problems raised most often with the *maquiladoras* are the absence of significant linkages to the Mexican economy, vulnerability to and dependency on swings in the U.S. economy, and the exploitation of women's labor and the consequent disruption of traditional Mexican family relations. The Women's Center arose out of the last concern.

Egalitarianism and Participation in a Mexican Women's Organization

The Women's Center is a grassroots development organization concerned with equality and democratic participation. The analysis presented here is based on systematic observation of the organization over a period of about twenty months—from the fall of 1982 through the spring of 1984.[45] In what follows I examine how class, absence of hierarchy, and charismatic leadership (which characterized the center in earlier years) affect organizational functioning.

INEQUALITIES OF CLASS AND EGALITARIANISM

Class relations have been a factor at the Women's Center since its inception in the late 1960s. A group of relatively privileged women, acting on their sense of social responsibility toward those less fortunate, formed a small philanthropic institution to assist the growing number of women in the *maquiladoras* who were confronting the dual roles of wage earner and family member. Their initial concern was with the morality of women swept up in the rapid industrialization created by the establishment of export-oriented assembly plants in Cd. Juarez. In their view, these young factory workers needed guidance to maintain the high moral standards of the traditional Mexican women's role.[46]

To the founders' credit, as they become more directly involved with women workers and listened to the concerns those women expressed—about the loss of sense of self that results from being an appendage of a machine and the need to rediscover dignity and value—they moved toward collaboration with the *maquiladora* women to create a center responsive to workers' own perceived needs.

Nonetheless, the nature of the center's genesis was such that little impetus existed for organizing women to force change in the conditions of the workplace; instead, the broad project of the center has been more ameliorative: to enable women to cope constructively with the fact of *maquiladoras* in their lives and to develop and channel women's potential as community change agents. Such a project is more in line with the upper middle-class location of its founders, which is not to imply, however, that the organization's activities do not speak to real needs of working-class women. Evidence that they have is discussed below.

The center's objectives, articulated in 1978 in a proposal to a U.S. donor agency for funding, included: providing counsel to the *mujer obrera* about her changing role as a woman and an employee; helping her resolve personal, family, and work-related problems; helping her understand her reality and her potential role in society; promoting solidarity, participation, social responsibility, and openness to change; and channeling the working women's *inquietudes* (anxieties) toward community-related activities.

The activities of the center's twenty-two staff members—seventeen of whom were women and half of whom had previously worked in the *maquiladoras* themselves—operationalized these objectives. A general understanding of the center's purpose—education and development of women, especially factory women—guided their daily work. Staff members believed they had a clear sense of the needs of women to which the center should respond. But this was not a unified sense: some advocated preparing women workers for better jobs, and others, taking a more abstract view, emphasized enhancing women's understanding of the world.

Without benefit of formal input from factory women regarding the center's programming, the legitimacy of the staff's assessment of women's needs as well as the center's claim to be a workers' organization rested on the members' own working-class experience. Some viewed this as the only valid experience on which to base the creation and carrying out of the center's project. This extreme position created a climate of "anti-intellectualism"—intellectuals being those who had no direct experience in the *maquiladoras* but who studied the situation in other ways—and gave rise to contradictions for some of the "workers-turned-intellectuals" on the staff.

The upper middle-class, graduate school–educated director ably deflected criticism of her own background by emphasizing to the staff the weight their experience carried in defining and implementing the center's activities. The result was further support for the anti-intellectual position. However, more problematic was the hint of paternalism it revealed, for practical manifestation of this position is an orientation, common among staff members, focused on helping factory women rather than on empowering them.

Although it is reasonable to raise the issue of the degree to which staff members themselves were empowered in their relations at the center, their helping orientation can also be traced to the institution's origin, which has been a continuing influence on the center's fundamental project.

Analysis of the formalized curriculum offered by the center reveals more about this issue of women's empowerment. It also illustrates that women's concerns do, indeed, cut across class lines. The process of *concientización*, embedded in Paulo Freire's approach to education and adopted by the center, leads factory women to question their situation as women.

The curriculum in use contained some radicalizing material, but the scenario most often presented was not one where class-conscious *maquiladora* workers act on their common interest against the dominant interests. Rather, it was a reformist scenario in which socially conscious women organize themselves to ameliorate the conditions of their lives and their communities. Reform and radical messages were both conveyed in the curriculum, but the course neither purposefully promoted ideologically inspired activism nor detailed strategies for effective reform—in terms of what does and does not "work" and how women can organize to influence the system.[47]

With only a fragile, newly found sense of empowerment, the women found that the result of the course was frustration, at times, and, in the extreme, immobilization, as they were presented with a complex reality they possessed few tools to change. Yet, personal transformation of women who participated in the center's courses has always been evident.

Through experiences at the center, factory women have gleaned an awareness of their rights as women and thereby begun to undermine the patriarchal relations within which they live. They have developed a more self-assured style based on enhanced self-respect. They aspire to be autonomous, equal actors having an effect on their world. Though male dominance, the devaluing of women, and artificial limitations on women's potential are all conditioned by class position, it is also the case that all women share these gendered experiences. The center's programs enabled working women to analyze their situation as women and start to grasp how the "personal is political."[48]

Factory women came away from the center with a foundation for the ongoing process of self-empowerment. However, strategies for making demands for wider changes in the institutions that shape their lives, such as government bureaucracies or work organizations, remained obscure to them. This was due, in part, to the nature of the center's fundamentally ameliorative project. It was also an outcome of problems with the center's own organizational structure and style of management.

PARTICIPATION AND THE CONSEQUENCES OF CHARISMA

The center's organizational structure was characterized by the absence of hierarchy, an expression of its democratic and participatory ideals. The structure was simple: a director assisted by a relatively undifferentiated staff; an advisory board existed but played no significant role. Beneficiaries compose an additional element of the organizational structure, but to begin with, this analysis pays attention primarily to center staff.

By definition, the informal management style that accompanied this organizational structure lacked specific procedures. Nonetheless, staff members did make internal reports: over half the staff reported on an almost daily basis to the director—verbally, not in writing. And though staff members did learn new skills, the most valuable training experiences were limited to the privileged few with whom the director worked very closely. Because organizational role definitions were not precise and no formal procedures existed, personnel evaluations were fated to be personalistic.

The primary basis for relations in the organization, then, was personal rather than positional—as exemplified by the informal management style. At one time this had been a strength, and there is no intent in this critique to suggest that staff members should be reduced to instruments merely for the use of the organization. However, as the center increased its dealings not only with the bureaucracies of the state and of industry but also international donor agencies, elements of the informal management style became liabilities.[49] The organization grew, and its tasks became more complex. This intensified the need for precise specification of tasks and responsibilities so that operations were rationalized rather than based solely on "good" personal relations.

Problems arose in the organization because job descriptions were vague and did not really reflect what staff members were doing. Thus, structurelessness, in the sense of little clear delineation of tasks, meant *not* that nobody was responsible for anything but that everyone became responsible for everything. That, in turn, led to serious overextension of some staff members and to their inevitable exhaustion. However, no mechanism existed to address the personal inequities resulting from organization structure, and the frustrations felt were further complicated by the importance of maintaining good personal relations in the organization. It does not seem an overstatement to assert that staff members were often victims of the tyranny of structurelessness.

The center's management style, which led to many of the problems of structurelessness, was conditioned by the nature of organizational leadership. Among the founders was a charismatic woman who became the organization's director and remained in that position until 1984. As a person with extraordinary qualities, she elicited strong commitment from the staff, who internalized her definition of the situation of women in the *maquiladoras*. She was illustrative of the leader who derives her right from people's conviction that they must follow her dutifully because of her mission. Her nearness to divinity in the eyes of the others was revealed when she suffered an apparently life-threatening illness that was followed by a medically inexplicable recovery, an episode that occurred toward the end of the evaluation on which this analysis is based.

Charismatic leadership is both a nonformal and an inherently unstable leadership style. For example, as happened at the center, the strong emotional commitment elicited by a charismatic leader made organization members more demanding of themselves and more critical of their colleagues, which led to internal conflict.[50] Complicating matters in this case was the importance of maintaining a personable work environment: in contrast to the *maquiladoras,* where workers were merely cogs in the wheel, relations between the director and the staff and among staff members were highly personalistic. Such a situation is not conducive to confronting and resolving conflict. Thus, not only was internal conflict very likely, it was also devastating, for the organizational relations associated with charismatic leadership contain no provisions for the constructive handling of conflict.

The case examined here contributes little to a comparative analysis of whether women's organizations have greater difficulty resolving conflict than do men's organizations. However, what observation of the center did demonstrate is that "it is as difficult to *remain* a democratic organization as it is to *create* one."[51] Without models for participatory and egalitarian organizational forms that operate through processes other than maintaining "good" relations (nothing in the hierarchical Mexican patronage system offers guidance), the charismatic director and the staff "ad hoced" an organizational form and process that limited effectiveness and ultimately exacerbated conflict.

In a change-oriented workers' organization such as the center, empowerment should be an ongoing and deliberate process. However, charismatic leadership comprises few of the elements of empowering leadership. Although charismatic leaders can articulate issues and mobilize people around goals (certainly true in this case), organizations, in turn, become identified with and dependent upon their charismatic leaders.[52] Leadership succession at the center became an ambiguous and highly charged issue.

The male pattern of the leader's choosing his successor, as in the succession to the Mexican presidency, provided the most visible model.[53] Though rejecting that process but still groping for a way to transfer power, the center never confronted the issue thoroughly. It was typically met with dismissive statements to the effect that "of course others are capable—the workers can run the center." Ultimately, the charismatic director departed and the organization experienced a diaspora.[54]

The dynamics of the center offer a lesson in the difficulties of empowerment and moving with others in self-empowerment. Specific aspects of the center's structure and processes acted as obstacles to actualizing the image of a nonhierarchical and participatory organization that empowers women.

Formal staff meetings were not scheduled regularly, and when they were held, they were more often reactive to some crisis rather than proactive. As center activities became more complex, the informal management style exacerbated problems already existing because information was centralized in the head of the director. Thus, because the director was the primary source of staff information about the center's ongoing work and she called meetings irregularly, staff members experienced considerable fragmentation of knowledge regarding organizational activities.

Few of them were able to articulate an integrated overall picture. In a sense, the anti-intellectual climate, with its emphasis on knowledge through direct experience, also limited the "sources" on which staff members could draw to explain the ways in which more recent projects were linked to the center's basic project of working with factory women or to elaborate the role of the center in the broader process of social change in the city or the region. This suggests the limits on the degree of empowerment experienced by staff members.

Yet, despite the irregularity of staff meetings, staff members did believe that they had a say in the organization. Unstructured observation and observation of center meetings revealed that the most influential and active participants from the staff were those people who had greater personal resources, such as more education, and who worked on a daily basis with the director. Meetings were periodically called to brainstorm about the organization and its activities, but little evidence exists of a fundamental role for staff members in defining the basic project of the organization. On the other hand, all center activities were undertaken by staff consensus. However, giving approval is not the same as empowerment.

The center's informal management style, based on charismatic leadership, engendered two interrelated problems: internal conflict became destructive in the absence of rules or strategies for confronting dissent, and without specific provisions for staff development, staff members were not empowered in their relations in the organization. Few staff members were prepared practically to take on responsibility and authority, and we must ask whether greater staff empowerment might have enhanced members' ability to advance the self-empowerment of the women the center served. Finally, with neither a forum nor any creative means available to the staff for managing and resolving conflict, high expectations and emotions contributed importantly to the center's virtual dissolution in 1984.

The director now heads an organization that carries out research. She has little formal contact with the center where, during the last few years, a core of staff members has undertaken various activities. Their organization will doubtless comprise a new form and processes. What can be extracted from earlier experiences that should inform the center's re-emergence?

Conclusions

Organizations opposed to hierarchy, especially those that strive to be egalitarian and participatory, struggle with particular problems. This study reveals that the issues of leadership and conflict resolution emerge as critical challenges confronting women's organizations as they attempt to create alternatives to bureaucratic domination. Although the center did not reproduce a "gendered" form, women's empowerment was limited because the organization did not find—in the maintaining of good relations under the wing of a charismatic leader—a workable alternative to dominance. Some aspects of organizational relations still reflected politics as men play it in the Mexican bureaucracy. Is it possible that rooted in women's experience are keys to resolving these difficulties and to creating democratic organizations? Linking concepts and observations, I first draw out insights into hierarchy and empowerment to be taken from this analysis.

Structurelessness has been one response by women's organizations to the negative assessment of hierarchy. Although structurelessness implies attention to process, the process in which organization members get involved seems to be one of personal accommodation rather than conflict resolution. Avoidance of risk and conflict—that is, accommodation—is rooted in values associated with women's subordination, not in the values of the caregiver/ mother who empowers. (This is not to deny the obvious, that gender subordination conditions mothering just as class and race or nation do.) Although both are part of female experience, they have different implications for women's organizing. Women need to develop tools for negotiating as equals. Accommodation has not facilitated conflict management and resolution; empowerment holds out more promise for fulfilling the democratic process in women's organizations.

Leadership by women can also be understood over against bureaucratic hierarchy. Any power the bureaucrat possesses is conditioned by her position in the bureaucracy. In contrast, the charismatic leader (common in women's organizations) exercises power because people feel a duty to follow her. Women's organizations have rejected hierarchy as perpetuating inequalities and limiting potential, but charisma engenders crisis management and highly emotional commitment, which have proven to be organizational liabilities of a different nature.

An alternative conceptualization of leadership is the ideal of the reciprocal (group to leader and vice versa) empowerment of rotating feminist leadership. Part of women's organizing project must be to develop ways of delegating authority and responsibility that do not involve relations of dominance and subordination and that do allow efficient accomplishment of tasks and effective promotion of women's interests.

Class divisions form part of the basis for bureaucratic hierarchy and organizational inequality, and the argument is compelling that equality in organizations, including women's organizations, cannot be achieved without more equality and the end of class divisions in society. Nonetheless, women's capacity to re-form organizations that are change oriented can be enhanced. And in working on that task, we can clarify the connections between gender subordination and inequalities that are due to class position (as well as race and level of national development).

All women as women share common interests around which to organize and mobilize, but women of relative privilege, especially, must guard against constricting the meaning of women's empowerment to gender relations alone. The other inequalities women experience condition the concrete meaning of gender. Development organizations enabling women's empowerment must confront all sources of women's subordination, for they are interconnected. To do that will require tremendous resources, but only then will women be treated as equals in society.

Notes

1. This is a premise of Sally Yudelman, *Hopeful Openings: A Study of Five Women's Development Organizations in Latin America and the Caribbean* (Hartford, Conn.: Kumarian Press, 1987).

2. Ibid., p. 3.

3. Ibid.

4. Elise Boulding, "Female Alternatives to Hierarchical Systems, Past and Present: A Critique of Women's NGOs in the Light of History," *Women in the Twentieth Century World* (New York: Sage, 1977).

5. Argued most notably by Kathy Ferguson, *The Feminist Case Against Bureaucracy* (Philadelphia: Temple University Press, 1984).

6. Within the context of an analysis of the U.S. Agency for International Development, this is argued by Kathleen Staudt, *Women, Foreign Assistance, and Advocacy Administration* (New York: Praeger, 1985).

7. Ferguson, *The Feminist Case*.

8. Boulding, "Female Alternatives."

9. Ferguson, *The Feminist Case*, p. 25.

10. Recent political events in Mexico notwithstanding, "the rules of the game" are elaborated in Peter Smith, *Labyrinths of Power* (Princeton, N.J.: Princeton University Press, 1979), esp. pp. 242–78.

11. Boulding, "Female Alternatives."

12. While recognizing that mothering is "implicated" in the creation and maintenance of male domination—see Nancy Chodorow, *Mothering* (Berkeley: University of California Press, 1978)—we must remember that the relations of mothering also comprise other attributes, as discussed below.

13. Jo Freeman, *The Politics of Women's Liberation* (New York: David McKay, 1975), esp. p. 105.

14. Charlotte Bunch, "Woman Power and the Leadership Crisis," *Passionate Politics* (New York: St. Martin's, 1987), pp. 122–33.

15. Staudt, *Women, Foreign Assistance and Advocacy Administration.*

16. Bunch, "Woman Power."

17. Sources of more elaborate discussions include ibid. and Freeman, *The Politics of Women's Liberation.*

18. Jackie St. Joan, "Female Leaders: Who Was Rembrandt's Mother?" in *Building Feminist Theory: Essays from Quest,* ed. Charlotte Bunch (New York and London: Longman, 1981).

19. Bunch, "Woman Power," p. 128.

20. More on shared leadership can be found in ibid.

21. Freeman, *The Politics of Women's Liberation,* p. 123.

22. Bunch, "Woman Power," p. 125.

23. The analysis by Max Weber on which this discussion is based appears in H. H. Gerth and C. Wright Mills, *From Max Weber* (New York: Oxford University Press, 1946), esp. pp. 245–52.

24. Ann Ruth Willner, *The Spellbinders: Charismatic Political Leadership* (New Haven: Yale University Press, 1984).

25. Yudelman, *Hopeful Openings,* pp. 98–99.

26. Ibid., p. 100.

27. Maxine Baca Zinn, Lynn Weber Cannon, Elizabeth Higginbotham, and Bonnie Thornton Dill, "The Costs of Exclusionary Practices in Women's Studies," *Signs* 11, no. 2 (1986): 290–303.

28. Charlotte Bunch, "Class and Feminism," *Passionate Politics* (New York: St. Martin's, 1987), pp. 94–102.

29. Baca Zinn et al., "The Costs of Exclusionary Practices."

30. Bunch, "Class and Feminism," pp. 94–95.

31. Myra Marx Feree, "The Women's Movement in the Working Class," *Sex Roles* 9, no. 4 (1983): 493–505.

32. Baca Zinn et al., "The Costs of Exclusionary Practices."

33. For more examples, see Bunch, "Class and Feminism," and Feree, "The Women's Movement in the Working Class."

34. The significance of diversity is presented in Charlotte Bunch, "Making Common Cause: Diversity and Coalitions," *Passionate Politics* (New York: St. Martin's, 1987), pp. 149–157, and Baca Zinn et al., "The Costs of Exclusionary Practices."

35. Gita Sen, *Development, Crisis, and Alternative Visions: Third World Women's Perspectives* (New Delhi: Development Alternatives with Women for a New Era, 1985).

36. Staudt, *Women, Foreign Assistance, and Advocacy Administration.*

37. Sen, *Development, Crisis, and Alternative Visions.*

38. Yudelman, *Hopeful Openings.*

39. Ibid.

40. Kathleen Staudt, "Women, Development and the State: On the Theoretical Impasse," *Development and Change* 17 (1986): 325–33.

41. Margaret E. Leahy, *Development Strategies and the Status of Women* (Boulder, Colo.: Lynne Rienner, 1986).

42. The most up-to-date bibliography is Leslie Sklair, *Maquiladoras: Annotated Bibliography and Research Guide to Mexico's In-Bond Industry, 1980–1988,* monograph series, vol. 24, Center for U.S.-Mexican Studies (La Jolla, Calif.: University of California at San Diego, 1988).

43. Gay Young, "The Development of Ciudad Juarez: Urbanization, Migration, Industrialization," in Gay Young, ed., *The Social Ecology and Economic Development of Ciudad Juarez* (Boulder, Colo.: Westview, 1986).

44. These estimates are projected from data provided by the Dirección de Investigación Económica, Banco de México, Serie Documentos Internos, "La Industria Maquiladora de Exportación (1980–1986)."

45. Chosen by the center's director, a Mexican counterpart and I took the lead in an evaluation of center activities funded by one of the center's donor agencies. In addition to offering programming for approximately 100 women workers—a program that included the "basic course," training in areas of paraprofessional employment, and community service/action research—the center also administered three cooperatives and four basic education centers (for school dropouts eleven to fourteen years old) during the period covered by the evaluation.

Nonetheless, almost every staff member was involved in the Women's Program in some way, either as her or his main job or in addition to the main job. The course director drew on other staff members (as well as the center director) as lecturers, discussion leaders, instructors in the areas of specialization, leaders of action research teams, and more. She even called on members of the small office staff, who beyond their typical clerical duties also had the task of assisting the many visitors (practitioners and scholars) attracted to the center. Staff members assigned to coordinate the workings of the various coops as well as to run the basic education program also played roles in the program for women workers. Finally, a group of staff (varying from two to four members), generally referred to as the Research Department, carried out descriptive analysis of data collected from program participants and clipped newspapers stories bearing on the *maquiladoras* in addition to their responsibilities in the Women's Program; two of them were given the job of working with us on the evaluation.

This analysis relies on all of the observational strategies employed in the evaluation—relatively unstructured observation of day-to-day activities, a field experiment comparing women in the course with other women in terms of course aims, and hours of interviews about the center with community and labor leaders, direct beneficiaries of the center's work, and with the staff and director. At the risk of oversimplification, the emphasis of this work, in contrast to the larger evaluation per se, is on how the organization operated rather than what it was doing and how well.

46. This is taken from Maria Patricia Fernandez Kelly, "COMO: A New Frontier in Popular Education" (unpublished manuscript, 1985).

47. Kathleen Staudt, "Programming Women's Empowerment," in Vicki Ruiz and Susan Tiano, eds., *Women on the U.S.-Mexico Border: Responses to Change* (Boston: Allen & Unwin, 1987).

48. Gay Young, "Gender Identification and Working Class Solidarity among

Maquila Workers in Ciudad Juarez,'' in Riuz and Tiano, eds., *Women on the U.S.-Mexico Border*.

49. A position also articulated in Yudelman, *Hopeful Openings*.

50. Observed as well by ibid.

51. Robert Wasserstrom, *Grassroots Development in Latin America* (New York: Praeger, 1985), p. 12.

52. Yudelman, *Hopeful Openings*.

53. Admittedly, the process may no longer be as clear-cut as presented in Alan Riding, *Distant Neighbors* (New York: Alfred A. Knopf, 1984), pp. 94–134.

54. This concept is used by Yudelman, *Hopeful Openings*.

International
Agencies

5/Can an Aid Bureaucracy Empower Women?

Karin Himmelstrand

Sara Longwe suggests that the "main problem in Africa is to shift women's development above the welfare level in the face of resistance from male dominated government bureaucracies." She also maintains that "women's welfare is not likely to be much improved until the affected women themselves achieve *control* in such areas as control over factors of production and distribution of income and benefits. . . . This dimension is concerned with women's power to control their own lives and become independent and self-reliant—both individually and collectively—on equal terms with men. Equality in control is the ultimate objective of the process of empowerment."[1]

How far from realizing this objective are the developing countries? Can a foreign donor country like Sweden facilitate the process? If so, is Sweden's contribution specific or unique, and are there constraints difficult to overcome? Looking ahead, can we envisage new alternatives beyond the present horizon of feasible implementation?

Objective with Impediments

Longwe suggests that the male-dominated bureaucracies in the developing countries are the main obstacles to the emancipation of African women. Undoubtedly, this is a significant and obvious factor to be reckoned with, but according to my experience it is only one symptom of a much more fundamental and basic dilemma. The constraints holding women back from taking their rightful place in society, on equal terms with men, are embedded in the overall socioeconomic fabric of these countries. The constraints are woven into the web of culture in such a way that the patterns—the economies—might fall into pieces if one tried to tamper with the threads holding it together.

The division of labor between the sexes in Africa is very strict and rooted in ancient as well as colonial traditions. Biological and social reproduction along with reproductive work are traditional obligations of women. Anything related to small children is regarded as belonging to the domain of women. Their reproductive work is constantly extended to include obligations to more people within the extended family, the community, and new related tasks. This means that women find themselves responsible not only for feeding the whole family, for supplying the household with water and firewood, and for taking care of sick relatives, but also for paying school fees, for growing food crops, for engaging in income-generating activities to earn cash. As men in ever-increasing numbers leave the rural areas in search of paid labor in urban communities, women have to shoulder their husbands' original tasks and responsibilities as well.

Of the common resources, a few trickle down to the women to ease their reproductive work, but these resources are meager and cannot match the contribution the women are making to society. This fact gives economies in developing countries their very special feature. With their unpaid reproductive work, the women subsidize society (usually the men in their own household). The reproductive value produced by this unpaid labor can be used by international and national capital to underpay men in industries and mines, and by the men (the husbands) to buy capital goods like bicycles and radios, or to acquire new wives.

The society at large may seem to profit greatly by the unpaid reproductive work women provide, as long as women are unaware of the value of their own contribution to the society and do not demand their share of the common resources. Instead, they take on more work and responsibilities without being given anything other than marginal assets, and without making sure they are in control of their own lives. But in Africa, where society seems to benefit so greatly from the unpaid farm labor of women, we can see another side of the coin as well: Society itself is also harmed by this lack of economic incentives for women to take on a growing and more efficient farm production—a negative feedback loop that probably explains a great deal of what we call underdevelopment.

Against this background it is unlikely that the status of women will be enhanced quickly in any substantial way. This is easily seen in the way the male establishment reacts to any attempt to improve women's socioeconomic conditions, for instance, by introducing new bills regarding marriage, inheritance, and ownership of property. Women have great difficulties acquiring land on conditions equal to men. Since women have no assets to be used as collateral, they cannot obtain money from ordinary credit institutions. Their inheritance rights are inferior to men's. If the husband dies, the wife's legal position is very weak.

Few African women are aware of their importance to everybody's day-to-day upkeep. And those who are aware are often reluctant to join together, to speak up forcefully, to start campaigns, and to apply pressure on the authorities for equal rights with men. They know it can be dangerous, too risky for them to disturb the traditional relationship between the sexes. Another severe problem is that women, and their nongovernmental organizations (NGOs), at times find it difficult to work together toward a common goal. Internal fighting gives men ample opportunities to disregard women's struggle for better conditions.

Surely, the women's decade and the women's conferences were powerful manifestations of women's will to achieve economic self-determination and control over their own lives. But today the momentum built up has gone—even in Kenya where the last, most successful U.N. conference was held. African governments would seem to have forgotten that they adopted the *Forward Looking Strategies* (see Chapter 1), if they or any country were ever aware of the implications of the adoption, for that matter.

Almost the only tangible result of the decade is the establishment of women's ministries, bureaus, and the like. Women in particular have attached great hopes to these government agencies. But they have been frustrated. These agencies have been given low status, very meager resources in terms of money and personnel. Without proper authority they have not been able to formulate policies, to coordinate activities, and to function as pressure groups within the government structure. Without proper resources they have been unable to serve the women of their countries as well as they would have liked.

It is within these frames that a foreign donor must work. It surely gives rather limited possibilities for achieving anything close to what could be called the empowerment of women. There are, however, some promising developments as well, and we will return to them. Let us first look at the donor's problems and what SIDA (Swedish International Development Authority) has contributed in spite of the constraints.

The Donor Perspective

Countries rarely have either national or sectoral WID (women in development) or gender policies. The absence of such guiding policy documents has forced donors to write their own WID strategies. These papers are limited in scope, usually products of the respective donor's own thinking and planned activities. Furthermore, various donors emphasize potentially different goals, strategies, and programs, thereby placing the developing countries in a position that requires a great deal of coordinating effort.

In Sweden the idea of supporting women in developing countries was formulated for the first time in the budget proposal that was approved by the Swedish Parliament in 1964. After a journey through Africa in 1963, Ambassador Inga Thorsson wrote that development was leaving women by the wayside. Twenty-five years have passed since she made that observation, yet it is almost as true today. At that time it was considered possible to help women significantly through inputs directed at specific areas such as higher education.

In 1972 SIDA made an analysis of the situation of women in developing countries. The lack of knowledge concerning women's opportunities to participate in social and economic development was pointed out. The idea of selected inputs for women in particular was rejected, and it was asserted that the situation of women "could apparently be improved only if the situation of all neglected groups in the society were to improve—groups in which women often were the majority." The importance of "integrating women in the development process" was enthusiastically emphasized.

Thus, in the early 1970s SIDA maintained that women would be included automatically in its aid efforts since these efforts were aimed at improving the situation for the less fortunate groups in any given society. At that time it was decided also that all SIDA policy documents should include a paragraph on women. However, during the women's decade these approaches did not show any tangible results. SIDA therefore adopted a more direct strategy to the issues involved. Making a long story short, I can summarize that approach in six steps (here listed in order of appearance):

1. setting up a WID office within SIDA,
2. providing special WID funds,
3. appointing a WID counseling group,
4. adopting a Plan of Action and country-specific plans,
5. appointing special WID officers at SIDA's field offices, and
6. setting up a regional WID office in Nairobi.

By the end of the 1970s SIDA somewhat reluctantly allowed one officer to be in charge of WID issues. Soon afterward one, at times two officers, were seconded to her. In 1980 it was clearly stated that the WID unit was a temporary arrangement. After two years it was to be evaluated. By then SIDA expected that the women's dimension would have been integrated in all SIDA's programs under the supervision of the program officers. At that time it was also believed, it seems, that WID belonged to that group of trendy issues that the U.N. system introduces from time to time to stimulate the imagination of the international community, to strengthen its sense of solidarity with less fortunate members, and to prevent opinion leaders from losing interest in matters of global concern.

Those working closely with gender issues knew that these issues were not going to disappear with changing fashions. Therefore, they struggled hard to obtain support for the strengthening and enlargement of the administrative WID structure (special officers) in charge of gender issues at the field offices, for more personnel and authority to the central unit, and for an advisory group drawn from the different divisions at SIDA headquarters. Furthermore, it was obvious that one top member of the executive ought to have an overall coordinating responsibility for gender issues within the agency.

The advisory group at SIDA headquarters was appointed early. More recently, locally employed WID officers have been appointed at the main field offices, and one person in the executive has now an overall responsibility for gender issues within. Furthermore, a regional WID office has been set up in Nairobi from January 1987 with coordinating responsibility for seven countries in Africa. However, the WID office at SIDA headquarters has not been strengthened up to now.

As do all Scandinavian donors, SIDA has prepared and adopted a Plan of Action for the Women's Dimension in Development Assistance. It was presented by the Swedish delegation to the U.N. End of Decade Conference on Women in Nairobi 1985. One and a half years of preparation preceded the adoption of the plan; it is thus thoroughly anchored in all relevant forums in Sweden. However, very soon it became evident that this Plan of Action was not concrete and operational enough. The idea of country-specific WID plans for each of SIDA's program countries was launched and resulted in a set of short papers indicating total Swedish assistance to each country and how the different programs ought to be changed, supplemented, or replaced so as to make them more WID oriented.

According to the Plan of Action "the objectives of SIDA's development cooperation" (in relation to gender issues) can be summarized as follows: that assistance as a whole become more women oriented; that special women's projects be initiated when circumstances warrant them; that women's productive work and responsibility for reproduction be facilitated so that women can support themselves, attain economic independence, and, in the long run, be accorded equality with men in social, economic, political, religious, and cultural respects; that assistance in all areas be designed in accordance with the special needs of both men and women; and that women on both the donor and the receiver side be given the opportunity to participate actively in and contribute to shaping the broad outlines of aid policies as well as the planning, implementing, and evaluation of individual assistance inputs.[2]

Let me elaborate on *women oriented*—another word for *integration*—as the key concept for SIDA as well as for many other bilateral and multilateral donors. This approach has different meanings at different levels. On a national level it implies that men and women should have equal rights and responsibilities in society, to include both decision making and access to common resources; that economic and social benefits are distributed on an equity basis to everyone; and that, consequently, no special measures are necessary for either of the sexes. Many countries can claim that they have come that far, at least in terms of legislation, but few if any can honestly maintain that they have reached that stage when it comes to *implementing* laws, distributing benefits, and inviting men and women to equally share decision-making power and economic benefits.

However, a donor's "integrated WID approach" does not go as far as to integrate the WID aspects in the overall development efforts of the developing countries. Even if these countries had adopted an overall gender strategy, it is still not possible for a donor country like Sweden to fit into this framework other than in a piecemeal sense since donors are confined usually to certain sector programs. These programs have been decided upon without discussing their overall particular merits for women, and until now they have rarely been planned in accordance with a needs-assessment analysis of the people involved. Usually, a woman's component (or several) was (were) added only at the implementation stage, when it was realized that the women's dimension had been missing already at the planning stage. This does not necessarily mean that the concerns of women have been properly integrated within the sector program, but only that a specific women's project or component has been loosely added to it.

In any country, men's and women's worlds differ. Even if the laws were to treat the genders alike, still the real world would go on resisting changes. This means that men easily are favored in agricultural projects since they own the land, are listed as heads of family, and grow cash crops. Furthermore, agricultural advisers and extension workers addressing themselves to these issues are usually men, and they may find it difficult to reach women even if they wanted to. When women in fact are in charge and work the land, their husbands, even if absent, still will decide in all matters of major economic importance. The same is true regarding credit. Men can provide security; women cannot. Health programs are designed to cater for the well-being of the family but often forget women's specific needs in relation to childbearing. In mother-child welfare programs it is particularly evident that the child component is favored, while the mother is left more or less unnoticed, except perhaps for the family planning part. This means that sector programs, in order to become women oriented, must identify women as a target group and recognize their specific needs from the very beginning.

The sector of greatest importance to women in Africa (and to the continent) is agriculture, food production in particular. This is a well-known fact, more and more recognized also among donors. Sweden has bilateral country agreements with twelve African countries in rural development, including rural water and health programs. Water programs are good examples of how far it it possible to go in integrating the concerns of women. Let me take an example from Kwale in the Coastal Province of Kenya.

Having experienced difficulties with a technically sophisticated water project in Kenya, SIDA decided to support a technically much less complicated one, called Kwale Water and Sanitation Programme. It first and foremost installs hand pumps, with participation from the local communities and a local NGO, KWAHO (Kenya Water for Health Organisation). Three Kenyan sociologists from KWAHO are employed, and they involve the people in each village as soon as it is decided that they are going to get a pump. Before the pump is installed, the villagers are asked to form a water committee of nine members, five of whom must be women. Usually the treasurer is a woman, since women are considered more trustworthy than men by the project manager. The chairman is often a man. The water committee holds meetings with the whole village in order to come to an agreement on pump location, maintenance, and local maintenance fees. Furthermore, some villagers are chosen to undergo training in pump use and in maintenance and minor repair. This whole process makes sure the village considers the pump its own property. Once the pump is installed, it is handed over to the village in a ceremony, with a document stating that the land where the pump is installed now belongs to the community. (If the land orginally was the property of one of the villagers, he must be in agreement, of course.)

In the Kwale Water Project women were integrated through mobilizing and involving the local community at an early stage. In this whole process, KWAHO has been instrumental as an NGO with a strong local base willing to invest time and effort.

Although there is a lot of talk of integrating women in country sector programs, the once fashionable talk of integrating women in the development process as such has faded away. In the 1970s this was SIDA's goal— a bit presumptuous for a small donor agency, of course. Now the goal is simply to integrate women into the sector programs in SIDA's program countries. The question is, however, if this objective is ambitious enough. Many sector programs supported by SIDA and other aid agencies do not cater to the specific needs of women, such as reproduction, protection against assault, and genuine guarantees of equal rights. These needs have now become the concerns of women's groups, associations, and organizations, in itself a very promising sign, and a first step toward the empowerment of women.

The gap between women's needs and donor sector programs shows that it is often necessary to support special women's projects. The SIDA Plan of Action opens some possibilities for this kind of approach. However, with a few exceptions, SIDA is reluctant to embark upon these kinds of projects. A special small fund has been set aside that, for instance, provides an opportunity for SIDA to support women's NGOs in the program countries. Although the projects upon which these organizations are embarking may not always have an immediate dramatic importance on the development process, they have been and will be of an immense importance for mobilizing women and for giving them experience, knowledge, and self-confidence that in the long run will benefit any society greatly. The Dodota project in Ethiopia is an example. Here follows a brief account.

After preliminary research on women's situation in two different districts in Ethiopia, SIDA decided to get involved in one of them. As a first step representatives from the government and SIDA went to the place and sat down with representatives for the local women's organization and asked them about their needs and priorities. After some discussion they came to the conclusion that, because they live on a dry plain, water was what they needed first and most of all. "Without water, no development," as they put it.

Finally, after all the red tape had been cut, they got their water. Women were involved in the planning of the project from the very beginning and, through a special project group, also in the implementation. Approximately ninety women were elected to be trained in how to take care and maintain the pumps and how to keep books, among other things. Finally, the whole project was handed over to the organization and became their own. The small fee that is now charged for the water is collected and saved by the women for future income-generating projects.[3]

In SIDA's Plan of Action two main strategies for women-oriented assistance are described. The first has welfare as its focus and is called the "Welfare Strategy." It is concerned with reaching women and children through social and health-care measures. In this strategy women are seen as receivers of aid rather than as active agents in a development process.

The aim of the second strategy is to strengthen the position of women in the economy by raising the value and productivity of their labor through increased access to and control over productive resources. This is called the "Strategy for Economic Independence" and is based on the notion of women as producers and active participants in the economy. These two strategies are not mutually exclusive, according to the Plan of Action, but rather are complementary strategies for integrating women in development. However, for me personally, the second is crucial if women are ever to approach equality.

I agree with Longwe when she maintains that the welfare approach is on the lowest level of a continuum that has "control" on its top.[4] She suggests that aid interventions may be assessed according to the following empowerment scale (in order of level of empowerment, the highest first):

- Control
- Participation
- Conscientization
- Access
- Welfare

These criteria are intended as analytically separate aspects of women's status, hierarchically ranked according to women's empowerment. The Dodota project reaches the highest level. Upon completion, the local women's organization was given the full control over the project, its resources and incomes. The Kwale Project reaches the participation level, and so do most of the NGOs' projects; some of them may go even a bit further. The so-called integrated sector support programs seldom go beyond the welfare and access levels, as far as women are concerned.

In her paper Longwe pointed out that "whereas there is opposition and resistance to women's development in some areas—most notably the government bureaucracies—the overall pattern is mixed. Generally, the UN agencies are moving quite fast towards increased interest in women's development, with agencies such as UNFPA [U.N. Fund for Population Activities] being very progressive. . . . Of the bilateral donor agencies the pattern also varies, with the Norwegian NORAD [Norwegian Agency for International Development], like all the Scandinavian countries' aid agencies, being very progressive."[5]

Sweden thus has not been doing so badly generally in regard to WID approaches. Probably, it has been among the most progressive bilateral donor countries. If we consider the empowerment of women as the ultimate goal of WID interventions, none of the donors, including Sweden, has been able to do very much to reach it.

The SIDA Predicament

The WID administrative setup within SIDA is similar to those that exist (if they exist at all) in other organizations, agencies, and ministries. They are usually characterized by inadequate resources, both with respect to money and personnel, particularly qualified personnel, but are still supposed to cover wide areas in terms of countries, sectors, and contacts. They are usually placed in a subordinate position in the organization (agency, ministry) and have superiors without experience in gender issues.

Those responsible for gender issues in the organization are often so absorbed in day-to-day routine work that they find it difficult to devote time to more significant issues and questions of strategic importance. The problems hereby created do not always facilitate but sometimes even prevent development toward the empowerment of women. It has happened that donor agencies with rather inadequate WID resources of their own for empowering women have demanded recipient countries to strengthen their women's bureaus as a condition for support.

Gender issues found most aid bureaucracies (as well as ministries in developing countries and other organizations) unprepared. These issues did not exist when the agencies were established, and they did not fit in naturally. But during the women's decade and the U.N. conferences, women all over the world mobilized so much strength that it became impossible to neglect them. Women, their organizations, groups, and activities, became fashionable; nobody dared to stop them. Thanks to the U.N. Decade for Women and its conferences, the women's cause became legitimized. In the middle of the 1970s the WID issues made a *breakthrough* within government bureaucracies. But the WID structures within the agencies were usually not yet defined, with no more than ad hoc resources. In the agencies the women who became involved did so because of their interest and devotion to the issue itself.

The next stage could be called the *temporary*. A few women were appointed to be in charge during the time the WID trend was supposed to last—no more than a couple of years, it was assumed. Therefore, the organizations did not feel it necessary to come to grips with the situation. Why bother if concern with this subject would fade away by itself anyway? On top of that, WID issues were difficult to fit in. A target group approach, like WID, involves virtually all sectors and must be dealt with by almost all program officers. But an aid organization is usually organized according to countries and sectors, and target groups may therefore acquire secondary importance. Signs of suspicion and withdrawal from WID issues were also present here and there.

By now, however, most agencies have realized that WID is not a trend of short duration; it is not going to pass by, not in Africa in any case. The pressure from inside and outside the agencies (for instance, from women's organizations) made it imperative to take some decisive and permanent measures: for instance, staffing the field offices, allocating some money, and adopting action plans.

We are now in the middle of a third phase, which could be called the phase of *cooptation*. A coopted organization wisely and cautiously turns around to define its demands so that they fit the established structure without requiring more than very minor organizational changes: it thus becomes integrated into the coopting establishments, being accepted by them as regular even if peripherally important members.

What effect does this organizational structure have on the WID officers and their ability to appreciate the struggle for empowerment that is now going on at many different levels? And what effect does it have on women and development in developing countries?

The pioneers in this field—and many of them are now retired or about to retire—made the WID issues their whole career, which usually meant that they failed to be promoted very far. They were genuinely interested in and devoted to the issue. Many paid heavily for that interest. They fought a hard battle for having the area recognized and for getting resources. They met suspicion, slander, gossip, and accusations for being part of the "women's lib" movement and therefore not really trustworthy. These problems may not have been so prominent in donor agencies as in organizations, agencies, and ministries in developing countries. On the other hand, most women in developing countries have been much more careful and withdrawn. Their slogan has been: move, but move slowly so nobody is upset or worried. They know how sensitive the whole gender issue is.

It is still not possible as a WID officer to make a full career to the top, or even to the vicinity of the top. Trying to integrate the concerns of women within the country programs involves being constantly occupied in persuading others within the organization to "integrate" the perspective of women in their work, in searching for ideas on how and what to do to attain "integration," and often in finally being rejected anyway. If you stay too long in this kind of job, you are stigmatized and stuck. In an aid agency a professional with an interest in WID issues should make sure that she works with that subject only for a short period, and that she becomes identified with other issues as well.

Some will argue that this development is not necessarily all that bad. It is realistic and falls within the possibilities of an aid bureaucracy. As it seems to me, empowerment of women does not. Too much devotion and involvement in any issue within a bureaucracy is often detrimental to those involved, and may even be so to the issues (the gender issues probably in particular).

However, without resources and authority and someone fighting for them, there is a risk that the whole matter slowly dies or totally loses importance. The aid agencies will not suffer; they will only be duller places to work in; but women in developing countries will lose important allies in the donor community, allies they badly need.

If aid agencies cannot contribute to the empowerment of women in any substantial way, from where shall the impetus come? It will most probably have to come out of the efforts applied by the women concerned.

What Is Beyond the Horizon?

In a recent report of the World Bank, Moeen Qureshi, senior vice president of operations, states, "In recent years, NGOs have been multiplying and expanding. In many developing countries, the poor are better organized now than they were 15 years ago when the Bank began to work more directly on poverty problems.

"In neighbourhood associations, women's groups, religious groups, environmental organizations, farmers' organizations and cooperatives—in such pioneering institutions as Dr. Yunus' Grameen Bank men and women have joined hands to shape their own futures. Growing networks of regional NGOs bring the strength of numbers to these grass roots groups. Confederations of the local groups, national voluntary organizations and think tanks on social issues are mobilizing new resolve and imagination."[6]

This observation by the World Bank is important. These national and local organizations and groups are noticeable, particularly in Asia, mainly India, but also in Africa, and they are almost exclusively concerned with empowering women economically. In Kenya, for instance, apart from the traditional women's organizations, new regional and national associations have been formed, for instance, Women's World Banking Africa Region, Tototo, Women's Finance Trust, Partnership for Productivity, Kenya Water for Health Organisation, the Green Belt Movement, and Shelter Afrique/ Africa Housing Fund, to mention just a few. Many of these organizations have both men and women as members. But women dominate since women are better organized at the grassroots level—the level at which organizations work.

When it comes to the empowerment of women, grassroots associations play an absolutely crucial role. It will take time before they reach that goal, but an important process has been started. Many times the process itself is more important for empowerment than reaching the specific goal. By solving problems, gaining experience, and working together, women will become aware of their own subordinate position in society and more capable of changing it. Nothing seems more important for an aid organization wanting to contribute to the empowerment of women than to support these groups to gain access to and control over economic resources.

One of SIDA's objectives emphasizes that women both on the donor and receiver sides should be given the opportunity to actively participate in and contribute to the shaping of the broad outlines of aid policies as well as to planning, implementation, and evaluation of individual assistance inputs. We are on our way to that point, but we are not there as yet. But I see here the possibility for women on both sides to join together for a real breakthrough for women. Women's empowerment is central to overall development, so those keen on supporting the latter should support the empowerment of women.

Notes

1. Sara Longwe, "From Welfare to Empowerment" (Paper presented at the NGO African Women's Task Force Meeting, Nairobi, April 11–15, 1988).

2. SIDA, "Women's Dimension in Developing Assistance," *Plan of Action* (Stockholm: SIDA, May 1985).

3. SIDA, *The Peripheral Centre, Swedish Assistance to Africa in Relation to Women, An Assessment* (Stockholm: SIDA, 1985).

4. Longwe, "From Welfare to Empowerment."

5. Ibid.

6. Moeen Qureshi, *The World Bank and NGOs: New Approaches* (Washington, D.C.: World Bank, July 1988).

6/The Adaptability of International Development Agencies: The Response of the World Bank to Women in Development

Nüket Kardam

The adaptability of organizations and their response to change have long been topics of concern to both academics and policy makers. By *change* I mean the conception, proposal, and adoption of new policy.[1] This chapter examines the adaptability of an international development agency, the World Bank, by exploring its response to women-in-development (WID) policy during the period of 1977–1987.

The research reveals that when the World Bank is part of a development activity in which different actors who are sensitive to WID issues participate, the likelihood of the consideration of women increases. So far, the World Bank has resisted a systematic adoption of WID policy, where WID is considered at all levels of agency activity (including policy negotiations with borrower governments, country and sector programs, and projects). This resistance can be explained by a combination of factors related to the World Bank's organizational ideology and structure. Strategies of change that have taken heed of the bank's particular characteristics promise to be more successful. Such strategies need to follow a dual path by working to adapt WID policy to the professional and technical frameworks of the staff, at the same time promoting close ties with management to wield influence. Indeed, these are the strategies that are followed by the current adviser on women in development in the bank. Their success is demonstrated in new resource allocations to the WID office and her position upgrade from adviser to division chief.[2]

The following analysis will focus on four matters: first, a brief history of WID in the World Bank; an explanation of WID policy adoption based on the bank's professional and technical expertise and on its organizational structure; third, the bank's interaction with external actors, and fourth, internal strategies of change followed by change advocates. The data are derived from the author's interviews with the World Bank staff, internal memoranda and documents, and publications by and on the World Bank.[3]

Women in Development in the World Bank

In the early 1970s WID issues were introduced by a transnational group of academics and policy activists into the development discourse within the context of changed priorities of development agencies.[4] As the inequities in the distribution of income in developing countries became an important issue and disenchantment with the merits of liberal growth theories increased, the World Bank's emphasis started shifting toward policies and projects that attack the problems of absolute poverty in the developing countries by increasing the productivity of the poorest 40 percent of the population of those countries. The new focus emphasized "basic needs," "people-oriented development," and the need to overcome the massive poverty in developing countries.[5] In fact, the bank claimed that the creation of the position of adviser on women in development reflected the bank's changing emphasis toward questions of distribution and poverty alleviation.[6]

At the same time, there have been a number of international women's conferences held under U.N. auspices and U.N. recommendations urging development agencies, including the World Bank, to pay attention to women in development. In 1970 the U.N. General Assembly passed a resolution titled "Programme of Concerted International Action for the Advancement of Women."[7] This resolution invited all agencies within the U.N. system to cooperate in achieving the objectives and targets of the program and to make available resources for that purpose.

In 1973 the U.S. Congress introduced a series of "New Directions" amendments to the Foreign Assistance Act that required focusing on aid programs in food, nutrition, health and population, education, and human resources.[8] To these amendments, the Percy amendment on "Integrating Women into National Economies" was added.[9] This amendment mandated the Agency for International Development (AID) to implement the program. AID was further mandated to encourage other development institutions to consider women in their development activities: "Bureaus and field missions [of AID] will encourage international development institutions and other donors and private voluntary organizations and foundations to give specific attention to the role of women in development."[10]

One of the earlier activities that the bank has participated in was the International Forum on the Role of Women in Population and Development, held in 1974.[11] President Robert S. McNamara's speeches also focused on the importance of fertility decline for economic development.

> The truth is that greater economic opportunity for women—and greater educational opportunity that undergirds it would substantially reduce fertility. . . . Schools must make the point to young women that the ideal role of a girl is not to be the mother of a large and poor family but rather have a double role as mother of a small family and as a wage earner who contributes to the well-being of her family by economic employment.[12]

Subsequently, the first report on women that the bank published was based on a paper the bank prepared for the World Conference of the International Women's Year.[13] It discussed World Bank–assisted projects in rural and urban development, education, family planning, and nutrition, and it provided examples of questions to be addressed in project design and implementation. In 1977 the World Bank appointed Gloria Scott, a Jamaican who had, before joining the bank, held the position of senior adviser, U.N. Center for Social Development and Humanitarian Affairs. In 1985 Scott retired and was replaced by Barbara Herz, a population economist who had previously been with the bank's Population and Human Nutrition Department.

The objectives of WID policy are phrased to fit the objective of the bank, that is, the efficient and effective use of bank loans. The bank's WID policy states that one needs to ensure that issues affecting women are integrated into project analysis and that not doing so will result in less effective projects. However, when it comes to the operationalization of WID, there is no systematic knowledge of WID issues in the bank. Two training workshops on women in development were held, but attendance by high-level management was limited.[14] There is no policy paper nor specific sectoral guidelines except for a paragraph that was added in January 1984 to the operations manual under "Sociological Aspects of Project Appraisal." Women are discussed in this section along with other specific target groups such as resettled populations and minorities that projects should pay attention to. There are also no guidelines as to how much weight should be given to WID relative to other criteria. To understand the reasons for this lack of attention to WID, one needs to examine the organizational context of the World Bank.

Professional Expertise and Women in Development

The World Bank prides itself for its high-quality technical specialists who are trained to achieve control of their environments through the mastery of technical knowledge based on objective and rational analysis. Technical control requires the employment of technical, financial, and economic analysis to help assess projects and programs for their efficiency and effectiveness. Effectiveness refers to the degree to which a given objective is achieved. Efficiency, on the other hand, is a measure of the relationship between given outcomes and their costs. The bank's priority lies in the efficient and effective use of its loans.

Technical, economic, and financial analyses are well accepted, but social analysis, within which the bank has placed WID, and institutional analysis are relative latecomers that are not as well accepted and integrated into the bank staff's work because they are less determinate, require some experimentation, and therefore are not compatible with the general goal of technical control.[15] Staff members have not favored social assessment and social impact analysis, which are necessary to ensure that target groups or others will cooperate with or benefit from a project and to minimize the unintended negative consequences on such groups. Staff members are usually not trained to conduct any social analysis; they perceive it as adding to uncertainty, leading them to an area where they have to admit to a lack of knowledge and forcing them to compromise the technically rigorous analysis that they are trained to conduct.

Interviews revealed that staff members felt justified in concerning themselves with WID issues if economic viability was involved, that is, when WID is linked to economic productivity and returns on investment. In other words, if the involvement or role of women was in any way instrumental to economic development in general and to returns on the bank's investment in particular, the bank is willing to consider them. The areas where WID issues are considered most are population, health, nutrition, and education. Studies conducted by the bank staff and others have shown that increased education for women, reduced fertility, and increased economic development are linked. Women's economic activity is considered mainly within this context. Income-increasing projects are designed for women so that they will have fewer children.[16] Women, then, are mainly considered in their reproductive roles in the bank's work. For example, WID issues were examined as part of the background research in two recent World Development Reports: in the 1980 report, as part of the human resources development theme, the importance of women's education in attaining developmental goals is established; in the 1984 report, as part of the population and development theme, the significance of improving women's status through education and employment for reducing fertility is documented.

WID has also been discussed in the context of achieving more equitable development. In other words, WID issues are justified as a strategy to empower a section of the population to whom fewer resources have been allocated or at least to make sure that they are not further disadvantaged. The bank, however, is much less willing to consider WID on grounds of equity and fairness than on grounds of efficiency and economic viability. Many staff members pointed out that whenever it was economically viable to do so, the bank would consider women, but not *because* they are women. Most staff members are not willing to discuss WID as a fairness or equity issue and do not see increasing women's status or women's empowerment as relevant to their work. This is in spite of the fact that the bank has been on the forefront of development thought in the 1970s on "poverty-oriented development," "basic needs strategies" within which the idea of "a more equitable development should include women" can be placed.

Although many staff members are interested in problems of social justice, welfare, and equity, they are uncomfortable with them. The consideration of women separately on the basis of their differential access to resources implies that they may be disadvantaged and that this imbalance may need to be corrected for reasons of social justice and equity. This is nothing less than asking for the empowerment of women. The issue of women's empowerment brings with it a whole host of uncontrollable factors in the environment. It shifts attention from the design and planning phase of project organization, where control may be exercised, to the implementation and evaluation phase, where the bank has much less control. The bank is not ready to push for such a goal, whether it is the empowerment of women or the empowerment of all project beneficiaries. Interviews showed that many staff members were skeptical about whether it was appropriate for the bank to push for women's interests on grounds of fairness.

There is, however, much less resistance to increasing women's status indirectly if it is instrumental for efficient development. If, for example, women's status increased as a result of an income-generating project for women, where the income-generation component is the means to decreased fertility, then it is considered justifiable.

The Organizational Structure and Women in Development

The implementation of a policy and the allocation of resources to it involves a political choice. Many staff members indicated that there is no conscious opposition to WID issues but simply a lack of attention. How does the bank's organizational structure affect this lack of attention, and what is the location and bargaining power of the adviser on women in development within this structure?

The World Bank is organized along geographical and functional lines. There are regional offices, country programs, and projects departments, on the one hand, and operations policy staff, on the other. The operations policy staff is divided into functional departments such as population, health and nutrition, agricultural and rural development, transportation, water supply, and urban development. The position of adviser on women in development is part of the operations policy staff and is located in the projects policy department. The offices organized along geographical lines are responsible for the design and appraisal of specific programs and projects; operations policy staff members work in advisory, monitoring, research, and other support capacities. For each project a lead adviser is selected from a functional department under operations policy, who then works together with the project and programs staff in specific geographical areas. The functional departments are supposed to play a quality-control role to projects and programs staff, and they have to approve projects related to their sectors before the projects can proceed. But their advice may sometimes be resented by the programs and projects staff. Those that are most likely to be interested in particular issues such as WID or the environment are the operations policy staff. Their interest, however, may not be received favorably by those with direct responsibility, that is, the projects staff. The projects staff members indicated that they, having to design projects and to go to the field, had little time left to be concerned with the many different issues, and they criticized operations policy staff members for "running crusades."

The position of an adviser is a sensitive one, and this applies to the adviser on women in development as well. The WID adviser can bring up problems with projects that she reviews, and the projects cannot advance before those criticisms are answered. However, as an assistant to the WID adviser indicated, she was hesitant about making too many criticisms, knowing that the projects staff was already overworked and that she might sound as if she was "policing" them.[17] The input of the WID office is also limited because it reviews projects at the appraisal stage, not the design stage. This limits the potential WID input while a project is being designed. The first WID adviser once pointed out that if she happens to hear about missions going out, she would call the relevant people and suggest possible issues to consider.[18] At any rate, there is no possibility of reviewing projects systematically by an office with one adviser and a few support staff in a large institution like the World Bank.

There is widespread consensus that if WID were taken seriously by the management, its operationalization in the bank's organizational structure would be very different. As one staff member in the projects policy department pointed out:

Management does not see this as an important issue that serious professionals have to consider; there is no serious mandate. It is never mentioned in regular management seminars. Among management, one's generation and individual orientation determines interest in women in development issues.

At the time of this research, the office of the WID adviser consisted of the adviser, a part-time assistant, and a part-time secretary. Many of the staff members said that in a vast institution like the World Bank, one person could not be effective, and the fact that more resources are not devoted to WID is an indication that it is paid only lip service. The staff members felt that there were no rewards for considering women, nor any requests in general from management to include WID in their work programs. The shortage of staff time and the definition of organizational output in terms of dollars loaned were mentioned by the staff as disincentives to consider women. In short, the post of WID adviser was seen as a political position, as window dressing that functioned as a good public relations ploy to show that the bank was doing something. In fact, some saw it as a tactic that let the management off the hook without having to do anything more substantial.

Procedures and Women in Development

Besides an alteration in the organizational structure initiated by the management, a meaningful response would also require that WID issues be made part of loan negotiations at the country level, of country programs, and of sector policies. Projects are prepared within the context of long-term country programs and sector policies so that in order to be effective, WID has to be part of national- and sector-level bank work. Issues related to women have begun to appear in some country programs and some sector policy papers in an ad hoc manner.

More and more, however, women's economic roles are being recognized in countries where women are already economically active (such as Nigeria and the Gambia), where women head families and men are employed elsewhere (such as Lesotho and Yemen), or where the worsening economic situation pushes women toward employment (such as Saudi Arabia, Kuwait, Jordan, Syria, and Turkey). Country program papers for some of these countries have started to include women. Studies are beginning to be conducted that examine women's situation. For example, an education economist in the Middle East Country Programs division mentioned that he is working on a proposal to be submitted to the bank's Research Department that would look at women's employment in five countries in the Middle East. If the proposal is accepted, the next step is to organize regional workshops and integrate the findings into the high-level policy advice that the bank gives those countries.

Once WID is identified in country programs and sector policies (assuming that it has been), there is still the issue of its consideration in specific projects. A bank mission to a country is made up of both country programs and projects staff. The project officers tend to be trained in a narrow, technical discipline, unlike country programs staff members, who are trained in broader disciplines and who negotiate with borrower governments. It is the projects staff who play a pivotal role in the identification of projects, and therefore the consideration of women is at the discretion of the individual project officer.

New projects that are identified are usually follow-ups to old projects or spinoffs from old projects. Usually it is a personal decision so the individual project officer decides whether, for example, there will be a health component to a project. Even though there are guidelines, there is a lot of discretion.[19]

Internal Change Strategies

Given the constraints posed by the bank's organizational structure, procedures, and the nature of the professional and technical expertise, what change strategies are most likely to overcome them? Strategies for change that are likely to be successful need to be internal strategies that aim to make WID acceptable to the professional and technical staff and at the same time to promote close ties with the management so that the management may provide incentives to staff members for including WID in their work.

Some staff members felt that the first WID adviser did not form networks with other WID advocates in the bank and isolated herself. She did not work inside the bank to prepare the ground for a more influential WID office but instead spent her time doing public relations, justifying the bank's work to the outside. Many staff, even those who had done WID-related work, mentioned that they had very little or no contact with the WID office. They felt that the WID adviser was much more effective in her dealing with outside in representing the bank than inside and suggested that more can be achieved inside the bank by attending project design meetings and talking to relevant projects staff "instead of attending women's conferences," as one staff member put it. Scott herself confirmed that her main achievement had been defending the bank to the outside:

I think perhaps one of the things I have taken some satisfaction from is how much I have been doing in the Bank is regarded as providing intellectual leadership to other agencies, little though it is. For instance, when I wrote the "Invisible Women" in 1979, I thought it was just a little progress report for the Bank. But it has become guidance material for other multilateral, bilateral and nongovernmental agencies because the material was specific and raised operational issues which had not been dealt with before.[20]

In short, Scott seems to have concentrated her efforts on defending the bank's WID work to the outside instead of building a position of influence inside the bank, thus contributing to the general perception that the post was a political or a public-relations position. Many staff members said that they perceived the position of adviser on women in development as a political, consciousness-raising position. This may have been the goal of the management. The bank management may have hired her precisely because of her qualifications. Scott, who was not an insider came from the Commission of Humanitarian Affairs of the United Nations, reinforced the suspicion that the bank was responding to outside pressure. She was not a bank staff member; she did not have any specific technical expertise and was seen as an "affirmative action" case. Some bank staff members felt that Scott did what she could under the circumstances with minimum support from the management. She did express desperation about the management's attitude in her last interview before she retired: "And although I've had to constantly defend the Bank as being really serious about these [WID] issues, it became increasingly difficult to do so over the years. Why? Because sometimes I myself doubted the Bank's commitment."[21]

The new WID adviser (chief of the Division of Women in Development since 1987), Barbara Herz, came from inside the bank, from the population, health, and nutrition department; she is a population economist. The recent strategies of the WID office have been twofold: to promote the legitimacy of WID among bank staff members and to promote close ties with management. Regarding the former, Herz has the credentials and the expertise to lend legitimacy to WID issues. Since the bank is interested in WID primarily as a population issue, her training in population economics gives her credibility. She has been instrumental in organizing the Conference on Safe Motherhood, cosponsored by the U.N. Fund for Population Activities, the World Bank, and the World Health Organization in Kenya in February 1987. Her efforts focused on outlining a new policy that is directed toward specific sectors (agriculture, education, health, and family planning) and specific geographical areas and toward making WID part of country policy dialogues.[22] She has started going on project identification missions, thus getting the chance to provide WID input at the identification and preparation stages of projects.

Regarding the strategy of promoting close ties with management, Herz has sat in on meetings of the operational vice-presidents and has followed internal strategies of close ties with management rather than concentrating on public relations efforts. President Barber Conable has also publicly accorded support to WID as a priority area:

Regarding population, the environment, and the role of women in development, the World Bank president said, "we should work on all three fronts at once. It is clear that population pressures are one source of heavy environmental damage, so we must provide training to give women the skills to take charge of their productive and reproductive lives. And it makes little sense to fund agricultural extension services and credit programs in Africa that do not reach the real farmers, the women who work the land." [23]

External Actors and Women in Development

How do borrower governments influence the bank's WID policy? After the preparation and appraisal of a project comes the negotiation stage, during which the bank and the borrower attempt to agree on the measures necessary to assure the success of the project. The bank may propose conditions in the loan agreements regarding women and development. Some respondents did mention this possibility but also expressed doubt whether the bank would be interested in using its influence in this area. Even those who thought that the bank should make WID a condition of loan agreements were not sure "how that would go if the Bank started running a crusade." Many thought that countries evolve at their own pace. The bank cannot force change; it can only push women and development to a certain extent. Ultimately WID consideration depends on the reaction of borrower governments.

The importance of borrower government interest and commitment to WID was mentioned repeatedly as a very important determinant of its consideration. The bank management takes the position that WID policy is ultimately the responsibility of the governments; without government commitment, women and development can be paid only lip service:

The legislative, policy and program decisions to improve opportunities for women rest with governments. But by paying increasing attention to women's needs in project design and by analyzing women in development issues, the World Bank is helping to create a more favorable climate to improve women's options. If concern for women is to be given more than lip service, it is essential that women's roles be considered seriously in policy discussion with development agencies, that women and their organizations take part in such dialogues and they obtain information about their results as well as information about development programs and projects about to be financed. [24]

In some cases where a bank staff member did make WID a condition of the loan agreement, the problem of borrower government interest and commitment remained. Since the bank has little leverage over implementation, it is possible for governments to agree and then bypass the issue. For example, one staff member in Latin America country programs mentioned that she had worked on an irrigation project for Kenya in which an attempt was made to provide funds for women, making it a condition of the loan agreement. She does not know, however, whether the government followed through with it or found a loophole so as to ignore it.

Host country governments generally do not see the consideration of women as a project design issue. A staff member in the agriculture and rural development department mentioned that government officials are cynical, and they laugh when WID issues are mentioned. For example, a staff member working in a forestry project in India asked the government to set a target of 30 percent for employing women as extension workers, but he related that the officials just nodded their heads and went on with their business. Another staff member from the operations evaluations department pointed out that host country officials denigrated women: "When you inquire about women, they say, 'you don't want to talk to women, they don't know anything.' "[25] Involved in a project in India, this particular staff member saw that there were no women extension agents for women's work. When she asked officials about it, they became defensive. In another case in Malaysia, where she was doing an evaluation study, she found out that 60 percent of the tapping of rubber trees were done by women, yet women did not get extension advice and men receive the proceeds of the work.

Resistance seems to come especially from those borrower governments whose societies are patriarchal and strongly discriminate against women. On the other hand, in countries where women are already economically and politically active, the governments display a more positive attitude. Examples of successful projects that specifically included women came from countries such as Malawi, Kenya, Sri Lanka, and the Tamil Nadu province in India, where women are economically and politically active. For example, in Tamil Nadu a current nutrition and health project for mothers and children is entirely women driven, with female project workers. This is because Tamil Nadu recognizes women; it has high-level authorities who are women, and government encouragement has made it possible for women to organize cooperatives and run their own project. On the other hand, a family planning project in Bangladesh is run by men because its society is more patriarchal and government attitudes are more traditional.[26]

Donor governments are also important external actors that influence the response of the bank to WID. They sit on the executive board of the bank and cofund its projects. Among bilateral donors, those that are known to be sympathetic to WID concerns are Norway, Sweden, Netherlands, Germany, and Canada. In projects cofinanced by these donors, the likelihood of WID consideration increases. These donors may finance, for example, the women's vocational training component of the bank's family planning, nutrition, and health projects. Since bilateral donors provide grants and not loans, the bank lets donors decide what they want to fund.

The possibility of WID consideration is also greatly increased if the bank is the executing agency for a particular project and the funding agency is interested in WID integration. For example, some projects in Sri Lanka, funded by the International Fund for Agricultural Development (IFAD) and executed by the bank, have special women's components; to illustrate, an income-generating component provides small loans to rural industries. In one project mentioned in the interviews, WID was incorporated because (1) the Sri Lankan government showed interest, (2) a specialized women's bureau was involved; (3) the funding agency, IFAD, was interested; (4) the project officer interviewed was sympathetic; and (5) his division chief asked his staff to include WID in the Sri Lanka country programming paper and sector analysis.[27]

Another project that was funded by IFAD in Yemen includes a women's component in its design and a WID consultant on the project team. As the mission leader explained, the women's component deals with agricultural extension and is designed to fill a gap in reaching women beneficiaries and improve production. It has been realized that many women head farmer households as a result of the men's migration, and male extension agents have not reached women farmers. This proposed project included a women's component because IFAD, the borrower government, and the bank staff all paid attention to WID. The bank has also shown interest in WID through the publication of technical papers that address WID issues. For example, a U.N. Development Program (UNDP) project that is executed by the World Bank has resulted in the publication of technical papers, addressed to engineers and other technical staff, that show them how to obtain sociocultural data and how to involve women in sanitation projects.[28]

Conclusion

As one bank staff member put it, women are not ignored on purpose. However, they are not purposefully included, either. WID is being treated as a residual issue that may or may not be addressed depending on interest, rather than as a matter of bank policy. As one staff member said: "The Bank has not yet seen the need to address women in development, and has not taken any initiative to experiment with it. No projects are designed around WID and there is no real commitment to increase women's status through projects."[29]

It is important to note that there are cases where WID is beginning to be considered seriously in the World Bank. Such cases are most likely to occur if various actors in a position to influence bank policy simultaneously demonstrate sensitivity to WID. Thus, external actors have influenced the bank's responses to WID issues. However, the bank itself has not employed its considerable resources and influence to initiate discussion on WID issues with other donors or with borrower governments. In short, any systematic consideration is still to come, and its lack can best be explained, first, by the nature of the professional and technical expertise and the fit of WID issues into this expertise, and, second, by the constraints posed by organizational structure and procedures.

The conceptual acceptance of WID issues is necessary; without it, bureaucratic strategies have little chance. Previous studies on the organizational response to WID support this conclusion. Staudt[30] and Rogers, [31] examining WID implementation in the U.S. Agency for International Development and the United Nation' specialized agencies, respectively, both reach the conclusion that the conventional gender ideologies of staff members and their lack of acceptance of WID as a legitimate professional concern have been the reason for the bureaucratic resistance encountered. On the other hand, the relative success of the Ford Foundation can possibly be explained by its goal of finding innovative solutions to social problems.[32]

This is certainly not to say that bureaucratic strategies to change organizations are unnecessary or irrelevant. In fact, the bank's current allocation of resources to WID is largely the result of an internal strategy that aims to make WID more acceptable to the professional and technical experts on the staff, particularly through women's link with population, health, and nutrition, while at the same time attempting to convince the management of the importance of WID. However, it is important to keep in mind that bureaucratic strategies are ultimately circumscribed by the nature of an agency's professional and technical expertise. In the World Bank's case, the nature of this expertise, with its emphasis on the economic success of projects, has defined the ways in which women may be considered.[33]

Notes

1. I have adopted James Q. Wilson's definition of change in *Approaches to Organizational Design*, ed. J. Thompson (Pittsburgh, Penn.: University of Pittsburgh Press, 1966).

2. With the restructuring of the World Bank in 1987, a Division of Women in Development has been set up in the new Population and Human Resources Department.

3. The interviews were conducted by the author at the World Bank headquarters in Washington, D.C., in April and May 1986. They were based on a stratified sample that sought to cover the staff and management in each regional office, country program, and projects department, as well as in each department under operations policy and operations evaluations staff. A total of fifty interviews were held; they were open-ended and lasted from twenty to sixty minutes.

4. See, e.g., Ester Boserup, *Woman's Role in Economic Development* (New York: St. Martin's Press, 1970); Irene Tinker, ed., *Women in Washington: Advocates for Public Policy* (London: Sage, 1983); and Georgina Ashworth, "The United Nations 'Women's Conference' and International Linkages with the Women's Movement, " in P. Willets, ed., *Pressure Groups in the Global System* (London: Francis Pinter, 1982).

5. See, e.g., Robert Ayres, *Banking on the Poor: The World Bank and World Poverty* (Cambridge, Mass: M.I.T. Press, 1983).

6. Robert McNamara, the introduction to *Recognizing the Invisible Women in Development* (Washington, D.C.: World Bank, 1979).

7. United Nations, General Assembly, 25th Session, "Programme for Concerted International Action for the Advancement of Women," Resolution 2716 XXV, pp. 81–83.

8. U.S. Congress, House of Representatives, Foreign Assistance Act, Pub. L 93–189, 93rd Cong. 1st Sess., S.1443, December 17, 1973, Sections 103–107.

9. U.S. Congress, House of Representatives, Percy Amendment, Pub. L. 93–189, 93rd Cong. 1st Sess., S.1443, December 17, 1973, Sec. 113.

10. U.S. Department of State, AID, "Integration of Women into National Economies," Policy Determination 60, September 16, 1974.

11. United Nations, *Newsletter on the Status of Women,* no. 46 (June 1974), p. 12.

12. World Bank, *The McNamara Years at the World Bank: Major Policy Addresses of Robert S. McNamara, 1968–1981* (Baltimore: Johns Hopkins University Press, 1981), p. 416.

13. World Bank, *Integrating Women into Development* (August 1975).

14. Interview with a staff member from the Western Africa regional office; Michelle Moriarty, "Women in Development," *The Bank's World,* March 7–8, 1983.

15. William Ascher in "New Development Approaches and the Adaptability of International Agencies: The Case of the World Bank," *International Organization* 37, no. 3 (Summer 1983): 415–39, also makes this argument.

16. Interviews with staff members from the Population, Health and Nutrition Department and South Asia Projects Department, World Bank, April 1986.

17. Interview with a staff member in the Office of the Adviser on Women in Development, World Bank, April 1986.

18. World Bank, *Report,* July–August 1977, p. 5.

19. Interview with a staff member in South Asia Projects Department, World Bank, May 1986.

20. World Bank, *The Bank's World* 4, no. 5 (September 1985): 6.

21. Ibid.

22. Internal bank document on the Work Program for Women in Development, 1986.

23. *Development Forum,* January–February 1987.

24. Atilla Karaosmanoglu, "The U.N. Decade for Women," *The Bank's World* 4, no. 9 (September 1985): 2.

25. World Bank interview, April 1986.

26. Interview with a staff member from the Population, Health and Nutrition department, World Bank, April 1986.

27. Interview with staff member in South Asia Irrigation department, World Bank, May 1986.

28. See, e.g., Heli Perrett, "Involving Women in Sanitation Projects," TAG Discussion Paper No. 3, UNDP Interregional Project INT/81/047, "Development and Implementation of Low-cost Sanitation Investment Projects," executed by the World Bank.

29. World Bank interview, May 1986.

30. Kathleen Staudt, *Women, Foreign Assistance and Advocacy Administration* (New York: Praeger, 1985).

31. Barbara Rogers, *The Domestication of Women: Discrimination in Developing Societies* (New York: St. Martin's Press, 1979).

32. Cornelia Butler Flora, "Incorporating Women into International Development Programs: The Political Phenomenology of a Private Foundation," in *Women in Developing Countries: A Policy Focus,* ed. Kathleen Staudt and Jane Jaquette (New York: Haworth, 1983).

33. See Nüket Kardam, "Social Theory and Women in Development Policy," *Women & Politics* 7, no. 4 (Winter 1987), for a discussion of the relation between the discourses of "development" and "gender."

7/The Inter-Amercian Foundation and Gender Issues: A Feminist View

Sally W. Yudelman

From 1972 to 1984 I worked for the Inter-American Foundation (IAF) as a representative, a director of the Office for Mexico, Central America and Panama, and a vice-president for program. IAF is a public corporation that was established by Congress in 1969 to support self-help projects in Latin America and the Caribbean. A small agency better known in Latin America and the Caribbean than in the United States, IAF has deliberately maintained a low public profile. Its only constituencies over the years have been the Congress and the organizations and groups it has supported.

This chapter tells how women have fared in a government agency that has always prided itself on being different—less bureaucratic and hierarchical, more participatory, responsive, and socially progressive.[1] It is a tale of three foundation presidents, and of changing times and an unsettling political climate. With regard to gender redistribution, it is a story of unfulfilled potential with the final outcome yet to be seen.

IAF, whose total staff has averaged sixty over the past sixteen years, has never had a women-in-development (WID) policy or program officer, but its track record on hiring professional women appears impressive, particularly in comparison with other donor agencies. The current president, selected by the board of directors in 1984, is a woman. I was a vice-president from 1982 to 1984. Women have been field staff (representatives) since 1972 and were office directors from 1979 to 1985, when that position was abolished in the course of a reorganization. The first general counsel and the first director of research were women. The personnel and budget and finance officers have always been women. Save for 1978–1980, there have been women on the board of directors since 1976.

With the exception of one brief period in IAF history, however, pro-

151

Table 7-1 / IAF Funding of Projects Directly Benefiting Women, 1982–1986
(*$ in thousands*)

YEAR	WOMEN'S PROJECTS		FUNDS FOR ALL PROJECTS	PERCENTAGE OF FUNDS FOR WOMEN'S PROJECTS
	Number	*Funds*		
1982	31	$1.5	$22.4	7%
1983	39	2.5	18.9	13%
1984	23	1.3	17.7	9%
1985	36	2.5	24.7	10%
1986	44	$2.6	$22.0	11%

fessional women have not found it easy to be hired, or once inside, to move into management positions. Perhaps more significant, the foundation has not been a major supporter of the women's organizations and projects involving women that emerged during the U.N. Decade for Women (1976–1985). Nor is the agency perceived as such by many Latin American women's groups and organizations.[2] During the first five years only 7 percent of all grants benefited women directly; after 1987 support began to rise but has never been higher than 13 percent in any year (see Table 7-1).[3] Despite IAF's vision of itself as socially progressive, a tradition of male preference is still strongly embedded in the agency.

IAF: What It Is, What It Does, How It Works

IAF was established to be different. As Robert Mashek pointed out in *The Inter-American Foundation in the Making:*

Its founders did not have in mind creating another standard government agency. Some of its uncommon birthmarks are its resemblance to a private foundation, its derivation of identity from the programs it would support rather than preconceived ideas, and its focus on human beings rather than on techniques or fields of endeavor. . . . There is no known analogue among public agencies.[4]

The foundation grew out of public and official disillusionment about foreign assistance programs in general and the Alliance for Progress in particular. The rationale for establishing a new agency was twofold: first, during the years of the Alliance for Progress, too little assistance had reached the poor in Latin America and the Caribbean; and second, Alliance for Progress programs had not proved effective in meeting the need for social change in the region.

Dante Fascell, chairman of the House Subcommittee on Inter-American Affairs, supported the idea to create a new agency for social and civic development and drafted the legislation. On December 30, 1969, Congress enacted Public Law 91–175 establishing the Inter-American Foundation as Part IV of the Foreign Assistance Act. IAF's legislated goals were "to strengthen the bonds of friendship and understanding among the peoples of the hemisphere; to support self-help efforts designed to enlarge the opportunities for individual development; to stimulate and assist effective and ever wider participation of people in the development process; and to encourage the establishment and growth of democratic institutions." The agency was also to be a "creative center and demonstration piece to encourage and test new concepts of what foreign assistance and development involved and how that might be best achieved."[5] More important, it was to operate independently of short-term U.S. foreign-policy interests.

IAF makes grants to Latin American and Caribbean organizations and grassroots groups for projects in education and training, agriculture and rural development, community services, urban enterprises, research and learning, and cultural expression. Grants to benefit women have been made in all categories, but very few have assisted women farmers.

The foundation has a seven-member board of directors appointed for six-year terms by the White House: four from the private sector and three from government agencies concerned with inter-American affairs. Staff is limited by law to one hundred and numbered sixty-eight in 1986. Within the agency work is divided among five divisions: the President's Office, Administration and Finance, Learning and Dissemination, the General Counsel's Office, and Program Operations.[6] There are no overseas offices.

Funds are appropriated annually by the Congress, and in 1986 the total budget was $26.7 million. Since 1974 the foundation has also had access to Social Progress Trust Fund monies. The fund, administered by the Inter-American Development Bank, holds repayments in local currencies for loans made under the Alliance for Progress to Latin American and Caribbean countries.

As in most small institutions with a flat organizational structure, the president is a key figure. He or she sets the tone and influences program directions and staff attitudes and practices. The history of IAF to date can be divided into three periods, each one reflecting the personality and style of the foundation's presidents: William M. Dyal, Jr. (1971–1980), Peter D. Bell (1980–1983), and Deborah Szekely (1984–).

The Early Years

1971–1975

In the late 1960s and early 1970s WID was an issue of little interest. There were few women professionals in donor agencies.[7] Poor women's economic role in the development process was generally invisible, and projects benefiting women provided services or enhanced their domestic roles. Peace Corps reflected the thinking of this period. As Staudt points out in the introduction, most women volunteers in Latin America and elsewhere were engaged in traditional social welfare activities. There were very few women country directors, or even associate directors, in the agency.[8] The Peace Corps' Latin American Division was deeply divided over whether or not women should be appointed country directors. There were doubts that they could work effectively in male-dominated Latin societies.

Bill Dyal, a former representative of the Foreign Missions Board in three Latin American countries, came to IAF from the Peace Corps, bringing with him several colleagues. Peace Corps attitudes toward women were thus incorporated into the fledgling new agency. The first four professional women hired for the Program Office were not allowed to travel to Latin America or the Caribbean on foundation business. Their job was to analyze and write up the project proposals that male representatives brought back from their travels. By late 1972, however, the situation changed, and the four were made representatives.

There are differing opinions as to how this came about. Some recall that the women themselves rebelled; others, that the new program director changed their status. In any event, the door was open for women to become representatives. From 1972 to 1975 there was an average of five women representatives each year out of a total professional program staff averaging sixteen, or 31 percent.

But it was not easy. The atmosphere around the foundation in the early years was heavily sexist. One male staff member recalled the "high testosterone level." Sexual asides, put-downs, and jokes were prevalent, and board meetings had the atmosphere of a men's club. Women representatives remember that they were held in low esteem and that their "abilities were not respected." They were assigned "the least interesting proposals" and those that their male colleagues did not want to handle, which included women's projects. They felt that they "had to be better than men to be hired in the first place," and once inside, that they "had to perform better." To move into senior management was not considered a possibility. As one female representative recalled, "senior management was an all-male club that women could not join."

Besides the internal machismo, other factors contributed to staff attitudes toward women. In addition to ex-Peace Corps members, early staff also included former Catholic clergy, lay activists, or men who had worked for Catholic nongovernmental organizations. These individuals were strongly influenced by the conference of the Latin American Bishops held in Medellín, Colombia, in 1968 in which the bishops committed their church to the cause of social justice.

Although it is widely acknowledged that the bishops urged a "preferential option for the poor," they certainly did not envision a changed role for poor women. These staff members, and the types of organizations and projects they funded, reflected the church's historical conservatism with regard to gender roles and the family. The few projects benefiting women approved during the first five years were developed by priests, Christian Democratic organizations, or social action arms of the Catholic church. Reflecting the influence of Medellín, they combined a strong *concientización* component emphasizing women's roles as citizens in the fight for social justice with the organization of traditional domestic activities such as nutrition, cooking, and home improvements that did nothing to improve poor women's economic status.[9]

In addition, traditional criteria prevailed in the project review process: "Past performance had to be good (credit references); matching funds were required in many cases (collateral needed); independence from continued financial assistance was expected in due course (solvency); and projects were expected to produce materials and/or learning that could be applied elsewhere (capitalization)."[10] The women's organizations and groups that existed in Latin America and the Caribbean during the early 1970s offered primarily social welfare services to poor women, and few could meet IAF's criteria. Most of their proposals were rejected. Further, a high percentage of the projects supported by the foundation were agricultural projects that provided credit, extension services, and new technologies to men only.[11] Women's productive role in agriculture was still invisible during this period, both to the organizations presenting projects and to IAF staff. Projects to benefit rural women emphasized their role as homemakers.

Finally, Dyal's decision in 1977 to transfer authority for project approval to the regional directors meant that the project portfolio of each regional office reflected the particular interests of the director and the representatives supervised by him. Perhaps the invisibility of women in IAF-supported projects during the agency's first five years can best be summed up by the staff itself in a statement written in 1977: "Our style is responsive and non-directive in the sense that we select for support those . . . activities designed to achieve conditions . . . under which all *men* [emphasis author's] will be offered the opportunity to develop their potential and to seek through gainful and productive work the fulfillment of their aspirations for a better life.''[12] During the first five years only 7 percent of all grants directly benefited women.

1975–1980

The International Women's Year conference in Mexico City in 1975 contributed to a growing awareness of gender issues. After the conference the number of requests for support from women's groups and organizations, or male-run organizations developing projects for women, began to rise. Within the foundation itself I took the initiative to raise consciousness among representatives and to actively search out and fund women's groups and projects in the country for which I was then responsible. A few others, including newly hired male representatives who seemed less threatened by the emerging women's movement and were more sympathetic to gender issues than the earlier generation, followed suit.

By 1978 when IAF published *In Partnership with People,* a study of the foundation's evolution and experience, staff members were generally aware that women were active participants in the development process and that their contributions were not recognized. In the course of their travels representatives had noted the growing numbers of women-headed households among the urban poor, the discrimination women faced, and their role in urban housing and in organizing communities to pressure the state for services. Most women's projects supported during this period were urban-based. The economic role of women in general, and the role of women in agriculture in particular, continued to be invisible. *In Partnership with People* never mentions the productive role of either rural or urban women. Still, the book concluded with a recommendation that "external funders . . . search out opportunities to support women's organizations directly or insist that they be provided with opportunities to take part in organizational activities."[13]

Nineteen hundred and seventy-nine was a landmark year in that a female colleague and I were promoted into senior management as directors of the Andean and the Mexico, Central America and Panama regional offices. Dyal deserves full credit for opening up management opportunities for women within the agency. Over time our appointments led to increased support for women, especially in the countries for which we were responsible.

The High-Water Mark: 1980–1983

By 1980 when Peter Bell, a former Ford Foundation officer, assumed the leadership of IAF, gender issues had become legitimate, and most donor agencies were providing at least token support to women's projects. Bell's presidency, preceding as it did the final conference of the U.N. Decade for Women held in Nairobi in 1985, coincided with the height of international attention to women. In 1980–1981 IAF granted about $1.8 million per year to women's organizations and projects directly benefiting women, a substantial improvement over previous years.

Although the timing was propitious because of the interest and momentum created by the women's decade, it was Bell's strong leadership that initiated the process of gender redistribution within IAF. He was strongly committed to the hiring and promotion of women, and he was intellectually interested in gender issues. He brought a degree of professional curiosity that had been lacking in earlier years. He also provided legitimacy to feminist advocates and sympathetic males, encouraging them to seek out and support women's organizations and projects benefiting women.

Following Bell's appointment, the proportion of professional women on the program staff rose to 35 percent in 1980, a 5–10 percent increase over the previous five years, and then rose again to an all-time high of 41 percent in 1983. Bell named me as the first woman vice-president in 1982, and by 1983 there were two women regional directors (Andean and Southern Cone) out of four, and seven women representatives out of a total of twenty-four. In addition, there were two women professionals in the Office of Evaluation and Research, and the financial and budget and personnel officers were women. A number of women were hired as consultants, and two of the seven board members were women.

Funding for women continued to rise. By 1983 the high-water mark in terms of numbers of women professionals in the agency, funding had risen to $2.5 million out of a total of $18.9 million, or 13 percent.[14]

But IAF still had to learn how to integrate women's projects into the wider processes of social change. In 1982 I hired a consultant to analyze the agency's track record. I was not satisfied with the level of support IAF was providing to women and felt uneasy about the number of income-generating projects that trained women in traditional sex-segregated skills and failed to generate income or to increase women's access to resources. The consultant's report, "In Support of Women: Ten Years of Funding by the Inter-American Foundation," examined IAF's experience and included eight brief case studies. Although the consultant's report was weakened by a lack of field research, she concluded that the foundation's experience had been a good one.

Two experts from the International Center for Research on Women (ICRW) did not agree. In their review of the report they pointed out that "there was no recognition of women's economic roles and their right to be given the same opportunities for economic development that men have."[15] Time and again the report failed, they concluded: "to assign project failure to IAF—failure to choose appropriate feasible projects; failure to choose appropriate implementing agencies; failure to closely monitor project progress; failure to link job training to job placement, and finally the determination to fund traditional activities . . . which naturally seem to result in project failure."[16]

Buvinic and Lycette were essentially correct in their analysis, but staff reactions were defensive and negative, reflecting the "laager" mentality inherent in bureaucracies and bearing out Staudt's observation that "if agency folk wisdom is challenged, personnel are threatened."[17] Lycette later commented, quite rightly, that she felt that ICRW was saying things IAF did not want to hear. Some male representatives reacted strongly to the challenge to their more traditional view of women's roles. In all fairness to the agency, however, IAF's reluctance to accept ICRW's criticism was also due to its strong belief that it should respond only to Latin American and Caribbean project initiatives, traditional or not. Despite the hostile reaction, IAF would have pursued ICRW's recommendations had external politics not intervened. A commitment to gender redistribution was sufficiently in place at that time to have assured follow-up.

Losing the High Ground: 1984 On

In December 1983 the political battle in which IAF had been engaged since 1981 with the Reagan administration in general and a conservative new board of directors in particular came to a head, and the board fired Peter Bell. Bell's dismissal was symptomatic of the changing times. The board's action heralded a paternalistic attitude toward grantees, as well as a private-sector orientation to development, a preference for small business rather than cooperative or collective projects, and a hierarchical and corporate approach to the management of the foundation itself. The fight to maintain the institution's independence from short-term foreign-policy objectives, as mandated by the Congress in 1969, continued.

Following a nine-month interregnum, Deborah Szekely, a prominent California businesswoman, became the first woman president. Unhappily, Szekely has exemplified Flora's observation that "there is no necessary corollary between being female and working to better women as a group."[18] In early 1985 Szekely initiated a reorganization in which the positions of the regional directors were abolished. Today, with the exception of herself, there are no women in senior management.[19] Although four of the eight senior representatives at the middle level are women, two of them former regional directors, the number of professional women in the Program Office has declined to seven out of twenty-six, or 26 percent of the professional field staff. The six new representatives hired since September 1984 are all men. A former staff member commented sadly that since there is no commitment to women, it is not important to hire them.

In 1986, 11 percent of all funds supported projects benefiting women, or $2.6 million out of $22 million, a decline from 13 percent in 1983. In the early 1980s the foundation initiated a process of gender redistribution. Why, despite the current lack of leadership on the issue, had the staff not continued to build on that record?

The Unfulfilled Potential

In the absence of strong leadership, patterns of male preference reasserted themselves in the agency's institutional culture. In addition, the lack of policy directives in general, and a gender-related policy in particular; limited interest in, or knowledge of, women's issues; and the failure of women within the institution to work together also conspired to restrict women's opportunities both within the agency and in Latin America and the Caribbean.

LACK OF POLICY DIRECTIVES

Because the foundation's operating philosophy is one of responsiveness to Latin American and Caribbean initiatives, there are no policies requiring support for particular sectors or particular types of projects. Further, the transfer of funding authority to the regional directors in 1977 decentralized operations, allowing representatives enormous autonomy. This autonomy permits them to pursue their own interests within the framework of IAF's funding criteria. There is a strong relationship between the interests of a representative and the kinds of projects he or she seeks out and encourages. Over the years such interests have included certain beneficiaries such as Indians, street children, or *campesino* organizations, or certain types of projects such as worker self-managed enterprises, appropriate technology, and legal aid. With few exceptions, women have not been a special interest.

Although it is true that most representatives have funded at least some women's organizations or projects benefiting women in all countries, this is due in large part to the flowering of women's organizations in Latin America and the Caribbean since 1975. Women in the region have gained confidence and experience in the course of the women's decade, and they have formed effective organizations with solid programs. They have learned to deal with international donors and are more assertive in pushing their interests. They have played an important role in raising IAF's awareness of practical and strategic gender issues.

There are two principal drawbacks to the lack of policy directives: first, only those representatives who are interested in and supportive of women will make the effort to find and fund women's projects. Second, representatives are free to work with groups and organizations in the countries that may not be supportive of women at all, or if they are, only in traditional roles—as Buvinic and Lycette pointed out in 1982. In the absence of leadership, decentralization tends to perpetuate male preference.

LACK OF A SPECIFIC GENDER-RELATED POLICY

Even though the foundation has never had a specific policy to support women, the president and senior staff play an important role by encouraging representatives to seek out and fund particular types of beneficiaries and projects. Bell's and my own interest in the early 1980s certainly contributed to a rise in the numbers of women hired and projects funded. At the same time, the autonomy of the representatives and the regional offices or units makes it difficult to implement any kind of agencywide initiative. The Percy amendment to the Foreign Assistance Act of 1973, which requires agencies to take into account the impact of their programs on women, has been largely ignored by IAF.

If the agency were to adopt a gender-related policy, it would require field staff to intervene more actively in the project preparation process of grantee organizations. From its earliest days, however, IAF decreed that it would not impose predesigned programs on local populations. Any policy or strategy that smacks of social engineering raises hackles. But fear of cultural imperialism can also be a "line of defense for field staff inaction."[20] The reluctance of IAF staff to confront the inequity of gender relations in Latin America and the Caribbean suggests not only an unwillingness to analyze the nature and causes of women's subordination, but also a strong resistance to substantial investments in improving women's access to resources, investments that would cut back on grants to men. Resistance clothes itself in general opposition to any policy that would require support for specific sectors or projects. In this sense the foundation is no different from other public and private agencies in not wanting to tackle the empowerment of women. It is time, however, that IAF recognized that support for women is not synonymous with cultural imperialism.

LACK OF INTEREST AND KNOWLEDGE

Several staff members interviewed commented that the "U.N. decade arrived but IAF never knew how to respond." No one from the foundation attended any of the three official conferences or the nongovernmental organizations (NGO) forums held simultaneously. IAF sent only two women from the region to Mexico City in 1975, no one to Copenhagen in 1980, and again only two to Nairobi in 1985. IAF was not involved in International Women's Year activities and as a general policy does not send grantees to Europe, but efforts to develop criteria to analyze the many requests from grantees who wanted to attend the Nairobi conference failed. Lack of interest prevented the development of an agencywide response.

A former staff member recalled that in 1978 IAF was unable to identify the productive role of women as a learning issue. Another reflected that "when we discovered women running projects, we didn't know what to do with the knowledge. We were unable to link women's problems to broader social issues." My own work, *Hopeful Openings: a Study of Five Women's Development Organizations in Latin America and the Caribbean,* is the only IAF-supported effort to set women's organizations in a broader social context. Fewer than 10 percent of the articles published in seventeen issues of *Grassroots Development,* the IAF journal, concern women.

The men and women interviewed for this chapter are generally aware of the obstacles that block women's access to resources and participation in the political and economic life of their countries. Even so, some representatives still assume that if men benefit from a project, those benefits will "trickle down" to the women and children. There is ample research to show that this is not the case.

But few representatives are familiar with the considerable research on gender issues that has resulted from the decade. Nor do they know how to integrate women into projects that are not women-specific, or the kinds of technical questions to ask. The foundation has prided itself on being a non-technical agency. The majority of staff have been sensitive, intelligent, open-minded generalists who are fluent in the languages of, and have extensive life and work experience in, Latin America and the Caribbean. For the most part, they have not been academics or technicians. Yet most of the research on gender issues to date has been carried out by academics and technical people. To a great extent the foundation has ignored this substantial body of work, which is unfortunate. Research is a powerful and useful tool, once absorbed into agency practices.[21] Because available knowledge about women's economic activities and potential has not been incorporated into program operations, the tendency to fund conventional and traditional women's projects continues. IAF's responsive posture further inhibits the agency from taking a hard look at the assumptions about women and their roles that the mostly male-run organizations that it supports hold.

The result is that gender issues are not systematically raised in the meetings held to review projects. This is a critical shortcoming because most of the learning within IAF takes place in project reviews. It is in these meetings that the accumulated knowledge and experience of the years is examined, processed, and digested. One female representative confessed that she could not remember when she had ever raised a question about women unless it was specifically a women's project. Another, one of the few who does know the questions to ask, commented that she does not raise women's issues in project reviews unless an female representative or a male with whom she "feels comfortable" is presenting the project.

Raising gender issues also forces representatives to confront feminism. One former staff member suggested that many representatives are uncomfortable with ideology in general and with feminist ideology in particular. The reaction to feminism on the part of many male and female representatives has generally been negative or an attempt to humor "all you women libbers." As a rule, the term is avoided, another example of what Staudt calls "a subtle personalized resistance" to gender redistribution.

WOMEN HELPING WOMEN

Some women representatives have consistently supported organizations and projects that benefit women, but they have done so in a quiet way, as if they did not want to draw attention to the fact. For example, a recent review of women's projects funded between 1982 and 1987 noted that "despite the disclaimers that the IAF portfolio in Colombia has shied away from women's projects *per se,* the portfolio shows the highest investment in organizations reaching low-income women, 18 grants for 1.6 million."[22]

In their support of women, female representatives tend to work alone, not as a group. As the introduction to this book points out, institutional culture and values influence women's positions and opportunity structure in bureaucracies. With the exception of the Bell years, the male-dominated institutional culture at IAF has not encouraged open discussion of gender issues. This explains women's quiet approach and the hesitancy of one female representative to raise these issues in project reviews.

With the possible exception of the rebellion of the four women hired as project analysts in 1972, female professionals have never worked together either to improve women's status within the institution or to increase the level of support for women in Latin America and the Caribbean. Efforts to organize female representatives around these issues have consistently failed, although when asked, several staff interviewed had no explanation. Others suggested that women were rivals for status and position. One disagreed, noting that "women who think alike make allies." In addition to the institutional culture, however, there are other explanations.

First, many women professionals in the foundation are not feminists or activists. One female representative commented that "we're all bureaucrats." Few have joined, or networked with, women's organizations or other groups in the greater development or feminist communities. For example, no professional woman from IAF participated in, or even attended, the last two conferences of the Association for Women in Development (AWID).

Second, at least until recently, women have not seen a need to improve their status. There is greater equality of relationships between men and women professionals. The sexist jokes, asides, and put-downs of the 1970s are long gone. Women who were hired in the early 1980s are there because of their professional qualifications and experience. As representatives they have autonomy and responsibility. It may be that if a woman does not have to fight for responsibility and autonomy in a bureaucracy, she becomes less sensitive to gender issues. In this sense, however, decentralization and line as opposed to staff jobs favor women.

Finally, and perhaps most important, not being feminists, many female representatives find women's organizations and projects of no greater interest than projects benefiting *campesinos,* Indians, or urban workers. The representatives for the countries with the highest numbers of projects benefiting women after Colombia—Bolivia, Brazil, and Costa Rica—are all men.

Conclusion

Fourteen of the twenty current and former staff members interviewed believe that the track record of the Inter-American Foundation with regard to the hiring and promotion of professional women is outstanding. This point was particularly stressed by staff who had worked in other donor agencies. Even so, most think that more women, and more minorities, should be hired.

The track record with respect to support for women in Latin America and the Caribbean has increased incrementally over the years, but, again, a majority of staff interviewed believe that the foundation can and should do better. They also believe that although there is an important role for women's organizations and women-specific projects in particular contexts, women should be integrated into projects benefiting men. Despite these beliefs, gender redistribution within the agency has retrogressed since 1983.

In the introduction Staudt writes that gender redistribution within bureaucracies can be initiated by men who are not threatened by the idea of sharing power or ceding male privilege and/or by constituencies that push for redistribution from outside. In IAF's case, change will have to come from inside, as in fact did happen in the early 1980s. It is unlikely that the Congress will push the issue, and with the exception of women's organizations, the foundation's Latin American and Caribbean constituencies are still bastions of male privilege.

The experience of IAF suggests that gender redistribution in a small decentralized agency is most likely to take place when there is strong leadership and commitment to bring about change, a gender-related policy to support that commitment, technical knowledge on the part of professional staff about how to integrate women and increase their access to resources, and an increasing number of professional women (and men) dedicated to improving women's status.

It is not clear whether or not the agency will make the necessary commitment to continue the process of gender redistribution initiated eight years ago. The potential is there, as indicated by the staff's belief that they should do better. Bureaucracies, however, tend to become smug. As long as IAF's track record is better than many, and as long as country portfolios include some projects benefiting women, the foundation runs the risk of complacency. But an agency that prides itself on being socially progressive and committed to the "ideals of justice, respect, equity and compassion"[23] surely has a special responsibility to concern itself more seriously not only with the gender makeup of its staff but also with the low status of women in Latin America and the Caribbean.

Notes

1. Much of the information in this chapter was gathered from interviews with twenty current and former IAF staff members. The chapter also reflects conversations with grantees over the years and the recollections of the author.

2. The foundation has played a more active role in the Caribbean. A respected Caribbean intellectual commented that there are two strong forces for change in the region and IAF is supporting both: women and cultural identity.

3. Statistics for 1979–1982: Ann C. Hartfiel, "In Support of Women: Ten Years of Funding by the Inter-American Foundation" (Rosslyn, Va.: Inter-American Foundation, 1982), p. 1. Between 1982 and 1986 IAF *Annual Reports* listed 173 grants, new and supplementary, that mentioned women as primary or direct beneficiaries. This number is somewhat misleading. The short project descriptions, or "blurbs," that appear in the *Annual Reports* are written by individual representatives. There is no methodological consistency to what a representative may label a women's project. Thus a women's project may be one implemented by either a male- or female-run service organization for poor women (from 1972 to 1980, 70 percent of women's projects were carried out by service organizations usually headed by a male but including female field staff); one carried out by a grassroots group; a project run by women that provides services to both sexes; a service program with women as secondary beneficiaries, such as a multifaceted community development project, or a program into which women have been integrated and receive the same services as men (in which case women may not be mentioned in the "blurb"). Projects that provide credit and technical assistance to urban microenterprises are an example of

the latter. In addition, supplementary grants provide support to organizations that may have received funding over many years. This means that the number of projects benefiting women may be higher or lower than the *Annual Report* suggests. For the purposes of this chapter, a women's project is one listed in the *Annual Report* as specifically benefiting women. It may or not be carried out by a women's organization or grassroots group. See Table 6-1 for an estimate of projects benefiting women from 1982 to 1986.

4. Robert W. Mashek, *The Inter-American Foundation in the Making* (Rosslyn, Va.: Inter-American Foundation, 1981), pp. iv–v.

5. Eugene Meehan with Thomas Ramey and Charles Reilly, *In Partnership with People* (Rosslyn, Va.: Inter-American Foundation, 1978), p. 3.

6. The structure of the Program Office has varied. Until 1985 it consisted of four regional offices: Andean (Bolivia, Colombia, Ecuador, Peru, Venezuela); Brazil; Mexico, Central America, Panama, and the Caribbean; and Southern Cone (Argentina, Chile, Paraguay, Uruguay). A reorganization in 1985 broke the regional offices into one regional (Caribbean) and one-, two-, or three-country units, of which there are eight. Each unit is headed by a senior representative, and the Program Office is presided over by a vice-president for program assisted by a small staff.

7. For example, women constituted 19.6 percent of the professional staff in the Ford Foundation in 1972 but were located primarily in the domestic division. Cornelia Butler Flora, "Incorporating Women into International Development Programs: The Political Phenomenology of a Private Foundation," *Women and Politics* 2, no. 4 (1982).

8. I was the regional program and planning officer in the Latin American Division of the Peace Corps from 1965 to 1968. By 1970 there were two women country directors in the division: one in Barbados covering the eastern Caribbean and one in El Salvador.

9. *Concientización* can be translated as raising an individual's awareness of the social, economic, and political conditions in which he or she lives.

10. Meehan et al., *In Partnership with People*, p. 39.

11. The highest percentage of IAF funds have always supported agricultural and rural projects: 42 percent from 1971 to 1986. IAF *Annual Report* (1986).

12. Inter-American Foundation, *They Know How . . .* (Rosslyn, Va.: Inter-American Foundation, 1977), p. 7.

13. Meehan et al., *In Partnership with People*, p. 126.

14. In 1979 only 3 percent of the total combined budgets of AID's four geographic bureaus benefited women. The WID budget of the Latin American/Caribbean Bureau was $13.7 million (5.5 percent of total), supporting sixty-five projects. By 1986 the total percentage of the four bureaus had risen to 4 percent. Kathleen Staudt, *Women, Foreign Assistance, and Advocacy Administration* (New York: Praeger, 1985), p. 5.

15. Mayra Buvinic and Margaret Lycette, "Review of 'In Support of Women: Ten Years of Funding by the Inter-American Foundation' " (Washington, D.C.: International Center for Research on Women, 1982), p. 2.

16. Ibid., p. 7.

17. Staudt, *Women, Foreign Assistance, and Advocacy Administration*, p. 118.

18. Flora, "Incorporating Women into International Development Programs," p. 90.

19. I resigned from IAF in September 1984.

20. Staudt, *Women, Foreign Assistance, and Advocacy Administration*, p. 96.

21. Ibid., p. 54.

22. Helga Baiteman, "A Review of the Inter-American Foundation's Support of Women's Projects" (Rosslyn, Va.: Inter-American Foundation, 1988), p. 10.

23. Inter-American Foundation, *Annual Report* (Rosslyn, Va.: Inter-American Foundation, 1984), p. 9.

8/The Feminist Agenda in Population Private Voluntary Organizations

Judith Helzner and Bonnie Shepard

Private voluntary organizations, or PVOs, have become important actors on the international development scene. Among the best known to the U.S. public are CARE and Save the Children, but there are many smaller PVOs based in local communities in Africa, Asia, and Latin America. PVO activities are generally oriented toward either emergency relief efforts or longer-range small-scale development programs designed to help people improve their standard of living. More recently, some observe a move beyond relief and small-scale development to a strategy in which PVOs disseminate their successful experiences among other development agencies.[1]

As compared with their government counterparts, PVOs are believed to bring benefits to development work, a result of their small size and field-level staff. In a typical assessment, the World Bank identifies PVO effectiveness to be "the result of many factors: commitment to poverty relief; freedom from bureaucratic procedures and attitudes; scarce funds, which force concentration on priorities and replicable technologies; and their small size, which makes it easier to understand and respond to the needs of local communities."[2]

Yet students of PVOs note that the numerous "articles of faith" about PVOs' impact on the poorest members of the communities in which they

The authors wish to thank the following people for making substantial comments on this article at various stages of its preparation: Susan Bourque, Judith Bruce, Elizabeth Coit, Ruth Dixon-Mueller, Judy Norsigian, Freya Olafson, Carolyn Stremlau, and Norma Swenson. Full responsibility rests with us, however; the reviewers did their job so thoughtfully that there are still many points we have yet to incorporate into our analysis. Preparation of the numerous drafts of the document would not have been possible without the cheerful assistance of Doris Bertzeletos, for whose perfectionism we are most grateful.

operate may not be borne out in reality. For example, do PVOs really deserve their reputation for reaching the poorest members of the communities where they operate? One scholar has observed that "the PVOs' self-proclaimed competence at reaching the poor may have been as much a function of the kinds of tasks they engaged in during the days of relief as it was of the character of the organizations themselves."[3] Looking more closely at the dozens of internationally oriented PVOs based in the United States, one finds substantial differences among them. Some government-funded PVOs are large and quite bureaucratic, managing millions of dollars; smaller PVOs may have minimal funding, perhaps mostly from private sources, and few staff members.

U.S. PVOs are becoming increasingly dependent on government funding. Brian Smith reports that "in the United States public assistance to PVOs for overseas work totalled only $80 million in 1964, but by 1973 had reached $207.9 million, and by 1979 amounted to $637.6 million. In 1981, 125 of the 156 U.S. PVOs registered with United States Agency for International Development (USAID) received public subsidies amounting to $742.3 million and this public aid accounted for 42.4% of their total revenues of $1.75 billion."[4] One of the political costs of this increasing dependence is that U.S. PVO assistance becomes linked to U.S. foreign-policy goals.

The PVOs involved in population programs are a subset of the broader community of private organizations working overseas. PVOs involved in population activities can be found based in the United States, in other developed countries, and in the Third World. Available data on funding for the years 1982–1985 show that private organizations worldwide were the channel for about one-third of the total population aid given to developing countries in those years. The PVOs' share of population funding in those years ranged from $120 to $152 million.[5] Population PVOs vary widely in size and scope. Though more than one hundred U.S.-based private organizations can claim at least some link to broadly defined population issues (research, policy, training), about forty PVOs have some significant involvement in service delivery activities in the Third World.[6]

The scientific and ideological influences to which these organizations have been exposed over the years have had an important impact on their approach to the women and men they intend to serve. Women—in their role as actual or potential mothers—are the majority of clients for agencies promoting family planning programs. A "target mentality" ruled in the 1960s— the early years of population assistance. Macro-level analyses of the consequences of rapid population growth were used to justify some programs that paid inadequate attention to ensuring medical safety and voluntary informed choice. The image of the "population explosion" generated scenarios of imminent disaster: famine, disease, ecological deterioration, political stress.[7]

However, attention to women and their needs was not considered essential to the resolution of the population problem.[8] In the 1970s a number of factors combined to increase attention to women, by PVOs and others in the population field: demographic research turned to the complex, micro-level determinants of fertility; the U.S. Congress in 1973 added the Percy amendment emphasizing attention to women in foreign aid expenditures; the United Nations promoted International Women's Year (in 1975) and the Decade for Women; and "basic human needs" became a theme of development programs at all levels.

Since only women have the biological capacity to reproduce, they must be recognized as the main clients in population programs. However, the design of family planning service delivery is often based on a medical model. There is some tension between this top-down approach, in which doctors (and other health professionals) believe they know what is best for clients, and the growing attention to the "user's perspective"[9]—the population field's equivalent to the move toward bottom-up community development.

Using a feminist lens to inspect current PVO family planning programs, we first define the feminist perspective as it applies to such programs and then compare that feminist vision with the reality found in the field. This paper examines the political dynamics of working for a feminist agenda within the community of population PVOs. The following case study illustrates these dynamics and leads to a discussion of both the obstacles to the realization of a feminist vision and the political strategies and attitudes that help implement this vision. Together, we draw on seventeen years of work with a variety of PVOs involved in family planning and reproductive health.

Feminist Vision in Family Planning

Work toward defining a feminist view of family planning programs has been carried out within the population field and through dialogue with feminist health advocates both in the United States and abroad. For example, in 1986 the International Women's Health Coalition and the Population Council brought together feminist activists and U.S.-based representatives of organizations engaged in international family planning. The report of that meeting covers points of consensus and issues for further discussion on the topics of contraceptive development and quality of care in reproductive health services, and it serves as a snapshot of where the large population agencies and grassroots feminist groups agree and differ.[10] For example, all participants agreed that they should not expect or look for the "perfect" contraceptive but should seek instead to expand the range of "good" methods. They recognized that more discussion was needed about the accountability of service providers to their clients. They concluded that, although differences are likely to remain between women's health advocates and experts in the population field, sufficient common ground exists for alliances to be built.

The occasion of a session entitled "Feminist Perspectives in Demography" at a meeting of the Population Association of America led Ruth Dixon-Mueller to analyze the "contradictory implications for women" of "the dominant ideologies and biases underlying the rapid spread of family planning programs at home and abroad": "demographic" bias, medical bias, male bias, legalistic and legislative bias, and class or race or Western bias.[11] On a more visionary note, she and others[12] have outlined the elements of a feminist perspective of family planning service delivery. These include:

- making family planning part of a comprehensive effort to transform power relations in the family, the community, and the society;
- providing the information needed to make informed choices;
- implementing programs designed, in large part, by women for women;
- opposing all forms of coercion;
- making contraception part of a holistic approach to women's health needs; and
- emphasizing the availability of choices: not only of methods, but also of service delivery systems.

According to Dixon-Mueller, "the essence of a feminist program is empowering clients as individuals and in groups—however poor—to *make demands* of themselves, their family members, and their community institutions."[13]

An example of the difference between the demand for a change that can be incorporated into an organization's program and one that cannot so easily be accommodated comes from the examination of the reproductive health perspective on family planning. Some women may be grateful for the availability of contraceptive methods alone, but feminists often argue that complementary services ought to be provided as well. The Pap smear and the more expensive regimen of tests for infertility are additions that have been incorporated in some family planning programs. The availability of safe abortion services—as backup in the case of contraceptive failure, or for women who misused or did not use a contraceptive method—is a much more controversial demand in most countries and cannot easily be accepted by population agencies. Restrictions placed by certain donors on their funds are only part of the problem; cultural and religious opposition makes abortion a taboo subject in many places even for those without the funding obstacles. Yet at least some feminists on every continent have raised the issue of safe abortion as a key component of a women-centered, complete program promoting reproductive health.[14]

It is not surprising that women's needs and desires have not yet been fully incorporated into existing population programs. Bureaucracies are hard-pressed to promote empowerment under the best of circumstances; when the changes desired are for women, poor or rich, mainstream organizations may trigger incremental reforms but they rarely promote radical change. Even in population PVOs, where the reproductive rights agenda of feminists over-laps to some degree with the perceived organizational mandate, various hur-dles obstruct the path toward the comprehensive woman-controlled programs promoted by feminists. The following case study illustrates how diverse ob-stacles combined to make it impossible to achieve part of one PVO's fem-inist agenda—the integration of family planning services with development activities for women.

A Close-up View of a Population PVO

The Pathfinder fund is a private, nonprofit funding agency that was estab-lished in 1957 by Clarence Gamble, a pioneer in the family planning field who was instrumental in helping found family planning associations around the world in the 1950s. Pathfinder is based in the Boston area, with eleven international offices. The organization's main mission is to give funding and technical assistance to local groups in developing countries whose work will directly or indirectly increase the availability of high-quality family planning services. Although the bulk of the support for the grants that Pathfinder makes now comes from the U.S. Agency for International Development (AID), it continues to receive substantial funding from individuals and pri-vate foundations; this increases Pathfinder's flexibility and autonomy in pro-gram development.

During the beginning of the U.N. Decade for Women and after severe criticisms of the population field were voiced at the World Conference on Population in Bucharest in 1974, Pathfinder was one of several population agencies to respond by incorporating women's programs into its program-ming. This response was made possible through the formation of the New Paths Committee by the chairman of the board and the input made by sev-eral key players as the committee deliberated. The committee's report ad-vocated a restructuring of Pathfinder to include three technical divisions: Fertility Services, Population Policy, and Women's Programs.

The Women's Programs Division (WPD), established in 1977, funded three categories of activities: (1) "Women-in-development projects" were development activities for women, which did not necessarily have a family planning component. Activities funded in this category ranged from manu-facturing and agricultural production by women's cooperatives to neighborhood-run childcare centers to research seminars on women's status. (2) "Integrated projects" linked development activities for women with family planning. These projects typically involved funding a women's organization to provide both income-generating activities and family planning education and services. And (3) "women and family planning" projects provided family planning information and services through women's organizations, some of which were feminist groups. A typical project of this type, funded in Brazil, involved starting a women's center that provided comprehensive women's health services, including family planning as well as a variety of educational and consciousness-raising activities.

This last category of projects fits under one of the WPD's mandates, which was to promote increased sensitivity to women's needs in all family planning services. The division's first strategy was to scrutinize every project for user sensitivity and to suggest changes where they seemed appropriate. This strategy earned them much resistance and enmity within the organization, since these comments held up the approval process. This strategy also cast them in the thankless role of being the nagging consciences of the organization. The second—and much more successful—strategy was to involve people from all three technical divisions in the User Perspective Committee, which was to promote more client-responsive and bottom-up programming agencywide by identifying and disseminating positive examples and practical strategies that already existed in the many programs funded by Pathfinder.

Unfortunately, the implementation of women's programs suffered from the tensions inherent in trying to introduce a completely new and divergent mission into a specialized agency. The main problems were these: (1) Development activities such as agriculture and micro-enterprises that would provide income-generating opportunities for women were outside of the expertise of most Pathfinder staff members, and therefore more time-consuming and anxiety-provoking: (2) AID's Population Office saw most of these projects as outside its scope of work, and AID's WID office was not receptive to funding projects with a family planning component, so most projects had to compete for scarce private funds. Furthermore, private donors were not as enthusiastic about women's programs as they were about family planning. (3) The projects could not be evaluated in terms of Pathfinder's traditional sense of mission, that is to say, increase in family planning use.

The history of integrated projects at Pathfinder illustrates another obstacle to the incorporation of women's programs—the need to serve two different agendas: that of the feminists, and that of the population field. This split agenda undermined the success of the projects themselves.

In the feminist view, women's programs enhanced reproductive choice and control for women by treating them as whole persons and serving needs arising from both their productive and reproductive roles. Feminists recognized that when motherhood is a woman's main source of status, mere provision of family planning is not enough to give her true choice with regard to her reproductive actions.

The population agencies' rationale for WID programs was based on the goal of lowering birth rates and increasing family planning use. The literature on fertility showed that women's level of education and other indicators of status are closely linked with fertility behavior. In most settings the more educated a woman, and the higher her status, the fewer children she is likely to want and to bear. In the early 1980s there was some sympathy within AID for the idea of integrated projects as a voluntary and politically acceptable way of promoting changes in women's fertility behavior. However, because development activities were an unorthodox use of population funds, the burden of proof fell on integrated projects to make the theoretical link between development activities and increased family planning use.

As a result, the programs were distorted to fit the funder's political needs. Logistically difficult experimental designs were added to projects run by relatively inexperienced local PVOs. These local PVOs did not want to prove anything with these projects; they just wanted to benefit local women. Therefore, they were not comfortable with denying the development activities to the control groups, who felt cheated; similarly, the PVOs lacked the necessary motivation for the difficult task of keeping track of the whereabouts of control group members, and of their family planning acceptance.

Not only were the projects distorted programmatically but also the design of the projects practically assured their failure to prove the links between production and reproduction. The number of women that could be accommodated in a development project was not large enough to produce statistically significant results.[15] Furthermore, the two-year project length was too short to produce the kinds of changes that population professionals were looking for. The path of a woman from successful income generation to increased status in the home, to a changed vision of her possibilities in life, to a desire for smaller families, to use of family planning is an extremely complicated and long-term chain of events that could break down at any point. It is unrealistic to expect the final step in the chain to show up for significant numbers of people in a two-year project. The entirely predictable failure of many of these AID-funded integrated projects to prove what they were supposed to eroded the support within AID for this type of project, and Pathfinder returned to the use of private funds for such efforts.

As a result of these problems, both within the agency and with AID, the WPD was dissolved in 1986 as part of an agencywide reorganization when a new executive director came on board. This reorganization was designed to focus Pathfinder's energy on the main mission of the organization, at a time when the right-to-life movement was threatening international family planning programs. The WID projects and "integrated" projects were then dropped from Pathfinder's portfolio. Only those aspects of WPD work that were closely related to family planning or population policy were continued. The emphasis on the user perspective, the openness to working with feminist groups, the deemphasis of the medical model, and the inclusion of women's status issues in population policy and adolescent activities still are present in the work of the agency. Only development projects, such as microenterprises for income generation, are no longer funded.

Critics could easily see the abolition of the Women's Programs Division and the end of funding for WID projects as a defeat for women's issues within this population PVO—a defeat that coincided with the end of the women's decade and that was a symptom of weakening support for women's programs. However, this is a misleading view of what happened. In Pathfinder's view the changes were positive for women's issues and for the organization because Pathfinder could now focus on those aspects of the feminist agenda that fit in more naturally with its main line of work.

Obstacles to Implementing the Feminist Vision

A variety of obstacles inhibit the full implementation of a feminist perspective in the programs of PVOs supporting population programs. The obstacles are grounded in disciplines, bureaucracies, religion, ideological difference, and the complex personal politics of gender.

Much has been written about the obstacles that are external to the PVOs. The medical and social science fields contributed frameworks of analysis that led to approaches that "made women the targets of family planning policies rather than providing the opportunity for women to take control of their own fertility."[16] The policies and politics of large donors in the population field (for example, AID, the U.N. Fund for Population Activities, the International Planned Parenthood Federation) set a context in which family planning is justified by demographic, health, or human rights rationales; none of these major agencies has an explicitly feminist mandate.

Other obstacles are bureaucratic: a small, flexible PVO with relatively few employees who share a consistent ideology can promote a feminist mandate more easily than can a larger organization with more formal procedures for obtaining funding approval for a given activity or approach. In a large organization the diversity of views among the more numerous staff members has a major impact on the success of efforts to integrate any new perspective—but particularly a feminist one—into the core beliefs of the organization.[17]

The case of integrated projects examined herein clearly illustrates how some obstacles to a feminist agenda can be related to a lack of a shared vision or goals by decision makers in a given institution, or by that institution's authorizing bodies. This ideological resistance is distinct from external or bureaucratic factors and bears its own analysis.

If the feminist vision were limited to benefiting women, there would be more of a shared vision between the feminists and the population agencies. The population community sees family planning (and rightly so) as a tool that provides enormous potential benefits to people in the developing world; much of the passion and motivation of professionals in this field arises from first-hand observations of the need and demand for family planning services, especially among the most disenfranchised group—low-income women. Although population professionals share feminists' wish to benefit women, that common goal does not necessarily lead to agreement on the best program to adopt. The objective of meeting family planning needs does not automatically entail any conscious efforts to upset the status quo in power relations between genders. A major difference, then, between the feminist agenda and most population agencies is that feminists see use of family planning within the context of sexual power dynamics that subordinate women, and *they place highest priority on helping women change these dynamics*.

This feminist priority theoretically fits in with strictly family planning goals, since research has shown that equality and communication within a couple leads to higher family planning use. Many U.S. family planners support raising women's status in principle, but when it comes to attempting to do so within the context of a specific program, efforts to alter the status quo often seem to be more political trouble than they are worth. Planners fear that these efforts might be seen as outside interference and that they could cause resentment among the local power brokers, who are usually men. Local contacts (also usually men) often argue that raising women's status is a western feminist standard inappropriately imposed on their culture. In this way, U.S. planners' nervousness and local contacts' resistance result in lower priority being given to efforts to raise women's status, and a higher priority to increasing the availability of family planning services within a given and accepted pattern of gender relations.

Attempts to change the status quo with regard to gender relations are fraught with political difficulties because the consciousness of unjust gender dynamics and the commitment to change them are simply not widespread in most societies. Even when the staff of a U.S. funder shares this commitment with the feminist movement, it is difficult to implement for lack of a similar vision among many developing country family planners. For this reason, male-female dynamics are rarely addressed when family planning providers counsel women, except for giving the woman a method that she can hide from her husband! Furthermore, local taboos may inhibit communication about certain methods—both between providers and clients, and between women and their partners. For example, the use of barrier methods such as condom, foam, or diaphragm may require a woman to touch her (or her partner's) genitals, which may not be accepted behavior in some cultures. Likewise, these methods can necessitate a woman's asking her partner to pause midway through their sexual relations—which the counselor may not be comfortable in mentioning, or the client herself in doing. Addressing these issues could help to improve the effectiveness of contraceptive counseling, decision, and practice; yet the controversy about confronting taboos and unequal gender relations makes it difficult to promote such efforts.

Ethics and Vision in User and Feminist Perspective

On less controversial aspects of the feminist agenda, population professionals within AID and the PVOs would agree that women should be treated with respect and sensitivity, that the services must safeguard women's health, and that women's choices should be voluntary and informed. So where is the divergence in vision between the user perspective in the population field and the feminist perspective?

One difference is the relative *priority* given to voluntarism, the quality of information, and the way women are treated in services, on the one hand, versus the number of people served and the contraceptive prevalence rate, on the other. These priorities are manifested concretely in monitoring and supervision checklists, in reporting forms, in evaluation criteria. Though population agencies in general may be alert for signs of coercion and for dangers to health, as a rule they are not *systematically* evaluating projects according to the quality of information given users and the way women are treated. One reason that these service characteristics are given lower priority in monitoring and evaluation is that they are more difficult to measure.

In fact, the need for quantitative indicators of results constitutes a major obstacle to the adoption of feminist programs. Feminist concerns tend to lend themselves to purely qualitative measures, which are not easily summarized or standardized agencywide. Feminists usually ask "how?" not "how many?" The results on reporting forms, which are reviewed when funding must be renewed, are mostly numerical. Although agencies like Pathfinder and the Population Council may make every effort to promote attention to qualitative indicators, the main funder in the field—AID—must use quantitative indicators for its reporting to Congress and must therefore emphasize these indicators with the PVOs it funds. Furthermore, the quantitative bent of public health schools—in which many population professionals have been trained—promotes an ethos in which numbers are the bottom line in determining "success."[18]

A crucial blind spot in the ideology of most population agencies is their failure to perceive that treating women with respect and sensitivity (the "user perspective") and overturning the traditional power dynamic between the genders are two intimately linked goals. User perspective literature and literature on informed choice speak of respect and "client-responsiveness" in limited terms that are hard to disagree with. (After all, who will advocate treating clients with disrespect?) However, this literature makes a key omission; it may be impossible to achieve respectful and sensitive treatment of women on a wide scale without correcting the power imbalance between male and female in the culture within which services operate. In the context of an actual service, the relationship between the provider and client can either reinforce the traditional power dynamic in which a woman is subordinate and passive, or it can give a women a hint of a wider vision of control over her life. The traditional medical context within which most family planning programs are located reinforces the unequal power dynamics between provider and client by adding a class dimension. The extreme case is when the provider is a male doctor and the client is a poor illiterate woman. Because deep-rooted and readily apparent gender and class relations are involved, most providers either are not conscious of treating female clients as subordinate or do not recognize this treatment as something that needs to be changed. Often, racial or ethnic differences between clients and providers simply compound the inequality of the relationship. Until these societal inequalities are addressed and opposition to them is widespread in a given culture, most providers will continue to believe that they are giving the best possible care and consideration to their female clients when in fact they are not giving their clients the information and emotional breathing room to think and decide for themselves. In the meantime, family planners can strive to deemphasize top-down service models that exacerbate the impact of these inequalities.

Population agencies such as Family Planning International Assistance, affiliates of the International Planned Parenthood Federation, Pathfinder, and others have actually had enormous success in removing family planning services from the medical context by implementing community-based distribution programs in which local villagers—usually but not always women—inform their neighbors about family planning and distribute barrier methods and oral contraceptives. The use of this model significantly increases the chances that a woman's choice of family planning method will be voluntary because the relationship between her and the provider is more likely to be characterized by equality and respect. Although this model certainly fits in better with a feminist ideal, feminists and other critics have serious doubts about the quality of the information provided and the advisability of distributing oral contraceptives with so little medical supervision. Therefore, feminists in the population field find themselves giving mixed messages about medical settings, since the modern, or high-tech, methods of contraception necessitate use of medical professionals if a program is to place a high priority on women's health and safety. One solution to this contradiction for most feminists is to emphasize the use of barrier methods such as condoms and foam, which can be provided safely outside of a medical setting. Another solution is to disseminate more information to women, so that they are better equipped to deal with medical professionals and the medical model. (This is an especially difficult task where illiteracy, geographical obstacles, and limited financial resources are problems.) A third solution is to emphasize the training of community health workers to take over some of the functions of medical staff.

Professionals with feminist agendas in U.S. funding agencies thus face an abundance of obstacles in addressing the power dynamics adversely affecting women within the family planning programs that are funded. In the absence of a strong local feminist movement and public consciousness, the human resources simply are not available to implement this vision in many countries. Furthermore, the quantitative evaluation criteria taught in most public health schools, and the emphasis on initial acceptance rather than continued use of contraception found throughout the population field, do not illuminate the real successes of feminist programs.

Digging In for the Long Haul—Strategies and Process

There are two main strategies for advancing a feminist agenda within the population field. One involves developing examples of projects and programs with a feminist perspective from which others can learn or that will have an influence on the programming of larger agencies. This has to be a primary strategy of agencies such as the International Women's Health Coalition (IWHC), which can not and will not seek AID funds and thus faces constraints in the amount of money available to it. The other strategy is to make incremental changes within large agencies. In agencies such as Pathfinder or International Planned Parenthood Federation affiliates, which have private unrestricted money as well as public funds, both strategies are used. Pilot projects are usually, but not always, funded with private funds, while the incremental changes are made through developing agencywide procedures and guidelines for both privately and publicly funded programs.

The two strategies have different political and emotional consequences for feminists working within these agencies. In large agencies the model projects may enjoy only lukewarm support because their numbers do not look good, or because their model is judged to be inapplicable to the large mainstream programs that provide services to the vast majority of the population. Unfortunately, this judgment is often correct; publicly funded services in developing countries often do not have the training resources or enough staff to replicate an ideal feminist service model. The challenge then becomes the identification of elements of a feminist model that can be widely replicated. In a small and more ideologically homogeneous agency like the IWHC, the challenge to realize a true demonstration effect is the same, but the internal political battles to continue funding such projects are fewer and less wearing. In both cases, supporters of these projects find a tremendous emotional and political satisfaction in funding a program that comes so close to their ideal. The emotional satisfaction is akin to admiring a small jewel that one has helped (in a small way) to cut or polish. The political satisfaction comes from supporting feminists in other cultures to adapt feminist ideas to their own society, and in the process helping each person involved to gain valuable experience that will contribute in the long run to the viability of the feminist movement in that country.

The incremental strategy is less dramatic and therefore in some ways less satisfying. Instead of big changes in small projects, there are small changes in large arenas. The product usually does not involve a radical change in consciousness: at best, there is a new training curriculum, a new set of guidelines, a different reporting form. Often, the main obstacle is not lack of good will, but institutional inertia. However, because the steps are incremental, they are built on commonly agreed-on goals, such as medical safety, informed choice, and better counseling; their achievement represents the co-ordinated efforts of many people, not just feminists. The political satisfaction from this strategy, then, comes not from viewing perfection, but from pulling together as a diverse team toward a common goal, dragging that stone one more foot forward toward the pyramid.

For all its lack of drama, each incremental step in a large agency may have many times the impact of the typical small model project that goes unreplicated. Even so, when viewed by outside critics, each incremental step may seem tiny and the result so far from the ultimate goal as to represent failure, not success.

The key to long-term survival for feminists within such institutions may be, then, to adjust expectations. What is counted as a success, and what as a failure? Each small step in the right direction represents an enormous investment of time and energy; it deserves to be greeted with rejoicing, as a victory. Those who made it happen deserve congratulations. Each model project is so small in the face of the problem it is designed to address that it is easy to say, "So what?" The answer is that it has ripple effects that can be seen or measured only sporadically, but it is almost certain that they exist, and that only a small portion of them is visible. The expectations of insiders have to be adjusted to the real possibilities of achievement, so that their professional work does not feel to them like a long string of failed initiatives and unmet goals. Too strict a definition of success is a sure road to burnout.

To many feminists, the process of working within mainstream institutions is fraught with ethical ambiguity and the difficulties of trying to please a variety of audiences: supervisors, funders, themselves, feminist colleagues outside the organization. Many subject themselves to constant self-examination: "Am I following a realistic long-term bureaucratic strategy, or am I caving in on an important principle?" "When I change my viewpoint on an issue that I am discussing with my colleagues, am I adjusting my views to a complex reality, or am I giving up my feminist vision?" When is a principle absolute, and when is one satisfied with small steps toward that principle? In order to maintain political legitimacy and effectiveness within the working environment, feminists have to choose their battles carefully and not engage in those that will make them appear to be on such a different wave-length that they are discounted. The battles that they choose not to fight nag at their consciences, yet they can find pride and satisfaction from bridging disparate views.

There is a long-standing and usually fruitless debate about the merits of working within any mainstream institution to effect change versus working with pressure groups from the outside. With the former road, the "insider" sacrifices independence and ideological purity, because no moves can be taken without the support and cooperation of a usually diverse set of colleagues. With the latter road, the "outsiders" usually suffer from shortage of funding, which limits the scale and type of interventions they can undertake. Furthermore, because their chosen role is to challenge the status quo within the "establishment," they risk being seen as adversaries by insiders, which leads to insufficient communication with the decision makers who will effect change, and therefore to lack of information on the complexities of an issue and on the constraints on the decision makers. This lack of information and the nature of the outsider role can in turn lead to self-defeating political strategies, in which denunciations of abuses or calls for reform can be used against the whole family planning movement by political forces opposed to reproductive rights. On the positive side, outsiders can generate a degree of political pressure for radical reform that can rarely be mounted by those in the inside whose jobs are on the line.

In fact, feminist insiders and outsiders need each other. Both groups—in completely different ways and under different circumstances—can stimulate change within an institution. Taking a wider view, the two paths are complementary, and probably both are indispensable.

Notes

1. John G. Sommer, *Beyond Charity: U.S. Voluntary Aid for A Changing Third World* (Washington, D.C.: Overseas Development Council, 1977); David Korten, "Micro Policy Reform: The Role of Private Voluntary Development Agencies," National Association of Schools of Public Affairs and Administration Working Paper No. 12 (August 1986).

2. *World Development Report 1983*, (New York: Oxford University Press, 1983), p. 95.

3. Judith Tendler, "Turning Private Voluntary Organizations into Development Agencies: Questions for Evaluation," AID Program Evaluation Discussion Paper No. 12 (Washington, D.C.: U.S. AID, April 1982), quote from p. 68.

4. Brian H. Smith. "U.S. and Canadian PVOs as Transnational Development Institutions," in *Private Voluntary Organizations as Agents of Development*, ed. Robert F. Gorman (Boulder, Colo.: Westview Press, 1984), pp. 115–64. Quote from p. 116.

5. Dorothy L. Nortman, "External Funding for Population Programs in Developing Countries, 1982–1985," *International Family Planning Perspectives* 14, no. 1 (March 1988): 2–8. The data below apply to all PVOs, including the largest one involved in population activities, the International Planned Parenthood Federation based in England. Funds (in current U.S. dollars) committed to population programs each year from 1982 to 1985 were as follows: in 1982, $378 million, of which $119.7 was from the private sector; in 1983, $380.7 million, $128.8 private; in 1984, $415.3 million, $139.6 private; and 1985, $472.5 million, $152.2 private. Adapted from ibid., Table 3.

6. U.N. Fund for Population Activities, *Inventory of Population Projects in Developing Countries Around the World 1986/87* (New York, 1988) and *Guide to Sources of International Population Assistance 1988* (New York, 1988). Also see Population Crisis Committee, "Non-Governmental Organizations in International Population and Family Planning," Population Briefing Paper No. 21 (Washington, D.C.: December 1988).

7. See, e.g., William Paddock and Paul Paddock, *Famine—1975* (Boston: Little, Brown, 1967); Paul R. Ehrlich, *The Population Bomb* (New York: Ballantine, 1968); Lester R. Brown, *The Twenty-Ninth Day* (New York: Norton, 1978).

8. Ieda Siqueira Wiarda and Judith F. Helzner, "Women, Population and International Development in Latin America: Persistent Legacies and New Perceptions for the 1980s," Occasional Papers Series No. 13 (Amherst: Program in Latin American Studies, University of Massachusetts, 1981).

9. Judith Bruce, "User's Perspectives on Contraceptive Technology and Delivery Systems: Highlighting some Feminist Issues," *Technology in Society* 9 (1987):

359–83. See also Judith Bruce, "Fundamental Elements of the Quality of Care: A Simple Framework," Population Council Programs Division Working Paper No. 1 (New York: May, 1989).

10. *The Contraceptive Development Process and Quality of Care in Reproductive Health Services* (New York: International Women's Health Coalition and Population Council, October 1986).

11. Ruth Dixon-Mueller, "Redefining Family Planning: Feminist Perspectives on Service Delivery" (Paper presented at the annual meeting of the Population Association of America, April 1988). Also see Betsy Hartmann, *Reproductive Rights and Wrongs: The Global Politics of Population Control and Reproductive Choice* (New York: Harper and Row, 1987).

12. Including Judy Norsigian and Norma Swenson of the Boston Women's Health Book Collective, personal communication, November 1988.

13. Dixon-Mueller, "Redefining Family Planning," quote from p. 24, emphasis in the original.

14. Adrienne Germain, "Reproductive Health and Dignity: Choices by Third World Women" (Background document for the International Conference on Better Health for Women and Children through Family Planning, Nairobi, Kenya. 1987). Also see Gita Sen and Caren Grown, *Development Crises and Alternative Visions: Third World Women's Perspectives* (New York: Monthly Review, 1977), pp. 46–49.

15. During this time, AID's Program and Policy Coordination Office funded Pathfinder to support five women's income-generating cooperatives in Latin America and the Caribbean. Ongoing intensive semianthropological research on the participants in these cooperatives focused on impacts in women's socioeconomic status and on productive and reproductive behavior. Although the two-year time frame and the small numbers involved made it impossible to draw any definite conclusions about impact, the evidence suggested that, for some women at least, the changes were profound. See Libbet Crandon and Bonnie Shepard, *Women, Enterprise, and Development* (Boston: Pathfinder Fund, 1985).

16. Jane S. Jaquette and Kathleen A. Staudt, "Women as 'At Risk' Reproducers: Biology, Science, and Population in U.S. Foreign Policy," in *Women, Biology and Public Policy,* ed. Virginia Sapiro (Beverly Hills: Sage, 1985), pp. 235–68, quote from p. 260.

17. Kathleen Staudt, *Women, Foreign Assistance and Advocacy Administration* (New York: Praeger, 1985). See chap. 6 on "bureaucratic politics as penetrating the core."

18. Even when service data are quantified, they generally focus on initial acceptance of a contraceptive method, ignoring the significant impact of continuation rates. The quality of family planning services has recently become a focus of attention; see Bruce, "Fundamental Elements." Also see Anrudh K. Jain, "Assessing the Fertility Impact of Quality of Family Planning Services," Population Council Programs Division Working Paper No. 22 (New York: July, 1988). Nevertheless, possible indicators of the quality of services have received relatively little attention from the population community to date.

9/The Malawi Case: Enclave Politics, Core Resistance, and "Nkhoswe No. 1"

David Hirschmann

The Avuncular State

In Malawi society an *nkhoswe* is a male witness to a marriage who acts as a guardian of the man or woman. The *nkhoswe* is of more significance in the case of a woman. Usually the *nkhoswe* is the woman's elder brother or maternal uncle, and he is supposed to represent her interests in marital disputes. Malawi's life president, Dr. Hastings Kamuzu Banda, has taken on the title of "Nkhoswe No. 1" for all the women of Malawi—"my women," as he refers to them. Since his return to Nyasaland (the British colonial name for the territory) in the late 1950s, Banda has consistently and publicly stressed his determination to raise the status of women in the country. He established a League of Malawi Women as a wing of the ruling (and only) political party, the Malawi Congress Party, and women are always present, in their thousands, at public gatherings, dancing and singing praises for the president. The purpose is not political participation, but manipulative paternalism. His protective posturing includes regular warnings that nobody should mistreat "his women"; endless calls for hard work, discipline, good behavior, and a strict moral code; and the enforcement of detailed dress regulations. Two characteristic exerpts from his speeches illustrate his tone:

> Don't allow anybody to mistreat you. . . . If anyone does [this] in the name of the Party or my name, report him to the Party. If you don't get an answer come and see Kamuzu himself. No one must mistreat my people . . . my women. . . .[1]
> I want you to learn to grow more than one crop. I feel very happy when I see how beautiful my women look . . . if you grow more than rice . . . if you now have two dresses and no shoes, next year you will have three or four dresses. . . . I want you to be proud . . . that is why I started that farm.[2]

185

Though it amounts to no more than a variation on the theme of patriarchy, the avuncular image of a seemingly benign but aggressively exploitative guardian uncle to Malawi's women seems an appropriate way of characterizing Banda's state.

To a very large extent the postcolonial Malawi state is in effect Banda's state. Several factors account for the comparative autonomy with which the state operates and for Banda's extremely personal control over it. First, the country is relatively unimportant to international capital. It is small, landlocked, and very poor, and it lacks minerals. Second, Banda has done everything to reassure international capitalists that he is on their side. He may be unique in his complete openness about making policy pronouncements of a nonprogressive, even reactionary type. He has been explicit about Malawi's friendship with South Africa and the Portuguese colonial authorities; its paying low wages to urban workers; its denial of freedom and the consequences of political opposition; his dislike of anything to do with socialism, communism, or the east; his hostility to Arabs; his openness to investment by multinational corporations and their use of Malawi's cheap, controlled labor force and repatriate profits; and the superiority of English to Malawian schoolteachers. Third, Malawi's local urban petty bourgeoisie in the early years after independence was miniscule, new, and primarily bureaucratic. It therefore lacked the economic independence, political muscle, and organizational experience to attempt to challenge Banda's control of the state apparatus. The few who did—"the dissidents"—were quickly dispensed with. Fourth, the settlers who remained were too few in number and too weak to resist him had they wanted to: in the event, his postindependence conservatism soon put their fears to rest. Finally, Banda's own considerable political skills must be noted. His energy in touring the country, attention to an amazing amount of detail, demand for total loyalty from those around him, selective ruthlessness in dealing with anyone who opposes or challenges him, and an unpredictability balanced by a singleness of purpose once a decision is made, have all served to create a somewhat nervous but relatively efficient bureaucracy, and an effective state.

It is effective in the sense that it has been used by Banda to make a strong impact on the economy and society of Malawi. He set out to bring about rapid growth by using foreign loans to build the infrastructure, foreign investments to create a small industrial base, and a peasant-created surplus to build a dominant estate sector; and by deemphasizing welfare responsibilities such as health and primary education. And he achieved this, at very great cost to the peasantry.

To do this he created a set of interlinking and reinforcing agencies that may be divided into four categories: (1) the public sector, made up of the party and the civil service (both operating at national and district levels) and the parliamentary and local council system; (2) the parastatal sector, public corporations using private management systems but under public sector control, of which the Agricultural Development and Marketing Corporation (ADMARC) has been the key agency in the transfer of surplus from the peasant to the estate sector; (3) the "presidential" sector, consisting of numerous companies owned by the president but given all the public sector supports, without the controls, of a public corporation; and (4) the "para-private" sector, nominally private but comprehensively dependent on the other three sectors—Malawi's only two banks fit into this category.[3]

Bureaucracy: The Male Core

The civil service bureaucracy (which will be referred to simply as the bureaucracy) is therefore only one component of the public sector of the state, and the public sector is but one of four such sectors. Yet in a state as tightly controlled as Malawi's, the bureaucracy probably has greater potential for influencing policy making and implementation than any other organization. Its size, complexity, and concentration of expertise and the range of activities it undertakes provide it with considerable administrative power. As the economy becomes more complex, as trade, aid, and investment decisions and negotiations become more detailed and problematic, and as the demands for data and statistical and technical analysis grow, so the Malawi civil service has taken on increasing responsibilities. This process was accelerated by events in the late 1970s and early 1980s, when the country was beset by an economic crisis. Poor rains and the effects of low official prices for peasant products led to a harvest failure in 1980. ADMARC's profits therefore disappeared and with it the main source of locally mobilized revenue. Too much foreign borrowing, too much of it on a short-term commercial basis, combined with a rising interest rate, caused a serious debt problem.[4] In return for a structural adjustment loan, the state submitted itself to the increased control of the International Monetary Fund (IMF) and the World Bank. The president has been required to place greater emphasis on economy and efficiency, rather than patronage and hunch in all sectors, and delegation of responsibility to technocrats has increased.[5] The president's age must also be a factor in limiting his capacity to oversee his empire: he is thought to be between eighty-six and ninety years old.

The bureaucracy has therefore been growing in influence in formulating and carrying out the details of policy. Outside Banda's immediate circle of advisers, it almost certainly provides the most meaningful point of access to state power that might be open to women. It is, however, dominated by men in terms of seniority and numbers and location: men control and protect the technical core of the organization.[6] (Women civil servants commented that the planners of the new government buildings in the new capital, Lilongwe, had clearly assumed that this would be the case: there are no women's restrooms on the floors that accommodate senior officers.)

In those agencies that constitute the formal planning machinery, women's issues were not assigned any specific attention and women had no representation. There was no department set up or given the task of preparing projects on women or of assessing projects or plans in terms of their impact on women. Among those ministries that had planning units, there was no section that specifically dealt with women's issues. Within the central planning agencies of the Office of the President and Cabinet, namely, the Economic Planning Division, the Development Division, and the Rural Development Division, there were also no sections dealing with women's issues.

There were no women in any of the three central planning agencies or in any of the ministerial planning units. All principal secretaries and deputy secretaries were men. The one exception was the vice-chairman of the Public Service Commission, who has deputy secretary status. (Although she had no planning responsibility, she was making a point of attempting to ensure that women were not being discriminated against in terms of promotion.) Neither the Treasury (which bears a major responsibility for negotiating aid projects with donors) nor the National Statistics Office (which provides much of the data on which planners rely) employed any professional women. In formal terms, therefore, women were effectively excluded from the planning and planning-related machinery.

In the Ministry of Agriculture there were no women in the Planning Division or in the Evaluation Unit and no women at a high enough level to be called into all planning and policy-making meetings. There were two women who were consulted from time to time. One was a nutritionist, a senior expatriate officer who was about to leave the country and to be replaced by a young Malawian woman graduate. The other was the women's program officer (the title had just been changed from home economics officer), also a young Malawian graduate. These two were being consulted because the ministry was giving attention to a nutrition program and a new women's program. This consultation was not in any way institutionalized, and its continuation was not assured.

In the Ministry of Education all positions of head of division and above were occupied by men. There were four women who held relatively senior posts, three as chief inspectors, one as a training officer. These had been recent appointments and were seen as indicative of women's progress in the ministry. Although these women were in a position to influence planning within their divisions, they were not represented at top-level policy meetings.

In the Ministry of Labor, which bears responsibility for working conditions in the private sector, there were no women at all in any of the medium- to senior-level posts.

In the Ministry of Community Development and Housing there was no planning unit, as it was a small ministry. Here there were two women who headed divisions—one for home economics, one for adult literacy—who were fully included in the planning and policy-making process. This was the most clearly established and effective participation by women in any of the ministries. In the Ministry of Social Welfare (also a small ministry with no planning unit) the under-secretary was a woman, and she was definitely fully involved in policy making. In health, the planning unit had no woman, but the senior nurse was in a position to influence decisions. In the Ministry of Youth and in the Ministry of Local Government there were no women at the senior level.

There were therefore a few women who had some direct and regular influence on policy making and implementation, but it was very limited in terms of small numbers and in terms of the rather traditional women's areas to which they were still restricted: mainly home economics, adult literacy, social welfare, and health.

This pattern was replicated at the district and local level. There were no women district commissioners or council clerks, the key figures on district development committees and local councils, respectively. As a result of men's dominance of senior district posts, men therefore also dominated the district development committees, which are made up of both political and administrative personnel. Most district development committees appeared to have four to six women (mainly party women, plus a community development assistant or members of Parliament) out of a total of twenty-four to thirty-six members.

Restrictive Documents

Men's overwhelming dominance of the bureaucracy comes through very clearly in the major planning and policy documents of the Malawi government. Examples will be given of the way women were dealt with in some of the major official documents. To make the point, some detail is essential.

Except for one very slim document produced in the early years after independence, Malawi has not made use of the type of medium-term planning documents so common among African governments. Instead, it has relied on three-year public investment programs. These are the principal planning documents. They deal in summary form with all government projects intended for implementation during the three-year period covered. In the document covering the years 1979/80–1981/82 women were mentioned under the following heads only:

(1) Community and social development: There were four projects where women were specifically mentioned: Macoha Rural Vocational Rehabilitation Training Center, New Community Development Training Center at Mzuzu, New Women's Hostel and Home Economics Teaching Block at Magomero, and Save the Children Fund New Headquarters. In each case the project linked women to home economics objectives.

(2) Education: One major project had as an objective the expansion of girls' secondary schools in order to enable more girls to be admitted to secondary boarding schools. The project aimed to improve and expand facilities at seven secondary schools. The summaries did not mention numbers. Although this project did emphasize girls, it seemed to be counterbalanced by British-aided projects in secondary education where all the new hostels (seven for 120 pupils each) were for boys, while the girls received assistance with three or four home economics units.

(3) Government buildings: A new hostel for women was included as a major part of the expenditure on the extension of the Staff Training College, used primarily for clerical and secretarial training.

(4) Health: All hospitals and clinics included a maternity ward, but other than that there was no special attention given to women.

(5) Agriculture: In all the summaries of projects women were mentioned only once, and that was under the National Resources College, which promised an intake of a certain number of farm home instructresses.

The Statement of Development Policies 1971/80 was another key policy and planning document laying down guidelines for the decade. The 140-page document contained the following chapters: (1) Development Strategy, (2) Proposals for Exports, (3) Agricultural Policy, (4) Transport and Communication, (5) Industry and Trade, (6) Manpower, Education and Training, (7) Health, Community Development and Housing, (8) Public Finance, and (9) National Income and Outlay. In this whole document only the section on community development mentions women. On page 106 the following paragraph is found.

The Department operates at the village level, for the personal involvement of every villager in efforts to improve his own way of life and standard of living, thus enabling him/*her* to require the maximum social and economic benefit arising out of Government development programmes. (Emphasis added)

That is it.

The National Rural Development Programme (108 pages, plus twelve appendixes and numerous tables) is also a key document, providing a broad national blueprint for agricultural development and covering strategies, objectives, and structures. No significant attention is given to women. Under structural arrangements at headquarters, nutrition and women's programs are mentioned. Under health services note is made of pre-natal services, mother and child clinics, and of homecraft workers who provide health education, especially on nutrition, childcare, and hygiene. In Annex 2 on Recommended Format for Regular Reports there is a minor suggestion that the number of women's groups formed be used as an indicator of development interests.

The Ministry of Community Development *Five Year Development Plan, 1981/2–1985/6* refers to a woman's program only under home economics, when it mentions the planned number of trainees and courses to be given. The same ministry's *Statement of Development Policies* also refers to women only under home economics (one of its four programs).

The Ministry realizes that individual families form the basis of the nation's socioeconomic structure and that therefore women have a prime responsibility in national development. Their full participation in homecraft activities must therefore lead to improved living standards and national development . . . the programme involves the teaching of women throughout the country in organized groups. Subjects that are taught in this programme include Food and Nutrition, Child Care, Housing and Home Improvement, Village Health and Sanitation, Textiles and Clothing, Poultry Keeping and Vegetable Growing.

The *National Health Plan 1973–1988* concerns itself with all aspects of health in Malawi for a fifteen-year period. Women do not arise as an issue of policy except in two respects: as a vulnerable group particularly during pregnancy and soon after giving birth, and as the people responsible for bringing young people to clinics. They are therefore the target group of nutrition education.

The proposals contained in the *Malawi Integrated Functional Literacy Pilot Programme* (1979) aimed at providing functional literacy to specific target groups. Although the recommendations constantly refer to the utility of the program, especially in enhancing the impact of agricultural extension in project areas, wherever it discusses women it returns to the same health and home economics theories. On page 36, in discussing the Lakeshore Rural Development Program, it says:

The literacy programme for women should be built around subjects like Health and Sanitation, Home Improvement, Food and Nutrition, Child Care, Textiles and Clothing, the Management and Development of Family Resources, Vegetable Growing and Poultry Keeping and other items of special concern to women. The Community Development Homecraft Workers and the Farm Home Instructresses of the Lakeshore Rural Development Project should constitute the main teaching personnel of the Women's Education Programme. For the men's literacy programme Primary School teachers, (Agricultural) Extension workers, and progressive farmers should be encouraged to offer their services to teach and for which they should receive remuneration.

It is possible to go on listing other documents. But it is clear from these that women have received precious little attention in the formal planning documents, and what reference to them exists is limited almost entirely to home economics and health. This neglect of women would emerge far more poignantly were one to note all the relevant areas in which they are ignored—in agricultural project after agricultural project, in research and evaluation on agriculture, in water supply projects, in the rural growth center projects, in small-scale industrial development, and so on.

Resistant Ideologies

In interviewing male civil servants on issues related to division of responsibility and labor between the sexes inside and outside the bureaucracy, terms and phrases such as "customary," "how it has always been," "women's own consciousness," "cultural," and, less often, "Christian" were regularly included in responses. The terms *natural* and *naturally* cropped up even more frequently and in a wide variety of contexts. "Naturally, women become nurses/secretaries, and men become doctors/bosses." "Naturally, men take decisions, and women follow them." "Naturally, girls don't want to be plumbers." "Naturally, women's fingers are much more flexible than men's; that is why they are much better as tea pickers then men." "Naturally, more women than men are illiterate." "It is a natural tendency for girls to see themselves as not as good as boys." Of course, *natural* means many things. It means biologically natural, for example, when referring to the fact that women give birth to babies and breast feed, but it also means traditional, cultural, accepted, habitual, and convenient. And *traditional* or *cultural* may refer to African or western traditions or some combination. The frequency with which these terms are used is equaled by the lack of specificity with which they are used, for this is the realm of resistant gender ideology, and the purpose is not to analyze, but to protect male dominance and men's control of the core from encroachment by a small but articulate group of women civil servants. For example, in discussing the possibility of women's taking more responsibility, making policy, leading, and the like, men would often refer to Malawi custom:

Our custom is that women should be subordinate to men. This is how it always has been and it won't change easily. We always have been a male-dominated society.

Men were hunters, but made most of the important decisions. Then they became migrant workers and brought home money. Ask any woman about decisions. They will talk but in the end they will say: you must ask the man. So this is a cultural thing.

This hunter–migrant worker–principal secretary argument has been extremely effective, for the ultimate test of effective ideology is its acceptance by those whom it is being used to dominate. Women civil servants confirmed that most women found themselves accepting or having to accept a position of inferiority.

Men are responsible for destroying women's minds. Men decide for women all things . . . who always has to drop out of a job? My career is not considered . . . we were given no place in the cash economy and in migrant labor. . . . Women are slotted into a role right from the start. The home role is exclusive to woman. She is completely tied to it. Right from the start boys are treated differently. Boys are allowed to go out and play. . . . Girls have to help mothers. Girls are denied the pleasure of play. In the family fathers have the final word. Woman just listen even if they know he is wrong and fathers teach sons that this is the man's rightful role.

Another element of this ideology, couched in positive terms, is the stress on, even the glorification of, the role of women in the home. A district commissioner explained:

Traditionally the woman must do the garden. She must produce food and look after children. Men will only marry a woman who is a hard worker. Even if she has been to school they will look at her output not her education. The family is the hub of the nation. If the family is poor the nation is poor.

Along the same lines a senior economist added: "If you educate a woman you educate the nation because women impart knowledge to the children and the husband is rarely home."

In the sense that ideology is used to protect an interest, strategy is very closely related. Sometimes it is difficult to distinguish which of them is at work. A case in point is the extent to which men credit women officials with a deep and abiding interest in home economics. This leads to a number of restrictive policy presumptions about programs for women (see the section above on documents) and about recruiting and training expectations for women. This was clearly illustrated in a survey of council clerks and district commissioners (all men) and of women local councilors and women members of district development committees. Women councilors put health as their main area of interest, followed—in order—by finance, staff, education, and community development. (Since the home economics program is administered by local councils, it is even more noteworthy that these women demonstrated little interest in the subject.) By contrast, nearly all the clerks saw home economics as the topic in which women showed the most interest; and although women placed finance second, the clerks seemed to be under the impression that the women had no interest in finance at all. The pattern of interest of women and their interests as perceived by the men officials was similar in the district development committees.[7]

Moving more clearly into area of strategy, one observes men seeking out and emphasizing apparent contradictions in the women's proposals. An example is the integration-segregation dilemma. It is pointed out that women are wanting to be "integrated into the development process"; at the same time they are calling for separate women's programs, women's bureaus, women's cooperatives, and the like. "They don't seem to know what they want," the men point out with some satisfaction, "segregation or integration."

Figures, used selectively, help to make bureaucrats more secure in the knowledge that women are being cared for, when these same figures, put into a different framework, illustrate the opposite. For example, a man in the Ministry of Agriculture asserted that women were getting their fair share of agricultural training. "In 1966 only 33 women received training. In 1975, 6,200 women did." When pressed further, the officer explained that in the same year, 1975, 33,000 men had been trained, and he acknowledged that the vast majority of women were trained in home economics and not in agriculture. The ratio of women to men receiving agricultural training was probably in the range of 1:30.[8] An absence of figures is also used to demonstrate that there is no problem. The Ministry of Labor, for example, kept no statistics and did no research on women in the private sector. It was therefore in a position to argue that there were no issues of specific concern to women of which its staff members were aware.

Middle-level women agricultural officers (at the workshop concerned with women in agriculture) complained that when they began to speak at meetings, men would often start talking to each other, shuffling papers, reading the *Daily Times,* and looking bored. A local council city clerk observed this same practice on his council: "Men do not take them seriously, and they therefore shrink and fade away in a heated argument. They are shy in debate, shy about making mistakes and they lack courage and confidence." Always being in very small minorities adds to the problem. A women local councilor remarked: "Being alone, I lack confidence to argue with men. I need to be able to consult with more women so as to make a better contribution." Women also noted that they were accused of trying to bring "women's lib"—a foreign issue picked up at conferences—to Malawi, where it did not belong.

Bureaucratic Politics of Gender

Schatzberg has observed that the Kenyan state "like Janus, has two faces," a democratic and an authoritarian one, and that the two were locked in a struggle, the final outcome of which was uncertain.[9] Samata has contrasted the supposed rural development concerns of the Somali state with the reality of its predatory nature.[10] Stein, among others, has pointed to this kind of duality in the case of the Tanzanian state: "the adoption of the slogans of socialism on a wider basis is linked to the proclivity of any ruling class that does not want to rule by naked coercion to legitimize its activities."[11] I have referred briefly herein and elsewhere to the contrast between the rhetorical concern of the Malawi state for the smallholder farmer and its practical backing for the estate sector.[12] Moving from questions essentially related to class to those of gender, one observes similar discrepancies. Urdang noted that despite protestations by the male socialist leadership in Guinea-Bissau of support for full women's participation, women were left to fight what she refers to as the second colonialism of "black patriarchy."[13] Parpart concludes her survey of women in postcolonial Africa: "Thus African states are run primarily by men for men. Socialist countries advocate political involvement by women, but fail to achieve it. Liberal capitalist states promise women equality through the vote, but men dominate it. Military governments advocate development, but ignore women."[14]

It comes therefore as little surprise to note that Nkhoswe No. 1, the guardian-uncle of all of Malawi's women, has two faces. Yet some refinement needs to be introduced into this pronouncement—reality contrast. There is a difference between the cynical mystification and cover-up suggested by Ake's phrase "defensive radicalism"[15] and situations where the conflicting pressures are substantive. Schatzberg is suggesting above (and not everyone would agree) that the democratic and authoritarian trends are both real in Kenya. And Saul has argued (and again many would not agree) that the Tanzanian state contains both exploitive and progressive factions.[16] Banda has done something for "his" women. His repeated pronouncements about raising the status of women and his token gestures toward women (at one stage in the early 1980s he appointed twenty-four additional women to Parliament) have raised the level of consciousness about women; the party and the civil service both know that they need to try to do something about recruiting women. However, in the same way as tokenism works for the president, so too it operates in these agencies. If the president does not appoint women to senior posts such as to the national executive of the party, the cabinet, managing directors of parastatals, and the like, they do not need to either. Also at the president's direction, the party has made an effort to get rural communities to send daughters to school, and some results can be observed in the first couple of years of school. Again, this may be a token response; for this to have an impact, the daughters will need to stay in school for longer. One-third of places at high schools and teacher-training colleges are reserved for girls (and this is far more than they would secure in open competition, given present social realities), and girls may get into university on slightly easier (but unstated) requirements than boys. On the negative side, the mass of women have suffered because they are peasants, and all peasants have been seriously disadvantaged and exploited. In addition, they suffer because the limited assistance directed to peasants is targeted on the upper level (from which most women household heads are excluded) and has a distinctly cash-crop and male orientation.

And inside the bureaucracy itself—as this chapter has made clear—his interest has not been sustained enough to elicit much more than symbolic responses in terms of recruitment, promotion, and policy formulation. Men dominate the bureaucracy and do not feel under pressure from the president to release control. In the face of a small but articulate group of women civil servants calling for change, they have resorted to long-established bureaucratic stratagems. Many years ago Merton observed that vested interests that characterize bureaucracies will oppose "any new order which makes uncertain the differential advantage" that they derive from current arrangements.[17] In the face of uncertainty, bureaucracies are said to respond either by closing the system boundary or (if that is impossible, as in the case of women today) by creating what Hoyle calls special cells to deal with and contain the disturbing elements.[18] And Staudt, in referring to James Thompson, is making the same point. By establishing what Thompson refers to as "boundary-spanning mechanisms" such as "advocacy offices, organizations respond to threats in the environment, coopt political energy, and seal off those offices from their technical core." She goes on: "Advocacy offices, often established to placate potentially troublesome constituencies, can be trapped in an enclave, and thus prevented from completing a mission that requires penetration of the technical core."[19]

Strengthened by numbers, experience, and seniority, by their continued dominance of the socialization processes, by their manipulation of gender ideologies and strategies, men have successfully kept women in peripheral enclaves of the civil service: homecraft, social welfare, health, and the like.

Without allies in the bureaucratic hierarchy and lacking the sustained support the president's promises may have led them to expect, women officials have sought to claim, rather than nurture, a constituency. They are here asserting a bureaucratic-public nexus. Reference is more and more frequently made to women smallholder farmers' tremendous contribution to agriculture through labor and decision making, and to the high percentage of women household heads who take full responsibility for agricultural production. Making a case for women to be included in the planning office, a woman educationist argued: "There are no women planners. In a country where women make up more than half of the population and much more than half of the farmers, how can that be called planning?"

The argument, in this author's opinion, is valid. Yet the real nexus between these women civil servants and the mass of women is tenuous. (There is no reason to suggest that the equivalent links between men would be any more meaningful.) Until women civil servants somehow cross the class divide and make an effort to actively nurture them as a constituency, rural women will remain an imputed political commodity, to be used in bureaucratic bargaining. The appeal to rural women has nevertheless become a fairly effective argument because the same case is being echoed by allies of the women officials, namely, international researchers, women's conferences, and women in aid agencies. In response, men cannot claim to compete for the same constituency. They therefore deny its existence.

Farming is a joint venture . . . it is not a profession that you can segregate into men and women.

You have noted the absence of "women" in the planning documents. This is because we don't have sex discrimination. We believe in human beings and we expect women to play as good a part as men.

Therefore: "If we have left 'women' out of the planning process that is an error, but it doesn't mean women have to do the planning."

Behind the controversy over reversing male preference lies another connection, the bureaucratic-private nexus, akin to Staudt's private family sphere concept. Writing of U.S. AID bureaucrats, she observes:

Complicating the normative foundations about gender still further are interpersonal gender relations, the familiarity they breed, and the subtlety of male-female conflict. These complications influence decision making through a personalization of issues. Those who make policy, predominantly men, live intimately with the group about which policy is made, and individual characteristics of that relationship carry over into work relationships and policy thinking in potentially distorting ways.[20]

The connection between the public and private domains surfaced in a number of ways. In the case of the public-bureaucratic nexus, men feared that a changed perception of rural women's roles would affect relationships within the civil service. In the case of the bureaucratic-private nexus, men were concerned that changes in the bureaucracy would disturb established patterns of behavior in the private sphere, which was something they clearly did not want. In discussing increased responsibility for women in the civil service, men frequently made analogies with family decision making and budgeting. "Ask any woman about decisions. They will talk but in the end they will say: you must ask the man." "We expect our wives to respect us and despite the talk of equality, we must lead—we can compromise a bit, but we must lead." A number of women acknowledge that they transferred their domestic sense of subordination to the bureaucracy. At home it was not proper for women to argue with men, and in public women still found conflict difficult. And nowhere is there any suggestion that men might take more domestic responsibility. Yet, this is basic to women's effectiveness in the civil service and in public (and this affects women of all classes), for this has a direct impact on a person's time, freedom, energy, perseverance, mobility, initiative, risk taking, and networking—all essential components of effective management.

Finally, in considering the strategies for building alliances and nurturing constituencies as ways of breaking through and around a wall of gender ideologies and so penetrating the technical core of the bureaucracy, one other element needs to be considered. Gender ideologies and strategies are not always on the defense; they may sometimes move on to the offense. Thus, while women may be attempting to nurture their enclave alliances, men may be cultivating divisions. And there is considerable potential for division. Whereas reversing male preferences is in the first instance gender redistributive in that it threatens economic stakes between men and women, it is in its secondary effects potentially redistributive between women and women in the bureaucracy. Those women who "man" the "home economics"–oriented departments and who benefit from the official perception of women as homemakers may well come to resist (and the resistance may be subtle indeed) the embryonic "women in agriculture" and "women in development" types of agencies. And they are not without resources. These are the only departments where there is the necessary critical mass of women to influence policy making and implementation effectively. They have firm supporters in two of the colleges of the university, teacher-training colleges and the community development colleges, and in overseas universities. Foreign home economics consultants and educationists were coming to Malawi at about the same rate as "women in development" advisers. Given their initial comparative strength, there is a real possibility that home economics personnel will expand their empire. When it comes to survival and growth of departments, restraint is difficult.

A second potential alliance, which is not being realized, is between the women bureaucrats and the League of Malawi Women (the women's wing of the ruling party). Partly this is related to class distinctions: in general, middle- to senior-level civil servants come from higher income groups and are far better educated in formal terms than are party women. But, possibly more so, there is considerable (and understandable) suspicion of the party among bureaucrats and particularly of its insidious potential to interfere and control the work of the professional women. This lack of support between party and bureaucratic women operates at lower levels as well. The ministries will not make use of the 4,000 women who have graduated from the party's Young Pioneer courses. In thirteen years, Magomero, the training college of the Ministry of Community Development, trained 1,000 home-craft workers, of whom 440 were still left in government service (this was in the early 1980s), and in fifteen years only 82 female community development assistants, of whom 52 were still with government. Despite a high drop-out rate of these trained women and a serious shortage of women in the field, ministries did not consider employing these party-trained women.

Another potential constituency and bargaining point that both deserves urgent attention and could be included in the effort to alter the male bias in the civil service are women on agricultural estates. Seemingly here, the women bureaucrats have been blinded by the Ministry of Labor, a totally male-dominated ministry, which has rendered these estate women invisible by not collecting data on them. Yet there are large numbers of these women who work as full-time, part-time, or peak-season laborers or as wives of tenant farmers on estates. They are productive, exploited, and unprotected participants in the rural economy, and they should be constructively included in the debate.

So the small group of women in the Malawi bureaucracy—maybe ten or twelve, or fifteen at most—capable, but not totally unified in purpose, have initiated some women-focused programs and have undertaken to try and reverse prevailing male preferences. While their numbers will increase and a few will take up more senior posts, they will remain (based on education statistics) for the foreseeable future a minority. The one or two who will eventually penetrate to the technical core will find it difficult to alter the nature of that core; they may well have lost the will to do so by then. Resocialization of their male colleagues therefore remains an essential but formidable undertaking. A few men appeared sympathetic, if not enthusiastic; a few seemed partly convinced. Most seemed resistant, and their resources are formidable. Donors and itinerant advisers have been of some help, but inconsistently and hesitantly so. And Nkhoswe No. 1, despite his public rhetoric, has left these women very much to their own devices.

Notes

1. Government of Malawi, *Malawi News,* No. 9 (Party Convention 1969, film).

2. Government of Malawi, *The President's Central Region Tour* (March 1969, film).

3. These are discussed in more detail in David Hirschmann, "State, Peasantry and Rural Poverty in Malawi," in Aruna Michie, ed., *Policy and Rural Poverty* (unpublished manuscript).

4. Charles Harvey, *Malawi's Adjustment Policies* (Paper presented to the International Social Science Conference, Chancellor College, University of Malawi, 1982).

5. Jonathan G. Kydd, *Malawi in the 1970s: Development Policies and Economic Change* (Paper presented to a conference entitled "Malawi—An Alternative Pattern of Development," Centre of African Studies, Edinburgh University, 1984).

6. David Hirschmann, *Women, Planning and Policy in Malawi*, (Addis Ababa: U.N. Economic Commission for Africa, African Training and Research Centre for Women, 1984), includes a fuller study of women's influence in the bureaucracy. Much of the material and all of the quotes are derived from that study and a subsidiary report. *Participation of Women in Local Councils and District Development Committees in Malawi* (Zomba: Report prepared for the U.N. Economic Commission for Africa, 1982).

7. David Hirschmann, "Women's Participation in Malawi's Local Councils and District Development Committees," *Planning and Administration* 13, no. 1 (1986): 43–52; also Michigan State University, "Women in International Development," Working Paper No. 98 (September 1985).

8. See David Hirschmann, "Bureaucracy and Rural Women: Illustrations from Malawi," *Rural Africana* 21 (1985): 58.

9. Michael G. Schatzberg, *The Researcher and the State: Reflections on Field Research in Kenya* (Paper presented to the U.S. African Studies Association Conference, 1985), pp. 3, 30.

10. Abdi I. Samata, "The Predatory State and the Peasantry: Reflections on Rural Development in Somalia," *Africa Today* 32 (1985): 41–57.

11. Howard Stein, "Theories of the State in Tanzania: A Critical Assessment," *Journal of Modern African Studies* 23, no. 1 (1985): 121.

12. David Hirschmann, " 'Starring Kamuzu:' Malawi's Life President on Film, 1966–1969," *African Studies Review* 9 (1986).

13. Stephanie Urdang, "Fighting Two Colonialisms: The Women's Struggle in Guinea-Bissau," in D. L. Cohen and J. Daniels, eds., *Political Economy of Africa Selected Readings* (Harlow: Longmans, 1981), pp. 213–20.

14. Jane L. Parpart, "Women and the State in Africa," in Donald Rothchild and Naomi Chazan, eds., *The Precarious Balance: State and Society in Africa* (Boulder, Colo.: Westview, 1988).

15. Claude Ake, *A Political Economy of Africa* (Essex: Longmans, 1981), p. 92; discussed in Aaron T. Gana, "The State of Africa: Yesterday, Today, and Tomorrow," *International Political Science Review* 6, no. 1 (1985): 130.

16. John S. Saul, *The State and Revolution in Eastern Africa* (New York: Monthly Review, 1980).

17. R. K. Merton, "Bureaucratic Structure and Personality," R. K. Merton et al., eds., *Reader in Bureaucracy* (New York: Free Press, 1952), p. 367.

18. A. R. Hoyle, "The Changing Environment of Administration," *International Review of Administrative Sciences* 1 (1976): 68.

19. Kathleen Staudt, *Women, Foreign Assistance, and Advocacy Administration* (New York: Praeger, 1985), p. 19. She refers to James Thompson, *Organization in Action* (New York: McGraw Hill, 1967).

20. Ibid., p. 7.

10/Farming Women, Public Policy, and the Women's Ministry: A Case Study from Cameroon

Barbara Lewis

Numerous ministries and bureaus of women's affairs have been formed since 1970 in Third World states. We have welcomed them as political and administrative voices for women marginalized in colonial and postcolonial development. We can now begin to look at the performance of such agencies. How have they defined the overbroad task of improving the status of women? What resources have they been able to mobilize? What are the results of their initial efforts and the pitfalls encountered? We can also look at the factors that have shaped these efforts: funding availability and substantive preference of donors, national party politics and ministerial politics, and the expectations of women constituents themselves.

This study draws on material from field work done in Cameroon in 1983 and 1985 on the needs of women food farmers in the area around the capital, Yaounde, and the impact of public policy on those farmers. The women farmers who produce most of the food consumed in the capital have received no government recognition—no agricultural extension workers, no farm loan programs, no improved inputs—with one exception. The exception was a small women's agricultural project in three localities, including

This research was conducted while I was a visiting Fulbright lecturer in Yaounde, Cameroon, January–December 1983 and April–May 1985 under the authorization of the General Direction of Scientific and Technical Research of the Government of Cameroon. I am very grateful to those in the Ministry of Social Affairs who graciously answered my questions in 1983, and to Mme. Yao, Minister of Women's Affairs, and those of her staff who were equally generous in May 1985 and in October 1986. The farming women of Sa'a who patiently explained how they earn their livelihoods showed me every hospitality.

Sa'a where I was conducting field research. I traced the project, reconstructing the first phase of the project through retrospective interviews, following it in its second phase in 1983, and then briefly during the third phase in 1985 after its relocation under the new Ministry of Women's Affairs.

The Sa'a women's agricultural project was initiated by the first president of the women's wing of the sole Cameroonian political party. This party militant had been given her own portfolio as minister of social affairs when the ministry of which she was second in command, Health and Social Affairs, was divided into two ministries. The Ministry of Social Affairs became popularly known as "the women's ministry" mainly because of its minister's party role.

In November 1982 President Ahmadou Ahidjo, the sole president of Cameroon since independence and unchallenged leader of Cameroon's ruling party, announced his retirement. His selection of long-time Prime Minister Paul Biya for the presidency gave every indication of political continuity. But the change in presidents led ultimately to extensive political housecleaning, including the replacement of the national leadership in women's affairs and the creation of new bureaucratic machinery to serve women. In 1983 the first president of the women's wing of the party and minister of social affairs (appointed by Ahidjo) was gradually eased out, as a new Ministry of Women's Affairs was created and another woman made its minister in 1984. In 1985 the minister of women's affairs became head of the women's wing of the party, and finally the original president of the women's wing of the party was relieved of her post as minister of social affairs. The small women's agricultural projects in Sa'a (and in two other localities), which had been started by the Ministry of Social Affairs a few years earlier, were quite logically transferred to the new Ministry of Women's Affairs.[1]

This case study focuses only on one activity of the new Ministry of Women's Affairs, although the ministry seeks simultaneously to address issues as varied as widows' property rights, vocational training among young urban women, questions of maternal health, and sex discrimination against female civil servants and salaried women. Thus the agricultural project discussed here cannot be seen as typical of the work of the new ministry. However, this case study focuses on women farmers, a group of great numerical and economic importance in Cameroon and throughout Africa. Moreover, this study emphasizes the fact that such institutions are not created on a tabula rasa, but are constrained and shaped by preexisting institutionalized partisan and administrative behavior. Finally, this study offers cautionary notes concerning expectations and constraints surrounding such a newly created women's ministry.

The Women's Agricultural Project in Sa'a

FIRST PHASE

The minister of social affairs started the Women's Agricultural Project with financial aid from international donors. This venture sought to improve the status of women by helping them earn money—an objective that went beyond the ministry's established responsibility for social work, assistance to the handicapped, and reeducation of delinquent youth. This project in Sa'a involved chicken- and pig-raising schemes. Women's groups from several villages as well as a town group were to grow crops on community fields that the groups would work one day a week. The cash from the sale of the crops harvested from these community fields was to be used to purchase feed for the animals, which in time were to be sold for profit. The profits from the whole enterprise were to furnish capital for further commercial agricultural ventures, the precise nature of this later effort to be determined through consultation with the minister upon successful completion of the first phase.

It is difficult to determine whether the project initially had the enthusiastic support of all its participants, both the town women raising the animals and the village women providing cash to buy feed through the sale of crops they grow. When several hundred chicks, imported from Cote d'Ivoire, died because of a failure to inoculate them, the morale of participants received a severe blow. Finding (male) landowners to loan fertile plots for each women's group to use as its community field had been difficult. Reputedly fertile land was finally obtained across the Sanaga River, but the distance from the women's villages meant that they needed transportation to work these fields. Although the project had been given a truck, the project's local leaders found other uses for the truck that conflicted with transporting the women's groups to the community fields. Women's attendance at their group's weekly work day became irregular, weeding was insufficient, and harvests from the community field were mediocre. The project created debts, not profits. Its only beneficiary seems to have been Sa'a's most notable woman, the president of the provincial women's wing of the party, who retained the project vehicle for her personal use.

SECOND PHASE

When the livestock scheme had been written off, the Social Affairs ministry launched a second phase of the women's agricultural project. This time the ministry bypassed the provincial party president to work directly with a newly elected president of the women's local (Sa'a) wing of the party. The new project retained the community field as its key vehicle. But this time proceeds from each village field were to be invested to benefit that group, rather than being pooled in a larger project fund.

The disastrous outcome associated with the lack of technical support to control disease in the livestock project was taken to heart by the women's national party leadership. This time the women's wing president and minister of social affairs secured the assignment of three young, well-trained agricultural technicians to the project's three localities—thus, one was to work exclusively with the women's groups in Sa'a. He was equipped with a mobilette and administrative housing but was no longer supervised by the Ministry of Agriculture hierarchy. Rather, he was answerable solely to the minister of social affairs. This direct access to technical aid for a women's agricultural project was an important new departure for women farmers and a significant innovation for the "women's ministry."

The new local team in Sa'a—the new president and her secretary and the young extensionist—set to work energetically. They were able eventually to overcome the problem of women's access to land by arranging temporary use rights in land in each of the villages of each of the six women's groups, rather than across the Sanaga River. The village women's groups rallied to clear and plant each of these plots of land. The extensionist initially worked hard with the women's groups, going to a different village field every day of the week. He did manual labor in the fields alongside the women and explained the advantages of various techniques and inputs such as insecticides and high-yield varieties of corn. He took care to warn the women of unfamiliar dangers such as the toxicity of the insecticide used to treat the high-yield variety corn, carefully explaining the importance of washing hands before nursing one's baby. His energy and his many relationships within the agricultural bureaucracy enabled him to provide resources not readily available to ordinary people.

Because the village women learned the purpose and correct use of modern inputs and used them in the community fields, the fields functioned like demonstration plots for village women. The assignment of the agricultural technician to the women's community fields sparked curiosity and interest among village women. Attendance during the initial months was good, and the work groups appeared socially cohesive. Some village groups formed *njangui* groups, the Cameroonian term for the rotating credit associations resting on solidarity and reciprocity so common in West Africa. In this case, each member brought a small sum, 100 cfa francs, to the weekly community field work day. The kitty was used to purchase a small toilet article for each member in turn. Thus, the women deliberately created an added obligation to the group as well a positive social purpose.

Within two years disillusion again crept into the project. Women's attendance declined, and poor yields were inevitable. Earnings from the first harvest had been disappointing, apparently because of both the severe drought of 1983 and the irregular attendance of the women. The party leadership took what earnings there were for safekeeping until more money could be saved and a good business chosen in which the women would invest. This outcome, reminiscent of the project's first phase, left some of the village women wondering if and when they would benefit from their labors: they would have preferred to divide up and distribute the money immediately.

A rise in local political restlessness had accompanied the change in national presidents from Ahidjo to Biya. Although the transition was initially peaceful, talk of democratization fostered diverse political ambitions and maneuvering to topple long-established party women. The factious atmosphere did little to advance community solidarity. The extension worker assigned to the women's community fields, taking advantage of the absence of direct ministerial supervision, demanded that the village women supply him with more and more "gas money" for his mobilette, putatively to ensure his presence at the various community fields. He also permitted himself to voice preferences among the women's local political factions, became increasingly irregular in his attendance at the community field work days, and failed to supply resources he had promised. By 1985 only two of the six community fields in Sa'a appeared likely to yield any profits, and morale was very low.

THIRD PHASE

The minister of the newly established Ministry of Women's Affairs inherited the Sa'a project and two other small agricultural development projects initiated by the Ministry of Social Affairs. Their transfer to Women's Affairs, under the new minister and eventual new president of the women's wing of the party, made sense. But the projects suffered from the break in administrative continuity. Furthermore, the political pressure on the new minister to deliver may have precipitated revival of the projects. For the new minister to launch a hardheaded reappraisal of the projects and to consider cutting losses by dropping the projects would be costly in scarce political capital.

The new minister of women's affairs was vulnerable in several respects when she inherited the women's agricultural project. She had no party or administrative experience. Her appointment to a cabinet post gave regional balance to the new cabinet, otherwise dominated by southerners, for she was a member of an important Fulani family from northern Cameroon. Her education, including an MBA from a good American university, credentialed her as a technocrat able to evaluate the project's history and future feasibility. But as the incoming president of the women's wing of the party, she needed to gain the support of party notables in the Yaounde area, a zone noted for its factious politics. She was very much dependent on the "technical advisers" the national presidency had urged her to appoint for information and advice. These women were long-term party activists from central and western Cameroon, women whose modest formal education was compensated by their extensive party experience.

It was these advisers who argued successfully that marketing cooperatives, like those existing in Cameroon's Anglophone provinces, would serve a real need and would revitalize the troubled women's agricultural projects in the Yaounde area. Despite the failure of prior efforts at state-sponsored food marketing in the Yaounde area (see the discussion of Mission pour le Developpement de Vivres, below), the new Ministry of Women's Affairs soon made a commitment to assist in the establishment of marketing cooperatives. Cement and sand for a building were delivered to Sa'a, and local members were invited to constitute themselves as a "pre-cooperative" according to Cameroon's legal requirements for cooperatives set up at the creation of Cameroon's coffee and cocoa cooperatives. The precipitous commitment of the Women's Affairs ministry to marketing cooperatives fit into the larger process of defining the ministry's purpose, specifying the ministry's organizational chart, and appointing personnel to the various ministerial posts. This process did not unfold in the calm of reflection on the long term, but rather while the minister was responding to immediate pressures inside and outside the ministry. In addition to the pressures to maintain the women's agricultural projects noted above, the new minister received an endless stream of demands for legal or financial intervention. These ranged from the pleas of destitute widows whose deceased husbands' kinsmen had stripped them of every piece of property to the visits and inquiries of regional officers of the women's wing of the party.

The Ministry of Women's Affairs had to work out personnel use and establish its internal structure while simultaneously adopting a strategy for inherited projects like the women's agricultural projects and responding to innumerable requests. Pressures regarding ministerial organization and staffing came most directly from those already within the ministry and those seeking appointments. Prevailing arguments regarding the function of each department, the number of departments, and their internal staffing tended to reflect the career interests of ministerial staff. The propensities of bureaucratic careerism are straightforward:

(1) An increase in the number of ministerial departments means more high-ranked and better paid civil servant posts—multiplicity of ministerial departments maximizes their chiefs' autonomy, particularly with no chief of staff ranked between the minister and the department heads to oversee departmental activities.

(2) The budgetary and administrative autonomy of the ministry as a

whole is limited by collaboration with other ministries. Access to technical ministries' services (in this case, agricultural expertise and technology) may seem essential to improving farming women's productivity, but the ministers and skills of ministerial personnel do not favor such interministerial collaboration.

(3) Ministerial personnel's low level of skill and experience in technical areas—such as agriculture—make interministerial collaboration difficult and unrewarding for staff from the women's ministry.

The dominant pressures within the ministry favored retaining the small localized women's agricultural projects and promoting other similarly small-scale, technically simple projects. Such projects complemented the trend toward multiple departments, each shallow in supporting personnel. They provide department chiefs with the small bailiwicks, which they are eager to administer. Small projects, funded by small grants from international donors, are more likely to receive prompt funding, permit complete control of budget by the ministry, and promote autonomy by the implementing department in the ministry. Planners and implementers will not become mired down in external negotiations, as must occur in projects in collaboration with or dependent upon slow-moving, even disdainful, large, technically specialized ministries. The career interests of department chiefs and the ministerial interest in commanding resources to serve constituents and to do so visibly and quickly are served by small, technically simple projects.

Small projects can be justified as "pilot projects," justified as proving grounds for the "women's ministry" and blazing the path for larger projects of much wider impact. But if, in the absence of strong technical staff and field support personnel such projects tend to be weak from their inception, their legacy may be deleterious.

Interpretation and Critique

The means chosen in the women's project—community fields and marketing cooperatives—represent choices of common, though not clearly successful, solutions to real and persistent problems in African agriculture. In my view, their conceptualization does not adequately weigh participants' individual gains and the benefits of collective action.

COMMUNITY FIELDS
The small women's agricultural projects depended on the mobilization of communal labor for the community welfare. Long familiar in Francophone Africa, they were used by the colonial government to build public works and by some chiefs in the colonial period for personal gain. Since indepen-

dence, the slogan *l'union fait la force* (unity makes power) has been invoked by the party as the key to development with human capital.

The community field is worked by community women to create a food surplus, usually without other inputs to increase productivity. The earnings from the field are to acquire some resource not otherwise available to the group. Community fields rest on the questionable assumption that women, and any farmer, are net beneficiaries when they devote one day per week to the community field—time that they very likely would otherwise have spent on their own family food farms, cultivating a surplus for sale. Women in this area of Cameroon work more hours in agriculture than do men, and those with access to food markets sell as much as 40 percent of what they grow.[2] Thus the community fields model for action repeats the common error of failing to explore seriously the producers' opportunity cost. This error occurs often in planning women's income-generation projects because women are seen, even more than are peasant men, as not rationally weighing the benefits of different activities.

The second phase of the women's agricultural project marked a significant departure from past practice: an agricultural technician was assigned to work with the women on their community fields. This meant that a trained technician was supplying his expertise to women farmers and also guiding women in its actual application. They were introduced to new varieties of corn, insecticides, fungicides, and new methods of planting and field maintenance.

But the farming techniques used on these community fields were not designed for adoption on women's individual food farms. Indeed, the extensionist told me that the women must learn that only through cooperative farming could they benefit from modern technology. Because women's methods on their own fields (notably, the practice of mixed cropping) generally precluded the use of (existing) new technology, extensionists regularly dismiss their methods as "archaic."[3] Not only is the disparaging stance typical of the extension service regarding traditional farming practices, but this appraisal is representative of the failure of Cameroonian extension services to meet the needs of women who raise food for family and for sale. The technology the extensionist introduced and the manner in which it was introduced required that women fit their farming practices to modern technology rather than the reverse. Given their labor and capital constraints, this expectation is not usually a practicable alternative.[4]

Whether or not village women's suspicions concerning the real destination of community field earnings were well founded, they certainly were a deterrent to collective action. The initial phase of the women's agricultural project in Sa'a had been two tiered, with party officers and townswomen managing the livestock tier, while the village women provided the field labor. The local leader's free use of the project vehicle did little to convince the village women that they were equal partners. Compounding this problematic hierarchy was the lack of care in defining how each member would benefit from the labor she expended. The failure to clarify whether a woman who worked twice as many days as another in the community field would get twice as much of the final profits created little incentive to be present. At the point when absenteeism begins to have a visible effect on yields, more women withdraw their labor.

The Department of Community Development presents an interesting comparison because it also uses community fields to mobilize labor to earn money.[5] But unlike the Ministry of Social Affairs projects, which presented community fields as generating income for women, the Community Development projects use the earnings for the construction of village safe water points. The earnings purchase cement, and village men, advised by a Community Development technician, build the safe water point. Thus the final output is truly a collective good and affords no way of rewarding individual participation (except by community approbation). Although these projects have not been free from irregular attendance, some of them have succeeded. This suggests that individual incentives are not the sole viable basis for mobilizing labor to increase production and acquire benefits. One might conclude that when the goal is individual income, in contrast to a truly collective (that is, an indivisible) good, it is more important that individual labor be directly related to individual gain. But a competing hypothesis is that the problem in the women's agricultural project's community fields lay not in intravillage relations, but in center-periphery ties, that is, in villagers' lack of confidence and anxiety regarding leadership outside the village.[6]

Probably both factors are related; analysis of the viability of community fields should not be restricted to intravillage dynamics. The worry that leadership may be unjustly privileged or exploitive will clearly alter group functioning. Farmers in Sa'a are part of the system of national cocoa and coffee marketing boards, which are both taxing devices and patronage hierarchies permitting some rural elites access to resources from the center. Thus, this patronage system both links rural populations to central authorities and undermines peasants' capacity for collective political action through the selective, and thus divisive, distribution of patronage goods. Village women certainly recognize the self-interested nature of political privilege in the men's world and in the women's wing of the party in their complaints that the community fields became "politicized." Their desire to divide up the proceeds of community fields immediately rather than banking the funds outside the village until an official decided on a project that would serve them suggests a similar interaction of several elements. Their wish to divide up their slim profits rather than letting them accumulate for some larger purpose and

their disquiet regarding the decision officials would make for them are reinforcing. Given the imprudence of a direct attack on anyone in the party
hierarchy, absenteeism from community field labor may be a passive protest
as well.

The failure of the project's planners and implementers to take individual incentives seriously was costly. In the face of the change in national
leadership and resulting maneuvers among local party leaders and those hop-
ing to replace them, careful delineation of how labor expended would be
rewarded was particularly imperative. Nor should village women be assumed to be a natural or preexisting communal labor force. They farm to
achieve family subsistence and a salable surplus: a diversion of their labor
for purported economic gain must offer payoffs clearly greater than current
gains from working their own individual farms.

L'union fait la force is an empty political slogan if the group effort
does not clearly benefit individual village women more than does their usual
practice. These village women's lives demonstrate both unmistakable economic individualism and the capacity for collective economic action. They
are commited to farming not only for family subsistence but also for income
they earn from surplus production. Taking labor from their own fields for
one day per week on a community field will endanger that income, and so
it must offer sufficient reward. Moral exhortations to community effort imply that they are ignorant of the benefits of collaboration—clearly an inac-
curate assumption to make about these women. They all belong to one or
more fairly large rotating credit and savings associations, and many join
with a few other women to work together on the farm of each member in
rotation. The carefully balanced reciprocity practiced in these groups demonstrates that the definition and the security of individual gain is essential to
collective action among them. This is at least as true among peasant women
as it is among other economic actors.

PRIVATE TRADERS, PRODUCERS' MARKETING PROBLEMS,
AND COOPERATIVES

The food-marketing cooperatives, which the Ministry of Women's Affairs
promoted as the means to revive the ailing agricultural project, seem an
oblique response to the project's disarray. Rather than addressing the structural defects in prior efforts to increase women's salable surplus, the new
initiative addressed women food producers' marketing problems. Like the
proposals to increase production, this proposal focuses on real concerns of
producers—the desire to find a buyer at a good price. But the model proposed evokes the marketing board–cooperative combination that purchases
and sells peasant-produced cocoa and coffee. The model is politically attrac-

tive but inappropriate for domestically consumed foods produced by small-holders.

The proposed cooperative's promise of an alternative to private traders and a greater producer share of the final consumer price echoes the cocoa and coffee cooperative movement of the nationalist period. Before independence, cocoa and coffee farmers rallied against the private traders, to whom they often became indebted and who refused to pay them full weight or top grade for their produce. The cooperative movement had wide popular support, for it was to replace the private traders, distrusted (and often expatriate) adversaries, with community members who represented the farmers' interests in grading and pricing. Although the cooperatives that emerged from this movement pay the farmer only about 40 percent to 60 percent of the (FOB) international price and support extensive patronage machines, they do ensure the seller a public and stable price. Thus the (male) export crop farmers' low marketing risk contrasts sharply with that of producers of domestically consumed crops.

The proposal of food marketing cooperatives for women farmers strikes a resonant chord: they would be the women's analog to the male farmers' cocoa and coffee cooperatives. The idea of food-marketing cooperatives certainly does not originate with the new minister of women's affairs: variations have been tried in Cameroon and elsewhere. I heard party women activists argue publicly when I first arrived in Cameroon in 1983 that the government should assist women in forming food-marketing cooperatives as it helped men form cocoa and coffee marketing cooperatives. The vision is very attractive: no-risk marketing at fixed prices. Such an arrangement would certainly take much of the sting out of women farmers' labor for market and perhaps even revive production on the community fields.

But though the food producers' problem in finding a purchaser at a good price is real, the analogy to export crops is wholly misleading. Food-marketing cooperatives are unlikely to protect food farmers from unstable prices and irregular sales. The food farmers' marketing problems are in part due to the nature of the food crops in question. Because the food crops grown in this area are perishable, market prices are highly variable in response to gluts and shortages. Private traders will not travel farther from Yaounde to buy produce than their margin for transport and for profit permits them to. A farmer a certain distance from the city cannot be sure for what price her produce will sell, or whether it will sell at all. When private traders dominate the market, the producer is forced to absorb much of this risk: women may well watch plantains or tomatoes perish for want of a buyer, or be forced to sell at very low prices lest the buyer at hand be the last to pass that way.

But a cooperative or a public agency buying these same crops must function according to these same parameters. When prices in Yaounde are down, the cooperative would have to cover operating cost out of the difference between purchase and sales price. The cooperative could attempt to maintain stable prices by paying less than private traders when prices are high. This would be intended to make up for artificially high prices for cooperative members when consumers are paying less. But this would require producers to forgo better prices from private traders when low supplies have driven prices up. When, under such conditions, producers sell to the private traders rather than to the cooperative, the cooperative would turn to government for coercion against the "disloyal competition" of the private trader.

Governments may respond by direct subsidy to the cooperative, but African governments can ill afford such a costly solution, nor are they politically likely to favor it. They are more likely to cap food prices in order to slow inflation and keep urban consumers politically quiescent.

Government may also create a marketing monopoly that buys at fixed prices. This is in essence the system of coffee and cocoa marketing boards in Cameroon, and most of West Africa. But black markets have not invaded coffee and cocoa markets because export crops must pass through the port to reach international buyers, which permits the state to maintain its monopoly. In sharp contrast, domestic food markets are made up of a multiplicity of dispersed buyers and sellers who easily elude state controls if government prices are artificially low. Governments that have imposed marketing boards for domestically produced and consumed foods (such as Mali and Upper Volta, now Burkina Faso) have witnessed burgeoning black markets controlling up to 90 percent of production.

In Cameroon the government attempted price controls of staple foods in 1972, triggering a retailers' strike. The Cameroonian government quickly dropped these price controls in the same year. Then, in 1973, the government launched a marketing parastatal, MIDEVIV (Mission pour le Developpement des Vivres), intended to outperform the private traders: it was to be so efficient that it would pay producers better prices *and* sell to consumers below the private traders' prices in Yaounde, thus forcing urban food prices down. But MIDEVIV could not pay producers more than private traders: indeed, when demand was strong, the private traders came to MIDEVIV's buying points and cleaned out the good quality produce before the laggards from MIDEVIV, the marketing parastatal, arrived. MIDEVIV never succeeded in forcing Yaounde prices down because its market share was so slight. By the 1980s it has ceased purchasing food in the Yaounde area, including Sa'a, without eliciting the slightest regret among producers.

It is hard to see how a marketing cooperative in Sa'a could succeed where MIDEVIV failed. One argument is that the cooperative would succeed because loyal members would forgo sale to private traders when they offered more because of the advantages the cooperative would offer. According to this perspective, producers (mostly women farmers) never felt MIDEVIV to be "theirs," never gave it their loyalty, as the women in the Sa'a women's marketing cooperative would. But some women in Sa'a, having perhaps learned from MIDEVIV, saw the cooperative's success lying in "someone's" (the minister) securing a contract to buy food, without fail and at fixed prices, for a state institution such as a school in Yaounde. Thus the producers in Sa'a would be ensured constant prices and regular sales. Moreover, the dream of owning a vehicle always wins supporters among those dependent on vehicles owned by others and obliged to pay the fees they charge. But operating costs and vehicle amortization are rarely perceived clearly, and the problem of maintaining a sufficient supply of goods to make the vehicle pay for itself is rarely appreciated.

The marketing-cooperative proposal was politically popular for some of the same reasons its real operating chances were poor: imprecision regarding its structure let it be all things to all people. How it would operate—whether it would be subsidized, whether and by whom management would be hired, whether buyers' contracts would be sought and arranged, whether Sa'a members would be free to sell to private traders if and when they chose—all these questions were to be answered once the cooperative was legally constituted. Thus everyone could envision the cooperative as she wanted. For some in Sa'a it meant access to a contract to buy, ending their marketing risk. For others it meant cheaper transport for their produce, and thus a greater share of the final purchaser's price for producers. For those public officials arguing that the cooperative would serve the public interest, it meant more and thus cheaper food for urban consumers. And, if the parallel with cocoa cooperatives applies, one wonders whether the patronage possibilities of distributing salaried managerial employment had some appeal as well.[7] What seemed lacking was careful consideration of how the cooperative would provide a better alternative than Yaounde's innumerable small traders, including village women themselves, many of whom travel regularly to Yaounde by bush taxi to sell three or four headloads of food. It was politically convenient to overlook these obstacles to the proposed cooperative.

The ministerial proposal of a marketing cooperative, despite the evidence from MIDEVIV's failure in food marketing, suggests an almost reflexive choice of a familiar and ideologically sanctioned instrument. There have been government-instigated cooperatives in Francophone Africa since well before independence, though none has served producers effectively.[8] The official penchant to attempt to "master" *(maitriser)* markets is longstanding in Francophone Africa, as is the scapegoating of the irrepressible small trading sector. Such "mastery" of export crops has proved to be a highly successful political formula, meeting a good share of the regime's revenue needs and tying clients to the state for all levels of society. Although food marketing is a false analogy, it has, here as elsewhere, promised to link center and periphery and to provide revenue for the center.

Setting Up the New Ministry of Women's Affairs

A women's ministry has as its constituency over half the population, and a nearly limitless range of expectations regarding appropriate activities. Women's interests range from problems of marital law and women's legal rights, de facto discrimination in access to education and to economic advancement, including employment and credit, to problems of women's health and family planning, wife beating, and so forth. How a women's ministry should tackle these numerous problems is such a thorny question that some have wondered whether such an omnibus women's agency is doomed to satisfy no one and to do nothing well. Some believe the selection of priority areas to be essential—whether maternal and child health or particular legal problems, improving the earning power of some subset of women, urban or rural, educated or uneducated—because too many campaigns will dissipate resources. Poor performance and failure run the risk of the loss of credibility before those whose support the ministry needs—political and administrative elites.

One important choice is whether a women's ministry will try to launch its own projects or whether it will seek collaboration with other technically specialized ministries or simply to try to influence or advise other ministries or agencies undertaking major projects. Those favoring projects "for women, by a women's agency" point out that projects run by an organization for which promoting women is not high priority often drop the women's component, or withdraw resources from it. In this view, a modest project focused solely on women is most likely to be implemented. Others argue that such women's projects will suffer irretrievably from the lack of resources, both financial resources and technical personnel, so that planning and implementation will be poor, and impact slight.[9]

From the latter point of view, it is better for a women's ministry to collaborate as an equal partner with a specialized ministry: for example, a project on women and children's health undertaken with the Ministry of Health, or an agricultural project or an educational project undertaken with the appropriate technical ministry. But a women's ministry is unlikely to have equal weight in commanding and controlling budget and must also depend on the other ministry for technical planning and administrative personnel.[10] In such scenarios, a women's ministry is likely to slip into junior partnership and lose control of the project. It will lose direct control over the technical staff implementing the project. Leadership in planning and implementing the project would be very elusive.

An alternative is for the women's ministry to cast itself as a watchdog seeking to protect and promote women's interests in policies and projects fielded by well-established specialized ministries. The danger of being an irritating but ineffectual presence may be staved off through the mobilization of constituency pressure or the provision of technical expertise at least compatible with that of the technocrats in the other agency, and preferably offering them a valued service. This strategy requires that the women's ministry develop such a technocratic and research capability. Furthermore, the corresponding ministry must be committed to the women-oriented objectives of the women's ministry. These conditions are difficult to meet.

The minister of women's affairs in Cameroon has gone on record placing considerable emphasis on this kind of interministerial action. Apparently speaking of aspirations for her young ministry, she said in 1985, "We have several study bureaus, made up of researchers, sociologists and practical people, which propose action to various implementing ministers. Then we monitor the result. . . . The Ministry of Women's Affairs can act as a focal point and a clearing house for ideas and action."[11] But these objectives appear difficult to realize. By 1986 the ministry had a number of small projects relying largely on staff from within the ministry for their implementation.

From its foundation, the new women's ministry faced well-established expectations regarding interministerial competition, party politics, and patronage. These expectations derived not only from women's familiarity with established practice in men's ministerial and party politics, but also directly from the presence of women activists in the women's wing of the national party. The new minister of women's affairs had been given her ministerial portfolio before the party congress at which she was elected president of the women's wing of the party. With the election pending, the minister had an incentive to consolidate support among elite party women, including provincial and local notables. The talk of democratization by the new president generated considerable pressure from aspiring politicians seeking to eject established party elites. But neither the new president of the Republic nor his minister of women's affairs was willing to permit wholesale grassroots challenges of the party. A careful mix of cooptation of old officeholders and selective promotion of local political newcomers has to guide official visits and the allocation of patronage. Small, locale-specific development projects offered a visible vehicle to demonstrate the new minister's ability to deliver to local party representatives and to tie constituencies to the ministry. I interpret the rapid proposal that Sa'a form a marketing cooperative to shore up its faltering women's agricultural project as a response to these political pressures.

To get significant numbers of women food producers included in the agricultural extension system, the Ministry of Women's Affairs must either establish joint policy and projects with the Ministry of Agriculture or it must function as a watchdog over that ministry. But neither alternative has payoffs for the Ministry of Women's Affairs in organizational or structural terms. Women's Affairs does not have the technically skilled and experienced personnel needed to interface those in the agriculture ministry. Indeed, some of the women's ministry's ranking bureaucrats, as long-term party militants, are somewhat alien to technocrats and, because of their modest educations, ineligible for the grands corps of the civil service.

In addition, interministerial lobbying and collaboration conflicts directly with the propensity to protect organizational boundaries present in all bureaucracies. This territoriality is particularly pronounced in Cameroon because ministries themselves are highly developed patronage organizations, each ministry jealously guarding its territory. Competition is well recognized between the Ministry of Agriculture, one of the biggest in the country, and the Ministry of Plan, which has successfully cut Agriculture's budget and personnel by creating many agricultural parastatals controlled directly by the Ministry of Plan. Three smaller ministries, the Ministry of Social Affairs, the Department of Community Development, and the Ministry of Youth and Sports, all have overlapping responsibilities but do not collaborate. All strive to have the greatest number of social workers, with the result that social workers' training and assignment is a saga of duplication and wasted resources. Permanent staff are among any minister's most reliable political advocates, especially in a one-party system, because they have a very concrete interest in ministerial aggrandizement. The newly created Ministry of Women's Affairs faces severe structural constraints predisposing it to opt for small projects aimed at women, which it can plan and implement itself.

Conclusion

The vision of interministerial collaboration, of the ministry as women's advocate improving policy in all spheres of government, is surely attractive. That a women's ministry should tap the technical, administrative, and field resources of other ministries to serve women appears essential, given the lack of specialized personnel within the women's ministry. But the preceding analysis of the Ministry of Women's Affairs in Cameroon suggests that a convergence of bureaucratic interests—within the women's ministry, within the women's wing of the party, and in the larger ministerial context—favors autonomous projects implemented by the new ministry. Ministerial personnel, including advisers, appear to favor projects managed by specific ministerial departments. Also, party notables are predisposed to familiar policy solutions that have had demonstrable patronage value in Cameroon. The established technical ministries have little to gain from incursions on their turf by this unproven women's advocacy group.

This interpretation of the Ministry of Women's Affairs foundation and initial efforts suggests that the ministry's political environment predisposed it to undertake small projects, "by and for women," somewhat reflexively conceived but with uncertain feasibility. Although this essay explores only the ministry's formative period, it raises questions regarding the real gains of International Women's Year and the women's decade. Has the publicity triggered the creation of resource-poor "women's ministries" with a vague mandate to reform public policy in numerous sectors and even to create good policy where none exists?

Jane Guyer reflects on the diversity of activities and roles that are surely needed to promote women's diverse interests, which she summarizes as policy research, representation, and technically specific expertise. She notes not only the diversity and range of activities entailed but also the incompatibilities these imply:

Women's offices seem to have intrinsically incompatible aspects to their mandates. Research in technical areas, from tax policy to crop rotation, requires integration into the rest of the technical community. Political action, such as advocacy of a women's perspective, lobbying for more funding for women's projects, or the maintenance of links to other women's groups, demand cross disciplinary organization and a somewhat more confrontational collective stance. Working on project administration involves yet another kind of structure defined by authority and cooperation.[12]

The Cameroonian Ministry of Women's Affairs illustrates how these incompatibilities have been played out in a particular bureaucratic and political environment. Cameroonian government policy is publicly presented as an entirely technocratic creation, in which interest advocacy, lobbying, and confrontation politics are not acceptable. But the quest for ministerial autonomy and patronage is in fact both entirely political and extremely inhospitable to the technical collaboration and problem solving required, particularly where the ministry in question does not have the resources, budget, and personnel to have a sizable impact alone. This structured competition between ministries imposes isolation on the new women's ministry, although it is wholly unequipped to implement policies to fill its mandate without access to and collaboration with other ministeries.

The fusion of party and ministerial roles in the minister of women's affairs may provide some leverage in overcoming the ministry's bureaucratic isolation. But the joining of technocratic and party roles is not an unambiguous advantage. As head of the women's wing of the party, the minister inherits the demands and expectations of party activists. In this one-party system, party activists are not so much a channel for popular demands as a middle-range elite with clear interests and expectations. The ministry risks becoming a patronage instrument to service this constituency—as some bureaucrats in technical ministries hasten to argue. We have seen the pressures to distribute resources to party personnel rather than to lobby or to collaborate with other ministries.

Responses to possible collaboration in applied research are also illustrative. In this case, Cameroonian agronomic research scientists needed to conduct on-farm tests of newly developed, disease-resistant seed for certain food crops. For the women's ministry to sponsor these tests would have been an innovative strategy with, I believe, a great potential impact on women food producers. Such applied research addresses one of women farmers' major problems: their low returns on labor. In addition, collaboration would improve communication between those designing and conducting agronomic research and advocates for the interests of women farmers.[13] But such an innovative strategy required the women's ministry to tread on the domain of two ministries: scientific research and agriculture. Indeed, the research technicians were very skeptical about working with the women's ministry, claiming that party women introduce faction whereas they, the technocrats, truly serve women. The women's ministry took no initiative, and there was no joint effort to test the new seed.

The minister views her party role as a great asset to her ministerial efforts. As head of a fledgling ministry with minimal resources, her party role, including a seat on the national political committee, provides the weight needed in all ministerial activities. The party role should also provide a part of leverage needed to overcome the resistance of older ministeries to interministerial lobbying or collaboration. Nonetheless, ministerial isolation is hard to overcome. The minister suggested that the barriers to access to other ministeries would be lower if, rather than a new ministry, a women's bureau attached directly to the national presidency had been created.[14] Such a bureau would be above other ministries and could then more legitimately play an oversight role. In Guyer's terms, such a bureau would have a clear representation or advocacy role, rather than fusing these functions together with the policy formation and implementation functions of a ministry.

Whether the minister of women's affairs will assemble sufficient political capital to achieve access to relevant technical ministries is, in my view, a key question. Whether the ministry seeks access as an advocate or a collaborator with such ministries, even more than a blessing of the nation's president will be required. Acquiring personnel with specific expertise in whatever policy areas in which the ministry wishes to have an impact will be necessary. The ministerial staff itself will have to learn to break with the existing mores of ministerial territoriality and establish new channels of interministerial communication. Finally, the ministerial staff will have to straddle several contexts, moving into the relevant technical communities, back into the advocacy orientation of the ministry as well as to interest mediation with women party activists.

Another model is to have committed and competent personnel dispersed in various agencies and roles, including the relevant technical ministries, and the relevant functional roles, such as project administration, technical research, advocacy, and lobbying.[15] Thus far, it is not clear that the few established women technocrats in ministries such as agriculture, education, and plan are willing to serve, or can easily serve, within their own ministries as women's advocates and allies of the women's ministry. To do so may be perceived not only as a breach of ministerial loyalty but as breaking technocratic rules through association with the women's wing of the party.

It may be possible to balance party role and ministerial portfolio in such a way that they enhance the minister's influence over policy. But the structural barriers to resources affording the ministry an impact beyond projects it can design and implement alone are formidable. Ultimately, the ministry's mandate can be achieved only if women's advocates and committed technicians are a real presence in a variety of ministerial as well as partisan contexts. The first step must be acknowledgment that the women's ministry cannot and should not be the sole avenue through which women can seek remedies to their diverse policy needs.

Notes

1. Paul Biya was President Ahidjo's handpicked successor, but in the course of the year (1983) following Ahidjo's resignation, relations between the two became increasingly strained. Ahidjo appears to have sought to retain power by continuing as leader of the party. Relations deteriorated, the government won out over the party, Ahidjo left Cameroon, and in April 1984 a coup was attempted by northerners in the military, purportedly Ahidjo's supporters. In this context, the removal of all of Ahidjo's lieutenants can be seen not only as politically expedient but imperative. Thus, quite independently of ministerial policy or administrative competence, the president of the women's wing of the party and minister of social affairs appointed by Ahidjo were removed from office.

2. For excellent studies of women's agricultural activities and food production, see Jane Guyer, *Family and Farm in Southern Cameroon* (Boston: Boston University African Studies Program, 1984); and Jeanne Henn, "Intra-Household Dy-

namics and State Policies as Constraints on Food Production: Results of a 1985 Agro-Economic Survey in Cameroon," *Gender Issues in Farming Systems Research and Extension,* ed. Susan Poats, Marianne Schmink, and Anita Spring (Boulder, Colo.: Westview, 1988).

3. Extensionists at several ranks all described peasant women's farming methods as "archaic," saying that women plant "pell-mell" to describe how they intercrop the numerous foods they cultivate. The use of identical phrases suggests an officially legitimated, if not official, view of traditional farming methods, of which women's farming practices constitute a large share.

4. Mixed cropping is a clear adaptation to the brief time in which fields must be prepared and crops planted. Until very recently, agricultural research has not recognized that mixed cropping makes ecological sense in these thin top soils. In addition, certain crops are complementary in the soil nutrients they use and provide, but this too is underresearched. Modern western monocropping is imperative only when planting, tilling, or harvesting are mechanized—which is both irrelevant to these women farmers and often dangerous for their soil. Research directed toward an understanding and modification of women's multicrop farming practices in order to improve yields does exist, for example at ICRASAT (International Center for Agricultural Research in Arid and Semi-Arid Tropics) in Ibaden, Nigeria. Research along these lines has been recently introduced at Cameroon's regional agricultural research centers and agricultural colleges. But results are limited, and agricultural extension is as yet unreformed. An alternative model of research, conducted directly on villagers' plots so that researcher and villager can see the results of modifications in farmers' techniques, is used by some development agencies, but this concept was unknown in the Cameroonian context I studied.

5. The Department of Community Development was in, but not integrated into, the Ministry of Agriculture in 1983. Originally created in Anglophone Cameroon before Anglophone and Francophone Cameroon joined in federation, the Department of Community Development has been something of an orphan since it became a nationwide organization. It was assigned to the Ministry of Youth and Sports, later attached to the presidency, and then switched to the Ministry of Agriculture. But Community Development appeared to have remained oriented toward enhancing communalism and promoting collective action for public goods such as safe water points and community pharmacies. It was little altered by its relocation in the Ministry of Agriculture, although its community field projects sometimes benefited from the advice of agricultural extensionists. The idea that only communities, not individuals, can mobilize the labor to benefit from modern agricultural techniques encountered in the Women's Agricultural Project was echoed in the Department of Community Development.

6. See Mancur Olsen, *The Logic of Collective Action* (Cambridge: Harvard University Press, 1965), for the classic discussion of collective action and the free-rider problem, that is, the barriers to achieving full participation of all members if individual members can benefit without meeting the obligation of membership. It is very possible that the community fields are hampered more by lack of confidence regarding how leaders (external to the village group) will use or misuse the community field profits, a problem apparently more acute in the party-sponsored Wom-

en's Agricultural Project than in the Community Development projects. See Samuel Popkin, *The Rational Economy of the Peasant: The Political Economy of Rural Society in Vietnam* (Berkeley: University of California Press, 1979), on risk factors in collective action and the nature of successful leadership.

7. See Robert Bates, *Markets and States in Tropical Africa: The Political Basis of Agricultural Politics* (Berkeley: University of California Press, 1981), for an excellent analysis of the political uses of marketing boards and state-sponsored cooperatives of export crops.

8. See Jane Guyer, "Feeding Yaounde," in Guyer, ed., *Feeding African Cities* (Manchester: Manchester University Press, 1987).

9. Barbara Lewis, "Women in Development Planning," in Jean O'Barr, ed., *Third World Women in Politics: Continuing Perspectives* (Durham: Duke University Press, 1982); and Ruth Dixon, "Assessing the Impact of Development Projects on Women," AID Program Evaluation Discussion Paper No. 8 (Washington, D.C.: U.S. Agency for International Development, 1980).

10. The ministry's weight in budgetary decisions for joint projects is finally a question of how funds are allocated and who implements the project. My reasoning derives from evidence to date that funding sources, whether Cameroonian or international, have not given the women's ministry power of command in any joint project between two ministries.

11. *West Africa* (May 1985).

12. Jane Guyer, "Women's Role in Development," in Robert J. Berg and Jennifer Seymour Whitaker, eds., *Strategies for African Development*, pp. 393–422 (Berkeley: University of California Press, 1986).

13. This conclusion, based on observations made during my 1985 field work, is debatable. Involvement in testing these resistant varieties, as yet not fully proven, might be seen as too risky for the Ministry of Women's Affairs. But to wait until the agricultural research and extension establishment has agronomic innovations for use by women carries, I think, the greater risk that the agronomic research and development establishment will never take the particular constraints on women farmers into account. For this reason, women in agriculture is a prime illustration of the need for a strong women's lobby that can penetrate such technical institutions.

14. Interview, May 1985, Yaounde.

15. Guyer, "Women's Role in Development."

11/Tough Row to Hoe: Women in Nicaragua's Agricultural Cooperatives

Rural Women's Research Team
Center for the Investigation and Study of Agrarian Reform (CIERA)

One of the unique aspects of the Sandinista revolution in Nicaragua is that its Agrarian Reform Law of 1981 is the first in Latin America to explicitly include women as beneficiaries. In contrast to the situation in other Latin American agrarian reforms, in Nicaragua neither sex nor kinship position is a barrier to becoming an agrarian reform beneficiary. Moreover, one of the objectives of cooperative development is the incorporation of women.

Agrarian reforms in most Latin American countries over the past several decades have benefited only men. Rural women have not been taken into account partly because they are not considered to be agricultural producers or full-time wage workers, and partly because it is often assumed that benefits for household heads—usually men—will be benefits for all household members as well. The result has been that where land has been redistributed to formerly landless households, only male heads of households have received land in their own names. Although women may farm alongside their husbands as unpaid family labor, they have no legal right to the land. If divorced or separated, they again join the ranks of Latin America's landless. Where governments have promoted production cooperatives

This is a condensed version of a monograph, *Tough Row to Hoe,* published by the Institute for Food and Development Policy (Food First) in San Francisco, to whom we are grateful for permission to reprint. The Institute for Food and Development Policy is a nonprofit research and educational center that focuses on food and justice issues around the world. Founders Frances Moore Lappé (author of *Diet for a Small Planet*) and Joseph Collins, along with institute staff, have played a key role in changing global debates about the causes of and solutions for world hunger. The institute accepts no contributions from government sources, enabling it to carry out independent research and dissemination.

[handwritten margin notes: traditionally women excluded from cooperative membership; Nic. is a counter example]

(based on collective or group ownership of land), the members have over-whelmingly been men. Thus, although men have been given the opportunity for full-time employment, women, excluded from cooperative membership, have remained part of the temporary, seasonal labor force, with no right to participate in cooperative decision making.

In Nicaragua women began to join the agricultural cooperatives that were formed immediately after the revolutionary victory. Their involvement was often the result of their active role in the revolutionary struggle. Women fought alongside men not just in the armed struggle but in the land takeovers and strikes that helped topple the dictator Somoza. As this study shows, many rural women considered that they had gained their right to participate in the new cooperatives because of their revolutionary role.

The research for this study began in 1982, a year after the agrarian reform and cooperative laws had gone into effect. A major objective of the study was to analyze the process through which women became members of the cooperatives. To what extent was women's participation a result of the law, reflecting a progressive state policy? To what extent did the law help to break down traditional views of the proper gender division of labor, with women at the hearth and men in the fields? What were the factors that encouraged women to participate in the cooperatives, and what were the barriers to their incorporation?

[handwritten margin note: Examination of process by which women are incorporated into cooperatives]

Among the more important findings of this study is that even in a rev-olutionary setting it is difficult to create the preconditions for female equal-ity. Traditional attitudes that undervalue women as producers continue to exist. Moreover, although many women might like to join a production co-operative they often find that they cannot take on a full-time job because of their household responsibilities. As long as women carry the full burden of childcare and housekeeping, they cannot participate on an equal basis with men. As a result of these and other factors, in 1982 women constituted only 6 percent of cooperative membership. Though women are still underrepre-sented among the beneficiaries of the agrarian reform, Nicaraguan women have fared considerably better than their counterparts in the other Latin American agrarian reforms, with the exception of Cuba.[1] This study shows the difficulty of integrating women into the cooperatives, but it also shows the difference that women's participation makes for successful cooperative development. Not only are women a source of cohesion within the cooper-atives, but the female members have been able to enhance their technical, organizational, and political development.

Research Methods

CIERA (Center for the Investigation and Study of Agrarian Reform) is the research arm of the Nicaraguan Ministry of Agriculture and Agrarian Reform (MIDINRA). From the inception of agrarian reform in 1980, it was recognized that the subject of women's incorporation in the reform required research and analysis. The Rural Women's Research Team was formed the next year with the objective of fostering research, analysis, and policy formulations regarding rural women's participation. The goals of the Rural Women's Research Team were to analyze rural women's role in both production and reproduction, taking into account the interconnection between the economic, political, and cultural factors that perpetuate women's subordination.

Carrying out research in the midst of a war is no easy task. By the time field research on the cooperative study was concluded in 1983, many of the cooperatives had themselves become targets of the counterrevolutionaries. A new cooperative form emerged, called the self-defense cooperatives, which combined military defense and production. By 1985 it was evident that one of the main effects of the war had been the feminization of agriculture. As increasing numbers of men have been called to the front, women have taken a greater role than ever before in agricultural production—be it on their own plots, in the cooperatives, or in the rural labor market. Quantitative data are not available, but it appears that the proportion of women members in the cooperatives is increasing. Moreover, the absence of the men has begun to call into question the gender division of labor in agricultural production, as women begin to carry out traditionally male tasks and to fill male occupations.[2]

The study is based on field research carried out in three phases during 1982 and 1983. In the first phase we investigated nine cooperatives with women members. Of these, six were production cooperatives (Cooperativas Agricolas Sandinistas) and three were credit and service cooperatives (Cooperativas de Servicio y Credito). In the second phase we studied four cooperatives with no women members, two production and two credit and service, in order to analyze in more detail the obstacles limiting the integration of women as members. In the third phase we analyzed three "self-defense" cooperatives in the central-interior region of the country. The "contras" specifically targeted the production cooperatives for military attacks and kidnappings, so that the cooperative members now had to work in the fields with weapons on their backs. Women were officially members in only one of the three armed production cooperatives studied. The case studies of cooperatives presented in this report, however, are not statistically representative of the wide spectrum of female participation in Nicaraguan cooperatives, but, rather, are illustrative of the different degrees of female participation.

The field research was conducted primarily through open-ended interviews with four categories of informants: the members of the executive council of the cooperatives, the women members, the male members, and the wives of male members. In the second phase of research we also interviewed members of the community who did not belong to the cooperatives and women who had been denied membership. In all phases, we interviewed the Agrarian Reform technician, the activist for the Union of Farmers and Cattlemen (UNAG), and, in some cases, Agrarian Reform trainers and Sandinista Front (FSLN) party members in the community (See Table 11-1).

Women's Work

Nicaraguan rural women not only maintain the household and family but also make important contributions to household income through their agricultural and commercial activities. This double burden is difficult for all women, but especially hard for the extraordinarily large number of women who are heads of households.[3]

Census estimates of Nicaraguan women's participation in the rural and in the agricultural economically active population (EAP) show a participation rate of 15 percent in 1977, a figure lower than the CIERA 1980 female agricultural EAP estimate, 18.3 percent, which was based on a survey of coffee and cotton harvest workers during that year. According to CIERA, even this higher figure underestimates women's economic participation in agriculture. CIERA has estimated that women constitute 25 percent of the agricultural EAP.[4]

No quantitative data are available on peasant women's participation in productive activities on family plots. The one study published focusing on women's agricultural work was conducted in the community of El Horno de San Ramon in Matagalpa.[5] In the two households studied in detail, where the families were engaged in both subsistence agriculture and wage work, women participated in most tasks required for basic grain production—the selection of seeds, the selection of corn husks and pods, planting, weeding, irrigation, harvesting of corn, loading, and grain storage. The only activities in which women did not participate were clearing land and plowing furrows in preparation for sowing.

Besides working in agricultural production and commerce, women are responsible for housework and childcare. A case study of time use in a peasant household in Matagalpa demonstrates that housework is both time-consuming and labor-intensive. It took seventeen hours daily to care for a family of two adults and four children. Most of the housework is done by

Table 11-1 / The Cooperatives Studied

COOPERATIVE	COUNTY	MEMBERS	WOMEN	PERCENTAGE WOMEN	AREA*	CROPS
PRODUCTION:						
Blanca Arauz	Tola	4	4	100.0	4	corn, soy
Rigoberto Perez	Cosmapa	10	8	80.0	36	cotton, corn
Carlos Nuembes	Nueva Guinea	36	13	33.0	463	coffee, rice
Camilo Ortega	Tipitapa	34	8	23.5	714	corn, sorghum
Arnoldo Quant	Leon	13	2	15.4	300	cotton
Carlos P. Areta	Matagalpa	29	4	13.8	291	corn, coffee
German Pomares	Tola	78	10	12.8	1,176	corn, beans
Pedro R. Narvaes	Jinotepe	23	0	0.0	152	corn, sorghum
CREDIT & SERVICE						
German Pomares	Matagalpa	38	6	15.8	143	coffee, corn
Pedro J. Chamorro	Tipitapa	53	3	7.5	400	basic grains
Gregorio Montoya	Nueva Guinea	25	1	4.0	1,071	basic grains
Laura A. Cuadra	Tisma	18	0	0.0	43	corn, yucca
Reynaldo L. Lopez	La Laguna	14	0	0.0	2	corn

*Size in hectares (1 hectare = 1.4 manzanas, the Nicaraguan unit).

the adult woman and her two daughters. Men spent only fifty minutes daily (5 percent of the time necessary to maintain the household) doing housework.[6]

The Agrarian Reform and the Cooperative Movement

Nicaragua is predominantly an agricultural society; its development depends on its agricultural production. As in most Latin American countries, land ownership under Somoza was highly concentrated: 76 percent of the farms encompassed only 13 percent of the nation's agricultural land, while the remaining 24 percent of the farms controlled 87 percent of the land.[7] The principal developments during the first two years of the revolution were the establishment of state farms (the Area of People's Property, APP) made up of the estates confiscated from the Somoza family and its closest supporters; the reduction of legal rental rates for land; the enforced rental of idle land held by large landowners; the transfer of state farm land to collectives of workers; the increase of government credit and state services to the peasantry; the strengthened political power of the rural lower classes through the Farm Workers Association (ATC) and UNAG; and the increase of the wages of rural workers and the enforcement of existing labor legislation.[8]

In August 1981 the Agrarian Reform Law and the Law of Cooperatives were promulgated. The Agrarian Reform Law addresses the problems of reordering and rationalizing the use of agricultural land. It does not establish a limit on the amount of land that may be owned privately, as long as the land is used efficiently. It affects property larger than 357 to 714 hectares (depending on the region) that is idle or inefficiently used, worked by sharecroppers, or under labor service arrangements (colonato), or that is abandoned or decapitalized. Among the beneficiaries of this law are poor and landless peasants, cooperatives, and state farms.

Whereas the initial agrarian policies sought to benefit the peasantry by increasing their access to credit and rental land, the Agrarian Reform Law established a policy of land titling. Peasants and landless rural workers now receive agrarian reform titles to land either collectively, as production cooperatives, or individually, as small private farmers. The intent of this policy is clear: it favors production and furthers the economic development of the country.

The rapid development of the cooperative movement was impressive. In 1978 only 22 cooperatives existed in Nicaragua; by the end of 1979, 1,976 cooperatives had been formed. In the first three years of the revolution 50 percent of all peasants joined cooperatives. According to the National Census of Cooperatives,[9] by October 1982 a total of 2,849 cooperatives existed in the country, with 68,434 members who worked a total area of 873,988 hectares. Two forms of cooperatives predominate: production cooperatives (Cooperativas Agricolas Sandinistas) and credit and service cooperatives (Cooperativas de Servicio y Credito). In the production cooperatives all the productive resources are collectively owned and the land is collectively worked. In the credit and service cooperatives members individually own and work land but unite to collectively receive state services, such as credit and technical assistance. All told, collective forms of production characterize 37 percent of all cooperatives and include 31 percent of all members.

The Integration of Women into the Cooperatives

According to the National Cooperative Census, by October 1982, 44 percent of Nicaragua's cooperatives had incorporated women as members, but only 6 percent of all cooperative members were women. The cooperatives with women members have an average of three women but an average of twenty-two men.

The Cooperative Law of September 1981 established the right of all Nicaraguans to participate in the new cooperatives.[10] It explicitly stated that "the production cooperatives will encourage the full integration of women into productive tasks of the cooperative, incorporating women as members under the same conditions as men, as one more example of the participation of women in the construction of the new society."[11] The Statute of Rights and Guarantees of Nicaraguans established the principle of "equal wage or salary for equal work in identical conditions of efficiency and adequate social responsibility, without discrimination based on sex."[12]

The Minimum Wage Law established minimum wage levels for the entire country according to occupation, eliminating wage differentials based on sex. Similarly, the labor regulation governing agro-export production reinforced the legal equality of men and women with respect to rights, wages and social services. It established that every person fourteen years or older must be registered in his or her own name on the payroll list. This ensures that a woman is counted as a worker—with wages paid directly to her and not to a male relative—and that she is eligible to receive social services and benefits in her own name. These measures represent a practical improvement in the legal and social status of women and, taken as a whole, should facilitate the participation of women in the agrarian reform.

Although the legal basis has been established for the incorporation of women into the agrarian reform and the cooperative movement, data on women's participation suggest that relatively few women have taken advantage of their legal right to participate. In the sections that follow we analyze why this is the case.

Which Women Join Cooperatives?

Women with different social and economic positions encounter different situations when attempting to become cooperative members. The attitudes of both men and women about women's work and women cooperative members also influence the possibility of women's becoming members. We focus on factors that influence the integration of women into cooperatives: women as wage earners, household heads, low household income, alternative economic activities, family ties, and people's attitudes.

Increasing landlessness among the peasantry changed traditional family relationships. Female members of poor peasant and landless households were forced by economic necessity to seek wage employment. In many cases the survival of the family depended as much on women's wages as on men's. The situation of women wage earners was worse than that of men, however, since they could often obtain employment for only three or four months of the year during the cotton and coffee harvests. In some cases a husband and wife also rented a plot of land for growing basic grains.

We found that landless women wage workers were more interested than peasant women in working collectively in agricultural production cooperatives. This may be due to two factors: (1) The previous experience of female wage workers in a more collective work situation, and (2) their traditional lack of access to land and their consequent impoverishment. Of the fifty-nine women we studied, thirty-three were from the rural working class.

The family position of women within the household is another factor that explains their integration into cooperatives. Both peasants and wage workers who are female heads of household join cooperatives to increase their incomes in order to support their families. Our analysis shows that in three out of seven production cooperatives and in two out of three credit and service cooperatives studied, the majority of women are either the sole or the principal support of their households. In many cases they are wives or daughters who for some reason are responsible for generating household income. A typical case is one in which the husband did not want to work collectively, yet had been unable to find a steady job. There are also cases of women members who live with and support their parents.

The integration of wives and daughters into cooperatives is often the result of the family's attempt to increase the household income. The low level of remuneration in most cooperatives means that all adult members of the household must work in order to support the family. This is due to the fact that the cooperatives are still getting established and have not been able to generate sufficient profits to raise the salaries of their members. Although the participation of these women may be motivated by low household income, at least it challenges the notion that women and men cannot be equal members, or that only those women who are heads of households can become members (as is the case in some countries).

Some women have alternative economic activities that are more profitable or prestigious than agricultural work in a cooperative. We found women who were very supportive of their husbands' involvement in a cooperative but who were not interested themselves in joining because their own economic activities were more profitable. That was particularly true of the women who ran country stores. They had no economic incentive to join a production cooperative as full-time workers, and limited time available to become credit and service cooperative members.

Our study and other CIERA research projects reveal that family bonds among the members have a positive influence on cooperatives. This has a special relevance for women, since family ties to male cooperative members have facilitated their integration and have provided them with support and confidence. Similarly, family ties among women cooperative members serve to encourage and support women's participation.

Reasons for Women's Exclusion from Cooperatives

Traditional peasant mores and beliefs tend to deny the value of women's productive work. This in turn results in the denial of the right of women to participate in agricultural cooperatives. The exclusion of women from these cooperatives was often due to the members' prejudices concerning the social role of women; these were usually reinforced by state officials. Economic reasons, such as the scarcity of land and the lack of sufficient employment in the region, were also given to justify the exclusion of women.

"WOMEN AREN'T AS PRODUCTIVE AS MEN"

This was one of the expressions that the men of the production cooperative Laura Amanda Cuadra used to justify the lack of women members in their cooperative in Masaya. Before the formation of this cooperative, some of the members had belonged to a work collective on state land and made up of two women and six men. The men said they had had a very negative experience working with the women, did not consider women to be as productive as they were, and, therefore, had found it necessary to organize a division of labor according to sex. The "lighter" tasks were assigned to women (that is, sowing, cleaning, pruning) and the "heavier" tasks were assigned to men. For this reason, when the cooperative was formed, the men did not want to allow women members.

The members' attitudes regarding the productivity of women were mirrored by those of the agrarian reform technician. At a meeting to discuss the entrance of new members and, specifically, the petition of one woman interested in joining, the agrarian reform technician argued that the petitioner was not capable of carrying out all of the tasks of basic grain production by herself, and that she would require the help of an older son.

In general, the members of this cooperative reject the integration of women into the cooperative. They argue that not only will women never be as productive as men but that they are incapable of assuming the responsibility of an agricultural plot since the work required is simply too hard. In their opinion, women can perform housekeeping duties and raise animals but cannot be agriculturalists. Nonetheless, the majority of women in the region have been engaged in agricultural wage work for years.

It is important to point out that the Masaya area is characterized by very high unemployment. Consequently, there are many women interested in joining cooperatives in order to gain access to agricultural resources and to a stable productive activity. The men note that participation in cooperatives is necessary to gain access to land and employment, but they justify male-only participation because, as they put it, men need to work to support a home. However, the woman who has petitioned this cooperative for membership, like many other women interested in admission, is a household head and thus the main income earner. These women do have the same economic responsibilities as the men but are barred from the cooperative because of their gender.

"WOMEN MEMBERS? ONLY IF THEY HAVE LAND"

In a credit and service cooperative in Esteli we found the most negative attitudes toward incorporating women as members. According to the president of this cooperative, it had never considered including women as members because women had little experience in agricultural work. "Here nobody pays attention to women," he said. "We don't give employment to women, only men." Other members shared the same opinion: "It doesn't worry me that women don't benefit" . . . . "I am not interested in women joining, at least not my own wife. As for other women, who knows?" Even the incorporation of female heads of households into this cooperative would be considered only under special conditions. First, a woman must make the request to join; she should not expect the men of the cooperative to invite her. Second, a woman must own land in her own name to be considered.

It is usually the case in Nicaragua that even if a couple has purchased land with money earned by both the man and the woman, the land is registered only in the man's name. As a result, he becomes the cooperative member. Even when the plot is registered under both names, it is assumed that the man is the household head and should represent the family within the cooperative. It is clear that social and legal customs reflect ideological norms about men's and women's work.

The agrarian reform technician in the Esteli credit and service cooperative held opinions similar to the members regarding women's participation, namely, that agriculture was not the proper type of division of labor: a man's place is on the agricultural plot and a woman's is in the home. There were few exceptions: as one farmer stated, "It might be possible if women had land."

"WOMEN ARE NOT INTERESTED"

The Pedro Ramos Navarez production cooperative has always had only male members. Women were never invited to the initial organizational meetings, although several women attended on their own. One of these women publicly declared her responsibilities in the militia and in the neighborhood organization. Because she missed the meeting, she was not considered for membership. Nevertheless, she is still interested in joining because she is a single mother and unemployed, and membership would partially resolve her economic problems.

According to the agrarian reform technician of this cooperative, it has no women members because agricultural work is the responsibility of men. His lack of interest in integrating women into the cooperative was evident. Several members systematically asserted that no women had ever attended the organizational meetings or shown interest in joining the cooperative. According to other members, women do not like to work in cooperatives because they do not know how to perform all the agricultural tasks. Moreover, they stated that "the hardship of organizing cooperative work during the initial stages" prevented women from participating. Nevertheless, a few men did admit that some women were very good agricultural workers.

Many of the male attitudes toward women members were expressions of the prevailing values and beliefs that perpetuate women's subordination to men and idealize the sexual division of labor whereby "the man works and the woman stays at home." However, this ideal has very little to do with reality. The development of capitalism in Nicaragua in this century resulted in the impoverishment of the peasantry and in the increased participation of women in agricultural work, either as wage workers or as part of the family's labor force on the household plot. Even when women were not directly involved in agricultural work, their contribution to the household economy, either through animal husbandry or food-processing activities, has been significant. The important productive role of women has been negated by the prevailing definitions of women's roles in society. This acute contradiction has turned women into invisible workers with no social recognition. Women have not been taken into account, whether in the decision-making process in the peasant smallholding or as applicants for cooperative membership.

The men do value the domestic work that women perform. Most of the men interviewed recognized the importance of housework for the maintenance and survival of the household. Nonetheless, women are denied recognition for their productive work outside of the home; this has significant repercussions on women's socioeconomic position. Women actually work two jobs, both of which are essential to the survival of the household, but only one of which is recognized. This lack of recognition is used to justify the women's exclusion from household decision making and makes them totally dependent upon men. Women—whether married, single, or heads of households—are thus limited in their ability to work and contribute to the development of the cooperatives and the household economy. These elements are among those that produce female subordination and discrimination against women, even within the revolutionary process.

WOMEN'S ATTITUDES

The fact that women have the primary responsibility for housekeeping and childcare acts as a barrier to women's participation in the cooperatives. The women we interviewed reported that childcare was the factor that most limits their ability to join production cooperatives. Some women said that they would be able to take on the responsibility of working full time in a production cooperative if childcare were provided.

Among the other reasons women gave for not joining the cooperatives were: (1) lack of previous experience in agricultural work, (2) dislike for field work, and (3) fear of competing with men in agricultural work. These reasons were more prevalent among women who were in smallholder households than among female wage workers in landless households. The lack of previous experience in agricultural work is closely related, of course, to the household's economic position and to the availability of working-age men for agricultural work, but it is also related to the subjective factors discussed above regarding what is seen as appropriate work for women.

The Process of Integrating Women into Cooperatives: Case Studies

Various economic, cultural, political, and organizational factors affect the integration of women into the cooperatives studied. Women's socioeconomic position and the attitudes of both men and women about women's participation in cooperatives are critical, as we have shown, but the following factors also need to be considered: (1) women's participation in the struggle for land; (2) the cooperatives' need to secure a sufficient labor force; (3) the political and organizational work of the FSLN and the mass organizations; (4) the influence of the agrarian reform technician; and (5) the political and ideological development of the cooperative.

THE CARLOS ROBERTO HUEMBES COOPERATIVE

The evolution of the Carlos Roberto Huembes Cooperative illustrates how various factors combined to encourage the full incorporation of women as members. Among the economic factors was the need of a number of landless women to find stable jobs and the cooperative's need to increase the number of members in order to meet crop production plans. Key political factors were the political awareness of FSLN supporters and the work of the mass organizations in promoting the collectivization of individual plots of land.

Women were present at the cooperative's founding meetings. In September 1979, seventeen peasant households participated in a meeting to discuss the creation of a production cooperative. Seven of the participants (six men and one woman), who had been long-time FSLN supporters, decided to collectivize their land. Among them was a widow with two daughters; she saw that collectivizing would free her from the problem of finding male laborers for the agricultural tasks that she could not perform. Another advantage for this family was that the new cooperative assumed the debt they owed to the bank. Joining the cooperative also ensured that family members of both sexes would have permanent employment.

The provisional steering committee of the Huembes cooperative included a woman, the wife of one of the peasants. She was in charge of education and cultural activities. This showed the willingness of the group to put both women and men in leadership positions and to let both persons in a couple become cooperative members. Another example of the mechanisms that encouraged the gradual integration of women into this cooperative was their participation in a technical and organizational seminar to which all farmers and wage workers in the community were invited. Out of seventy-eight people who completed the seminar, eighteen were women.

Since the cooperative had sufficient land but not enough workers to carry out its projects, it decided to accept landless workers, both men and women, as members. From the start of collective production, women had the same rights as men. The ATC, UNAG, and FSLN activists played a key role in developing a clear understanding within the cooperative of the importance of equality between men and women members. This process was also reinforced by the fact that the agrarian reform technician assigned to help create the cooperative was a woman. The members say that her example as a revolutionary woman was an inspiration for everyone. When the cooperative began to prepare its official constitution in 1982, thirteen out of thirty-four members were women. As a result of all these factors, the Carlos Roberto Huembes cooperative is one of the most cohesive of those studied.

THE GERMAN POMARES PRODUCTION COOPERATIVE
The German Pomares Production Cooperative began when four communities took over a small area of the hacienda belonging to the Pastora family. Entire families settled on the occupied land to defend it. Initially they formed five separate cooperatives, each affiliated with a different community. Although women had taken part in the land takeover, the level of female integration into the cooperatives was not uniform and in no case equal to that of men. In some of the cooperatives men refused to let women participate in collective production, arguing that women "could not produce equally." The cooperative finally agreed to assign a plot of 5 manzanas to five women, who planted the area in corn and beans. In another of the cooperatives six women were allowed to participate in the collective work, but here, too, some men resisted. Eventually they relented, but the women were paid only three-quarters of what the men earned.

In 1982 four of the five cooperatives joined to form a single unit, which became the German Pomares Production Cooperative. During this merging process the topic of the role of women was again discussed. Some of the members defended the participation of women on the grounds that they were good workers, that they had always worked in agriculture, and that they could perform most agricultural tasks. This position was supported by the FSLN delegate from the area, a woman. After long discussion the majority put into their cooperative law that women had "earned their place in the cooperative" because of their role in the struggle for land, and that "all members of the cooperative had the same rights and duties regardless of whether they are women or men." The contribution of the FSLN delegate was a positive influence on the integration of women into this cooperative.

THE ARNOLDO QUANT PRODUCTION COOPERATIVE
In the Arnoldo Quant Production Cooperative in Leon, women also participated in the initial land takeover, but their full integration has been slower. The problem lies in the cooperative's own requirement that all members be heads of households; thus, only two female household heads became members. Although the wives and daughters of the male household heads participate in agricultural production as wage workers, they are not considered cooperative members.

Another factor is that the widows who are heads of households send their sons to do field work rather than participating themselves. As a result, many cooperative members think that it has only male members. Although four of the seventeen male members also send others to do their field work, the fact that women members engage in this practice has given them a certain stigma. The cooperative has not even recognized the existence of women members, nor initially did it encourage their integration.

However, because of the need for field workers, the cooperative uses a high percentage of women workers. Over half of those who work daily in the fields are not cooperative members but female relatives. In this case it is the high demand for workers that has helped female family members to participate in production. Because of the active participation of the women, the cooperative assembly finally had to recognize their contribution, and it was decided to distribute the profits in accordance with the labor contributed. This was considered the most egalitarian answer to meeting the needs of most households. At that point those who worked in the cooperative but were not household heads were given the title "associates," as distinguished from "members." The status of associates is being legalized and will be officially listed on the agrarian reform title. This means the integration of nine women, who will represent close to one-third of the membership.

Although women were not initially accepted with equal rights in this case, the high demand for workers has resulted in some progress toward the increased integration of women. The agrarian reform technician has played a decisive role in integrating women by recognizing the capability of the women and their right to participate as members. Finally, it is important to note that the cooperative itself has developed politically and ideologically. The importance of equal rights, regardless of gender, has gradually been accepted by both men and women.

THE CARLOS PEREZ ARETA PRODUCTION COOPERATIVE

In the Carlos Perez Areta Production Cooperative in Matagalpa women were not involved in the land takeovers. The hacienda that was taken over was located far from population centers, and only men participated in its occupation. Women remained in their communities taking care of their homes, their children, and their livestock. One year after the occupation of the hacienda the families moved there permanently. At this point the cooperative was functioning without the participation of women. It was not until two years after the land occupation that a few women joined the cooperative at the urging of the agrarian reform technician working with this cooperative.

ALL-WOMEN PRODUCTION COOPERATIVES

In 1982 there were four all-women production cooperatives in the country and sixteen where women represented more than 50 percent of the membership. The Blanca Arauz production cooperative, located near San Ignacio de

Tola, is one of the cooperatives made up exclusively of women. The cooperative was formed as a by-product of a soybean promotion project of MI-DINRA. A group of women was initially trained as promoters to teach soybean preparation for household consumption. A year later they demanded that they be trained in the cultivation of soybeans as well, and that they be given access to land to form a cooperative. One of them commented: "We could see that men got together in collectives; that is why we talked to the UNAG about getting land." In 1981 this cooperative obtained 6 manzanas (4.3 hectares) through UNAG (of which only two can be cultivated). Despite its small size, production problems, and the relative lack of government assistance, the cooperative survived because of the determination of its members.

The experience of the women in the Rigoberto Lopez Perez production cooperative has been somewhat different. This cooperative received its impetus from the efforts of ATC to promote collective production on state-owned lands. When the ATC began to organize the residents of the Cosmapa area in Chinandega in March 1980, women and men were invited to the first meetings. Most of the men were opposed to the proposal to collectively organize production on state-owned lands. They argued that many problems would arise because not everybody would take their responsibilities seriously. Moreover, they did not agree that women should be part of the collective because they considered them less efficient than men and unable to cope with the very demanding work. Finally, ten women and five men decided to form the cooperative and rented 50 manzanas from the state farm. They received technical assistance and a loan for their first corn crop. Later, however, the five men withdrew and only the women remained in the cooperative.

This cooperative now has its agrarian reform title to the lands previously rented from the state and is receiving strong support from the Agrarian Reform agency and the National Development Bank. Both institutions say that given the women's sense of responsibility, they are confident that their financial support is being well used. The cooperative now has a tractor and, with the profits, is able to give pregnant women a forty-day pre- and post-natal subsidy equivalent to half their salary.

These examples show how various combinations of factors and situations have had different effects on the integration of women. Even when the situation is favorable, however, women must continually struggle to transform the ideological values of their milieu and the roles to which they as women have been assigned. The desire to overcome obstacles is essential if women are to assume equal roles as producers in the agrarian reform.

Women's Participation in the Agricultural Work of the Cooperatives

In this section we analyze the different levels of participation by women cooperative members and female relatives of members in production and credit cooperatives.

In most production cooperatives with women members, the women are fully integrated into the collective enterprise with the same rights and responsibilities as the male members. They must work every day or provide a substitute when they cannot work, and they receive wages equal to the men's for a day's work. We encountered three forms of organization of agricultural work in the cooperatives, corresponding to different sexual divisions of labor: (1) sexually mixed work teams, (2) groups segregated by sex, and (3) groups of women engaged in work different and apart from the principal activity of the cooperative, which is done by men.

Theoretically, among the three forms of organization, the most advanced is the mixed work team; when men and women work together on the same task, their work is more likely to be equally valued. Although there may be a sexual division of labor within a given task, this tends not to be as marked as the sexual division of labor between tasks. When women work in separate crews, their tasks are *assumed* to be, but not always are, lighter and the men's heavier; the sexual division of labor is thus reinforced and women's work undervalued. Yet in one coffee cooperative women are firmly convinced that it is preferable to work in sexually segregated work teams, for they develop solidarity among themselves and are proud of their collective work.

Although mixed teams appear to be superior, they are not free of problems. For example, when men and women work together, jealousy has often developed among the nonmember spouses. In several cases this situation has resulted in women's having to resign their membership in the cooperative. Segregated work crews can avoid this problem. Moreover, in segregated teams women develop confidence in themselves and their work.

Women cooperative members are generally considered to be "good workers" by agrarian reform technicians. Although it is usually assumed that women cannot do all the tasks men do, it is recognized that women are as productive as men in doing certain tasks and, in some cases, are even more productive.

The majority of the production cooperatives studied give priority to family members in the hiring of seasonal or temporary wage workers. The nonmember workers are generally paid the same daily wages as members. Most women relatives view this opportunity to earn additional income very favorably and consider it one of the main advantages of having a family member in the cooperative. Nonetheless, some of the production cooperatives have expected wives and children to work in the cooperatives for free. This situation was found on several of the self-defense cooperatives; since the men were increasingly required to be on military alert, families had to take on a greater share of the field work.

In the three credit and service cooperatives studied, the majority of the women members were heads of households and solely responsible for farm operations. Nearly all of them managed the farm, made all the decisions, and also participated in field work. We found only one case of a woman farm manager who relied totally upon hired wage workers to do the field work. She was from the city and had moved to the countryside only four years before. Generally, the women members of credit and service cooperatives work their land with the help of sons and daughters. For heavier tasks, such as plowing, they rely on hired labor or the help of adult male relatives. Yet hiring male workers is often problematic for female household heads. Not only is it expensive to hire wage workers, but sometimes male workers do not respect a woman "boss" and are thus unreliable. Several women members have now made special arrangements with male cooperative members, often a reciprocal labor exchange, to assure themselves of male assistance during critical periods.

In all the credit and service cooperatives with women members, women who are not members contribute to household-based agricultural work. Among other tasks, family members plant corn, weed and harvest beans, and harvest and dry coffee. We found contradictory attitudes among some male credit and service cooperative members who valued the work of the women members but undervalued the work done by their own wives. One member of the German Pomares cooperative in Matagalpa asserted: "I'm the only one who works, she only brings me lunch. Women are not used to working in the field and they must care for the children." However, this same member expressed admiration for the women members: "They started a coffee renovation program, and their plantation is the envy of all of us." Women also negate their participation in agricultural work and undervalue the work that they do. Two women who worked almost daily in the cultivation of cabbage, with the help of younger children, said: "Here, there are no women doing agricultural work, they only work in the kitchen."

In both production and credit and service cooperatives, women members have a number of advantages over nonmembers, namely, the possibilities for growth and learning offered by the cooperatives' training program. Cooperatives train their members in both organizational and technical skills, and women members participate equally with men in these programs. Women had a keen interest in the training programs and in developing their technical competence. Household responsibilities, however, often prevent women members from attending special workshops held outside of the cooperative that require spending a night or two away from home. Young women seemed more willing to leave their children with neighbors to attend training sessions. Technical and organizational training, however, is rarely available to the women relatives of members. Moreover, male members seldom tell their wives or other relatives what they have learned. Therefore, only women members are able to develop technically and advance on a par with men.

The participation of women in cooperatives exposes them not only to technical and organizational training but also to politics. The level of political awareness shown by the women members in the majority of cooperatives is impressive, especially when compared with the level of awareness of female relatives of male members. Women members have a great commitment to the Sandinista revolution. In cooperatives that have militias, the majority of female members participate in them, but not the wives and other female relatives.

The self-defense cooperatives, however, are exceptions. The threat of contra attack has required that an increasing number of rural women participate in the defense of the cooperatives, be they members or relatives of members. In these cooperatives in the interior region of the country, the members are organized into squadrons that alternate production with round-the-clock guard duty. Female family members have been increasingly integrated into production and into daytime guard duty. The majority of women participating in defense are young women without children or older women with grown children.

The Participation of Women in the Management of Cooperatives

We have already examined the participation of women—both members and nonmembers—in cooperative agricultural work. But how much of a role do women play in cooperative decision-making processes? Are women in positions of leadership?

It is principally those cooperatives that have a high percentage of female membership that have elected a woman to the executive council of the cooperative. An executive council has five members: general secretary, financial manager, production manager, defense coordinator, and education coordinator. These positions are rotated every year, unless circumstances require changes earlier. Only the Carlos Roberto Huembes Production Cooperative in Nueva Segovia has an explicit policy of always having a woman on the council (due to the fact that women constitute 33 percent of the membership). Some factors that have facilitated the participation of these women on the councils are: (1) a higher degree of education and training of a particular woman as compared with the majority of the membership, and

(2) recognition by both men and women of the quality of a given woman's productive labor.

In general, members of both sexes had positive attitudes toward women's filling leadership roles. The cooperative members believed that the women performed their duties well and that they resolved problems collectively with the other members of the executive councils. One man stated, "From our point of view, we hope and expect that as women become leaders they will improve the cooperative." As one woman member said, "With time and training women will be able to become presidents and vice-presidents" (of cooperatives). The implication is that gender is not a limitation to occupying a leadership role, but, rather, that training is required to properly fulfill the duties of the position. We consider this attitude important because it represents an opening for women to assume these positions, even within cooperatives that presently do not have women on their executive councils.

In contrast, in cooperatives where women are not family members, gender is considered a limitation to exercising leadership duties as well as to membership. This attitude is reinforced by the values, prevalent among both men and women, that sustain women's traditional roles. The presence of women in cooperative leadership positions ensures greater attention to those problems specific to women and, therefore, encourages greater participation of women in the cooperatives. Through their understanding of the problems specific to women, women leaders have proposed different forms of work organization that permit women greater flexibility in work schedules and have paid more attention to the issues that make for successful mixed or segregated work teams, according to the wishes of members of both sexes. Councils composed solely of men, on the other hand, often have difficulty in understanding the specific problems of the women members.

In general, however, women are prevented from acquiring the same educational development and leadership training as men. Consequently, there are very few women overall who come to occupy leadership positions in the cooperatives. The problems that women confront are the "double" work day (necessary to the household's survival), childcare (which is neither shared nor valued by men), and limited access to education. As one woman said: "It would be difficult to attend more meetings than I already do, because of the small children and the things to do in the house." Moreover, the domestic duties that fall on women also restrict their ability to attend adult literacy classes, perpetuating their lower level of education in comparison with men.

In addition, the traditional social values concerning the appropriate role of women have also discouraged women from taking on leadership responsibilities in cooperatives. In the Pedro Joaquin Chamorro Production Cooperative in Tipitapa, for example, a woman was nominated for a leadership position, but she did not accept it in order to avoid personal criticism, primarily from her neighbors.

The participation of women members in cooperative decision making in general is closely related to the organizational structure of the individual cooperative and its degree of decentralization of decision making. We found two broad patterns in this regard: (1) the principal decisions are made by the executive council and then discussed and confirmed by the general assembly of the membership; and (2) the principal decisions are made in a decentralized fashion by production, finance, and education committees and subsequently presented to the general membership for approval.

In the second form more members participate in the decision-making process, which improves the likelihood that the women members will also participate. Women play the greatest role in decision making in those cooperatives that require every member to participate in a committee. Here, the women have a much deeper understanding of decisions than in other cooperatives. Sometimes, however, committees are composed of only a small portion of the membership; thus, in one cooperative only one of the ten women members sat on a committee. Since she had mathematical abilities, she was a member of the finance committee. A superior form of organization would allow all cooperative members to take part in decision making through committee membership.

When decision-making power is centralized in the executive council, the participation of women depends upon their participation in the general membership assemblies. But, in general, it is not common for women to participate actively or express their opinions in these assemblies. Many women are afraid to speak and think that "people will laugh at them" if they do. Among the few women who regularly offer their opinion, older women (usually mothers of male members) and those with a high degree of political awareness are the most outspoken. In some cooperatives the president or the technical adviser makes a special effort to ask for the opinion of women members. This practice seems to have a positive impact, since many women will share their opinion during meetings only if they are so asked. In general, many women members express their views only when there is a disruption in the meeting, with all the members talking at once.

Conclusions

The implementation of an explicit policy designed to incorporate women into the cooperatives would have a positive impact on the consolidation and expansion of the cooperative movement. It is not a coincidence that of the cooperatives studied, those with the most advanced organization were also those with high proportions of women members. This reflects their high level of political development and commitment to creating a more egalitarian society based on equality between the sexes.

It appears that family ties among cooperative members have played a positive role in the organizational consolidation of the cooperatives. They have helped create group identity and confidence among the members. This is particularly true in the production cooperatives studied where the majority of women members are wives of male members. Among these couples we found a very strong commitment to the collective process. The wife who is a member not only gives her husband moral support but also political, economic, and technical support, since she is developing equally with him.

The participation of women members also has a positive impact on production. The women are considered excellent workers; they are careful in their work and very responsible. The male members frequently commented that the women are an example to them, and that the women are considered a force of stability and cohesion with the cooperative.

Under conditions of labor scarcity—which some of the cooperatives face—the incorporation of women as members can increase the labor pool. Many cooperatives also need to diversify their productive activities if they are going to generate profits, and the incorporation of women into special projects might be a way of both offering employment to women and expanding the cooperative's activities.

Until now, the Cooperative Law has provided for the incorporation of women into the production cooperatives, but it is not explicit regarding women's participation in the credit and service cooperatives, the ones made up of small and medium-sized farmers who usually own their land. In the majority of cases, the members of the credit and service cooperatives tend to be household heads, usually men. The only women participating in them are female heads of households (usually widows or single women who own land in their own names). The incorporation of female family members would be an important step in the consolidation of these cooperatives as well as in the economic and political development of rural women.

Although women's membership in cooperatives is small, men's and women's lives are beginning to be transformed in them. Political activists and state technicians do not consistently encourage women's participation, as policy might predict. The incorporation of women into cooperatives as members is a necessary, but not a sufficient, condition to ensure that women will develop equally with men. As we have seen, the actual situation of women departs from the stated goal of the Cooperative Law to fully incorporate women under the same conditions as men.

Our findings suggest the importance of undertaking educational work in the countryside. It is important not only to make the provisions of the

Cooperative Law known but also to carry out a systematic consciousness-raising campaign about the position of women. This campaign should initially target state bureaucrats and the activists in the rural mass organizations. The first item on the agenda must be the social recognition of women's work. The second, if the goal of creating a more egalitarian society is to be reached, is to recognize women's demands not only as workers and farmers, but as women.

Notes

1. See C. D. Deere, "Rural Women and State Policy: The Latin American Reform Experience," *World Development* 13 (Fall 1985): 1037–53, C. D. Deere and Magdalena Leon, eds., *Rural Women and State Policy: Feminist Perspectives on Latin American Development* (Boulder, Colo.: Westview, 1987).

2. See Martha Luz Padilla, Clara Murguialday, and Ana Criquillon, "La Reforma Agraria Sandinista: su impacto sobre la situación de subordinación de la mujer rural" (CIERA–ATC, June 1985; Paper presented to the 45th Congress of Americanists, Bogotá, Colombia, July 1985).

3. Maxine Molyneux provides the figure of 34 percent female heads for Nicaragua (60 percent in Managua) in "Mobilization Without Emancipation? Women's Interests, the State, and Revolution," *Transition and Development: Problems of Third World Socialism*, ed. Richard Fagen, Carmen Diana Deere and Jose Luis Coraggio (New York: Monthly Review, 1986), p. 296.

4. Luz Padilla, Marta Perez, and Nyurka Perez. "La Mujer Semi-Proletaria" (Managua: CIERA, 1981).

5. Ibid, pp. 4, 59, 60.

6. Ibid.

7. 1971 Agricultural Census.

8. For a fuller discussion of Sandinista agrarian reform policies in the first two years of the revolution and how these changed with the Agrarian Reform Law of 1981, see Joseph Collins, *Nicaragua: What Difference Could a Revolution Make?* (San Francisco: Institute for Food and Development Policy, 1985).

9. National Census of Cooperatives 1982; UNAG-BND-DGRA-CIERA. This area increased markedly in 1983 because of the land titling.

10. Agricultural Cooperative Law, chap. III, art. 8.

11. General By-Law of the Agricultural Cooperative Law, art. 132.

12. Art. 30.

IV

Tinkering with Bureaucracy: Internal Politics, Procedures, and Plans

12/Women in FAO Projects: Cases from Asia, the Near East, and Africa

Alice Carloni

Since the International Women's Year (1975) and the World Conference on Agrarian Reform and Rural Development (1979), efforts have been made to see that attention is given to the needs of rural women who are doing much of the work involved in Food and Agricultural Organization (FAO)–assisted agricultural field projects. A variety of techniques have been tried: women's projects, components for women within larger projects directed to men, and projects addressed to "people" on the assumption that women will automatically benefit when the sector is one in which they are involved.

How are women integrated into mainstream FAO projects? At what stages of the projects' cycles, from design through implementation and evaluation, are attempts made to learn about or involve women? Ten case studies of selected FAO field projects were carried out in 1982. The projects selected were in sectors where women were known to be involved: poultry, post-harvest processing and storage of food grain, sheep and goat production, and irrigation. Also, the projects selected were those in which the role of women was brought to the attention of project staff at some time during the project cycle. The cases, therefore, are a highly select group. Written reports, and discussions with concerned staff members, including those from the field and FAO headquarters, were the basis for analysis. The full 103-

The case studies of rural poultry projects are based on a report by Elizabeth Mollard, the PFL projects on a report by Lauren Lissner, the livestock and the integrated rural development projects on a report by Clare Oxby, and the case study of the irrigation project was prepared by Alice Carloni. Special thanks go to the FAO Prevention of Food Losses Programme, the Animal Production Service, the Water Resources Development and Management Service, the Home Economics and Social Programmes Service, and the Agricultural Operations Service for their generous and painstaking support throughout the entire period.

page, single-spaced report, *Integrating Women in Agricultural Projects: Case Studies of Ten FAO-Assisted Field Projects* (1983), was never widely disseminated. This highly condensed version contains three of the cases from Asia, Africa, and the Near East, rather than all ten cases. In each case, women were addressed at different stages of the project cycle: in Asia, belated attention with potentially hopeful yet fatal follow up; in the Near East, limited attention throughout; in Africa, early design attention but subsequent marginalization of efforts to reach women. For each case, I describe project goals and operations. I then analyze the work the women do in each area that is relevant to the project; women's work varies tremendously and generalizations about that would be hazardous. Finally, I provide an overview of each project cycle. First, however, I examine some conventional answers to women's integration.

The process approach used herein involves dissecting all stages of project design and implementation to determine how, when, and where adjustments can be made to include, benefit, and give voice to women. As such, the analysis provides guidance about how to change existing mainstream projects or how to recast project administration. In the course of analysis, the limitations of conventional answers for administrative reform will become apparent.

Some Conventional Answers to Women's Integration

What are some action recommendations that have been enthusiastically put forth as possible solutions to women's integration in agricultural and rural development projects? In various development agencies, people focus on staffing balance, improved information, design and evaluation procedural adjustments, and local participation. Readers might reflect on these issues as I dissect the cases to shed light on what works, what does not, and why, in order to consider how strategies might be refined for action.

USE MORE WOMEN TO IDENTIFY AND FORMULATE MISSIONS?
In overwhelming numbers, men staff many development agencies, from top-level decision-making positions to field-level management and operations. Male colleagues commonly voice objections to efforts to assist women in agricultural production. These range from "I'm an agricultural expert; integration of women is not my job"; "Concern with women's control of income is Western influence"; "Benefits to households trickle down to women automatically"; to "All this emphasis on women's role in production undermines the family." Still, some male project staff members recognize the

need to include women, however late this may have been in the project cycle.

Will the inclusion of women experts on project identification and formulation teams be a panacea? Women's programs often advocate this strategy for reasons of equity and expertise. Women in development (WID) experts sometimes work in isolation from the rest of the team members, or information on rural women's work goes unutilized.

HIRE CONSULTANTS TO DO BASELINE STUDIES ON RURAL WOMEN?

Information on social structure, culture, and gender is not always available to management and technical staff. Knowledge about the division of labor in local farming systems can be useful in clarifying assumptions about the characteristics of the intended beneficiaries and their interest in the solutions proposed by the project. Where this is not done, project efficiency will decrease, as inputs and assistance will be directed toward men when the producers are women.[1] Yet, will the information collected be used rather than overlooked, and who is responsible for assuring its use? The *linkage* of baseline information to evaluation is crucial.

Along with this, explicit mention of rural women in project documents is important because it reduces the chance that they will be overlooked during project implementation. In FAO's projects none of those that made explicit reference to rural women in the project document overlooked them entirely during implementation. On the other hand, all of the projects that made no reference to women in the original project documents for the longer study on which this chapter is based overlooked them, some for as long as ten years.

EMPLOY BETTER TIMING IN THE PROJECT CYCLE?

It is generally accepted that when women are taken into account early in the project cycle, their integration in projects is more effective. For this reason, FAO has given more attention to integrating women in new projects than to reorienting existing ones. Yet opportunities are also available in later stages of the project cycle, shedding new light on the importance of timing. Without attention to ongoing projects (not to mention routine program implementation), gender gaps would be perpetuated and aggravated in the vast bulk of agency resource allocation. After periodic reviews, new components can be added or whole projects can be reoriented. A good example of the former occurred in a large-scale agricultural project in Jamaica. By the time the project ended the women's component was one of the few items in the project deemed unequivocally successful by people in the area and project reviewers.[2]

INCREASE LOCAL PARTICIPATION?

Local people's participation in project design, implementation, and evaluation has long been discussed as means by which to improve management, to secure better information, and ultimately to empower people. Rarely, however, are gender dimensions of such participation articulated.[3] If only men participate, obviously these positive outcomes may not occur.

MONITOR PROJECT EFFECTS ON WOMEN?

Projects typically have a formal system for reporting progress toward achieving their objectives: distribution of inputs, completion of activities, listing of outputs, and periodic evaluation of adoption rates or changes in yields. In addition, the reports of the project directors and field staff often touch on matters of substance, for example, the finding that incentives for the adoption of the technical package may be less than anticipated. Rarely, though, do projects have formal systems for monitoring and evaluating the effects on women's workload, employment, income, and access to resources. Were such systems present, project management and staff would regularly receive the kind of information that could prompt reorientation toward involving and benefiting women.

How can project management be motivated to seek such information? One strategy is through official policy to disaggregate all evaluation data by gender. Then, to the extent policy is enforced and to the extent "people-data" are collected, information on women will be available. Another strategy emphasizes making project managers aware of the relevance of women for project objectives, so that they do their work more effectively. If project managers are held accountable for project performance, they will have a stake in using such information. The same project director who lacks interest in reaching women or in monitoring project effects on them then has a reason to be interested in women's incentives for adoption of the technical solutions proposed by the project. Women's incentives, in turn, depend on their returns for investment of time and resources in relation to the risks. If the new cropping system increases women's workload without adequate compensation, their incentives will not be great.

EMPHASIZE WOMEN'S PROJECTS OR WOMEN'S COMPONENTS?

There is no inherent reason why a large-scale agricultural project cannot recognize women's role in production and then design baseline surveys, technical solutions, training, and extension with village women's needs clearly in mind. A limitation of women's projects is that they typically have smaller budgets. A comparison of the budgets in the larger study on which this chapter is based is instructive: the women's project was US$62,000. The others were between US$225,000 and US$500,000. In other agencies, such as the U.S. Agency for International Development (AID), the gap is even more glaring.[4]

A women's component is a kind of transitional strategy toward full integration in mainstream activity. It, too, faces difficulties, for example: delays in recruitment, which reduces the component's effectiveness; deletion or rejection when the need for them is not appreciated; their vulnerability to budget cuts when funding is tight.

Case Studies

When small-scale traditional production is in women's hands, the success of the project depends on whether or not women adopt the technical solutions proposed. For this to be possible, rural women must be informed about innovative practices, have incentives for adopting them, and have the time and resources to invest in production. None of this is automatic: first, reaching rural women with extension advice poses different problems from that of reaching men—problems whose solution requires planning. Second, the question of women's incentives raises a complex set of issues regarding the distribution of returns to their labor depending on who controls the crop and its sale. Third, the problem of time availability takes on a different meaning when women's competing production, household, and family roles are included in the analysis. Fourth, factors that, although they do not openly discriminate against women, inadvertently restrict their access to land allotments, loans, or farmers' organizations pose challenges for project design and implementation, if the broadest possible spectrum of producers is to benefit.

NATIONAL PROGRAMME FOR RURAL POULTRY (ASIA)
Project Goals. Within the context of government efforts to increase the supply of animal protein available in rural areas, the project aims to raise the productivity of commercial and backyard poultry production.[5] This is to be accomplished by:

- establishing poultry disease and diagnostic laboratories and poultry demonstration and multiplication centers;
- improving local breeds through research;
- multiplying improved breeds and distributing them to commercial poultrymen and village poultry keepers;
- improving veterinary assistance and implementing a nationwide poultry vaccination campaign;

• training poultry technicians, livestock assistance, commercial poultrymen, extension workers, and villagers; and
• providing assistance in marketing poultry products.

At the village level the project aims at transforming traditional scavenging systems—where birds roam freely during the daytime, feeding on wild
plants and household scraps—into semi-intensive systems, where birds are
kept in an enclosure and feed is brought to them. This will require the
construction of enclosures and houses for chickens to roost in. It also means
that some land must be set aside for on-farm production of feeds. Someone
will have to grow the feeds and take responsibility for the daily feeding and
watering of birds and cleaning the enclosures. Villagers' dependency on
outside veterinary and marketing assistance and outside sources of feed in-
tegrators and vaccines will increase. The aim is to upgrade traditional systems of production and transform them into viable commercial ventures.

Women's Work. Of rural households throughout this Moslem country,
80 percent keep an average of twelve chickens scavenging on the ground.
These chickens are cared for by women and girls, who do all of the work,
make decisions regarding production, and dispose of the chickens and eggs.
For some women, the sale of eggs is an important source of income. Wom-
en's husbands are often absent from the farm for prolonged periods because
they are doing off-farm work elsewhere.

Project Cycles. During the first three years of project operations all
attention was focused on establishing poultry multiplication centers, poultry
disease and diagnostic laboratories, and poultry demonstration centers. Research into improved breeds was undertaken, and multiplication of breeds
began. The first groups of poultry technicians, veterinary officers, and commercial poultrymen were trained.

Meanwhile, plans were made for the distribution of improved breeds to
commercial poultrymen and villagers, together with a package of extension
advice aimed at raising productivity. But before the improved breeds could
be distributed, a massive poultry vaccination campaign was needed at the
village level to eliminate sources of contagion that might wipe out the new
breeds.

Typically, a livestock assistant would make the rounds of each village
once every ninety days to vaccinate all of the local birds. After some time
it was found that the birds kept by village women were being missed. Male
livestock assistants were able to visit only those homes where a man was
present, because purdah restricts contact between village women and men
who are not their relatives. Therefore it was culturally inappropriate for the
livestock assistant to visit women's homes to vaccinate their birds when
their husbands were not around. Many men had migrated in search of work.

The livestock assistants' busy schedule did not permit them to make a return trip to the village to vaccinate the birds that were missed during the first visit.

Because the unvaccinated birds were a potential source of contagion for all of the rest, the introduction of improved breeds had to be delayed until all of the villagers' birds had been vaccinated. The success of the project strategy as a whole depended on reaching village women.

Since male livestock assistants could not make contact with village women, the project director decided to train women. In the province where the initial discovery was made, a pilot project for the establishment of rural development centers at district level was just getting under way. Each center was to have a female extension worker coordinated by the Ministry of Social Welfare, however, and not by the Ministry of Agriculture. Before these female extension workers could be used by the poultry project, an interministerial agreement had to be reached.

After discussions between ministries, the following arrangement was made: the Ministry of Social Welfare was to provide thirty-eight female trainees and absorb the costs of training; the poultry project was responsible for providing the actual technical training. The women would then be used in the poultry vaccination campaign and related extension activities. In this way, a solution was found at no additional cost to the poultry project.

In the other four provinces there were as yet no plans for establishing rural development centers, so an alternative solution had to be found. A pilot project for "Women's Participation in Rural Poultry Development" was formulated, as follows. A female poultry technician would be appointed as coordinator. A local woman who had received training at the National Poultry Research Institute in connection with an earlier FAO project was identified as a suitable candidate. Four female extension supervisors would receive six months' training at the Poultry Research Institute. Upon completion of their course, each would train three or four village-level female extension workers in her district. After completing their in-service training, each village-level worker would launch extension activities among women in two villages, under the guidance of her supervisor.

During the implementation of the pilot project an unanticipated problem arose. The mobility of the female extension workers was hampered because unaccompanied female travel is frowned upon in rural areas of this country. The problem could be solved by hiring female chaperones to accompany them, but the proposal that the ministry pay their salaries met with some resistance.

An as-yet unresolved problem remains that of motivating the female extension workers to spend more time in the villages. The difficulties appear greater for female extension workers than for males. The ministry also expressed concern about the relatively higher dropout rate of female extension workers trained by the program, but this fear proved unjustified, as only one woman dropped out before completing the course.

Project evaluation data produced as many questions about what remained unknown, as what was known. When the project ended 390 female extension workers had received training. The project trained a total of 4,693 villagers in the five provinces, and a substantial but unknown proportion of these were known to be women. The training of 3,344 students was also reported, without separate figures for girls' schools. The project also trained 368 veterinary officers, 70 poultry technicians, and 552 commercial poultrymen, but no separate figures were available for women to document the unlikely proposition that women were among them.

The project director's terminal report contains no information regarding the impact of the project on poultry keeping at village level. Have village women switched from traditional scavenging systems to semi-intensive production? The only information regards the number of crossbreed cockerels distributed to villagers and the number of birds vaccinated. There is no information on rates of adoption, and no way of knowing whether only the wealthier women in the villages have found the package attractive.

In other words, it is not known whether the effort to transform backyard poultry into a commercially viable and sustainable enterprise has been successful. The project marketing component was never implemented because of lack of funds in the final years of the project. Therefore, villagers received no assistance in marketing their eggs. Yet most women do not go to the market because of purdah; they have always sold eggs to neighbors within the village.

A great deal more information is available regarding the impact of the project on the activities and yields of commercial poultrymen. However, there is no information on how the increase in the supply of eggs from the commercial sector has affected the market for eggs produced by village women. There is no way of knowing whether rural families set aside some of their eggs for home consumption as opposed to selling them all, or whether the increased supply has increased their consumption by poor households.

A project continuation proposal was formulated for "Development of Women's Participation in Rural Poultry," with the aim to train a cadre of 150 female extension workers during the first year of operation. Those extension workers would then be posted to villages to initiate poultry-related extension activities, under the supervision of the coordinator and the four female extension supervisors trained in the original pilot project. During the second year fifty poultry units were to be established in each village, with a minimum of fifty layer hens per unit, along with fifty vegetable production units. Presumably, the women would use the chicken manure to fertilize their vegetable gardens. Training in nutrition, health, and home economics would also be provided. Instead of the Ministry of Agriculture, the Women's Bureau would coordinate the project.

Strong government support for the follow-up project appears to have been expressed when the project was located in the Ministry of Agriculture, but the Women's Bureau was anxious to take it over. As soon as the project was transferred to the Women's Bureau in the Ministry of Social Welfare, it was dropped from the government's list of priority projects in the U.N. pipeline.

FIELD LOSS ASSESSMENT AND PREVENTION (NEAR EAST)

Project Goals. The overall aim of the project is to reduce food losses at farm and village levels in two populous and agriculturally fertile regions. Specific objectives include: the assessment of storage losses at farm and community levels, the organization of an in-service training program in storage technology for extension officers, and practical demonstrations in villages on the storage and management of grain, including insect and rodent control.

The steps outlined in the project work plan include: the development of a viable technical package based on improvement of existing storage facilities; the construction of prototypes; the training of extension workers for the loss-assessment survey; the implementation of the loss-assessment survey; planning and implementing demonstrations in four pilot villages; the evaluation of the experience as a basis for planning the in-service training of other extension personnel; the preparation of educational materials and a training manual; the implementation of the in-service training program for extension workers.

Gender and the Division of Labor. Though women supervise the keeping of grains once they are moved to the house, it is men who control most cash expenditures, even when working abroad. Therefore a program for improved storage practices must reach both men and women, whose complex work dynamics and interactions are worth discussing in some detail. Between one-third and one-half of all adult males have emigrated to the oil-producing countries of the Arabian Gulf. As a result, the country has a surplus of capital (from incoming remittances) and a shortage of agricultural labor. Some of the highest rates of emigration in the country are found in the areas where this project is being implemented.

However, because deep-seated cultural and religious attitudes restrict women's participation in activities outside the household, the shortage of adult males has not led women to assume tasks formerly performed by males. On the contrary, families have used cash remittances to hire tractors to substitute for male labor in preparing land for sowing. Furthermore, the new cash wealth has allowed those households with more capital to hire others to do the work their own women previously did. Women are withdrawing from agricultural work in the fields to spend more time secluded in the household, in emulation of women in higher socioeconomic groups.

The emigration of men has not increased women's voice in household expenditures and farming decisions because the absent men either dictate decisions on expenditures and other matters from abroad or delegate their authority to a male kinsman present in the village.

The current cash surplus together with the government policy of unrestricted imports has had a startling effect on the local diet. Whereas in the past this consisted of breads and porridges made of locally produced sorghum and millet, imported wheat is now rapidly replacing sorghum as the staple food grain. Decisions regarding household food expenditure are in male hands, as men do the marketing. Moreover, most of the incoming remittances are being spent on consumption, such as bridewealth, house construction, luxury goods like televisions, radio-cassette players, and gold, or on the construction of new business, such as purchasing taxis and trucks. Little productive investment has been made in agriculture, especially in the drier rain-fed areas where agricultural holdings are small and located on mountain terraces.

Statistics point to declining agricultural production and increasing reliance on imported foods. However, households give continuing care to grains they produce once harvested, dried, threshed, and brought into the household for storage. Grains are still an important form of security and savings. Sorghum is important as a reserve stock. Grain harvest and storage—the focus of the project—is largely in women's hands.

The harvesting of the major cereal crops, sorghum and millet, is predominantly the work of women, though male labor is used in some areas. It is done by hand, with simple (imported) sickles. For most varieties of millet and sorghum, the heads are cut and transported to the threshing floors for drying by men, women, and children. Losses during the transport are not perceived by farmers.

Threshing is, in general, a male task. Even before the emigration-induced labor shortage, low-status males from other communities were brought in to thresh on a day-hire basis, and women have always done some of the threshing. Given the present labor shortage, however, adequate labor for this task is a serious problem. Threshing methods involve the use of long sticks, though sometimes animals or even tractors are driven over the grains. No loss assessment has been conducted on the various methods.

Winnowing is women's work; they sit in groups on rooftops, picking out stones and excess chaff to clean the grain. Grains to be used as seeds are separated from the rest at harvest time and given preferential treatment throughout the drying, threshing, and winnowing process.

Placing the grains in storage is a cooperative effort among all household members, with differential treatment given to the various grains. Where grains are placed depends on whether they are intended to be kept as seed, as human food in the household, as grain to be marketed, or as imperfect produce to be given to animals. The first two categories of grain are most carefully stored in an assortment of plastic and metal containers, ranging from plastic jerrycans to oil drums. Grains to be marketed, if there are any, are often dumped in the corner of a room on an upper level of the house or are, at best, placed in gunny sacks ready for transport. Grains to be used as animal feed are stored loosely near where the stalks are stored, as these are the most important element in animal fodder. Women are the caretakers of the grain once it is stored in the household. Most villages have local mills where women take the grains to be ground into flour on a weekly basis.

Project Cycles. The final project document states in sparse fashion: "since farm women have a role in activities related to the storage of grain, efforts will be made to involve them in the demonstration of improved storage techniques." None of the corresponding inputs, activities, and outputs described in the document specifies the participation of women; no funds are earmarked for special women's activities. Home economics extension workers are not named in the project document as beneficiaries of the project's pre-service and in-service training program in storage technology, nor does the document specify women as a target audience for the practical, village-level demonstrations of grain-management techniques.

The project's three major activities have been a farm storage loss-assessment survey, training programs for extension workers, and practical village-level demonstrations. The evaluation mission found that the loss-assessment survey was successful in providing "the necessary experience and knowledge . . . of current farm storage practices and problems." However, the technical report describing the survey *makes no mention of the division of labor* in storage-related tasks or of socioeconomic factors to be considered in the selection and introduction of simple improvements in traditional storage facilities.

On the other hand, reports of the training program on storage technology provide evidence that special efforts were made to include women in project activities: nine training courses were conducted, one of which was "for ladies only." A group of home economists was given an in-service refresher course on "how to store food grains," which included a slide story on food grain preservation with "37 colored slides, commentary in Arabic and set to music." The participants also were given free supplies of pesticides for use in village demonstrations.

Despite conflicting reports concerning the number of female participants (six versus fifteen), there appears to be no doubt that men received more attention in training activities; 165 male extension workers were trained.

Their courses were considerably longer than the one-day session for home economists, and official reports of the training courses were produced. The comparatively low numbers of home economists trained is probably the consequence of the scarcity of suitable personnel for such training.

When asked to comment on the scant involvement of women in training activities, the project manager made the following comments:

Till date, 127 candidates have been trained at the Central Agricultural Research Station. Of course, not a single lady has been trained. These candidates are selected by a powerful committee, and the project does not have the required status to argue forcefully before that committee. Secondly, the Rural Development Project has 73 extension officers; none of them is a lady. . . . How can the training to ladies be given when ladies are not being selected for training?

With reference to village demonstration, the review mission report made no mention of any special effort to promote women's participation. The project manager's report on demonstration programs noted that only one of the thirteen village demonstrations had any female participants: "For the first time, six ladies attended this program, besides 20 people *[sic]*." This is his only mention of female participation.

In the final stages of the project a consultant was recruited for a two-week consultation in which she was to make a critical assessment of the socioeconomic implications of project activities and to assist in planning improved demonstrations and extension activities, particularly with respect to women's role in post-harvest activities. Her observations on patterns of land ownership, family decision making, the division of labor in post-harvest operations, and knowledge and attitudes toward post-harvest tasks provided the only available background information on the social and economic context of the project, especially in relation to the female target audience. Ideally, of course, the socioeconomic information should have been made available much earlier in the project cycle.

Although the consultant did not attempt to assess the project's impact on women in the target villages, she did comment that post-harvest mechanization may have a positive impact because family labor is often insufficient as a result of migration, and "cultural norms put a high value on seclusion of women which is related to both religiosity as well as to high social status. . . . Women would welcome mechanization for it would mean relief from an already arduous workload and the luxury of leisure. This, to them, is development." However, this particular project does not focus on mechanization, but rather on farm and community-level grain storage.

The evaluation mission did not report the existence of any data that could be used to monitor the effects of the project on women. They did recommend that "efforts should be continued to reach farm families, especially women, through the mass media.'' The project director submitted a second project proposal to follow up and expand on the activities of the first two phases, providing more effective storage facilities such as improved oil drums and introducing collective storage facilities at village level. Although women are identified as a target audience for extension activities at village levels and female extension workers are to receive training, women have not been consulted about their interest in and reservations about transferring household grain stocks to a village center.

TECHNICAL ASSISTANCE FOR LIVESTOCK DEVELOPMENT (AFRICA)
Project Goals. The FAO technical assistance project is only a small part of a larger investment project for livestock development whose overall objective is to produce a marketable surplus of meat products for urban markets and export. The immediate objectives of the FAO technical project are to contribute to the socioeconomic development of arid zones by organizing herders' associations, by introducing improved livestock production techniques, and by increasing forage capacity through provision of water. The project is being implemented in two areas.

Although activities vary somewhat in the two project areas, the technical solutions proposed by the project focus on drilling wells and boreholes to develop pastures; improving pasture management through control of brush fires, research, and development of land use regulations; improving animal health through extension advice; establishing a temporary fund for credit; and studying potential market outlets for meat products.

The target group is intended to be the small herders and sedentary farmers in newly formed herders' associations. Emphasis is on cattle, although draught animals and small ruminants (sheep and goats) are included at one site. The overall approach of the project is described in the project document as "participatory, endogenous and integrated." The extension component will focus on improved methods of herd management, pasture management, and animal health, with herders' associations as the main vehicle.

Women's Work. A detailed baseline study conducted in the project areas by the women's extension expert in collaboration with the project extension specialist revealed that among pastoral peoples, all women own animals, which they acquire by gift (birth or marriage), inheritance, or purchase. This includes milk cows in addition to sheep and goats. In the eastern project area most of the herds of small ruminants belong to women.

Among sedentary agricultural peoples women may also own animals, but not as many. They are purchased out of the savings from the sale of grain from women's own plots, handicrafts, or milk. Women also inherit animals according to Moslem custom. Although sheep and goats are the preferred form of investment, the deterioration of ecological and economic conditions since the Sahel drought in the early 1970s has forced women to use their savings to buy food for their families and left no surplus with which to buy animals.

Even where women own animals, men intervene in their management. Household heads pay all animal taxes, usually by selling young males from the herd. Herdsmen (different ethnic groups for small ruminants and for cattle) follow herds in return for a certain quantity of grain per head of livestock per season and rights to all milk on the evening before the Moslem holy day (Friday). Women do not herd animals.

In the northern area milking is done by the shepherd or by young boys, or in their absence, by girls. Women are responsible for going each day to get the milk from the shepherd, but this task is often delegated to children. In the eastern region women and children milk sheep and goats.

Whoever does the milking, women control the milk and its processing. They determine how much to retain for household use and how much to sell or barter. Production is usually barely sufficient for household consumption and the needs of nursing animals. Milk is sold only when herds are large or sometimes during the rainy season when production is abundant. Women have a monopoly of goat and sheep milk from the family herds, whether the animals are owned by their husband or themselves.

Pastoral peoples exchange milk for grain: one bowlful of fresh milk or two of sour milk are exchanged for a bowlful of sorghum or millet. Butter is made primarily for home consumption, but cooked butter with onions and millet brings women a nice profit in village markets.

The ownership of animals plays an important social security function for women. It assures them a supply of milk for themselves and their children. Animals can also be readily converted into cash in time of need. Women sell young male animals to get females for milk production. They also sell animals to buy clothing for themselves and their children, to buy gold and jewelry, or to help family members in times of need. They have had to sell animals more often to help meet family expenses since the Sahelian drought.

Among pastoral peoples a woman has the right to sell animals she owns on her own initiative, even against her husband's will. Among sedentary peoples the husband cannot sell his wife's animals without consulting her, but she cannot sell them against his will. Although the decision to sell rests with the woman, the husband handles the actual transaction for her.

Whether among pastoral or sedentary peoples, men are responsible for supplying the basic household staples of millet and sorghum, whereas women are responsible for supplying the condiments for these staples such as beans, onions, vegetables, peppers, and salt. Men and boys grow family-consumed grains on the husband's plot. Women have their own individual plots on which they and their daughters grow grains and condiments. The millet and sorghum that women grow is their own, to dispose of as they wish.

The husband's grain is kept in one granary; the wife's, in a separate one. The wife keeps the key to her own granary; the husband's mother or sister keeps his key. In polygynous marriages each wife has her own granary, and the wives take turns supplying the condiments depending on whose turn it is to cook.

Only when the husband is unable to supply grain for the family is the wife expected to dip into her own reserves to come to his aid. She is free to sell her own grain for cash and is more likely, among sedentary peoples, to have a surplus to invest in animals than men. The drought has lowered yields, and surpluses are no longer available for the purchase of animals.

In addition to their contribution to animal production and agriculture, women are responsible for daily grinding of grains, fetching water, spinning cotton into thread and weaving cloth for garments, preparing food, and replastering mud huts. Fetching wood is women's work among agriculturalists but men's work among pastoral peoples.

The efforts of the project to build up herds to predrought levels should recognize traditional ownership by women as well as men and understand the mechanisms by which women accumulate a cash surplus for investment in animals; these include the sale of grain from their own plots, milk, cooked butter, and handicrafts.

Project Cycles. At the time the project was formulated the future project manager visited FAO headquarters. During his visit he was introduced to a home economics officer who was knowledgeable about the country where the project was to be implemented. After learning of the project's objectives and scope, she stressed the importance of women's role in livestock production and the transformation of milk products, and proposed that a component for women be included.

Since the project document had already been drafted and there was no time for an integral revision, the two of them agreed to amend it to add reference to "women's extension" in the section of the project document that specified the "contributions required by the present project," and a U.N. volunteer post for the women's component was tacked on to the project without specifying its relationship to the project as a whole.

Upon returning to the country, the project manager discussed the women's component with the government, and a decision was made to upgrade the U.N. volunteer post to that of a full-fledged expert. The terms of reference for the women's extension expert were drawn up in consultation with the headquarters home economics officer. They state that the expert will be responsible for organizing the female population in the project area for participation in animal production and the marketing of animal products; promoting action to raise the level of living of herders' families through activities such as vegetable cultivation, crafts, sewing, basic literacy action, and the introduction of appropriate household technologies; developing a women's extension program and training two national counterparts; and contributing to all other project activities as needed.

The first activity that the women's extension expert was to carry out was a study on the role of women in the two project areas, to shed light on the division of labor and decision-making roles of men and women in crop and animal production as well as household tasks, the ownership and management of herds by men and women and the way animals are acquired, the division of the products of crop and animal production among members of the household and between home consumption and sale, the potential for including women in improved systems of animal husbandry and related project activities, and the constraints and complementary activities required to improve women's working and living conditions.

Although the baseline study was to have served as a basis for identifying ways of assisting and strengthening women's traditional role in production and family life, recruitment of the women's extension expert was delayed for an entire year. This meant that detailed information on women's role in animal production was not available during the first year and a half of project operation.

In the expert's absence, the local woman who was assigned to the project as her national counterpart went ahead on her own, without much supervision, and developed a work plan that emphasized women's household and family roles instead of their roles in crop and animal production. Plans were made for improving traditional techniques of pounding and processing millet, introducing donkey carts to transport water, constructing demonstration hearths, and providing nutrition and health education. Vegetable gardening, introducing home technology, improving fuel gathering, and organizing women's groups were also considered as possible activities.

The baseline study in the first project area was carried out eighteen months behind schedule, for the women's extension expert arrived a year late and then waited until the end of the rainy season before roads were passable for travel to the villages. The project extension expert assisted her in study formulation and implementation, contributing greatly to pertinent questions, the recommendations follow-up, and the extension activity coordination.

The baseline study in the second project area was sharper in its focus. Questions were guided by a deeper understanding of the technical strategy of the project and of women's place in it. So the second baseline study was used to find out whether village women would be interested in forming groups to increase the production of goat's milk that would be used to make cheese for sale.

In order to increase the surplus of milk for transformation into cheese, the plan was to sensitize women to the need to concentrate on the births of animals during the rainy season when forage is most plentiful. In the absence of refrigeration, women's groups would make this product into cheese. Upon receiving the earnings from the sale of cheese, the women would reinvest them in goats (which are the most common way of keeping savings in the local area).

The project would also sensitize women to the need to renew their herds through the sale of animals that were past their productive prime and the purchase of young animals. Women would also be a target of a campaign for the vaccination of sheep and goats and the reduction of the death rate of calves. The project would prepare audiovisual aids for use in teaching women the proper hygiene when milking and handling milk products to make cheese. The improvement of rural poultry production through the introduction of cross-breed cockerels was also considered.

The success of this strategy depends on women's interest in having a large supply of milk during the rainy season for processing into cheese for sale rather than having a smaller but steady supply of milk for themselves and their children throughout the year. The nutritional impact of this strategy was not considered. Neither was the fact that women's workload is already extremely heavy during the rainy season, because all agricultural work from land preparation to planting, weeding, and harvesting is concentrated in one short season.

When faced with a choice between spending more time with lambing, milking, and making cheese for the market or growing more millet and sorghum, women may opt for the latter because of the greater security it provides for their families. The cost of purchased grain is also a key factor in this decision in comparison with the revenue from cheese, which is not a traditional product with a ready local market. Because of the cultural value placed on goats as a way of keeping savings, women may nevertheless be attracted to the idea because it allows them to build up their herds, even if it makes their food supply less secure.

The recommendations that emerged from the baseline studies were that the women's component should adopt a two-pronged approach. On the one hand, it would emphasize women's role in goat and goat cheese production. At the same time, it would focus on ways of introducing appropriate technology to lighten women's work burden in other areas such as milling grains, fetching water and fuel, and preparing meals, thereby increasing the amount of time women have at their disposal for income-generating activities.

Upon completion of the baseline studies the women's extension expert returned to her residence in the capital city, at a great distance from project headquarters. Her national counterpart was left to coordinate extension activities for women at village level on her own. In spite of the project managers' efforts to link the women's extension component with the men's, the women's component has gone ahead on its own in isolation from the rest of the project. This led the evaluation mission to recommend that the women's extension expert post be cut in Phase II and replaced with several months of consultancy funds.

CONVENTIONAL STRATEGIES: THE CASES SUMMARIZED

A comparison of all three cases reveals clearly that women's work was central to project missions but that its incorporation was grafted onto projects conceived and managed almost entirely for men. Attempts were made, usually belatedly, to change project operations using conventional strategies. In none of these three cases, nor in the full ten on which this chapter is based, did adjustments substantially improve project operations.

Is staffing the issue? Sooner or later, men who are project managers become aware that project goals go unrealized for inattention to women's work. Whether this is belated recognition, with a promising shift in design (though ultimately strategic mislocation) as in the Asian case, a weak concern about the "ladies" as in the Near Eastern case, or initial good intentions as in the African case, men sought advice from women or, more appropriately, a woman. These women were expected to develop a component or a sideline to redress gender problems that were squarely at the center of project activities.

In no case was gender staffing balance even a distant possibility, yet even if it were, outside "experts" and managers in the multilayered administration could remain oblivious to the implications and importance of a gendered conception of the division of labor and incentives. Women's work, resources, and power varied from case to case, and even from project site to project site. The generation of knowledge *about* the people to be involved, or *from* the people involved, rarely occurred at the time of the project's conception (even if the project document had wording on women). Even when knowledge came later, in the form of baseline studies or evaluations, incentives were necessary to encourage managers and staff to use that information.

What voice do local people have in project design, implementation, or evaluation? If by *local* we mean member government staff or in-country consultants, the answer is some. In the Near East case, "powerful committee" members decided who was to be trained; presumably none had an interest in recruiting women or in taking steps to increase the pool of women from which recruitment could occur. National staff may share a gender ideology that meshes with that of international agency staff. If by *local* we instead mean presumed project beneficiaries, then rarely do opportunities occur for such voices to be heard.

Conclusions: What Are the Answers?

Evidence from these case studies suggests that the *starting point* for integration of women in agricultural projects should be an understanding of women's work and incentives in local farming systems and their relevance for the particular set of technical problems addressed by the project. This will differ from project to project and must be thought through afresh in each case. Although such understanding will mean more effort for the people responsible for project design, it will make certain that the project rests on sound logic regarding the situation "on the ground" and the incentives and constraints affecting the villagers.

Some of the questions that the project formulation team should address are the following:

- What is the role of men and women in local farming systems and who is responsible for project-related activities?
- What traditional techniques do they use and why?
- What is the rationale for the current allocation of land, labor, capital, and assets within the household?
- Who makes decisions affecting the adoption of innovations?
- What are their resources and constraints?
- What is their incentive to adopt the technical solutions proposed by the project in comparison with alternative uses of their time and resources?
- What are the anticipated spread effects to disadvantaged groups?
- Do alternative technical solutions exist that would increase rates of adoption and provide greater benefits to disadvantaged groups?
- Who can reach the intended beneficiaries for training and extension?
- How can these persons be trained by the project?

The relevance of these questions depends on the nature of a given project and women's work in agriculture. Rural women should be identified as a target group of project components when they do the work or make key decisions that affect the project. When the productive activities addressed by the project are exclusively the responsibility of women, project efficiency will dictate that they be identified as the priority target group. When some tasks are the responsibility of women and others, men's, women can be identified as the target group for one project component and men for another. In this way the question of separate women's projects as opposed to integration in larger projects is no longer an issue. Mainstream projects should address mainstream work; all staff, male and female, are responsible for serving the rural people at hand.

Notes

1. Alice Carloni, *Women in Development: A.I.D.'s Experience, 1973–1985,* vol. 1 (Washington, D.C.: AID, 1987).

2. Elsa Chaney, "Women's Components in Integrated Rural Development," in *Rural Women and State Policy: Feminist Perspectives on Latin American Agricultural Development* (Boulder, Colo.: Westview, 1987), pp. 191–211. Sonja Harris-Williams, "The Second Integrated Rural Development Project (IRDP–II) of Jamaica: A Review of Project Area Residents' Experiences and Responses to the Project," in *Planning for Women in Rural Development: A Source Book for the Caribbean* (Barbados: WAND [Women and Development Unit], UWI/Barbados and Population Council), pp. 15–24.

3. David Korten, "Community Organization and Rural Development: A Learning Process Approach," *Public Administration Review* 40 (1980): 480–510. Milton Esman and Norman Uphoff, *Local Organization for Rural Development* (Ithaca, N.Y.: Cornell University Center for International Studies, 1974).

4. For the classic treatment of "separate vs. integrated" projects, see Barbara Lewis, "Women in Development Planning," in *Perspectives on Power: Women in Africa, Asia and Latin America,* ed. Jean O'Barr (Durham, N.C.: Duke University Press, 1982), pp. 102–118. On paltry funding for separate women's projects in the U.S. AID, see Kathleen Staudt, *Women, Foreign Assistance and Advocacy Administration* (New York: Praeger, 1985) p. 98.

5. Precise projects and country names are not used.

13/Getting to the Third World: Agencies as Gatekeepers

Katherine Jensen

One of the most formidable problems in addressing gender issues in development projects must be that of dealing with the successive gates in bureaucracies themselves. If we take as an assumption that the bureaucracies are populated mostly by men, the chief task is for women to have their issues heard, if not to infiltrate the organizations personally. However, usually that task requires "getting there." The first problem is that getting through the gates does not simply refer to the hierarchical structure of any one bureaucracy, but also to the multiplicity of bureaucracies involved in any Third World development project. The resulting maze turns Max Weber's view of the possibilities of bureaucratic rationality into a complexity prone to chaos or recalcitrance and vulnerable to personal idiosyncracies as well as organizational inertia.

What follows is a narrative of a personal journey into Third World gender redistributive research and the bureaucracies encountered along the way. It is not possible to analyze in full the organization and agenda of each, even in this case study focusing on Women in Development (WID) programs through U.S. Agency for International Development (AID) projects. Rather, I aim to enumerate them and to describe the typical gatekeepers in the path from a home university through development consortia and AID at home and abroad as well as implementing agencies in a host country. In addition, this path requires a recognized WID program at each junction, lest one be left climbing the fence in unofficial and probably unapproved ways. The point of this journey is to analyze the possibilities of improving the opportunities for women less advantaged than those of us who can afford to make getting to the Third World part of our work.

University Organization

Speaking as an academic, I start with the university. Participation in work abroad ordinarily takes months, even years to plan, and may well be part of a sabbatical leave, which is ordinarily requested a full year in advance and increasingly requires confirmation from a host institution that one has indeed already made arrangements and secured approval for a visiting position of some sort.[1] At a minimum, professors must arrange to get themselves out of classes, typically scheduled four months in advance of the following semester or quarter, having secured permission from a department head and dean before that time. Usually, the faculty member will also have to find funding for travel and probably also for salary replacement for the instructor who teaches in her stead, and maybe find that person as well.

The point of this description is to emphasize the timing that characterizes academic bureaucracies. Planning tends to be done in a routine that moves quite predictably, but slowly. Gender is not so much an issue here, except that few faculty women are in a position to simply leave their students, their departments, or their families at a moment's (or even a few weeks') notice. Power and seniority, the issues here, do have plenty of gender differentials.

In addition, in most AID projects an academic will not only be dealing with his or her own university but also the project "lead" institution, which may be a different university or at least a different college. Here the entry to the bureaucracy is at least at the level of the project, but one must still negotiate all the issues of credibility and utility in strange territory, which may at least be more readily assumed in the home institution. In addition, WID personnel are often social scientists, seen either as interlopers or extraneous baggage on otherwise purely technical agricultural or engineering teams—female "soft" scientists among male "hard" builders and doers. A recent example from my own university demonstrates the resistance of men to WID efforts and the ways bureaucracies can ensure there be *no* correct way of proceeding with work on women's issues.

Our WID coordinator, Sandra Halverson,[2] arranged for two faculty researchers from other schools to participate as WID fellows on a Wyoming project in an East African country. Both researchers were, in this case, from agriculture faculties, one a soil specialist looking at women's farming techniques. Halverson herself had not only worked on a three-couple team doing baseline social science research on the project, but also had experience in a neighboring African country, so she possessed a clear awareness of the personal demands of the research, as well as extensive scholarly expertise. A long telex to Barney Shaw, the project campus coordinator, from Sam Feldman, the in-country representative, had expressed initial support for the new additions to the team. Feldman, however, advised one WID fellow, Lois Baker, with the mixed message that the sample size for her proposed research should be enlarged by a factor of five and offered that female researchers would be assigned to facilitate the expansion; otherwise "MISSION CONSIDERS THAT RESEARCH TIME AND PROJECT SUPPORT COST CAN BE BETTER SPENT ON MORE WORTHWHILE ACTIVITIES AND WILL RETRACT COUNTRY CLEARANCE."[3]

In addition, the telex specified that Lois Baker should coordinate all her activities through Barney Shaw in the Agriculture College and that she would be "DIRECTLY RESPONSIBLE TO AND DEPENDENT ON" Sam Feldman, the university's in-country representative. It continued by pointedly excluding the WID coordinator from the orientation process in stating: "MISSION IS SOMEWHAT CONCERNED THAT [Baker] WILL BE UNDULY INDOCTRINATED REGARDING CID/WID ISSUES OF THE REGION BEFORE ARRIVAL, AND HENCE ARRIVE WITH MANY PRECONCEIVED IDEAS, INSTEAD OF FORMING THOSE IDEAS FIRST HAND WHILE ON SITE. . . . IDENTIFYING THE WID ISSUES OF THE REGION SHOULD BE DONE IN COUNTRY."[4] (This approach would seem to make a revised sample size methodologically premature.)

Three months later Feldman sent a long letter to WID coordinator Sandra Halverson complaining about the entire experience, starting with the date of arrival and the failure of Baker's luggage to arrive, the fact that she had travelers' checks rather than personal checks, and that she was unprepared for camping (the original proposal had specifically selected villages suggested by Halverson within commuting distance of a major town). The letter ended with the accusation to Halverson: "Since you had six months in [the country] in similar circumstances, I feel your orientation and screening did not adequately prepare her for this experience. Please do not do this to us again. We do not have the time to babysit."[5]

In fact, the orientation that had been set up by Barney Shaw did not include any time with any of the four social scientists on campus who had worked in the project, other faculty who had traveled to the site, or any of the indigenous students who were affiliated with the project, including one woman. Baker had met with WID coordinator Halverson only at Baker's request, but "indoctrination" as well as travel arrangements had been specifically removed from Halverson's responsibility.[6]

In sum, although universities are mandated and often do support basic as well as applied research on women in development, the association of one large bureaucracy with another inevitably complicates arrangements necessary for work to be done, and the resistance of individual men can easily sabotage good intentions and prior agreements, especially over long distances and long time lags. Private contractors, who can summon specialists in a matter of weeks or even days, are often preferred for their efficiency in getting high-priority work done. Whether women's programs ever fit that criteria is a separate matter.

U.S. AID and WID

As I have not had experience with a wide range of AID offices, my description must be specific and tentative. However, the AID mission in Egypt, one of the largest in the world (employees often remark that their enterprise is "bigger than Washington's"), provides an excellent example for analysis. I was often surprised that the organization and range of personnel reminded me so much of another large U.S. government agency, the Bureau of Indian Affairs, with which I had had long-term contract.

Kathleen Staudt's analysis of AID demonstrates generally why "WID survives, but it does not thrive in AID."[7] My observations will speak to the specific issue of resistance to WID within AID. I saw this resistance, or gatekeeping, by both men and women in three areas: resistance to WID as a program, resistance to "stateside" women's participation, and resistance to university people in general in terms of their goals and working styles, as well as their schedules.

My field notes record that some of the men in AID in Cairo assumed that WID was a feminist fad, and others saw it as another Washington political mandate, a stumbling block to get around.[8] However, because having a WID officer was required, some woman would be chosen for the title, whether or not she felt committed to WID's aims, and most often without reducing the demands on her of her "real" job. But this person, and other available women who were sometimes simply unaware of the basic issues, were consulted about WID fellowship proposals. I was told that WID assessments were sometimes even made by wives of AID officers who had never been in a village and who at best knew the kinds of traditional literature interested tourists read.[9]

It cannot be said that only ethnographies of traditional Egyptian social organization are available to interested personnel. The Cairo AID library contains a sizable number of critical sources on Egyptian women. The Population Council in Cairo has even more. One of the most important pieces in the AID library describing the problematic relation of WID to AID may be the September 1984 report "Women's Access to Productive Resources: Recommendations of AID Program Strategies; Report to the USAID Mission in Egypt" by Janet Self, Minouche Shafik, Cheryl Compton, and Salwa Soliman Saleh. This report (1) summarized the marginality of WID in AID and its focus on family and social welfare programs, (2) assessed project case studies, including the cereals project in which I participated, demonstrating the inclusion of some economic analyses but an overall emphasis on vocational training for women, and (3) made conclusions and recommendations claiming both opportunities and a mandate for financial and technical services for women in rural Egypt. I found no evidence of these materials' use in policy decisions, by women or men, in the AID mission.

Because women's work, women's economic potential, or even division of labor by sex have never been key concepts in agricultural research and development, AID personnel—most especially the conspicuously anomalous women in AID—do not see it as advantageous to their career to publicly support research on women, although they may express interest privately. That does not mean that nothing of merit or utility is done to improve the lot of Third World women. It only speaks to the difficulty of institutionalizing the work.

The problem is not only that WID responsibilities are thrust upon uninterested and unwilling workers simply by virtue of their gender. Some actions are clearly related to the uses and protection of power, where WID programs are perceived as jeopardizing rather than enhancing power, or at least prestige. Deprecation of women by women is commonplace. Gatekeeping also takes more concrete forms, reflecting both the sensitive nature of international bureaucratic relationships and very finite view of opportunities, rather than the expanding pie I imagined to be central to the idea of development. One group of WID fellowships was denied on the grounds that mission personnel did not want stateside women, whom they worried might have done "faulty research," coming over to "use up their chips with the Egyptians." [10]

This resistance to "outsiders" reflects a more basic conflict between people in the AID bureaucracy (along with the people with whom they contract on particular projects) and university people. On both sides of the ocean I detected a general distrust of university-associated personnel and university grants. It would be false to assert that faculty members are resisted because they are smarter or harder working. AID people are themselves a very mixed lot, ranging from some bright, adventurous, and caring Peace Corps alums to an assortment of former university people and those who, as in the Bureau of Indian Affairs, have found a comfortable niche in a government bureaucracy quite apart from work in a particular culture or region. [11] It seemed that regardless of the AID person's background, most feel that regular university faculty are greenhorns and temporary, too idealistic and demanding. They expect to plan ahead and to work hard for a short time, and they do not "know the culture."

More than most bureaucratic organizations, AID makes its own world, with its own language. This characteristic goes beyond the basic (often military) acronyms—to include frequent references to PIDS, PPs, TDYs, and the like. The words change, the rules change, the deadlines are short, and the stakes are high—in what appears to the outsider as a total and secret society.[12]

The best example of that appeared in the recent RFP (request for proposal) for a consolidated agricultural program in Egypt (a National Agricultural Research Program or "NARP," of course) to replace four programs that previously had been operating independently from each other. Even though the lead university sponsoring the largest of the four projects was selected to provide technical assistance in the new project with some of the same key personnel, it become a crucial point to know that after several years, "farming systems research" was no longer the key idea; the new buzzword was "adaptive" research. So, everyone who "knew" changed the wording in their titles and proposals, in part to signal that they were on the inside.

Meanwhile, stateside WID programs themselves tend to be very cautious in working with AID. At present, their efforts are almost always add-ons to major projects. Every WID fellow and WID inquiry is potentially challenging to the initial direction of the project and easily eliminated, since there exists no prior commitment to the person or effort, only a vague understanding of the concept. Therefore, in order to avoid being eliminated altogether, most WID directors feel they must take a relatively conservative stance in administering their programs. Indeed, the portion of my final report that questioned the utility of WID add-ons as well as my feminist analysis of AID-Cairo was excised by a WID director for politically understandable reasons. The relationship between WID and AID seems tenuous at best, even within one bureaucratic level.

Host Country Bureaucracies

Were it necessary to deal only with one or more universities, AID in Washington, and AID abroad, with their WID subprograms, it would be complicated enough. But aspiring Third World researchers are only halfway there at this point. Development projects rightfully work in cooperation with a foreign government and are managed in fact by a host country director and staff. This management is usually located in one or more agencies of the state. Bureaucracies in Third World countries, especially where there has been a long history of education for the elite with limited opportunity for career advancement, tend to be as proprietary, protective, and jealous as imaginable. None of these characteristics enhances efficiency, innovation, or political challenge. Although the intricate politics of these agencies are less accessible to most researchers than those of our own, they are no less important, because these are the ultimate gatekeepers to the project. And even when decisions are justifiable, they may seem arbitrary to those outside the often informal host country political process.

In my first foray into Egypt I immediately encountered two different aspects of this phenomenon. In the first place, the project to which I was assigned was between annual renewal contracts, held up for several months in the AID mission. The host country project director determined that no short-term researchers, fellows, or any other American personnel would be approved (lack of cost to the project notwithstanding) until a new contract was signed. I happened to arrive in Cairo from Australia, after many months of work on arrangements by the WID director, to find that my stay and my work could not be officially approved. Although I was most cordially treated by Egyptian and American colleagues alike, my status remained unofficial.

The second major lesson in host country bureaucratic organization came in my transfer from an irrigation project to one in cereal grains. Somehow, since both of these efforts were aimed at the problem of increased agricultural production, I assumed that they might work in concert to address questions of women's participation and effectiveness in agricultural production. I had to learn that the ministries of Agriculture and Irrigation had no formal connections and were at times quite at odds and very much in competition with each other, making the chances of a coordinated effort highly unlikely.

Nevertheless, some progress had been made in the direction of institutionalizing women's components within the cereals production improvement project, which has implications for a future consolidated agricultural project, for the Egyptian extension service, and perhaps ultimately for some Egyptian farm women. The degree to which these efforts hover between long-term personal commitment and ongoing organizational routine can best be illustrated by a description of the work itself.

Within the Ministry of Agriculture

The Egyptian Food Grain Project—a five-year, $52-million U.S.-dollar investment in increased food production that had no program emphasis on women—was headed in Egypt on the American side by a woman whom I will call Nora Black and on the Egyptian side by a man, Dr. Ashad, both of whom worked extraordinarily hard to implement research and training of women in agriculture. Further, the project was coordinated stateside by a very competent woman. As the administrative arrangement itself is unusual in terms of gender, one can make few structural generalizations until women routinely fill posts as administrators. However, some of the processes are typical and some outcomes even give cause for hope.

Nora Black initially joined the project in an ambiguous assistant-level position. Only through her demonstration of multiple talents, in addition to her persistence as compared with the general attrition to the States of her superiors, had she come to the position of influence and authority as chief of party. Dr. Ashad's support for this work came partly from his professional respect for some of the perceptive and hard-working Egyptian professional women in the Ministry of Agriculture who made up the Women's Committee he appointed. He was also more willing to spend time out in the field than is true of most bureaucrats and so was able to see women working. He had, however, endured continuing harsh criticism from his male colleagues for the stands he had taken with regard to women's farm work.[13]

The Women's Committee for the project was composed of two female Egyptian Ph.D.s in agriculture (a horticulturist and a plant pathologist) and a M.A.-level female rural sociologist with the National Extension Research Department. They had initially been recruited in an advisory capacity but increasingly became committed to doing primary research on Egyptian rural women while holding full-time laboratory research jobs in agriculture. They worked closely with both Dr. Ashad, a Ph.D. in agriculture, and Nora Black, whose background was in extension and sociology. Although the Women's Committee therefore had an "official" capacity, the kind and amount of work it accomplished had more to do with the mutual respect held by the three committee members and two administrators, as well as an evolving commitment to rural women whose lives were far removed from the Cairene professional elite.[14]

The second crucial component of the WID effort was the nurturance of the connection with the National Agricultural Extension office, whose director personally escorted me to several governorates (the local administrative units) to interview female extension workers. Although these workers and the Egyptian university professors attached to them nearly all reflected imported western assumptions that identify female extension work with home economics, the friendly administrative link was certainly crucial.[15]

Ultimately, the best access to Egyptian food producers came through the Extension Field Office in one Delta governorate, directed by an extraordinarily competent and receptive man, whose wife also worked as an extension worker and whose energy drove the village-level research and training programs. Whereas the national connection had *permitted* field projects in several governorates, here the efforts had *taken*. This office, its director, its extension staff, and its surrounding villages had become involved in a set of long-term cooperative commitments to improving agricultural production by farm men and women.

Again, a combination of bureaucratic relationships and personal perceptions created an optimal access point. The office director was obviously well connected within the national extension service. He had traveled widely in the United States on agricultural training projects while maintaining the respect and devotion of the field workers employed on the minimal, guaranteed government salary for secondary school graduates. His wife spoke no English and had just borne their fifth daughter, but she worked tirelessly in making sure surveys were translated correctly, that field workers understood the intent of the research, and that the efforts made sense to the villagers.

The Status of Research on Rural Egyptian Women

Having traced the logistical road from my home university to Egyptian farm villages, I should now look at what was actually going on there, not only to assess the merits of this sort of enterprise but to suggest further bureaucratic pitfalls in the process of doing gender-based research and training. Even if those problems (of bias and blindness) are constructed in ways western scholars and bureaucrats have trouble comprehending, their mystifying qualities hardly disappear once the westerner is actually in the Egyptian village. And, once data concerning those biases are collected, analyzed, even published, they do not necessarily enter the body of "established fact." This part of the journey, then, explores both some findings of field research and the political fate of that information.

First, the Women's Committee has had to verify more than once that there are indeed women farmers in Egypt. Traditional wisdom has it that Egyptian women are secluded in the home and that only men work in agriculture. Previous research and government statistics prove to be relatively useless. In her introduction to *The Women of Kafr al Bahr*, Sonja Zimmerman notes the improbable government statistics on the total percentage of women in agriculture, showing 43 percent in 1961, 6 percent in 1966, 22 percent in 1969, and 2 percent in 1974.[16] Aboul-Seoud and Farag estimated 46 percent in 1979.[17] Though hers is not a comparable statistic, Zimmerman's research in 1980 showed that 15 percent of the total number of farmers in Kafr al Bahr were women.[18]

The Women's Committee was not only skeptical of these data, given the large difference in ages of marriage partners (averaging more than ten years), the committee was sure that there was at least a sizable number of widows with considerable economic authority.[19] Second, sons are more likely than daughters to be away in school, in the army, or in wage work, leaving younger females to do the farming. Beyond that, an increasing proportion of work by Egyptian social scientists analyzes the effects of labor migration outside the country and the consequences for families left behind.[20] This research reports male out-migration for particular villages ranging from 30 percent to 70 percent, similar to estimates reported to me by various local government officials.[21] Yet, as of January 1986, the dominant view among agricultural specialists in the AID Cairo mission was that few women were engaged in farming, and if they were, they made few decisions anyway.[22]

Meanwhile, the committee had proceeded with some other questions of its own. Even though a large number of the agricultural extension agents employed in each of the governorate extension offices are women (and women with degrees in agriculture), they are typically assigned tasks in home economics research and demonstration in food preparation. Here the pattern results from a combination of lack of appropriate transportation resources in getting women out to the farming villages, an oversupply of underpaid extension employees who are required to report to the government office each day, as well as additional western assumptions about rural women's work and women's needs. The committee conducted a survey in 1985 that indicated a low level of participation of extension workers, especially female ones, at the village level. Although 76 percent reported that they worked in the villages, 24 percent had visited villages fewer than ten times in the preceding year and half did not declare the number of their visits.[23] This information is essential, since both the Food Grains Project and Women's Committee are essentially dependent on the extension workers for the distribution of new technical information in agriculture and the gathering of new data, for women are presumed to be able to contact women in the villages more easily than men are.

In addition, the committee administered year-long case studies of four farm families to evaluate more precisely the time-labor allocation of all family members to agricultural tasks. These data indicate that even in families in which men are named as the principal farmers, the hours in agricultural labor spent by women and girls may often exceed that of the "farmer" himself.

THE NATURE OF EGYPTIAN WOMEN'S AGRICULTURAL TASKS

Perhaps the most important contribution of the research is not only that it demonstrates how many rural Egyptian women work in agriculture, but more that it shows how many tasks assume female participation and how *few* tasks are *not* done by women. Women are most heavily involved in the demanding seasons of planting and harvesting. They do most of the milking, marketing, and processing of milk and milk products, with some assistance from girls and less from boys. More women than men participate in cleaning the fold and in feeding and watering the animals. Women and girls predominate in taking care of all kinds of poultry and animals used in transportation.[24] However, it must be noted that the wildly ranging results of previous research on women's participation comes not only from a clear tendency to provide "appropriate data" for the frequent government and university surveys but from indigenous (emic) definitions. Taking care of livestock is not in Egypt considered agricultural but, rather, as household work. Whether that work is "household" work because women do it or because the animals live in the house remains at issue. Nevertheless, even the tasks of loading the manure into baskets and leading the loaded donkey to the field is not unambiguously farm labor. It is, in part, "cleaning house."

Sonja Zimmerman also points out that collaborative work with husbands is *traditional,* recalling a familiar pattern whereby labeling women's work as "helping out" eliminates their claim to it as real work. Zimmerman lists typical female tasks as loading manure, sowing seed, weeding, watching the *gamoosa* turn the water wheel, picking bugs off the cotton, and harvesting activities such as bundling the maize stocks and cutting and carrying *berseem,* the latter task being one that will take place several times a day for all but the hottest part of the summer, when the annual clover does not grow. In addition to livestock work, women are heavily involved in storage work: drying the wheat on the roof, taking it to the mill, storing flour, storing the straw for fodder, drying the maize stocks for fuel, and shucking the corn cobs.[25]

There are at least two problems with the naming of women's agricultural work here: one is a surprisingly indistinct sexual division of labor; another is a lack of clear demarcation between consumption and production activities.[26] But also one finds the common pattern whereby even agricultural tasks that are claimed to be strictly men's work require significant female participation.[27] Finally, we will return to the difficulty in the integration of this information about women into a bureaucratic perspective.

A good example is plowing. Men typically guide the plow pulled by a draft animal, but the women go to the field and feed the animal *berseem* while it is pulling the plow. *Berseem,* the lush green annual clover, must be consumed a little at a time, so the animal must eat during the process of plowing to avoid wasting valuable time or risking bloat. Girls and women run alongside the draft animal with the loads of *berseem* they have cut and carried to the field being plowed. Also, because the draft animal cannot pull the plow to the very edge without ending up in the irrigation ditch, the women plow the ends of the field by hand. These two traditional tasks, in addition to extensive male migration, explain why even in 1979 Abou-Seoud and Farag found 40 percent of women reporting participation in plowing. Nevertheless, it is still widely held in official reports that women never plow.

FARMING WOMEN'S TECHNICAL INFORMATION AND
DECISION MAKING

Given the extensive involvement of Egyptian women in agricultural work, the Women's Committee felt it important to determine the sources and level of information about agricultural practices to which women who farm have access. Second, what kinds of agricultural decisions are based on this information or lack of it? Ultimately, how can an understanding of the reality of the process of knowledge transfer improve the chances of Egyptian food sufficiency? This is the research phase in which I participated directly, in designing and pretesting a structured interview instrument to assess the access to information among women who farm independently compared with those farming with their husbands and among those in villages with high female participation compared with villages where women's participation is generally low.

Most of the data was collected in my absence—I had returned to the States. The Egyptian rural sociologist shortly thereafter took a position in another country. Access to a mainframe computer with the capability of analyzing such a large data set was uncertain, so analysis of data was limited to statistical summaries. However, preliminary analysis demonstrated several things: that women farmers know more about new agricultural techniques than anyone expected, and that female heads of households have almost as much knowledge as women sharing production responsibilities with husbands. Whether formal or informal communication channels are more effective in reaching women as well as men in agriculture remains to be seen.[28]

Ironically, this field experience also showed the mechanism by which women become invisible. I say "ironically" because, if women are secluded anywhere in Egypt, it is not in the supposedly conservative villages. In addition to their early morning treks to the fields with the animals, women gather daily to both buy and sell produce (mainly vegetables) for the day's meals. Our village contact person would lead us to the homes of women selected for the sample only to find that they had gone to the fields, leaving the children and household to other women. Women of all ages were visibly apparent everywhere. Nevertheless, direct information from women still tended to "disappear" in a number of ways.

We had trained female extension engineers to do the interviewing, but, because of their limited proficiency in English and mine in Arabic, I often had to rely on a male interpreter. These men from the extension office usually assumed that they should do the interviewing, rather than simply helping me know what was being said. In addition, it was very difficult to interview just the woman farmer. If she worked with her husband and he was nearby, he was very likely to appear and begin answering questions. Even if the woman was the principal farmer, sons or neighbors were likely to show up and participate, even though we explained that there was to be another (comparative) interview with the men in the family. It was not that the women themselves were reticent. In the first thirty-six interviews we had only one refusal, even with our cumbersome entourage. Nevertheless the same study, conducted under more normal conditions, eventually yielded data from 180 village women farmers about what they know about farming techniques and how they decide which to use. The Women's Committee hoped, on the basis of these findings, to implement some applied projects demonstrating direct knowledge transfer to women in a new consolidated agricultural research program.

To What End? Women in the Development Structure

I would like to think that this research will change forever the "traditional" image of rural Egyptian women and will bring some important positive shifts in development policies affecting women.[29] I cannot be very hopeful, even though the Food Grains Project had done more than most to bring concerted attention to women's issues. Moreover, this project has now ended, to be absorbed by a consolidated National Agricultural Program, which formally was committed to no particular women's component nor an integrated effort to attend to women. The preliminary proposal from the Women's Committee to the Cairo AID mission was in fact returned by the agricultural project manager (a woman) with the question as to whether it wasn't a "dead issue" because the old project was ending, even though the new project contained no references to WID efforts either.[30] However, in November 1986 Dr. Ashad was named to direct the consolidated project, so it promised to have at least the informal support for women's programs that the Food Grains Project demonstrated.

However, in summer 1987 it was suggested that I might do a comparative literature-based proposal on demonstration projects for training women, rather than the data analysis from the previous project, as a rationale to reappoint the Women's Committee on the new consolidated agricultural research project, at that time lacking a formal mandate for a women's component. The Women's Committee might legitimately be used to demonstrate farming practices to women, but they were not themselves social science researchers. This reflected, on one hand, the continuation of informal good will but, as important, the lack of official in-house AID commitment to the integration of women's issues in the new project.

A year later, continued work on women's issues was still held hostage in a two-year dispute between the AID mission and the Ministry of Agriculture over the role of extension efforts in the new project, partly because women's farm work still seemed related to vocational training, not a research issue relevant to increased food production. Meanwhile, the stateside WID program director, under time pressures to field WID teams, announced that the gate would be closed on Egypt as a site because it was "too difficult to work with such large bureaucracies."[31] Although the bureaucratic linkages had not yet unraveled all the way back to my home university, it remains a foregone conclusion that a faculty member does not receive a paid sabbatical leave without a research site or program. More important, there was no mechanism in place to utilize information about Egyptian women's agricultural work in this "consolidated" effort to increase food production.

In a more general political view of the bureaucratization of WID, this huge project is a good example of how little formal effect the Percy amendment of more than a decade ago has had. A consolidated agricultural program in the second largest AID budget in the world ($750 million annually) could hardly be said to have slipped through the bureaucratic cracks. The lack of formal status of WID in the new project means that whatever will be done will be done informally, a precarious situation to be sure, but not a hopeless one.

WID, then, is forced to proceed as women's programs and women's studies have most often in other institutions—with the good will and concerted energy of a few people in places who can make an important difference. And the role of women in producing women's programs must be regarded as a necessary but not sufficient condition. This and other institutional experience suggests to me that women's programs require the active, persistent commitment of professional women in the presence of men with feminist sympathies. It is rare that men will take the lead, and as rare that women have the critical mass or enough authority to go it alone. But a female presence, especially in the youngest cohort of professional women who benefited from feminist battles without fighting them, who are unsupported in their professional roles for doing "women's work," is unfortunately no guarantee that the image of women, knowledge about women, or policies toward women will change in significant ways.

On the other hand, time and experience can make a difference. Barbara Rogers pointed out that the presence of women does not automatically reverse processes that discriminate against women's issues in development, but that their presence makes it less likely that *men* will be used as a synonym for *people*.[32] In the case described herein, two of the women in the AID mission who had been relatively unsupportive of WID in 1986 had two years later taken both hard lumps and real career risks in order to assist some of the same initiatives.

This discussion is not meant to lead to the conclusion that we should do nothing until we have the perfect feminist collectivist, process-oriented means to attack issues of poverty and exploitation of Third World women.[33] Few would disagree with Asoka Bandarage when she says that "the long term solution to the feminization of poverty lies not in the greater integration of women into the exploitative structures of the capitalist world economy, but in changes in those structures themselves."[34] The question is whether those structures are alterable, on the one hand, or whether feminist resources have any hope of providing a viable and timely alternative, on the other. The bureaucratic gates from Laramie to Kafr Abo-Dawood form a long, complicated set. Human beings with real human (and feminist) sympathies exist at both ends and are sprinkled all the way through the middle. Perhaps the expedient answer is to find ways of assessing and utilizing those sympathies and resources, while criticizing and exposing the mechanical and sexist roadblocks. We have plenty of evidence that development programs have hurt women, usually resulting from the unintended consequences of gender-biased efforts toward technological progress. That knowledge demands not the withdrawal from participation when the investment and the stakes are so large, but the continued involvement of feminist workers. Neither the revolutionary nor the gradualist approach is without toll, but helpless abandonment provides the greatest likelihood of human loss.

Notes

1. Once considered a sort of rest and recuperative period, sabbaticals are now nearly always paid research leaves. University of Wyoming guidelines seem representative in that regard.

2. In this essay I have struggled long with the politics of giving people credit for their institutional work and field research versus protecting them in sensitive situations. At first I identified names, places, projects, and offices, but reactions from field personnel encouraged me to remove identifiers. However, using only bureaucratic titles proved not only cumbersome but meaningless to anyone outside the AID network. I have therefore chosen to employ pseudonyms in order to identify actors by gender and nationality, both important variables in this multilayered system of interactions. I want to thank Janice Harris, "Nora Black," and Garth Massey for helping me to clarify this and myriad other questions in earlier versions of this essay.

3. Telex, March 10, 1986, photocopy in author's collection.

4. Ibid., March 10, 1986. CID/WID denotes the Women in Development Program within the Consortium for International Development, the eleven-member association of land-grant schools in the West that bid for AID projects in arid regions of the Third World.

5. Personal letter, May 26, 1986.

6. Personal letter, WID coordinator to in-country representative, June 5, 1986.

7. Kathleen Staudt, *Women, Foreign Assistance, and Advocacy Administra-*

tion (New York: Praeger, 1985), p. 44; also Kathleen Staudt, "Bureaucratic Resistance to Women's Programs: The Case of Women in Development," in Ellen Bonaparth, ed., *Women, Power and Policy* (New York: Pergamon, 1982)

8. This, I must admit, is a less sophisticated description of gender redistributive advocacy administration than Staudt provides, but I think it basically accurate.

9. Interview, field staff, Cairo, January 1986.

10. Field trip with mission personnel, January 15, 1986.

11. Staudt says that "the agency is far from monolithic; its diverse personnel reflect its pluralism. It employs bureaucrats, scholars, and field-oriented people; staff from numerous disciplines ranging from agronomy to anthropology; and people of varying ideological persuasions. While AID has its share of proverbial dictionary readers, like any other bureaucracy, it also contains some frantically ambitious, creative and committed individuals" *Women, Foreign Assistance, and Advocacy Administration,* p. 37.

12. Staudt, ibid., chap. 6, gives an extensive description of AID process, including a description of the project paper (PP), the project identification document (PID), p. 89, and temporary duty personnel (TDYs).

13. Personal conversation, February 10, 1986.

14. For another excellent example of this commitment see "Aziza Hussein: Family Law and Family Planning in Egypt," in Marion Fennelly Levy, *Each in Her Own Way: Five Women Leaders of the Developing World* (Boulder: Lynne Rienner, 1988).

15. The difficulty in making policy transitions from recognizing women's reproductive roles to assessing their productive contributions is demonstrated in the UNESCO publication *Women and Development: Indicators of Their Changing Role* (New York, 1981), especially in the introduction by Mayra Buvinic, or, using a different distinction between childbearing responsibilities and managerial responsibilities, in Martha F. Loutfi, *Rural Women: Unequal Partners in Development* (Geneva: International Labor Office, 1980). Other links between production and reproduction, the allocation of household resources, and the evaluation of unpaid work have hardly been considered by the extension offices I visited in Egypt.

16. Sonja Zimmerman, *The Women of Kafr Al Bahr* (Leiden: Leiden University, 1982), p. 1.

17. Khairy Aboul-Seoud and Flora Farag, "The Role of Women and Youth in Rural Development with Special Emphasis on Production and Utilization of Food" (1979, unpublished).

18. Zimmerman, *Women of Kafr Al Bahr,* chap. 4.

19. Yeldez Ishak, Zeinab El-Tobshy, Naima Hassan, and Coleen Brown, "Role of Women in Field Crops Production and Related Information," Egyptian Major Cereals Improvement Project (EMCIP) Publication no. 91 (July 1985), pp. 11–15.

20. Interview with Fatma Khafagy, director, Program on Women's Development and Education, UNICEF, January 27, 1986, and February 9, 1986; also her dissertation, University of London, discussed in Galal Amin and Elizabeth Awny, "International Migration of Egyptian Labour: A Review of the State of the Art" (1984, unpublished); Hind Abou Seoud Khattab and Syada Greiss El-Daeif, "Impact of Male Labor Migration on the Structure of the Family and the Roles of Women,"

no. 16 (Cairo: Population Council); Ingrid Palmer, *The Impact of Male Out-Migration on Women in Farming* (West Hartford, Ct.: Kumarian Press, 1985); and Nadia Youssef and Carol Hetler, "Establishing the Economic Condition of Woman-Headed Households in the Third World: A New Approach," in Mayra Buvinic, Margaret Lycette, and William Paul McGreevey, eds., *Women and Poverty in the Third World* (Baltimore: Johns Hopkins University Press, 1983).

21. Interviews with Mustafa Abdel Wahab, director of extension, Ministry of Agriculture, January 22–23, 1986; Ahmed Ged El-Karim, agricultural extension director, Menya Governorate, January 22, 1986; Ammer Fatah, Department of Rural Sociology, Agriculture College, Cairo University, February 1, 1986.

22. Articles by Maila Stivens and Deborah Fahy Bryceson in *Women, Work and Ideology in the Third World,* ed. Haleh Afshar (New York: Tavistock, 1985), address the issues of increasing feminization of agriculture in developing countries.

23. EMCIP Women's Committee (1985, unpublished).

24. Ishak et al., "Role of Women in Field Crops Production," p. 10. It should be noted that Ester Boserup had begun documenting women's typical work in agricultural divisions of labor as early as 1970, in *Woman's Role in Economic Development* (New York: St. Martin's Press, 1970).

25. Zimmerman, *Women of Kafr Al Bahr,* chap. 4.

26. Elise Boulding and other task analysis researchers demonstrate this phenomenon among North American farm women as well. See Boulding, "The Labor of U.S. Farm Women: A Knowledge Gap," *Sociology of Work and Occupations* 7, no. 3 (August 1980): 261–90. Lourdes Beneria, "Conceptualizing the Labor Force: The Underestimation of Women's Economic Activities," *Journal of Development Studies* 17 (1981): 10–27, makes a general theoretical argument about the intertwining of domestic labor and production in agricultural societies.

27. Corky Bush and I have discussed the phenomenon of "helping out" in two volumes on women and technology in which we have articles on American rural women. See Bush, "The Barn Is His, the House Is Mine: The Impact of Technology in Sex Roles on the Family Farm," in George Daniels and Mark Rose, eds., *Energy and Transport* (Beverly Hills, Calif.: Sage, 1982), and Jensen, "Mother Calls Herself a Housewife But She Buys Bulls," in Jan Zimmerman, ed., *The Technological Woman* (New York: Praeger, 1983).

28. Yeldez Ishak, Zeinab El-Tobshy, Naima Hassan, and Coleen Brown, "Egyptian Women in Agriculture," EMCIP Publication no. 105 (January 1987).

29. The possibility of negative effects must not be ignored, as development now seems clearly to generally have had negative effects on the relative status of women in Third World countries. See, for instance, Roslyn Dauber and Melinda Cain, eds., *Women and Technological Change in Development Countries,* (Boulder, Colo.: Westview, 1981), or Martha Loutfi, *Rural Women: Unequal Partners in Development* (Geneva: ILO, 1980).

30. AID memo to chief of party, January 1986.

31. Telephone conversation, July 1, 1988.

32. Barbara Rogers, *The Domestication of Women: Discrimination in the Development Process* (New York: Tavistock, 1981), p. 52.

33. This view is particularly well articulated by Kathy Ferguson, *The Feminist*

Case Against Bureaucracy (Philadelphia: Temple University Press, 1984), though she speaks very little about addressing international women's problems in that book. (See her article in this volume.)

34. Asoka Bandarage, "Victims of Development," *Women's Review of Books* 5, no. 1 (October 1987): 3; also "Women in Development: Liberalism, Marxism and Marxism-Feminism," *Development and Change* 15, no. 3 (1984): 495–515.

14/Planning Social Change: A Misdirected Vision

Cathy Small

This paper presents the results of a long-term study of an active, aid-funded women's self-help organization that has successfully redistributed village wealth into the hands of women. The organization was administered by a sensitive bureaucracy, largely in the hands of women, and implemented in a country where local tradition was supportive of women's development roles. However, rather than examining the impact of bureaucratic structure on development efforts, this paper proceeds from the "ground up," analyzing development, in the anthropological perspective, from the standpoint of the everyday behaviors and relationships that constitute development activity. What it shows by its analysis is the comparative irrelevance of the bureaucracy and the primacy of indigenous social processes in the development enterprise.

The basic research was conducted between 1981 and 1984 and, again, in 1987 in the Kingdom of Tonga, South Pacific, where a national network of rural women's groups—called the *fakalakalaka* or "moving forward" groups—had generated income for village and home improvement since 1978. Although village-to-village study of the "Moving Forward Organization" (MFO) was conducted, the mainstay of research consisted of intensive participant-observation study of groups in a single village.

By any measure, the MFO was an unqualified success. Within its first two years, moving forward (MF) groups had been established in thirty-one villages on Tonga's main island, and the Foundation for Peoples of the South Pacific (FSP) estimated that the organization was realizing well over 1,000 percent return on every aid dollar. The tangible results of group activities during this period included the building of 623 toilets, 336 dwelling houses, 390 kitchens, 157 water tanks, 497 fences, 261 pig pens, and 1,819 vegetable gardens[1]—accomplishments that have multiplied proportionally with the increase in membership and groups. The MFO quickly spread from Tonga's main island to its numerous outer islands, by 1984 reporting a membership of 400 groups in ninety-seven villages and a return of more than $57,500 from grant funds totaling $5,883.86.[2] These figures are nothing short of incredible, given that Tonga has a total of some 150 villages and an official annual per capita income of less than T$500.

Under pressure of budget cuts, funding for the organization on the main island was withdrawn in 1985, with the expectation that the MFO would continue operating on a "self-sufficient" basis. In 1987, however, the main island organization showed signs of general collapse—declining membership, irregular meetings, severe curtailing of income-generating and building activities.

This paper will neither provide a formula for the "successful" development bureaucracy nor a critique of development planning decisions. Quite to the contrary, the aim is to show how, once a development institution has been integrated into village life, it is then subject to the economic and historical forces that shape all social institutions. Indeed, the successes and failures of the development institution will have less to do with the goals, structures, and policies of development planners than with the deeper conditions affecting the choices and relationships of village women and, hence, the shape that any village institution will take.

I will show in this article that, although the MFO was initially constructed on a profit-making, self-help model, it became an institution of another order—one that converted traditional prestige and kinship obligations into a development fund and thereby redistributed village wealth into the hands of women. As the reader will see, the ability of the women's organization to do this underlay its success and the special nature of its construction. This ability, however, was based, not on development planning nor bureaucratic structure, but on the deeper social and economic conditions that fostered this conversion and redistribution process, themselves the product of a long history. The same conditions that allowed women to draw and escrow resources for development, also, over time, came to increase the investment necessary for women's participation and, ultimately, to divide and fragment the membership. This created an institution of diminishing returns and increased infighting, eventualities that explain, better than do changes in administrative policy, the ultimate decline of MFO participation and accomplishment.

I will first describe the basic operation of MF groups in one village in Mu'a[3] and provide an overview of the historical changes that have shaped the contemporary socioeconomic context in which these groups exist. I will then analyze the bases for the successes and the failures of the MFO.

A Portrait of Moving Forward in the Village

Officially, the roots of the MFO trace to 1974 when a group of seven Tongan Roman Catholic sisters, who had been relieved of their teaching duties, began the Tonga Village Women's Development Program.[4] In the village of "Mu'a" these first groups, begun by a resident Tongan nun, were organized as the Education for Religious Life Program, having a Catholic membership and a domestic focus on improving household nutrition, hygiene, and living standards. Such groups throughout the main island of Tongatapu became known as Moving Forward Organizations after 1978, when the FSP became involved in monitoring and supporting the nuns' activities, using U.S. Agency for International Development (AID) grant funds. The new name(s) reflected the organization's shift in status to a bona fide, fundable development institution based on the characteristics of the self-help model: nonsectarian, democratic, income generating, and self-sufficient.

When I came to the village of Mu'a in mid-1981, the MF movement was well in place on the main island of Tongatapu. There were nine active MF groups in Mu'a, with a total of sixty-six women. This represented approximately half of those households with a potential MF woman, that is, a married woman of sufficient maturity that the time-consuming demands of childrearing are either over or have devolved on older children.

At the beginning of each year all nine MF groups in the village met together as a joint body to elect a slate of officers and decide on their annual goals. Although individual groups could take on additional projects of their choosing, usually the nine groups focused their efforts on the same goal— building cement rain catchment tanks, bamboo kitchens with raised eating tables, new and more sanitary toilets, and the like. Each group proceeded with its plans by electing a chairwoman and treasurer and devising their own strategies and income-raising activities for the year but, every Sunday, the nine groups met as one large group to discuss their problems and progress. In Mu'a group meetings were originally presided over by the Tongan nun, resident in Mu'a, who supervised district MF activities, but, in keeping with self-help tenets, leadership was since officially handed over to a duly elected chair.

The MF groups accomplish their goals ostensibly by means of cash earnings from their various income-raising activities. MF women in Mu'a have the advantage of controlling a Women's Hall, built with AID money and local labor. The Women's Hall is used as the staging area for MF income-raising schemes. Each week, one of the MF groups, in turn, controls the hall. During its week the group stages various events to earn money— dances, movies, feasts, fund-raisers, and kava-drinking evenings, where the women prepare the mildly narcotic traditional drink for sale to circles of male drinkers. In each year the earnings from a group's rotating control of the hall are used to buy the lumber, cement, nails, and other materials needed for the women to accomplish group goals. The MFO also rents its hall for community and individual functions, receiving additional income through these rental receipts.

Within and among themselves, MF groups in Mu'a have worked out a number of innovative arrangements for cooperation and mutual aid that have become characteristic of the MFO as a whole. One group worked out a rotating system of labor and cash use. Each year the group devoted its total earnings, as well as group labor, to the construction of water tanks for a portion of its group—the number of tanks depending on how many can be funded that year from group receipts. After three years of ongoing cooperation, this group completed tanks for all its members. Other groups have taken out group loans to provide supplementary funding for their activities.

In 1981 the Mu'a MFO voted in a new arrangement among village groups that operates as sort of a rotating credit association. Every week, each group contributed T$10 to a central fund. The total fund of T$90 was given as a "gift" to the one group who was controlling the Women's Hall during the week. The system was designed to ensure that, at the end of every year, every group would have a minimal base fund with which to work.

Cooperation among groups is not limited to groups of the same village, or even of the same island. Mu'a's MF groups maintain cooperative relations with a handful of villages on the eastern side of the island and support MF events in those villages often by sending a busload of paying attendees. In turn, when Mu'a groups hold an event, invitation will be made to the cooperating village to attend.

Interisland mutual aid is evident as well. In 1982, when an outer-island MF group wanted to build rain catchment tanks on their home island, they appealed to their counterpart groups on the main island. The outer-island women sailed to Mu'a, where local groups staged a fund-raising evening attended by hundreds of women and their kinsmen. Funds were raised as each Mu'a group danced, and friends, kin, and well-wishers placed Tongan bills on the bodies of the dancers. At the end of this one evening, the outer-island group was able to return home with T$1,100—this in a country where the daily wage was T$2 to T$3.

The accomplishment of MF goals is timed around what are called "inspections." Inspections have a long history in Tonga,[5] but today serve as devices for the public display of group accomplishment. During an inspection an invited team of inspectors—typically composed of important figures in the community, the government, the church, and the MFO—formally views the achievements of women's groups. The inspectors are invited by

MF women—often by written invitation—to walk from house to house and view the year's achievements. There is usually a formal roster of events, sometimes presented as a printed program for distribution to the inspectors; these events include opening and closing prayers, the house-by-house inspection rounds, celebratory feasting following the inspections, and formal speeches, in which officials praise the energies of participating women, their husbands, and their families.

Inspection times are preceded by a flurry of activity. Group earnings accumulated throughout the year are typically divided in December. Building materials are purchased and husbands, children, and relatives are enlisted for construction tasks. Where funds fall short, group loans or family resources will be used to supplement group earnings. The end result is a visible change in the village: free-standing bamboo kitchens, sealed water tanks, renovated toilets, and new fencing.

The accomplishments and activities of the MF movement, however, have come to extend beyond individual household improvements. In 1981 Mu'a women built a small store, with a refrigerated unit, in the Women's Hall. Known as the Canteen, the store sells dry goods, snacks, and other refreshments most hours of the day and night. Tongans place a premium value on education, and this prompted MF women to begin the village's first preschool program—a staffed kindergarten operating three days per week in the Women's Hall. The organization voted to open the "kindy" to both member and nonmember families. And, in the name of family nutrition, MF women even entered into the agricultural domain of men. After a hurricane severely damaged Tongan crops in 1982, MF women organized a replanting scheme in which manioc, a resilient and fast-growing food crop, would be grown by all members.

MF members decided in 1982 that the local organization should visit sick members and voted additionally to send T$5 to the ailing member's home as a token of support and solidarity—a policy later extended to births by members. Mu'a women subsequently voted that the MFO should be publicly represented at the funeral of a member's mother, father, husband, or child and that a gift of T$10 should be made to the grieving member to help with funeral expenses.

One must conclude that the MFO in Mu'a has been not only successful but remarkable as a development institution. Though members presumably join for the personal benefit they will derive, the membership has managed to maintain a strong ethic of cooperation that has resulted in increasing networks of reciprocity and mutual aid. And while MF participation has made substantial changes in the material lives of member families, it has also contributed to the life of the village and enjoys a place of community prestige and support.

The Background of Social Change

The MFO seems a sterling example of how small-group entrepreneurship can be instituted for local development and, by its profit-generating success, attract an ever-increasing number of participants and a place of community importance. In fact, though, the success of the MFO in drawing members, in generating community support, and in making development improvements is based on a whole different kind of economic and social foundation, as the details of its economic operation will attest.

To understand "moving forward," one must first know something about Tongan social structure and the past one hundred years of Tonga's social history. Precontact Tonga was based on a complicated redistributive economic and political system in which a chiefly class, itself stratified into higher and lower chiefly ranks, was vested with spiritual, military, and economic control over Tongan commoners—fishermen and farmers residing on chiefly land. A Tongan kinship system cross-cut rank strata. Both for chiefs and commoners, one's kin group, reckoned bilaterally, defined a person's universe of economic and social cooperation. However, the kin group was also constructed hierarchically, with individuals "higher" and "lower" relative to each other, and these relative kinship positions implied a set of social and economic responsibilities.

Women have had a special place in Tongan kinship hierarchies, anchored by the important kinship principle that defines "sister" as higher than "brother"—a principle that extends as well to the children and grandchildren of sisters and brothers. Thus, for instance, the highest ranking chief in Tonga—the Tu'i Tonga—was the supreme political leader and title holder, but his eldest sister, as well as her children, were of higher social prestige.[6]

Throughout all strata of Tongan society, a sister's social prestige had enormous social, economic, and even political ramifications. A sister's prestige was the basis for ongoing obligations of economic support from her brother, as well as from her brother's wife. A woman's children could legitimately appropriate any and all property of their maternal uncle.[7] Conversely, a woman had considerable power over her brother's children, including the right to determine their marriage partners, veto their decisions, receive and control ceremonial wealth associated with their lives, and even adopt their children.[8] In political arenas, the rights and status of sisters and sisters' children over brothers and their lines were often leveraged to influence power and claims to titles.[9] Because of these often complex social dynamics, not only women, but all Tongans had a real investment in the superior status of women as sisters.

The powers behind kinship hierarchies and obligations, including those reinforcing the position of women, have always been bolstered by the system of rank. This is because it was through kinship hierarchies that people of rank could manipulate their political status, and it was through these same hierarchies that chiefs asserted their rights over commoners. The bilateral kin group, and the hierarchies contained therein, served as the vehicle through which chiefs appropriated commoner produce and labor. By the same token, it was the avenue through which land, wealth, and privilege were redistributed by chiefs to those high in the kinship unit for further redistribution to those below. In practice, kinship supported rank with labor, produce, and mobility while rank reinforced kinship hierarchies through redistributed wealth, chiefly favor and sanction. Modern Tonga represents the current status of a long-term process in which this kin and rank-based redistributive system has moved toward a more equalized, individualized, and commodity-based form of production, family, and village. Over the past century, the major thrust of social change has been the decline of chiefly involvement in commoner affairs, greater personal and economic freedoms for commoners, and also the decreasing importance of kinship hierarchies and constraints that had been reinforced by rank. The precontact Tongan system has given way to a more individualized, productive form of smallholder commoner farming that operates within an active but a narrower and less obligatory set of kinship obligations and constraints.

These changes have had different effects on the status of men and women. Because of the systemic connections between kinship and rank and the primacy of women in Tongan kinship, the waning powers of rank have weakened women's leverage as a class. Women's collective position has suffered as a result of the fact that kinship obligations to superiors are less strict, the group to which those obligations obtain is smaller, and the economic ramifications of status are fewer. Thus, for instance, sisters can less easily assert their superior status over brothers for economic gain, and what kinship leverage women do maintain now applies to a shrinking kin network, leaving women with a diminished base of material support.

Though women's position has been undercut by the changes of the last century, it has not been totally compromised. This is because the process of social change in Tonga has not resulted in the wholesale replacement of older Tongan values and productive forms with western ones. Rather, as the economy has become more individualized, market oriented, and cash based, all Tongans have attempted to use their traditional position in rank and kinship to commandeer new economic privileges and new forms of wealth. Women—like everyone with kinship or rank clout—have responded to the declining power of their kinship status by attempting to convert traditional prerogatives into their control in the modern sphere. At the same time, those whose fortunes have been favored by modern education and economic opportunity attempt to use their position in the modern realm to manipulate and control kinship relationships.

The reasons for these contemporary dynamics relate directly to the current state of the Tongan economy, which both reflects and depends on the opportunities of the market economy and on the labor, land, and resources of kinsmen. Modern aspirations, such as owning a village store or successful farm, are not easily secured without the support of kin, while kinship obligations, such as the provision of Tonga's elaborate funeral feasts, can no longer be satisfactorily fulfilled without the use of cash resources. Even the national economy depends both on capitalism and kinship. It is now kept afloat by a pattern of overseas migration for wage labor jobs that returns remittance dollars to resident Tongan kinsmen. And although land—the basis of Tonga's domestic and export economy—is in short supply, leaving almost 60 percent of Mu'ans landless, it remains the case that, through their kinship relationships, more than 90 percent of Mu'an households have regular access to land or agricultural produce.[10]

In short, the alternative paths to Tongan mobility are interdependent and uncertain, making it difficult to proceed in any sphere—modern or traditional—without attending to both. The result of this is the contemporary dynamics that reproduce both kinship and commodity relations, and in which Tongans generally are attempting to convert control in one sphere into power over the other.

The balance of "cash" and "kin," however, is a precarious one because the conditions for its reproduction are in flux. Kinship has long served to mitigate the effects of the privatization and commoditization of production that has occurred in Tonga, as well as the change toward social class structure that normally accompanies these economic changes. Nevertheless, wealth differences have begun to appear among commoners in the Tongan village, and these differences now affect individual life-styles and attitudes[11]— a sign of the growing importance of private wealth and the market economy in rural Tonga.

The dynamics of change throughout twentieth-century Tonga have been embodied in its social institutions. A good example of this is the precursor of "moving forward" groups, *kautaha*—indigenous women's groups for the cooperative production of bark cloth. Bark cloth is the most important form of traditional wealth in Tonga and is exchanged at all important life occasions to assert and cement kin relations. Earlier in the century these important property-owning groups were kin-based institutions in which leaders were chiefly women, membership was elitist, and where member's extraction of group labor and the group product depended on kinship and rank status. In processes detailed elsewhere,[12] these institutions gradually shifted

in organization as kinship obligations weakened and land tenure individualized.

In post–World War II Tonga, these groups are characterized by the
absence of noble women in leadership, the strictly equal distribution of labor
and group product, and a membership open to all who are able to procure
raw bark for manufacture. The traditional organization has become "modern" in structure, as well as commoditized in its production. Eighty percent
of women now buy raw bark to supplement their supplies, a function of land
shortage, and many women now sell tapa cloth to other Tongans—a market
created by the fact that the buyers of tapa cloth, being an outgrowth of
commoditization and wealth differences, are nevertheless using their cash to
fulfill kinship obligations.

The traditional wealth institution, thus, has come to contain the social
changes and social dynamics of the day. Traditional cloth manufacture, though
still the major productive activity of Tongan women, is now carried out
within an institution whose character is modern and commodity based. And
although the bulk of tapa manufacture remains devoted to kin obligations,
women are converting an increasing portion of their traditional wealth production into cash wealth through the sale of their cloths. It is an institution
that like all others in modern Tonga depends on and perpetuates both commodity and kinship relations, and even a "traditional" institution will be
progressively refashioned over time to reflect this.

The dynamics that have shaped the current form of the indigenous,
unplanned, traditional wealth organization have been no less influential in
the planned and funded development organization. Just as the traditional
wealth institution has been pulled into the orbit of a system that reproduces
the contemporary relationship of "cash" and "kin" principles, so too has
the modern development institution. How prevailing social dynamics have
reshaped the self-help development model within the MFO is the subject of
the next section.

The Economic Foundations of Moving Forward

In 1981 I joined an MF group in the village of Mu'a and regularly attended
group meetings and work sessions, joint group sessions, inspections, and
income-raising events, remaining a member until 1984. With the kind in-
dulgence of member women, I was able to audit all nine MF groups for a
full year. The task involved me in counting up all the chickens, pigs, and
kava roots donated by members for MF feasts and events, and in totaling
the various cash outlays made by members throughout the year.[13]

Yet even when I excluded labor time from the calculations, the audits

Table 14-1 / Annual Revenues, Outlays, and Profit or Losses in Mu'a's Moving Forward Groups

GROUP	REVENUES	OUTLAYS	DIFFERENCE	PROFIT/LOSS PER WOMAN
1	T$188.80	T$280.90	−T$92.10	−T$9.21 (10)
2	220.20	170.00	+50.20	+5.02 (10)
3	184.00	202.50	−18.50	−4.63 (4)
4	263.52	232.34	+31.18	+6.23 (5)
5	235.52	363.70	−128.18	−21.36 (6)
6	168.48	102.00	+66.48	+7.39 (9)
7	194.00	264.00	−70.00	−8.75 (8)
8	440.12	297.00	+143.12	+14.30 (10)
9	230.00	231.40	−1.40	−.35 (4)
	T$2,124.64	T$2,143.84	−T$19.20	−T$.29 (66)

Both revenues and outlays were less in this year than in subsequent years because the rotating contribution fund was not fully in effect.

of MF groups showed that, after a full year's work, the nine groups together had essentially made no money at all. As Table 14-1 indicates, four groups showed a minimal profit, an average of T$8.56 per woman for the year, while five of the nine groups lost money, costing their members from T$.35 to T$21.00 each for the year. As a whole, the finances of the MF groups can be summarized by saying that members almost broke even.

Despite the fact that each group had accumulated a cash fund to distribute for building and development purposes (column 1), the fund actually amounted to no more than the outlays made by member and member families through their various contributions throughout the year (column 2).[14]

Thus, reported statistics on the achievements and profits of the MFO can be said to be accurate in the sense in that end-of-year accomplishments are substantial. However, they fail to represent that, at least in the case of Mu'a, so-called profits are nothing more than the sum of member contributions. In fact, there was no income-generation at all—a fact that proved more surprising to me than to member women.

MEMBER ENTHUSIASM AND HOUSEHOLD SUPPORT

If, after a year of hard work, members had no more resources than they would have had anyway, then why did Tongan women continue to join the MF movement? As members themselves assert, they join and would continue to join because they would have never gotten their kitchen or water tank or bathroom if they had not joined. Individual women simply would never have been able to siphon off household income individually for the purpose of development or home improvement. They would have had to contend with the demands of household and kin in the use of household income—demands that, in contemporary Tonga, make the accumulation of resources a difficult task.

Women's groups, in effect, provide a charter for individual women to control a portion of household income that they would not easily be able to control without the group. This is an important feature in the success of Tongan women's groups and their attractiveness to women. Through the MFO, women could accumulate a fund of resources for development and design its use.

The development fund created each year by MF groups depends, then, not on profits, but on the ongoing contributions of member women to the organization. But from where did these contributions come? My survey of the source of member contributions to their groups showed that husbands, as well as children and siblings, in that order, were significantly involved in the funding of MF activities. In 1981, twenty-nine (52 percent) of fifty-six MF members interviewed reported that their own outlays to the MFO were provided in part or whole by their husbands. An additional thirteen households received resources from close kin both living in Tonga or overseas (children, siblings, parents, or some combination thereof). Only one-quarter of the membership indicated that they funded their MF participation through their own means, and this discounts the sometimes sizable labor and material resources that must be used to supplement MF revenue in final building projects.

What accounts for the tremendous household support of MF women? I suggest that husbands and nuclear family kin so willingly funnel available funds to women because, by doing so, they are able to withhold family resources from the demands of kinsmen. A husband's contributions to the activities of his wife may have ambivalence attached because he must give over resources to his wife's immediate control, but his support has the ultimate effect of staying the distribution of resources to the wider kin unit and recycling those resources back into the household. Membership then can be thought of as a partnership between husbands, wives, and immediate family to accumulate resources for the use and benefit of the nuclear family and, by extension, to remove resources from kin distribution. It is a partnership that derives, not from good planning, but from the right historical conditions.

COOPERATION AND MUTUAL AID

The MFO, then, operates as a kind of escrow fund, managed and controlled by women, that accumulates household income for development purposes. Many rules and practices of group organization, in fact, function to support the ability of MF women to extract and earmark resources for household improvement. The features of cooperation and reciprocity that distinguish the MFO as a model development institution are often little more than mechanisms to increase the accumulation and escrow of resources.

Consider, for instance, the system of rotating gift giving conceived and established by Mu'a women, where each group controlling the Women's Hall is given a cash gift in turn from the remaining groups. Although no member or group will end up receiving any more in "gifts" than they themselves contributed, the advantage of such a system is the accumulation of resources that it forces. By making weekly gifts to others a requirement of MF participation, it uses the charter of the group to extract resources from the household and then returns those resources for development use. Even intervillage and interisland mutual aid works on similar principles in that contributions to other groups, requiring elevated levels of contribution by household and kin, will, in the future, be returned by those same groups—not to the kin of Mu'an MF members—but to the Mu'an development fund. In these examples, as well as many other MF structures, model "self-help" behaviors of mutual aid and reciprocity operate really as an elaborate system of self-assessment designed to increase the final development fund.[15]

Other forms of MF cooperation serve to augment the degree of felt obligation in a household to commit resources. The common practices of funding MF projects through initial group loans, or using group revenues over several years to build water tanks for members in turn, make household and kin support a matter of social obligation and prestige. Joint arrangements of this kind mean that any member's failure to meet her obligations could threaten the future credit possibilities of her entire group and their households or jeopardize building projects for her group as a whole. These are socially volatile and disruptive matters in the close-knit village communities of island Tonga. For this reason, group borrowing, rotating use of resources, and other such cooperative schemes effectively increase women's ability to secure household resources by producing a more binding and ongoing sense of member commitment and a more urgent sense of family and kin group obligation.

In summary, one can see that neither the popularity, the household support, nor the ethic of cooperation enjoyed by the MFO is a result of the effective implementation of a self-help bureaucratic vision. The organization makes household improvements, not from profits, but from its ability to transfer resources from one pocket to another. Its popularity with women depends not on entrepreneurial spirit but on women's ability to increase their personal control of household income. The MFO is supported by households and husbands, not because of sensitive family enlistment strategies, but because it allows the household to salvage its resources from the demands of

the extended kin network. Mutual aid abounds, not because of group training seminars, but because cooperative schemes reinforce the escrow functions of the institution.

COMMUNITY SUPPORT AND VILLAGE PARTICIPATION

The only missing piece of this puzzle is why the community at large would
support an organization that operates to withhold resources *from* the community. It is important to realize that, not only is the village sanctioning an
escrow of resources that it would not condone outside the organization, but
it is also directly participating in the funding of the organization. To see
this, one must understand that the development fund available to MF members at the end of the year may equal the sum of their household contributions, but it is not the same money. What really occurs is a conversion of
resources, in which member contributions are applied to diverse obligations,
including feasts, capital costs, building maintenance, and the like, and re-
created and returned as revenue in the form of paid attendance or donations
at MF events. In the final analysis, MFO "profits" can be realized only
through the financial support and direct participation of the local community
at its events.

From the standpoint of the self-help bureaucratic model, community
purchases and attendance at MFO dances, movies, feasts, and other events
would seem based on the entrepreneurial notion that the organization provides desired goods and services to the village. In practice, though, cash
revenues from community attendance are largely the product of solicited kin
obligation and support. Most MF events, especially the larger functions,
involve the distribution of tickets to each member that it is her obligation to
sell. Members, in turn, approach their own extended kin group for support,
and villagers will exclusively buy tickets from their member kin. MFO revenue, then, is essentially extended kin group money transferred to the organization through relationships of kinship and obligation. Given this, one
can see why women, particularly in their role as sisters, are in an ideal
position to run rural development efforts: women's traditional kinship status
bolsters the strength of their petitions to kin for participation.

Most accurately stated, the MFO's end-of-year development fund represents the revenues provided by members' extended kin networks—the very
people from whom resources are being withheld to enable the accumulation
of development funds. MFO women are seemingly accomplishing what all
Tongans today are trying to do: withholding resources from kin so they can
use it for private mobility while at the same time enlisting kin to help them.
In the end, though, women can be no more successful at working the system
both ways than any other Tongan. To earn its charter, the MFO has had to
reproduce the various relationships that underlie wider kinship support and

community sanction and, importantly, to do so in accordance with the changing basis for their reproduction.

THE INSTITUTIONAL PRICE

Reproducing village sanction and kin support explains why, despite a year's worth of income-generating activities, the MFO earned no profits. To elicit kinship support and community sanction, MF women have had to do the same thing that any Tongan wanting the support of kin must do: they have engaged in material reciprocity with the village; they have maximized their own social prestige. Accomplishing this, however, has required the outlay of considerable resources—resources that, together with capital expenditures for events and hall maintenance, proved in the audit year to be equal the income earned from MF events.

The resources needed by women to reproduce relations of prestige and reciprocity in the village, and thereby draw kin support, are a product of Tonga's social history. As the power of Tongan kinship status has weakened in its scope and material impact, and as traditional spheres have themselves become commoditized, the wealth necessary to secure the support of kin has both escalated and changed in kind. Whereas women could once command support on the strength of their kinship prestige and access to traditional wealth, they must now, like all Tongans, reciprocate the flow of wealth and labor to them with greater levels and amounts of countergifts. These countergifts, moreover, increasingly involve the cash domain. In all, it now takes more resources, and more cash wealth, to sustain the prestige and reciprocity necessary for kinship support.

The price tag of prestige in MF operations can be seen, for instance, in the inspection, an occasion that elevates the importance of the MFO by drawing traditional and modern figures of importance to its ranks. The written invitations, printed programs, and traditional feasts provided by MF women require, not only enormous labor input, but outlays of hundreds of dollars. These outlays make sense only when one understands that the prestige value of the organization enables MF women to draw the support and resources of their kinsmen.

Prestige is also the logic behind the MFO's decision to act in a patron role, taking on activities often consistent with chiefly "philanthropy." Providing cash gifts to members during times of funerals, births, and sickness; contributing to ceremonial events in the village; extending excessively liberal credit to canteen customers; making gifts to the church in its own name; and donating the Women's Hall without charge for important village events are just some of the prestige-seeking gestures that drain the MFO of resources.

Reciprocity has also had a monetary value. Continuing to stage less lucrative but popular activities and lowering the price of hall rental to accommodate the village pocketbook are just two of many "community spirited" decisions that have clearly affected profits. Although such public shows of reciprocity and prestige generate the environment necessary to reproduce the community's sanction and participation, by the same token, they are what assures the MFO's lack of profits.

SUMMARY

One can conclude that, although the MFO was planned and designed on a self-help and profit-making development model, it has become an elaborate "break-even" escrow fund that converts reciprocity and prestige into resources for a women's development fund. Women, as the carriers of traditional prestige, have been in a unique position to draw resources in such a system—a fact that accounts for the primacy of women in Tongan rural development. Yet women's ability to draw and hold modern resources has, under changing economic conditions, demanded significant material outlays, resulting in the break-even nature of the MFO's "profit-making" activities.

The MFO has been successful, not because of its planned development role, but because its character and operation has been restructured. The MFO has been a success for women because it has allowed members to parlay their personal and institutional prestige into control of modern wealth. This has served to counter the declining material import of women's traditional status and allowed member women to gain greater control in the "modern sphere." The MFO has worked for member husbands because it successfully diverted household income from the demands of the wider kin group and directed it to private household mobility while the organization has enlisted the participation and sanction of wider kin and community groups by investing heavily in prestige and reciprocity.

Despite the content of the development plan, the MFO has come to reproduce the same dynamics embodied in the unplanned institution for traditional wealth production and in the social fabric at large. The importance of the MFO in Tonga today is not as a bona fide development group but as a sanctioned institutional agent for private accumulation under social conditions that reinforce the distribution of resources and as a vehicle for women's control of resources in a system in which women are increasingly losing their social and economic clout. In the end, it is these historical conditions and indigenous dynamics—rather than the structure or content of the development enterprise—that underlie the popularity, the character, and the success of the MFO.

The Decline of the Moving Forward Movement

I returned to Mu'a in 1987 to find that a number of changes, centrally and locally, had occurred in the MFO. The FSP had moved from a monitor to a supervisor of the development agenda, while the Tongan Catholic nuns, no longer officially associated with the program, offered assistance on a sporadic and volunteer basis, as their schedules allowed.

Overseas budget cuts for small-scale women's programs had forced some new funding decisions. As the FSP administrator told me, the main island groups already had a long history of success. Moreover, group representatives were now petitioning the central organization for seed money to generate income for nonessential household improvements, such as vinyl flooring for their homes. Given the fact that many main island members now had water tanks, kitchens, pig fencing, and other basic improvements, the central organization turned its attention to the outer islands and ended the main island assistance, inspection, and monitoring program.

The changes I encountered at the village level were startling. Infighting and lack of interest had led to a number of member dropouts that left many of the groups with only two or three members. As a result, and at the suggestion of a local nun, the MFO in Mu'a reformed into two groups. The organization suspended the regular Sunday meetings, and there was notably poor attendance at even those infrequent meetings held.

Most surprising was the fact that there were no more group-based income-generating activities. Without these weekly activities, MF women also ended their rotating contribution fund. The MF Canteen was rented to a family, who operated the store as a family business in exchange for a minimal rental fee of T$20 per month plus electricity. The hall itself was given over to a men's group who ran kava-drinking parties for profit six days a week. They paid a rental of T$60 per month, an amount that often simply covered electric costs, and agreed as well to provide free labor for the hall's varnishing and repairs. Movies, still held regularly, were run by an entrepreneur from Nuku'alofa, who gave the MFO 10 percent of the gate for each movie—an arrangement that resulted in minimal, if any, profit for the organization. The kindergarten continued to operate, officially under the auspices of the MFO. However, it was now run by a committee of kindergarten parents, composed of both member and nonmember households, and on a separate budget with independent overseas funding.

In short, the MFO in Mu'a divested itself of all of its income-raising group activities, and there was no development fund for use at the end of the year. Accordingly, the organization ended its program of development inspections and reverted to one annual inspection, conducted locally, of traditional wealth, that is, bark-cloth and pandanus mats, produced outside the organization itself.

At first glance the MFO seems a familiar portrait of project failure, characterized by funding constraints and undercapitalization on the part of planners, coupled with a lack of self-sufficiency and infighting on the part of participants. Indeed, seen from a short-term factor-oriented perspective, one is led to the conclusion that the withdrawal of central leadership and funding support resulted in the collapse of the rural development organization.

However, the processes of MF decline were in effect well before the planning decisions and funding cuts of 1986, as evidenced by membership rolls in Mu'a. Original groups were begun in 1974 with one hundred women. By 1978 there were eighty-eight active MF members. In 1981 the membership count was sixty-six, and by 1983 membership rolls had dropped to fifty-five. When I returned to Mu'a in 1987, only thirty women remained active members. Clearly, a pattern of waning membership had been occurring throughout the 1980s, and the withdrawal of funding in 1985—which amounted to only $30 annually for a group of ten—was not the kingpin of membership decline.

The factors that *can* account for the drop in membership involve both the internal dynamics of the MFO and the changing economic context in which these were occurring. If we reorient the analysis to the long-term contextual perspective of this discussion, it is clear that the MFO was a successful, vital organization, based on very particular social conditions that, themselves, were in flux. The institutional successes and structures of the MFO were contingent on the continuing importance of kinship, prestige, and reciprocity, set in a context of growing commoditization, personal mobility, and wealth differences. Although kinship had long served to mitigate the formation of bona fide social classes, wealth differences among Tongan commoners had already begun to appear and to affect both life-style and attitudes. These indigenous conditions, much more so than the vagaries of development planning and funding, can account for the changes that occurred in the MF movement.

In 1983 I conducted interviews with women who had dropped out from the MFO during the previous two years to determine their reasons for discontinuing their participation. Although overseas migration had claimed some members and infighting others, the overwhelming consensus of dropouts was that the *kavenga,* that is, the responsibilities or burdens of MF membership, had become too much for their household to bear. The demands of membership on their time and their pocketbooks had caused women to reevaluate their membership or caused their husbands to withdraw their support, many demanding that their wives sit out.

If one understands the true basis of MFO economics, then one realizes that an increase in the economic burdens of membership was neither a peculiarity of one village nor the product of inadequate central planning. It was, rather, a direct consequence of the MFO's success. In a development institution whose accomplishments are really based on the escrow of personal resources, it stands to reason that the elevation of goals or the growth of functions will necessitate complementary increases in the level of personal resources contributed. And as MF women added functions like funeral gifts to members, as they invested in permanent structures demanding constant capital outlays for upkeep, like the store, hall, and kindy, and as they elevated their group goals from a clean toilet area to a free-standing wooden kitchen, so too did they elevate the amount of resources they needed to divert to the MFO. Given the basis of institutional economics, the spiraling of *kavenga* was built into its success and growth.

The upshot of MFO success was, thus, increased economic pressures on the membership—pressures that eventuated in the loss of members. More specifically, under conditions of growing rural wealth differences, the consequence of economic pressure was the loss of its poorer members.

By 1984 the MFO was disproportionately drawing on the wealthier segment of the community. Tables 14-2 and 14-3 compare the economic status of MF households with the economic status of the village as a whole in 1984. Table 14-2 compares the economic status of households (high, high-middle, low-middle, and low) on the basis of rough indicators of disposable wealth (household type, toilet type, and the presence or absence of electric-

Table 14-2 / Economic Status in MF Households and the Village as a Whole

	MF HOUSEHOLDS		VILLAGE	
ECONOMIC STATUS	N	(%)	N	(%)
High	20	(40)	62	(24)
High-middle	15	(30)	82	(31)
Low-middle	10	(20)	55	(21)
Low	5	(10)	57	(22)
Not classified	N	N	77	(2)
Total	50		263	

Table 14-3 / Landholding among MF Households and in the Village as a Whole

	LANDED		LANDLESS		
	N	%	N	(%)	TOTAL
MF HOUSEHOLDS	43	(86)	7	(14)	50
VILLAGE	168	(64)	95	(36)	263

ity).[16] Table 14-3 compares MF membership to the village as a whole on the basis of landholding.

Whether seen by indicators of economic status (Table 14-2) or by land-holding (Table 14-3), MF members are not representative of the village as a whole. Poorer households, some 22 percent of the village, are underrepresented in the MFO, contributing only 10 percent of the total membership. Conversely, the 24 percent of the village with high economic status are overrepresented in the organization, constituting 40 percent of membership rolls. And though 36 percent of village households hold neither registered nor unregistered land, a full 86 percent of MF households are landed. Thus, when FSP administrators received group petitions for help from members whose goal was vinyl flooring—an occurrence that contributed to ending the main island funding program—these petitions represented nothing less than a product of organizational dynamics. It was an expression of the general fact that the MFO was drawing on an increasingly narrow and wealthy segment of the community.

The immediate consequence of the organization's declining membership was not only that the participant base was wealthier but also that institutional responsibility devolved on a smaller and smaller core of women. There were fewer women to stage activities and fewer member households and kin groups to support the organization, despite the fact that many capital expenditures of the organization remained constant, for example, electricity and hall maintenance. In a development institution truly based on entrepreneurial capitalism, a smaller membership would simply result in greater per capita profits. However, in an institution whose funds come through the conversion of household income through community attendance at regularly staged events, fewer members meant fewer contributions, fewer events, and fewer funds to defray the costs of maintaining organizational functions or to escrow for a development fund. The MFO became an institution of diminishing returns, with many of its activities beginning to lose money.

The burdens of membership, coupled with the growing economic division in the village, had other consequences for those who remained members. Where economic differences existed in the membership, it became harder for groups to cooperatively decide on mutual goals or to cooperatively bring those goals to fruition. While wealthier women might have wanted an annual goal of water tanks, poorer women simply wanted to rethatch their latrine area. Some groups, thus, decided to individualize member goals, inspecting different items for different members—a change that often made cooperative efforts, like building water tanks in rotation, untenable.

And even where groups agreed on the same goals, there often were problems based on economic differences: a member who must sit out during an inspection because the desired goal proved too ambitious, a woman who could not follow through on her group loan obligations. Invariably, the repercussions of such events involved the ongoing cooperative relations within the group. As I witnessed, the woman who could not meet inspection goals gave up her membership in the following year; the group in which one woman reneged on her group loan split angrily.

Even when members can decide and follow through on their goals, their arrangements to do so have become increasingly differentiated. While the wealthier woman can supplement group income with personal income for building projects, women with more moderate resources may need to take out supplementary loans, often with others in the same economic circumstances. Poorer women may have to opt out of loan arrangements altogether, choosing instead to engage with others in some additional income-generating activity outside the MFO, such as the sale of prepared food in the village. The result, therefore, even when groups agreed on and accomplished their goals, is that many MF groups maintained groups within groups that made their own loan arrangements, formed their own savings associations, or conducted their own "businesses" or other economic activities.

Leadership, and its relationship to membership, has also been affected by wealth differences. Although MF women continue to elect high-prestige figures to the more public village offices, they have begun, at the more local level of groups, to choose their wealthiest women as leaders. In 1984 the majority of operating groups had chosen the wealthiest woman as their leader, and they did so with the common Tongan understanding that the leader would "help" them with group obligations. Thus, for inspection feasts, the leader is expected to shoulder the more onerous obligations, such as the provision of a pig.

In itself, new leadership patterns and expectations create new forms of social division. Some wealthier women approach their involvement with the idea that they really join to "help" others not so fortunate. Often such women feel they are giving much, for little in return, especially when they have the personal resources to build kitchens or water tanks on their own. When group decisions do not go their way, or when personal slights occur within the group, these women tend to drop out in anger, feeling the group is ungrateful for their efforts. As one wealthier woman told me about leaving her group, "I can paddle my canoe alone." Members, on the other hand, may feel that their leader is not doing enough as a "patron," or is "eating group money," that is to say, using her leadership to her own advantage rather than for the benefit of the group.

The growth of rural wealth differences, then, in concert with the spiraling burdens of MF membership, has had the overall effect of fragmenting the MF effort. Development efforts have become more divided and individualized, reducing the arenas for cooperative action. Internal relations among members and between leaders and members have become increasingly strained. And, together with the loss of cohesiveness, waning membership numbers have placed the cost of maintaining the organization on a shrinking core of women, with the result that even the possibility of breaking even by one's membership is threatened.

It is no wonder that MF women were content to end their "profit-generating" activities, to revert to inspections of traditional wealth only, and to hand over control of the Canteen, the hall, and the kindergarten to other interested parties. All these decisions are consistent in that, although they generate minimal income for the members, they eliminate the possibility that members will lose resources through their participation. The changes also obviate the need for close cooperative effort and mutual-aid schemes among members—arrangements that have been frought with increasing difficulties and strains.

The members, in effect, have become caretakers of an institution that, as before, no longer lost or gained its members anything, but also that no longer generated a development fund. It has come to be, in other words, a development failure.

Summary and Conclusions

The MFO is a case study of a sensitive bureaucracy, a favorable cultural environment, and a successful development institution that enabled the re-distribution of wealth to women. However, the success of the MFO was never really based on the effectiveness of bureaucratic structure nor even on the content of the development plan. The socioeconomic context of the contemporary Tongan village very quickly infused the planned institutional model of self-help—just as it did unplanned traditional wealth organization—reformulating its structure and operation to reproduce indigenous social dynamics. And it was these same social dynamics—rather than changes in development structures and policies—that ultimately resulted in the decline and failures of the MFO.

Although my case study argues for the benefits of long-term, contextually oriented project evaluations and development research, the most important implication of this analysis is to call into question the entire development agenda—whatever its bureaucratic context. Development planners and agencies differ on the correct formula for Third World development, but they converge on the notion that a "correctly" conceived, structured, and implemented plan will work. Thus, as programs continue to fail, they attend to the problems in their own organization and conception (for instance, the local and unconnected nature of women's small-group rural projects) or to the implementation problems (for instance, the resistance of men) that need to be addressed in the future so that the program will be successful. The solutions, thus, would seem to be to "integrate" women's projects with national development efforts or to include efforts toward "educating men" with the project implementation guidelines.

The question raised here, however, concerns the core assumption of the development enterprise: Can socioeconomic change—the ultimate purpose of all development—be planned? The answer, I suggest, is that it cannot; the factors that are really affecting institutional successes and failures at accomplishing change exist at a social and historical depth that is beyond the ability of development planners to affect—at least, not given the economic and political limitations of the development enterprise.

It is, indeed, a form of arrogance to believe that the administrators, bureaucracies, and programs of the international planning community, without the political or economic clout to significantly change a nation's social order, can transform or reverse social realities that proceed from that order. Thus, for instance, most development agencies are in the untenable position of attempting to alleviate the effects of class development—a process associated with growing wealth differences between men and women, rich and poor—in a society undergoing class formation. And when our programs do not work, we look to improve our plans and bureaucratic strategies. It is, in my view, equally arrogant to presume that failures in Third World development proceed from some flaw in our own thinking or organization. Without both politicizing development efforts and recognizing the import of indigenous social processes (and, for instance, devoting support to indigenous movements like unions that tend to counter class inequities), development efforts will be futile. It is important to understand that, even if planners were able to assume more revolutionary directions, an unlikely scenario given the source of most development funding, planners can no more make "revolution" than they can make social change. Revolutionary programs can succeed only when there are indigenous revolutionary movements underway.

If there is a prescription here for planning and development, it is to recognize its limitations. As this volume attests, there may be better and worse bureaucratic structures through which to carry out development plans, but no development bureaucracy will itself provide the solution to instituting social change. This shift in the conception of the potency of the development enterprise would not only reduce the billions of wasted aid dollars that threaten to undermine any future support of the Third World but, more importantly, more honestly represent the inflated promises of Third World development planning.

Notes

1. Tonga Office, Foundation for Peoples of the South Pacific (FSP), Evaluation Report (Nuku'alofa, Tonga: unpublished manuscript, 1980); David C. Wyler, "Case Studies on Women in Development in the Kingdom of Tonga" (unpublished paper submitted to the School for International Training, Brattleboro, Vt., 1981).

2. Lorraine Sexton, "Women in Development Documentation Project: Evaluation Paper" (submitted to the Foundation for Peoples of the South Pacific, New York, 1985), pp. 8, 26.

3. Mu'a is the actual name of the general area in which the case study village is located, but it is a pseudonym for the particular village.

4. Sexton, "Women in Development Documentation Project," p. 379.

5. Inspections were always associated with prestige and the monitoring of household resources by people of rank, but in preconstitutional Tonga they were conducted for the purpose of chiefly appropriation of commoner production.

6. Adrienne L. Kaeppler, "Rank in Tonga," *Ethnology* 10, no. 2 (1971): 183.

7. Ibid., p. 177.

8. Garth Rogers, "The Father's Sister is Black: A Consideration of Female Rank and Powers in Tonga," *Journal of the Polynesian Society* 86, no. 2 (1977): 157–82; Christine Ward Gailey, *Kinship to Kingship* (Austin: University of Texas Press, 1987), p. 60.

9. Gailey, *Kinship to Kingship,* pp. 63ff.; Adrienne L. Kaeppler, "Me'a Faka'eiki: Tongan Funerals in a Changing Society," in *The Changing Pacific: Essays in Honor of Harry Maude,* ed. N. Gunson (Canberra: Australian National University Press, 1978), pp. 174–202.

10. Cathy A. Small, "Women's Associations and their Pursuit of Wealth in Tonga: Study in Social Change" (Ph.D. diss., Temple University, 1987), pp. 243–44.

11. Cathy A. Small, "Sociocultural Foundations for Environmental Health Planning in the Kingdom of Tonga" (report submitted to the World Health Organization, Office of the Western Pacific, Manila, Philippines, 1984).

12. Small, "Women's Associations."

13. Donations involving animals and agricultural produce were assessed at their market value and figured into the calculations as cash.

14. Outlays and revenues, though equal in amount, were not necessarily the same in kind. Outlays included such items as donations of produce for inspection feasts, expenses for staging events, contributions made to member families at funerals, and the maintenance and repair of the Women's Hall. Revenues were composed of cash receipts from paid attendance at MF events or donations at MF fundraisers.

15. The requirements that members purchase tickets for their own attendance at major MF events amounts to a similar technique for securing resources. Despite the fact that members fund, stage, and work these events, MF women elect to charge members for their attendance. In fact, MF women have elected each year to establish two price structures for major affairs—one for members and one for nonmembers—

with the seemingly curious provision that members pay more than nonmembers. The logic behind the practice, however, is that by charging themselves more, the women will have more to divide at the end.

By contrast, in contexts where accumulation is not the tacit purpose behind the rule, MF women establish rules that favor members. For instance, when a member is intending to privately raise cash through rental of the Women's Hall, charges to members will be less than to nonmembers.

16. Indicators represent features that are the contemporary markers of wealth to most Tongan villagers. A household of high economic status was considered to be one with a wooden or concrete house, electricity, and western plumbing with a flush toilet. Middle-status households had wooden dwelling homes with a thatched-covered pit latrine toilet; the high and low divisions of this category were distinguished by the presence or absence of electricity. Low economic status or poor households were characterized by a thatched dwelling house with no electricity and a pit-latrine toilet.

15/Mainstreaming Women in Development: Four Agency Approaches

Rounaq Jahan

Introduction

The world has witnessed a remarkable surge in the women's movement that has put forward over the last two decades a bold vision of social transformation and challenged the global community to respond. This article reviews the response of one set of key players: the international donor agencies dealing with women's development issues. It focuses on the actions of four donors, two bilateral (Norway and Canada) and two multilateral (the World Bank and the United Nations Development Program) and attempts to assess their performance in the last twenty years in broad strokes. It asks three basic sets of questions. First, what were the articulated objectives of their special policies and measures to promote women's advancement? Were they responsive to the aspiration of the women's movement? Second, did the donors adopt any identifiable set of strategies to realize the policy objectives? Were they effective? And finally, what were the results? Was there any quantitative and qualitative evidence to suggest progress?

The two bilateral donors—Canada and Norway—were selected because they have a reputation among donors of mounting major initiatives for women. They number among the few agencies who adopted detailed women-in-development (WID) or gender-and-development (GAD) policies. In contrast, the two multilateral donors—United Nations Development Program (UNDP) and the World Bank—were chosen not on the strength of their WID/GAD mandates and policies, but because of the influence they wield in shaping the development strategies of the countries of the South. The World Bank through its conditionalities often dictates policy reforms to aid-recipient governments. The UNDP, as the largest fund, has a big presence within the United Nations system. The actions of these two agencies—what they advocate and what they omit or marginalize—have a strong impact on the policy analysis and investments of the aid-recipient countries.

The study is primarily based on published and unpublished data collected from the four donor agencies.[1]

The Analytical Framework

I use a relatively simple analytical framework to conceptualize and compare the policy objectives, strategies, and measures of progress (see Figure 1). To compare policy objectives, I differentiate between substantive and process-focused instrumental objectives. In their various policy statements and documents, donors have referred to substantive objectives such as women's advancement, gender equality, women's empowerment, and so on. They have also committed themselves to process-focused instrumental objectives such as women's "integration" and "mainstreaming." Generally, donors have highlighted process-focused instrumental objectives. Early on in the Decade for Women (1975–1985), donors chose "integration of women in development" as the objective of their policies. But many feminists, especially those from the South, rejected the goal of integration. They argued that women did not want to be integrated in an unequal and exploitative system—they wanted to change the prevailing system. Dissatisfaction with the concept of integration led many development agencies to shift to a new term—"mainstreaming" women in development. Mainstreaming was chosen as a goal because it was felt that WID ghettos were being created during the Decade for Women in the name of integration.

MAINSTREAMING: INTEGRATIONIST AND AGENDA-SETTING

But what does mainstreaming mean? Mainstreaming as a concept obviously reflects a desire to be at the center-stage, part of the mainstream. Two broad approaches to Mainstreaming can be identified.[2] The first, which I call "integrationist," builds gender issues within existing development paradigms; the overall development agenda is not transformed but each issue is adapted to take into account women-and-gender concerns.

The second approach, which I call "agenda setting," implies transformation of the existing development agenda with a gender perspective. Women participate in all development decisions and through this process bring about a fundamental change in the existing development paradigm. Women not only become a part of the mainstream, they also reorient the nature of the mainstream. It is not simply women as individuals but women's "agenda" that gets recognition from the mainstream.

Figure 1 / Analytical Framework for Assessment of WID/GAD Policies and Measures

1. **Objectives**

   (A) Substantive
   Women's advancement
   Gender equality
   Women's empowerment

   (B) Instrumental
   Integration
   Mainstreaming

2. **Approach**

   Integrationist
   Agenda-setting

3. **Strategies**

   (A) Institutional
   Responsibility
   Accountability
   Coordination
   Monitoring
   Evaluation
   Personnel policy

   (B) Operational
   Guidelines
   Training
   Research
   Special projects
   Country programming
   Macro-policies
   Policy dialogues

4. **Measures of Progress**

   Mainstreaming
   Resources
   Discourse

WID STRATEGIES: INSTITUTIONAL AND OPERATIONAL

Again two broad categories can be used in comparing WID strategies of donors: institutional and operational. Institutional strategies are the input-side interventions that aim primarily at structural changes within agencies to facilitate the implementation of WID policies and measures. Operational strategies on the other hand are the output-oriented measures designed to bring about a change in the work program of agencies.

MEASURING PROGRESS

Assessing progress is difficult because agencies do not have systematic data on the impact of their interventions. They collect primarily input data. Based on available data, two rough indicators can be constructed to gauge progress in mainstreaming. The first, mainstreaming resources available in donor agencies, uses quantitative data about women's representation on the staff and women-oriented assistance. The second indicator is primarily based on qualitative information to assess achievements over time in mainstreaming gender issues in development discourse.

Policy Objectives

Donors varied in their articulation of policy objectives for women. The two bilateral donors—Norway and Canada—spelled out their objectives in some detail when they adopted their WID policies. In contrast, the two multilateral donors did not elaborate or even adopt formal WID policies for a long time, and started implementing WID measures before adopting formal documents.

Over the years the articulation of policy objectives changed. Prior to the Decade for Women the emphasis was on substantive objectives, but during the Decade the emphasis shifted to process-focused objectives. Policy approaches also gradually changed from "women in development" to "gender and development," the former implying a consideration of women's roles only and the latter paying attention to the socially constructed roles of both women and men. Within this broad framework, however, there were considerable differences between the four donors.

Norway's WID policy goals have changed over the past three decades from a straightforward emphasis on women's welfare to an amalgam of women's welfare, integration, and mainstreaming. Parliamentary *White Paper* no. 29 (1971–1972) for the first time raised the question of women's issues, calling for improvement of women's weak social position. The 1984–1985 Parliamentary *White Paper* gave a more comprehensive WID mandate. The WID policy—set in 1985—clearly endorsed an agenda-setting mainstreaming objective. It called for "placing women in the mainstream of development" as well as changing the mainstream "to make it benefit women." The policy underscored the importance of building on "women's strengths, needs, and interests," urging a stronger focus on the "human and social aspects of development" as well as "reconceptualization" of some aspects of "the economic and organizational models on which traditional development strategies are based."[3]

Following an overall national policy to achieve gender equality, the Canadian International Development Agency (CIDA) announced a WID policy for the first time in 1976. In 1984 CIDA adopted a more detailed WID policy framework, and in 1986 a five-year WID action plan. In 1992 CIDA came forward with a revised WID policy framework. The 1976 WID policy guidelines emphasized women's equal participation as agents and beneficiaries, and their "equitable integration into the mainstream of the agency's work."[4] The 1984 WID policy pledged that "the full range of its development assistance will contribute substantively to the realization of the full potential of women as agents and beneficiaries of the development process." The revised WID policy of 1992 emphasized women's decision-making roles, as opposed to their roles as agents and beneficiaries of development, thereby indicating a growing sensitivity towards an agenda-setting approach. It underscored the need for CIDA to work toward "empowerment of women." The revised 1992 policy was termed "women in development and gender equity."[5]

Though UNDP issued WID project and programming guidelines in 1976 and 1977, respectively, a formal WID policy was articulated only in 1987. The agency stated its concern as ensuring "the integration of women as participants and beneficiaries in all of its development program and projects."[6] The policy statement did not pledge gender equity, nor did it identify any feminist agenda. In recent years, UNDP has started to refer to "mainstreaming." It has also highlighted national capacity building as a priority objective. Although starting with a WID approach, UNDP officially shifted to GAD in 1992.

The World Bank came forward with a policy paper on women only in 1994, though it established a WID-responsible office nearly twenty years earlier. Like UNDP, the Bank referred to a broad objective, namely, "enhancing women's participation in economic development."[7] The Bank's substantive policy objectives have not changed much since 1987, when its operative WID policy statement called for "enhancing the role of women in economic development."[8] The 1994 policy paper, however, underscored shifts in the Bank's instrumental objectives and approaches. It has committed itself to "mainstreaming gender concerns into its operations" and stated that its analytical framework would change from WID to GAD; changing male roles and responsibilities is also explicitly recognized. The approach is, however, primarily integrationist.

Institutional Strategies

In the last two decades donor agencies have adopted a variety of measures designed to institutionalize WID/GAD in their organizations. These measures were detailed by the two bilateral donors in their five-year WID action plans. The two multilateral donors on the other hand, adopted measures gradually, on an ad hoc basis. The institutional strategies included a variety of procedures relating to WID/GAD responsibility, accountability, co-ordination, monitoring, evaluation, and personnel policies. Not all donors adopted all the instruments and procedures.

It is difficult to assess the efficacy of various institutional strategies because of a lack of systematic data about the actual workings of different measures. Still, enough information is available to identify some common patterns and draw a few conclusions.

RESPONSIBILITY

WID gained a tentative institutional foothold only after the first UN Women's Conference in Mexico, which urged national governments and international organizations to establish specific administrative responsibility structures for women. Agencies experimented with different structures and functions. They started with single WID advisory positions in the late 1970s, increased WID resources and created separate WID divisions in the mid-1980s, but by 1992–1993 the agencies had moved away from separate WID divisions to either single advisory positions or the so-called flat structure in which the program team is coequal with several other teams working on cross-cutting themes.

The mandate of WID/GAD offices also changed over the years. Generally, they were mandated with advocacy, co-ordination, and monitoring roles, leaving responsibility for implementing WID policies in the hands of the program managers. Although WID responsibility was formally allocated to program managers, many of these officers had neither the time nor the expertise to address gender issues, and in reality it was the WID offices that had to shoulder the main responsibility for providing technical support to operational managers.

The resources allocated to WID responsibility structures were far from adequate. WID offices were generally given two to four regular-budget, professional positions, buttressed by consultancies and extra-budgetary resources. WID positions, especially in field offices, were created at the junior level, which was often a constraint on influencing operational programs. In many cases WID specialists were assigned responsibilities outside the official bilateral country program framework.

It appears that structural location made very little difference to WID efficacy. The critical factors are the definition of mission, resources, commitment, and accountability measures to ensure agency compliance.

ACCOUNTABILITY

The donor agencies have experimented with several instruments to ensure internal accountability for WID, including staff performance appraisal, project/program screening, approval, evaluation, and so on.

CIDA and, to a limited extent, UNDP have used annual staff performance appraisals to hold staff accountable for WID. The CIDA's WID assessment, however, found that performance review did not work very well. It was "too vague and diffuse." The evaluation report argued that, rather than making all agency staff accountable, it would be more effective to hold only key managers (operations, vice presidents, and country program directors) accountable for WID achievements.[9]

Project/program screening was another instrument used by donor agencies to increase WID compliance. WID advisors and offices in the Norwegian Agency for Development Cooperation (NORAD), CIDA, and UNDP participated in project approval boards that could be used as checkpoints to hold operational programs in line with WID goals. CIDA's WID office appears to have exercised a strong authority in project approval decisions and the agency's WID evaluation noted that many existing projects in CIDA were "WID retrofitted."[10] The World Bank did not introduce any project screening procedure, nor did the WID office have any voice in project/program approval.

Public accountability was stronger in the two bilateral agencies than the two multilateral ones. Both the Norwegian and the Canadian development agencies reported through their ministries to parliament, whose debates were held in the public domain. In contrast, the work of the two multilateral agencies—UNDP and the World Bank—was largely shielded from the scrutiny of public interest groups.

COORDINATION

In the 1980s and 1990s the donors have not been able to come forward with satisfactory co-ordination mechanisms. Only the two bilateral donors established separate WID co-ordinating bodies; the two multilateral agencies did not have any formal co-ordination mechanism. CIDA's co-ordinating mechanism—the WID Steering Committee—was relatively more successful than Norway's.

MONITORING

Generally, three types of monitoring device were used by donors: annual reporting requirements, WID action on project-reporting formats; and statistical reporting on donor assistance. The annual reporting requirements were generally descriptive, and as such they had limited value in measuring progress towards WID policy objectives. The other two tools—WID action on project-reporting formats and statistical reporting of donor assistance—could be used as measures of "integration" and "mainstreaming."

All the donors introduced annual reporting requirements. The two bilateral donors introduced a mandatory WID classification system on projects as well as adopted the statistical reporting format of the Organization for Economic Cooperation and Development/Development Assistance Committee (OECD/DAC) on WID assistance. The OECD/DAC format classified women-oriented aid into two categories: "WID specific" and "WID integrated."[11] The two multilateral donors adopted neither mandatory WID classification of projects nor a system of statistical reporting of WID assistance. The WID divisions of the UNDP and the World Bank monitored projects for their WID contents for several years but later gave up their efforts.

EVALUATION

Donors adopted several measures to include gender considerations in their evaluations: guidelines, checklists, and specific methodologies, for example, that were included in their evaluation manuals. Agencies were required to include gender issues in the terms of reference (TOR) of evaluations and to include women in evaluation teams.

Despite corporate mandates, guidelines, and methodologies, however, only a small percentage of evaluations have addressed gender issues systematically. For example, a recent assessment of DAC donors found that, notwithstanding terms of reference addressing gender issues in 70 percent of a sample of agency operations, only about 40 percent of evaluation reports contained a full discussion of gender issues.[12] Similarly, a desk review of fifty general UNDP evaluations conducted in 1987 found marginal treatment of WID/GAD issues.[13]

PERSONNEL POLICY

The donor agencies adopted several policy instruments to increase the number of women on their staff: quotas, targets, and career development policies were the three most frequently used. The two multilateral donors did not formally adopt any of these three instruments, although their corporate leadership publicly expressed a concern to increase women's numbers in their agencies, particularly in management positions. The two bilateral donors, by contrast, adopted either a system of quotas (Norway) or targets (Canada).

They also took on gender-responsive career development policies to retain female staff.

Operational Strategies

Along with institutionalization, WID operationalization was a major concern of donor agencies. Guidelines, training, research, special projects, country programming, macro policies, and policy dialogue were used over the years to influence agency operations. A few donors, including Canada and Norway, adopted a coherent set of strategies to influence operations as part of their WID action plans, while others developed instruments and procedures gradually. It is difficult to assess the actual use of these tools and their influence on operations, since they were not systematically monitored by agencies.

GUIDELINES
This was one of the earliest strategies used by the donors. All four donors developed detailed guidance for their operations. Some donors, such as UNDP, classified their guidelines under "special considerations"; others, like CIDA, integrated the guidelines in the program and project cycle. Both general and sectoral guidelines were used. Donors such as NORAD established targets and timetables; others used only broad programming directions.

Despite detailed guidance, there were gaps between the guidelines and their actual use. For example, successive reports of the CIDA WID Steering Committee pointed out that gender issues often were considered too late in the process of program/project development, that technical gender expertise was not sought early enough, and CIDA's development partners, particularly Canadian executing agencies (CEA), had little gender expertise and commitment.[14] CIDA's WID policy assessment found similar limited use of the guidelines.[15] UNDP's 1989 review of the implementation of its WID measures showed that during the previous country programming cycle (1987–1991) "advisory notes in only 4 field offices referred to gender issues."[16]

TRAINING
Training was identified by the donors as an effective instrument to raise awareness and expertise of agency staff on gender issues. CIDA and the World Bank prioritized training in the initial years of their WID programs; in contrast the UNDP and NORAD started staff training only in the late 1980s. Generally agencies have focused on training of their own staff though some of the agencies, CIDA for example, have organized training of their development partners. CIDA also succeeded in putting most of its staff

through WID training. In other agencies only a small fraction of staff was exposed to some type of WID/GAD training.

RESEARCH

Research played a significant role in making gender issues visible and it continues to be a critical programming strategy. By generating quantitative and qualitative data, research not only raised awareness about gender issues but also served as the basis of developing all other operational tools. All four donors emphasized research and disaggregation of data by gender as important programming tools. CIDA, NORAD, and the World Bank prepared country-by-country WID profiles or situation analyses as part of their preparation of country WID/GAD strategy. The two bilateral donors, CIDA and NORAD, used OECD/DAC's statistical reporting format on women-oriented assistance and required that management information on "agents and beneficiaries" of projects be broken down by gender. UNDP and the World Bank, on the other hand, did not require such a gender-desegregated breakdown of management information. Donors used operational research to draw lessons about the best practice in a wide variety of sectors. The World Bank, especially, focused on policy analysis to elaborate gender issues in sector and macroeconomic policies.

SPECIAL PROJECTS

Special projects for women was one of the initial operational strategies pushed by the donors. The rationale for the special projects was to demonstrate on the ground approaches to overcome obstacles to women's participation. Indeed, action projects, usually developed by non-governmental organizations (NGOs), showed innovative approaches to reaching women and linking them with development resources. But despite the demonstrated success of a number of special projects, this approach faced strong criticism from many feminists. They argued that instead of leading to replication and mainstreaming, the special projects in most cases were creating an alibi effect.[17] Critics pointed out that the special projects focus had deterred consideration of gender issues in macro and sector policy frameworks and in major programs.

COUNTRY PROGRAMMING

Country programming was identified by all the donors as one of the most promising strategies to mainstream gender issues. Generally, three instruments were used by donors to address gender issues in country program exercises: preparation of WID/GAD country strategies, action plans, and a package of WID components in major sectoral projects and programs.

NORAD, CIDA, and more recently the World Bank have used all three instruments in a systematic manner.

The WID/GAD country strategies and plans prepared by the donors had mixed successes. The country WID/GAD profiles and situation analyses were useful for program analysis. But WID country plans were often treated as annexes to the bilateral aid programs rather than as guides to shape and change these programs. For example, only 14 percent of CIDA's bilateral staff reported that the CIDA/WID country strategy and the general CIDA/ WID policy have had a major influence on their country programs, and 33 percent reported that there had been no significant influence.[18] UNDP's 1989 review found that though 41 percent of country programs during the previous programming cycle referred to WID issues, only nine country programs actually translated this general reference into concrete programs and projects.[19]

MACRO POLICIES

In the last decade, donor assistance has increasingly shifted from projects to policies, largely due to the IMF and World Bank's focus on structural adjustment programs (SAP). At present SAPs constitute nearly a third of the total aid package. Donors have developed two types of gender-responsive approaches to structural adjustment.[20] One approach has emphasized measures to mitigate the adverse impact of SAPs, often through retargeting of public expenditure to poor women. Another approach has highlighted the barriers that gender relations create against the operations of adjustment measures (such as women's unremunerated reproductive labor) and recommended public provisioning of childcare and care of the elderly, and supply of basic needs like water and fuel to reduce market distortions.

Donor agencies have started sponsoring research on macro economic policies from a gender perspective, but further work is required before it is possible to draw firm conclusions about gender-responsive interventions.

POLICY DIALOGUE

As aid negotiations focused more on policy reforms, policy dialogues emerged as a key area for setting agendas. However, until now WID/gender issues have tended to be largely ignored in the policy dialogues. There were two major constraints. First, the structure of representation in dialogue virtually ensured women's exclusion. Generally, policy dialogues were carried out between donors and partner governments; very few women had attained the senior decision making level to represent either the donors or the partner governments in the dialogue. CIDA's WID evaluation found that the agency had been least successful in addressing gender issues in policy dialogue and structural adjustment.[21]

Measuring Progress

What has been the impact of the WID/GAD policies and measures implemented by the donor agencies in the 1980s and 1990s? Have they succeeded in bringing about a major shift in overall policy priorities, investment decisions, and agency behavior? More important, could one demonstrate that as a result of the WID/GAD policies and instruments, progress has been achieved in improving women's condition and realizing the goal of gender equality? What are the measures of progress?

Until now donors have generated quantitative data in three areas: gender distribution of agency personnel, WID classification of budget, and WID classification of projects. But the donors have not yet systematically assessed the impact of their assistance on improving women's condition and achieving gender equality in the partner countries. Part of the problem in measuring progress stems from the donors' failure to establish key indicators to track achievement of WID policy goals.

Assessment of progress has to be part quantitative and part impressionistic. To assess progress in mainstreaming, two broad indicators are used: mainstreaming resources and mainstreaming discourse. Personnel and budget data are analyzed to see whether women are being mainstreamed in agencies' resources. And public documents from donors are scrutinized to find out whether gender issues are gaining visibility and transforming the development discourse.

MAINSTREAMING RESOURCES

During the 1980s, most of the agencies succeeded in creating and maintaining a small WID-specific staff and budget, though these perpetually faced the prospects of withering away in the name of successful integration and mainstreaming. The number of female staff in the agencies also registered a slow and steady progress in the 1980s as a result of affirmative-action personnel policies. WID budgets—WID-specific as well as WID-integrated—also increased gradually, though calculating WID budgets was methodologically problematic.

Women's Share of Personnel

Personnel data from the four donor agencies indicate that women's share of jobs in the professional categories improved slowly from approximately 20 percent in 1975 to roughly 30 percent in 1992–1993—only a 10 percent increase over twenty years! Generally, the greatest increase was in the category of junior and senior professionals; women's numbers in management positions, however, still remain low. On the whole, the bilateral donors have a better record than the multilateral organizations: by 1993, the two bilateral donors had achieved near-parity for women in professional categories, and approximately one-fifth of management positions in these two agencies were filled by women. In contrast, by 1993 in the two multilateral organizations women constituted only about a quarter of the professional staff, and less than 10 percent of management positions were occupied by women.[22]

Of the four donors, the World Bank has the lowest percentage of professional and managerial women. Starting with a low base, women's representation at the Bank increased at a slow pace—from 12 percent in 1985 to 16 percent in 1993. Counting all job categories, women constituted 28 percent of the Bank's employees. At senior management levels, women's share rose from 1 percent in 1985 to 8 percent in 1993. At junior professional levels it increased from 17 percent in 1985 to 24 percent in 1993. Women did not fare any better at the UNDP. Women's share of professional and managerial jobs crawled from 20 percent in 1975 to 29 percent in 1993. In nearly twenty years, women's representation at senior management levels increased from 3 to 10 percent, and in junior professional categories it actually declined from 46 percent to 35 percent.

In contrast, by 1993, the two bilateral donors were close to achieving parity for women at least in professional categories. NORAD had the highest percentage of professional women. In 1985 already half of NORAD's professional positions were filled by women, two-thirds of junior professionals and a little over a quarter of senior professionals and junior managers were women. By 1992 the biggest change in NORAD was the significant increase in women's share of senior professional positions—from 28 percent in 1985 to 43 percent. Women's participation at senior managerial levels also rose— from 7 percent in 1985 to 16 percent in 1992. Of all donors, CIDA followed the most systematic approach of setting targets for each category of jobs, and it registered a steady progress in employment equity for all categories. In the fifteen years between 1977 and 1992 women's share of administrative and foreign service personnel more than doubled from 21 to 45 percent, in technical categories it tripled from 16 to 50 percent, and in executive and senior management positions it rose from no representation to 16 and 18 percent, respectively.

Personnel data from the agencies indicate some common patterns. Despite improvements in the last two decades, the pyramidal pattern of women's representation—concentration at the bottom and declining presence at higher grades—still holds for all the agencies. The improvement in women's participation in field positions, either as regular staff or as experts, is much slower than in the headquarters jobs; women's representation is also particularly low in senior management categories.

While WID advocates within agencies have emphasized women's share of agency posts as an indicator of mainstreaming, feminists in the women's movement, particularly from the South, have pointed out the limitations of simple body counts, arguing that advancing women's careers and advancing a women's agenda within agencies were two different objectives—there might not be a strong link between the two. Having more women professionals and managers would not necessarily result in making the agencies operationally more gender-sensitive.

WID Assistance

The two bilateral donors, following OECD/DAC/WID's statistical classification format, reported their WID assistance, which amounted to approximately 20 percent of their development assistance, most of which was "WID-integrated."[23] The two multilateral agencies, by contrast, did not adopt any statistical reporting format for their WID budgets, and hence it was not possible to calculate their WID assistance. In both NORAD and CIDA, social sectors have generally fared better in mainstreaming WID assistance, though some of the economic sectors such as rural development and banking in NORAD appear to have a fair amount of success at mainstreaming resources. Surprisingly, education and agriculture, two sectors of vital importance for women, have not shown much progress in increased WID assistance in either of the two agencies.

While a greater proportion of assistance can be classified under WID, agencies have generally allocated a much smaller WID-specific budget. For example, in NORAD special WID funds are less than half the size of the special environment funds and the special AIDS grant. It is interesting to note that though a concern with the environment emerged within agencies much later than WID, the agencies started their environmental work with a much greater financial allocation than they did with WID.

As with women's share of personnel, use of WID budgets as an indicator of progress faced some criticism. The protagonists argued that since in the final analysis it is the budget that defines priorities and commitment, a WID budget classification is a powerful monitoring tool in the hands of managers within agencies and governments: an increased share of assistance indicates the agency's commitment to WID. But the critics pointed out the imperfections of the methodology. For example, that a large portion of the aid budget was not people-oriented and hence fell outside the purview of the WID budget classification. They also argued that a simple money count, like the body count in personnel, did not give any clear idea about the progress of a women's agenda.

MAINSTREAMING GENDER ISSUES IN THE DEVELOPMENT DISCOURSE

Early in the 1970s, WID advocates identified invisibility and marginalization as major barriers to women's equality. In the 1950s and 1960s, development literature and agency documents simply did not refer to gender differentials. It was assumed that men and women benefited equally from development.

Visibility

Gaining visibility and avoiding marginalization thus became a key concern of WID advocates. Within agencies, a conscious strategy was adopted to make gender issues as visible as possible in agency documents. Visibility as well as integration was sought through multiple means: separate WID reports or sections in agency reports, raising gender issues in macro and sectoral policy discussions, pictorial display of women in productive activities, case studies highlighting "success stories" of working with women, and so on. As a result of these multi-pronged efforts, gender issues have become increasingly visible in donor agency documents since the 1980s. The annual reports of the donors generally included a separate WID section, and increasingly the donors made an effort to raise gender issues in macro and sectoral policy discussions. WID/GAD was accorded the status of a priority theme by at least three of the four donors: NORAD, CIDA, and UNDP. The use of women's photographs and case studies of women's initiatives grew dramatically in agency publicity materials. Indeed, it often appeared that poor women from the South were rendered visible in order to sell "development" in the same way that glamorous women models are used to sell commercial products.

Over the years in all agency documents gender issues have gained visibility and sectoral policy debates have increasingly become gender sensitive. The most significant progress was in the recognition of women's economic roles and contributions. In the donors' development discourses in the 1970s, women were portrayed only in their reproductive roles, as mothers and as a disadvantaged group needing welfare benefits. But now women's growing responsibility as the sole or primary income-earners of their families are openly acknowledged. Data about female-headed households, showing that up to a third of households are headed by women, have gained visibility. Women's roles in agriculture and in providing household food security are by now well documented.[24] There is open acknowledgment that donors' policies and practices, by ignoring women's roles in agriculture and targeting resources to men, have contributed to economic disasters, particularly in Africa. Women's contributions, especially in manufacturing and export-oriented industries, have also drawn widespread attention in recent years.[25] Women's roles in various economic sectors—such as micro enterprises, energy, infrastructure, urban and rural development, employment, and natural resources management—have similarly gained acceptance within agencies.[26]

Integration

To avoid marginalization, WID advocates within agencies have attempted to integrate discussion of gender issues under relevant sections of agency documents. Again they have gained some success. For example, in addition to the mandatory WID section, NORAD's 1990–1991 aid review presented to OECD/DAC mainstreamed discussion of gender issues throughout the report under each sector: agriculture, rural development and food security; energy; health and population; and natural resources management and environment. WID was listed as one of the six priority areas of assistance.

CIDA's reports to OECD/DAC indicated similar attempts to mainstream gender issues. For example, its 1988–1989 aid review, in addition to the WID section, referred to gender issues under the sectoral theme of agriculture, rural development and food security; identified WID as one of the six priority themes of assistance; and noted that 35 percent of projects met all WID requirements—an improvement from the previous year, when 24 percent of projects met such requirements.

UNDP's annual publication, *Human Development Report,* consistently mainstreamed gender issues in the discussion. The creation of the gender-disaggregated human development index and presentation of gender-disaggregated human development data had been a very imaginative tool to measure progress toward gender equality. In contrast, the World Bank's annual development reports had not made any effort to highlight gender issues in the discussion. For example, the *World Development Report of 1992,* which focused on the environment, completely ignored women's roles in natural resource management.

Agenda Setting

There was also slow progress toward agenda-setting. In the 1980s and 1990s, social-sector analysis, which had traditionally highlighted women's concerns, turned more consciously toward an agenda-setting approach. The exclusive focus on women as mothers gradually shifted to a human-development and human-rights perspective.

It is not clear, however, how much of the shift simply reflects a change in agency language and how much has actually been operationalized. Indeed, in recent years the donors have been very adept in co-opting the language of feminists and the women's movement. Agency documents frequently use such terms as "empowerment," "participatory development," "self-determination," "autonomy," "self-reliance," "choice," and "voice," which were coined and are used by feminists. But it is hard to gauge from the shift in agency language how much change has taken place in agency operations. Evidence from field-level assessment is needed to judge whether the changes in agency language reflects only rhetorical shifts or implies real changes in policies, programs, and investment.

Agency discourses have slowly embraced evidence from research and action projects about women's actual and potential economic contributions, but their policy debates and prescriptions have not yet given commensurate weight to removing gender-specific barriers to women's equal participation. The donor agencies not only underemphasized the issue of the cost of reproductive labor, they also did not focus on some other key gender-specific constraints: for example, the lack of property rights, particularly the right to inherit agricultural land.

Conclusion

The Fourth World Conference on Women (FWCW) held in Beijing in 1995 generated unprecedented enthusiasm among the world's women. They were energized by the Beijing process that attempted to link the grassroots with the international. But the reluctance of the global community at Beijing to pledge additional resources for women indicated that the policies of donor agencies would not change dramatically in the foreseeable future. Under pressure of cost cutting, the agencies would have to expand their work while maintaining or reducing their current level of staff and budget. In the name of mainstreaming there would probably be a push to promote a few women in managerial positions in the donor agencies, but the thrust of operational programs would remain the same.

Notes

1. For more details see Rounaq Jahan, *The Elusive Agenda: Mainstreaming Women in Development* (London: Zed Books, 1995).

2. Rounaq Jahan, "Mainstreaming Women in Development in Different Settings," paper presented at Mainstreaming Women in Development seminar organized by OECD/DAC/WID Expert Group, Paris, 18–19 May 1992.

3. The Royal Norwegian Ministry of Development Cooperation, *Norway's Strategy for Assistance to Women in Development* (Oslo: NORAD, 1985), pp. 5–6.

4. Canadian International Development Agency, *CIDA's Women in Development Program,* Evaluation Assessment Report, Annex 2 (Ottawa: CIDA, December 1990).

5. Canadian International Development Agency, *Women in Development and Gender Equity,* Administrative Notice No. 92–26 (Ottawa: CIDA, 21 April 1992), p. 1.

6. United Nations Development Program, *Women in Development, Policy and Procedures* (New York: UNDP, 17 November 1987).

7. The World Bank, *Enhancing Women's Participation in Economic Development* (Washington, D.C.: World Bank, 1994).

8. The World Bank, *Women in Development: A Progress Report on the World Bank Initiative* (Washington, D.C.: World Bank, 1990), p. 1.

9. Canadian International Development Agency, *Gender as a Cross-Cutting Theme in Development Assistance—An Evaluation of Canadian International Development Agency's WID Policy and Activities, 1984–1992,* Executive Summary (Ottawa: CIDA, July 1993), p. 11.

10. Ibid.

11. Organization for Economic Cooperation and Development/Development Assistance Ccommittee, *Methodology for Statistical Reporting of Women Oriented Aid Activities* (Paris: OECD/DAC, 1989), pp. 3–4.

12. Zulia Z. Paton, *WID as a Cross-Cutting Issue in Development Aid Evaluation* (Ottawa: CIDA, 1994).

13. United Nations Development Program, *Women in United Nations Development Program Supported Projects: A Review of How United Nations Development Program Project Evaluations Deal with Gender Issues* (New York: UNDP, May 1987).

14. Canadian International Development Agency, *Annual Report of the WID Steering Committee to the President's Committee* (Ottowa: CIDA, 1988–1989, 1989–1990, 1990–1991).

15. Canadian International Development Agency, *Gender as a Cross-Cutting Theme.*

16. United Nations Development Program, "Analysis of the Field Office Response to Women in Development Questionnaire," 1990, mimeo.

17. Mayra Buvinic, "Projects for Women in the Third World: Explaining their Misbehavior," *World Development,* vol. 14, no. 5 (1986): 653–664.

18. Canadian International Development Agency, *Gender as a Cross-cutting Theme.*

19. United Nations Development Program, "Analysis of the Field Office Response."

20. Diane Elson, "Gender Issues in Development Strategies," paper presented at Integration of Women in Development seminar, Vienna, 9–11 December 1991.

21. Canadian International Development Agency, *Gender as a Cross-Cutting Theme*.

22. Rounaq Jahan, *The Elusive Agenda*.

23. Ibid.

24. United Nations, *The 1989 World Survey on the Role of Women in Development* (New York: UN, 1989).

25. Ibid.

26. Ibid.

Conclusion

16/Strategies for the Future

Kathleen Staudt and Kristen Timothy

The diverse contributions in this collection reveal the bureaucratic mire women's policies and programs are still in, a phenomenon that transcends political and institutional contexts of various ideological stripes. Where data are available, we know that no more than 15 percent of funds are allocated—a magical ceiling that stunts the gender redistribution of resources. Feminist staff on the inside and constituencies on the outside range from nonexistent to barely audible. Yet they sometimes are heard, seize an opening, ally with other forces, and solidify places on the institutional agenda. We are, in other words, in transition, but the transition is a murky one—so murky that some activists cannot even use the word *feminist*. Gendered bureaucratic resistance, however, can no longer be discussed in absolutist terms.

Under what conditions do bureaucracies begin to empower women whom they are supposed to serve? In this closing essay, focus is placed on the three factors highlighted in the introduction: the engulfing statist apparatus; bureaucratic structures and staff, including gender imbalance; and constituencies outside the official apparatus. Following that, research questions are posed for this valid, crucial, but thoroughly underexamined part of the political process. The conclusion raises questions about our world of disparate resources and opportunities.

State Apparatus

International agencies exist in an amorphous world of states, private organizations, and the United Nations. National agencies, however, operate inside a state apparatus that facilitates or hinders their work in intricate ways.

The analysis herein represents the authors' views, not the official view of the United Nations.

Both Brazil and Nicaragua appear to have moved furthest in institutionalizing a feminist agenda into a limited number of core operations, though they have done so in different ways and for different reasons.

Nicaragua, in revolutionary-redistributive oriented transition, espouses an ideology that legitimizes female empowerment. It established a more far-reaching agrarian reform than its western hemisphere neighbors. As important, people who were once relatively powerless now engage in organized economic and political participation. Finally, women's economic integration jibes with the national development agenda. Yet, with this seemingly firm foundation, women represented only 6 percent of agrarian cooperative members. Some state officials reproduced male privilege as they interacted with actual and potential cooperative members, while others confronted prejudice and provided support for women's participation; dominant FSLN political party activists also articulated women's entitlements. The locus of resistance was found among many peasant men, for whom women's work was invisible or inadequate; some women had internalized these sentiments as well. Yet women's integration into cooperatives proceeded, as the Rural Women's Research Team documents, with profound transformative effects on cooperative process and outcome. Why doesn't the state go further? Will it undermine its base of support among men? Under what conditions will women demand more participation?

Brazil was in process-oriented democratic transition after long years of authoritarian rule. Many women's organizations had already emerged, by class and across class lines. With democratic opening, organizations were ready to fill the vacuum—a vacuum that also contained undefined policy agendas that had the potential to, on one hand, control women and, on the other, empower them. Sonia E. Alvarez portrays savvy political women, both on the outside and inside state commissions on the status of women, who were able to insert feminist discourse into state-supported family planning more successfully, however, than child care initiatives. Feminists found "points of access" in this nonmonolithic state, from which they maneuvered from within and outside to create selectively some "women's space." Early democratic transition was not the same as late consolidation, as dangerous tendencies existed toward compromising a feminist agenda and preempting or warping feminist organizations with a top-down or partisan orientation.

Authoritarian rule is rarely conducive to women's empowerment. For one reason, it often rests on an ideological "family" foundation in which women's labor and reproduction are under firm male control. For another, it inhibits independent political organizations, thus silencing women's collective voice or limiting audibility to sectors inside the dominant party.

The Cameroonian political women, about whom Barbara Lewis writes, affiliated with the party as a women's wing. A "captured" constituency, women nonetheless merited some of the spoils of political victory in the women's ministry. To their credit, they initiated the only women's agricultural project in a country where women work extensively on farms and where the Ministry of Agriculture ignores women farmers. Yet the women's ministry was stretched beyond its technical capability in a political world with little interministerial coordination. Even more devastating, the ministry operated in a top-down fashion without regard for constituencies. Rural women producers had little voice in determining the design of projects that could respond to their own felt needs; to them, state-dependent, collective projects lowered returns on their individual labor.

Cameroon is an authoritarian regime, but political openings exist from a new political generation now succeeding the "Founding Fathers." Malawi's authoritarian regime is a highly personalistic sort, attentive to the whims of an aging founder, an autocrat who on occasion opens opportunities for "his women." Female officials are few, and women's programming is directed toward mothers and homemakers with special health needs. Home economics, an approach with roots in the colonial years, is now a firmly institutionalized, though marginal unit in government; its staff hold different visions about what women's empowerment might mean from those who focus on women's economic production. Yet, as David Hirschmann analyzes, the relations that female officials have with either rural or party women are tenuous. Class and ideological divides separate women.

Bureaucratic Structures and Staff

International and national agencies are a diverse lot, yet we lump them all under the umbrella of bureaucracy. Though smaller and (technically) nonofficial, private voluntary organizations (PVOs) legitimately fit into this category as well. Insider activists pursue strategies in these miniature political worlds but sometimes find themselves stuck with insufficient staff, money, allies, or credibility.

Often out on a limb, women's units lack the leverage necessary to overhaul the larger bureaucratic incentives and penalties that impel the kind of broad agency- (or government-) wide behavior necessary to prompt the redistribution of resources between men and women. They are caught on the inside, by necessity making political compromises that may compromise their ultimate mission. Bureaucracies without women's units often ignore or fragment attention to gender. Such fragmentation may doom gendered "subversion," unless policy leadership or technical missions compel attention to women. That attention may be unrelated to or even antithetical to women's empowerment; the familiar bureaucratic lingo on "targeted" clienteles is ample warning.

Certain structural characteristics would seem conducive to incorporating a female empowerment mission: for example, flat hierarchy, a generalist as opposed to technical bent, balanced staff, small size, and decentralization. Yet a comparison of cases in this volume reveals that optimal structure, or structural reform—when mixed with the special dynamics of gender conflict—does not produce its predicted outcome.

The U.S. Inter-American Foundation (IAF) was an organizational child of the late 1960s. Born of negative reaction to technical, top-down, and bureaucratically bulky foreign assistance, it aimed to reach the Latin American "grassroots" through limited hierarchy and size. IAF's mission was a progressive one that proclaimed sympathy with the ethics of liberation that began to take hold in the Americas during that era. Staff did not see what some called "women's lib" in the same way, however. It took a decade before a critical mass of women professionals worked in the agency at various decision-making levels. Yet correlated with a 40 percent high point of women professionals was the disappointingly low funding figure of 13 percent directed to women. This bears out the introductory chapter's comments on "balanced' gender participation; it affects internal gendered interaction process, not necessarily outcome. Sally W. Yudelman certainly makes that point as well about female political appointees.

Still, the Pathfinder Fund's small size and committed staff, devoted to a highly specialized mission, did appear to make a transition toward greater responsiveness to women. The issue of family planning itself puts focus squarely on women, though "controlist" (as Brazilian feminists term it) and target mentalities have sometimes prevailed in other agencies. Pathfinder's ideological alliance with a "user focus" brought programming closer to a feminist agenda, despite the elimination of its women's division. Pathfinder experimented with production and reproduction linkage in projects, a format that clashed with the method and approach of the funding host on whom it depended. Women's programs that aim to do everything are perhaps doomed to do nothing exceedingly well. Feminists who have the successes in this volume are selective in their strategies and the tasks they take up. Technical specialization is compatible with women's empowerment, but the danger always lurks that technicians will capture and control the agenda. PVOs represent alternative bureaucratic means in development activities, as Judith Helzner and Bonnie Shepard argue, though insiders are as beset with dilemmas, compromises, and contradictions as anyone inside officialdom.

Seemingly ethical populists control the IAF agenda. Coupled with a decentralization that allegedly responded to initiatives from Latin America,

IAF bears out the observation about on-the-spot field bureaucrats' policy making that reflects their own sentiments or mere continuation of past operations. Ironically, top-down directives and follow-up, associated with big, bungling bureaucracy, could provide some incentives for staff to rethink gender assumptions.

The Swedish International Development Authority (SIDA) illustrates how feminist work from within can begin to transform an overall development mission. Various processes worked to facilitate agency action—a Plan of Action, country and sector plans—for results that Karin Himmelstrand terms as not so bad. She warns, though, about a cooptation stage through which WID efforts can pass.

Directives are no guarantee that agency technicians transform or even alter slightly long-standing "normal" operations that allocate resources to men through men. Katherine Jensen's chapter offers chilling reminders of this phenomenon in the U.S. Agency for International Development (AID), under official congressional mandate since 1973 to "integrate" women in development. The depth of hostility that still exists in some pockets of AID is borne out in an arrogant field mission director's reference to "babysitting" in official cable communication. Yet to expect ambitious women—who as Jensen puts it, benefit from but never fought feminist battles—to work for other women under these conditions would border on the naïve. Together with AID's closed, secret-society-like atmosphere, readers must surely wonder: Aren't other means available to transfer "development" resources?

AID's work through PVO intermediaries is an alternative. And AID's alliance with land-grant universities also represents alternative means, though the relationship was born of AID's hiring ceilings and its perennial political unpopularity. Universities, which have large stakes in securing outside funding, populate dispersed congressional districts and states, building a political support base for AID. In this alliance, hierarchy was rendered even more elaborate, down to reproducing tiny WID units and magnifying the complexity of interorganizational relationships. Whether development or university, these organizations are dedicated to using knowledge for rational decision making, but ironically, relevant studies sit piled on shelves, requiring political strategies for dissemination and use.

The mission of the U.N. Food and Agricultural Organization (FAO) is seemingly amenable to integrating women who work extensively in agricultural production, processing, and trade. The introductory chapter cites the miniscule amount of programming directed toward women; Alice Carloni, focusing on the unusual group of projects with some attention to women, carefully documents the peripheral or belated attention to women. She concludes that bureaucratic overhaul is necessary—the kind that gives technical offices the incentives to include women and, in so doing, to manage economically successful projects. Women's units rarely have this capability, but even if they did, the spread of accountability is not necessarily in their self-interest as visible, thriving, or even surviving units.

The World Bank's mission and staff of economists make it the "worst-case scenario" among resistant organizations in this collection. As Nüket Kardam analyzes, bank economists see no particular connection between empowerment and their central missions: increasing economic productivity and returns on investment. Economists have never understood women's work outside the wage economy very well; they have long been able to count people and the costs of children, however. It is through blinders like these that the bank views women. The bank's women's unit always emphasized an integrationist approach but was historically so understaffed and underresourced that it could barely influence any internal processes. More recently, changes in women's unit staff and structure appear to increase internal credibility, though Safe Motherhood—certainly a worthy campaign issue of concern to women—is not among the bank's core concerns.

What sorts of strategies will initiate the overhaul of bureaucracy? The brief IAF-Pathfinder comparison overturns some common assumptions about optimal bureaucratic structures that could serve progressive intents. No easy conclusions can be drawn about what works best to redistribute resources between men and women and, ultimately, to empower women. At this point, there is no substitute for "casing out" each organization, within its state or international context.

Contributors have surely raised skepticism, however, about the effectiveness of women's units within bureaucracy. Rather than advocating wholesale the creation of women's "machinery," as has been historically common in the United Nations, feminists need to advocate women's structural representation in contexts that facilitate first, connection to and authority over other technical units and agencies; second, majority feminist staffing; and third, accountability to outside feminist constituencies. Otherwise, a women's unit can become, on the one hand, a "bureaucratic ornament" (as some Brazilian feminists note), a statist device to define and preempt women's organizations or, on the other, an easy target for demise, for the threat it provokes to the historic institutionalization of male privilege.

Constituencies

The international agencies discussed in this collection reveal very little attentiveness to constituencies, whether in their own political context or the contexts of those they support with resources. IAF made a conscious decision to avoid political entanglements, understandably, for the sometimes short-term or self-interested distortions they could bring to IAF's mission. Yet IAF certainly needed political "protection" in the early 1980s. Perhaps feminist constituencies could have helped "protect" IAF's liberation mission from its inception.

U.N. agencies display even less connectedness to political constituencies, for they are not accountable to them with any democratic semblance. They respond to nation-states ("borrower governments," as the World Bank terms them), to funders, to the paper-laden, byzantine U.N. world of resolutions and mandates, and to the realization that they must project a good image, like any large institution, public or private. "Window dressing" on women comes cheap, as cheap as one and a half professionals amid a technical cast of thousands.

The states with which U.N. organizations interact do make a difference; the combination of technically uninterested staff and government officials who snicker when women are mentioned is a devastating one. Yet support is there, even weakly institutionalized in the numerous women's bureaus and ministries whose connections with other ministries are obviously tenuous. At one or another of the three U.N. Decade for Women conferences in 1975, 1980, and 1985, states officially voted for the consensus resolutions to end discrimination and empower women. Egypt, with its women's committee in the Ministry of Agriculture, seemed far more advanced on women and extension programming than the typical U.S. AID technocrat. Gendered bureaucratic resistance is sometimes worse in western international or bilateral assistance agencies.

Most tragic of the failed or underdeveloped constituency relations is that portrayed in connection with ostensible beneficiaries of programs. Fundable projects are not simply plucked from a political vacuum, but are set in as complex a context as agencies within states. Both Lewis and Jensen note competition among ministries in Cameroon and Egypt. Certainly the chapters of Alvarez and Cathy Small bear out the politically charged and dynamic set of relationships that any project or program lie in, whether in Brazil, Tonga, or anywhere. The "international connection" to projects may bring added resources, legitimacy, or credibility for family planning, WID, and the host of other program examples mentioned in this book, but the connection also bears the burden of matching the timetables, internal politics, and feminist or western ideological "taints" of institutions set in widely diverse contexts. SIDA's attentiveness to community power is welcome, but rare.

States and bureaucracy are only part of the picture, as Small reminds us. If there is any thorny complexity left hanging in this collection, it is the bureaucratic mire that women's own organizations are sometimes in.

Usually, development organizations are made up of women and men, with all the complexity that implies for gendered interaction and hierarchy. Rare but intriguing alternatives are found in separate women's organizations where women have the possibility of empowering themselves in ways they see fit. Such organizations, however, are not magically democratic, egalitarian, or nonhierarchical. The U.S. women's movement has long struggled with these process concerns, both in theory and practice, as Gay Young analyzes. Of course, the peculiarities of gender in the United States—only 6 percent of the world's population—is of questionable transnational relevance. Yet issues of class and hierarchy do transcend national boundaries, given women's attachment to class structure and their experience as daughters and mothers. Collective organization is imperative for empowering women to obtain public accountability, to ally with like-minded forces, and to augment their limited resources.

Yet women's organizations are beset with problems, some of them typical and others unique in women's experiences. Young analyzes how charismatic leadership and personalistic interaction in the Mexican women's center led to difficulties in resolving conflict, coping with staff burnout, and facing a total halt to operations. Cameroonian women farmers collectively—if informally—disengaged from the state in order to appropriate their own surplus, though this made no dent in state action on gender. Tongan women's organizations were complex reflections of kinship hierarchy, about which the international development organization was oblivious. The Moving Forward Organization served as leverage for women to appropriate money from husbands and kin for household consumption. In the midst of long-standing class accumulation processes, the stage was set for privileged women to use the organization to benefit themselves. Was this women's empowerment? For which women? The case reveals the importance of distinguishing means and ends, not just for bureaucratic organizations but for women's organizations as well.

A Post-Beijing Bureaucratic Roadmap

In preparation for the Fourth World Conference on Women in Beijing, 1995, women/gender advocates in bureaucracies prepared a flurry of reports to inspire action, to build coalitions, and to showcase at the meetings and thereafter. In that ten-year period between two major United Nations women's meetings, 1985–1995, the reports of many multilateral and bilateral development bureaucracies used politically correct editorial language ("men" and "women") and a balanced picture in their reports for public dissemination. By the early 1990s, *gender* terminology was in place, for better or worse, and most agencies also had in place pronouncements on policies to support a gender perspective in their work.

SOME LINGUISTIC MUDDLES

By gender, advocates meant to emphasize the *social construction* of male and female in its global diversity, the *relations* between men and women, and the lingering *disparities* between women and men. As Goetz and Baden point out in this volume, however, for some women in the South, this language seemed to depoliticize the process, provoking worry that men would once again be privileged in the distribution of development opportunities. For others, gender was just another Northern-driven language shift, a shift according to Jahan, that does not translate well into all languages.[1] But to respond to opportunities in what was felt to be a less threatening way, *gender* began to supplement *women* in development.

Use of the term gender in the draft Platform for Action to be agreed at Beijing was a major sticking point in March 1995 at the last preparatory meeting for the Conference. It was resolved by agreeing that it meant nothing more and nothing less than the Oxford Dictionary definition. This was intended to allay suspicion that use of the term gender was meant to muddy the distinctions between male and female so critical to arguments by fundamentalists seeking to preserve masculinity and femininity as first premises.

Gender training emerged as a movement to fix agencies in technical ways. Agencies sponsored gender training programs for staff to sensitize them to the often overlooked male/female division of labor, power relations, and earnings differentials that impinge upon development program effectiveness.[2] Some gender trainers diagnosed whole institutions to assess points of leverage for procedural and attitudinal change.[3] At 1991 and 1993 international meetings in Norway and the Netherlands, respectively, gender trainers showcased their divergent approaches and agonized over outcomes, such as hoped-for gender-sensitive attitudes and behavior.[4] In two of the bilateral agency success stories on women/gender, Sweden and Canada, gender training was once mandatory for all staff.

Yet nagging questions remained about whether, once staff are "trained," women/gender became institutionalized and mainstreamed, and if mainstreamed, on new terms or the old style development paradigms.[5] Trained staff complained of being isolated and of having too many seemingly competing add-ons to consider—women, environment, social development. The impact of gender training has yet to be fully assessed by most agencies.

At the same time, at the Cairo population conference in 1994, forces trying to appease others more resistant acquiesced to using the term "equity" in place of "equality," thus sliding backward in the struggle that had brought the term equality into general acceptance. As such, it was a slip into a relative concept that had long been rejected by such bodies as the Commission on the Status of Women and was in contradiction to the call for equal treatment of women in the Convention on the Elimination of All Forms of Discrimination Against Women, the first international "Bill of Rights" for women. Eventually the compromise to use both terms appeared in the Cairo Plan. Subsequently, efforts to reinstate equality have been made, and the Beijing results clearly avoid such equivocation.

Language is packaged, distilled, and used in multiple agency cultures. Since the 1985 women's conference in Nairobi, advocates have called for *mainstreaming* rather than separating and relegating women's projects to the margins. But what is "gender mainstreaming," and does it transform agency missions and outcomes? Jahan makes distinctions between agency mainstreaming strategies in her book[6] and in this volume. Those that mainstream women in "integrative" terms do not challenge existing goals and processes. Those agencies that mainstream in "transformative" terms broaden a gender-central development agenda that challenges a growth-oriented, natural resource destroying, concentrated-power paradigm. While increasing attention is being given to a convergence of such issues on the global agenda, including gender, the fever for reform that is sweeping most organizations generally fails to reflect the need for a gender perspective. Downsizing and re-engineering are in most cases decidedly lacking in attention to the need for mainstreaming gender.

PREPARATIONS FOR BEIJING

Several years before Beijing, some high-profile efforts brought renewed visibility to women. Nearly a decade had passed since the 1985 U.N. Conference in Nairobi at the close of the U.N. Decade for Women. Research had moved knowledge forward, particularly in comparative institutional terms. Focusing on the United Nations Development Programme (UNDP), the World Bank, and changes in the central secretariat of the United Nations itself, the Division for the Advancement of Women (DAW) revealed shifts in the paradigms from a development to a rights framework for gender analysis and advocacy, and shifts in the focus of the U.N. intergovernmental body that addresses women's issues, the Commission on the Status of Women, from women to gender.

At the UNDP those who compile the annual *Human Development Report* (HDR) focused entirely on gender for the 1995 edition. In his many speeches, the UNDP's executive director repeatedly emphasized that UNDP philosophy is pro-poor, pro-jobs, pro-women, and pro-environment.[7] HDR staff solicited background papers on topics not heretofore prominent in the women/gender field, including political representation. Only once before in 1989 when the U.N. Division for the Advancement of Women organized an Expert Group meeting on Women in High-Level Decision Making, had gender-imbalanced political power landed on the international agenda. The Inter-Parliamentary Union has also contributed a growing body of data on women in parliaments. The latest information shows that less than 10 per cent of the world's legislators are women.[8]

The UNDP's *Human Development Report* is a veritable competing companion piece to the World Bank's annual *World Development Report*. For "The Bank" (a shorthand term for what is perhaps the most powerful international development financial player), economists' discourse and values have predominated, even in discussions about good government, gender, and workers. As a reasoning principle, efficiency considerations reign supreme in cost-benefit terms that render long-term and nonmeasurable consequences less meaningful in calculations of "moving money" and evaluating money's payoffs. James Ferguson calls the Bank's domination of development analysis an "industry."[9] Moreover, Bank loans are conditional on reducing national governments' size and spending, or what has been termed structural adjustment. More recently, emphasis has increased on participatory democracy as a framework for the market economy, thus combining greater attention to civil society with the on-going support for capitalist strategies.

In a methodical ten-country study, the United Nations Children's Fund (UNICEF) traced the effects of adjustment programs, which nearly always resulted in lower education and health funding, but left military funding untouched.[10] As Diane Elson has argued, the real issue is not rolling back the state, but transforming it toward democratic politics.[11]

Inside the Bank, dialogue occurred about whether to feature gender in its 1995 *World Development Report*. Such a feature would recognize not only Beijing but also the maturation of its former women in development, now gender analysis cross-cutting organizational team, working under a formal policy that emerged almost two decades after it instituted an office, the history of which Kardam so ably analyzes in this volume. "Workers" was the thematic focus of the 1995 *World Development Report*. In it, readers learned that development benefits women, perhaps a surprise to the many researchers and activists who had documented otherwise. The primary source of this assertion was a Bank-sponsored study of six countries (not named in the title) in which consultants substantiated findings for five countries. Yet like many large bureaucracies, the Bank "speaks with many voices,"[12] and muted voices richly speak to women's experiences under structural adjustment.[13]

In great contrast, the UNDP's *Human Development Report* stresses human considerations and budgetary inattention to education and health spending. It ranks countries on a Human Development Index. Several HDRs weave gender throughout their thematic reports. In 1993, for example, the HDR's "people-friendly development agenda" subsumed women in its redistributive agenda. By 1995, the HDR launched two new indicators for those in the development community who are obsessed with numeric metaphors: the Gender-Related Development Index (GDI), which takes gender inequality into account in the Human Development Index, and the Gender Empowerment Measure (GEM), which focuses on women's ability to participate actively in economic and political life, including decision making. Once the GDI is factored together with the Human Development Index, country rankings always go down. The "simple, but far-reaching message of this Report . . . [is that] human development, if not engendered, is endangered." [14] Yet within this bureaucracy, which not only "speaks with many voices" but wherein country programming prevails, [15] divergent activities continue, only some of which mainstream women/gender.

Readers hungry for numbers, or for accountability, will no doubt wonder and ask: What *do* these bureaucracies do for women, in what amounts? Where are the action points, in which bureaucracies at international or national levels, including increasingly bureaucratized non-government organizations? *Can* bureaucracies empower women, or do we give up the ghost of hope? Increasingly, studies oriented toward action aim to make connections *between* the multi- and bi-lateral development agencies and women in various country contexts. Jahan's chapter in this volume compares the modest actions of both the UNDP and World Bank with the empowering actions of Norway's and Canada's bilateral agencies; her book traces considerable consequences with women in Bangladesh and Tanzania. [16] The U.N.'s social think tank, the United Nations Research Institute for Social Development (UNRISD), sponsored a study of numerous agencies that are connected to women in six countries, documenting mixed results. [17] The U.N. Division for the Advancement of Women (DAW) sponsored a study just prior to Beijing that also set the stage for moving toward accountability, responsive government, and women's shared political voices about development decisions.

DAW teamed up with the World Bank to work with women/gender advocates in more than a dozen U.N.-affiliated agencies to obtain information about mainstreaming strategies. [18] Advocates responded in detailed questionnaires and in interviews. Importantly, no agencies were named in the final document, for the aim of the analysis was neither to applaud nor to criticize. Such anonymity also reflected the continuing precarious nature of advocacy inside bureaucracies, advocates being expected to be both loyal team players and simultaneously bureaucratic transformers, whatever the paltry amount of budget and staff they control, if any.

The monograph focused on the culture of development assistance organizations and the institutional strategies to transform those cultures. A centerpiece chapter summarized cases from the "field," the term used to describe activities at the country level. Its high point was the widened gender agenda, beyond work and reproduction to violence and political voice. Yet another important finding served as a reminder of the difficulty of establishing outcomes of bureaucratic action, whether in financial or detailed country-case terms.[19] We still do not have the organizational memory that the first edition of this book called for. Among many recommendations, the report called for "accountability-based approaches" that "shift responsibility from a women's unit to other parts of the agency, including personnel units, evaluation offices, and managers and country-level staff . . . [including] dialogue with women's and women-friendly advocacy organizations to spread responsibility to governments for responsiveness to women as well as men."[20]

Bureaucratic reports have their own special life cycles, distinctive from academic analyses, peer reviews, and publication in more or less obscure journals. After being edited and duly numbered by paragraph, in accordance with U.N. style, the report was internally and externally distributed. It was one among 25 documents to be distributed to an Expert Group Meeting on the "Institutional and Financial Arrangements for Implementation and Monitoring of the Platform for Action" in November, 1994, sponsored by the DAW in its role as organizer of the Fourth World Conference on Women. This group consisted of bureaucratic insiders and outsiders, in terms of constituency representatives and people who had stakes and expertise in international gender issues. The report was also placed on the agenda for the 39th Session of the U.N. Commission on the Status of Women in March/April, 1995, from which it was in some cases internalized and then moved forward to and beyond Beijing, as part of the body of recommendations that influenced policy makers and U.N. bureaucrats.

BEYOND BEIJING[21]

Beijing is now history, but it lives on in a Platform for Action to which virtually all countries (189) agreed, in new networks (people and electronic),[22] in mounds of paper, and in people inspired to use whatever bureaucratic leverage and paper necessary to keep pushing for transformation. Crowded among many reports, but many reinforcing one another, the Platform for Action's recommendations, all 41 single-spaced pages of them, made their way six months later in April 1996 into "Draft Resolutions, Draft

Decisions, Resolutions and Agreed Conclusions Adopted by the Commission on the Status of Women at its Fortieth Session."

The proposed five-year plan of action contains the broadest agenda thus far. Strategists have laid out in some detail specifics from work and reproduction to education, communication, and sexual violence.[23]

Inside and outside official bureaucracies, people take Beijing-level ideas and move them into new settings in government, NGOs, and universities. The UNDP's *Human Development Report* national rankings, including gender-depressed ranks through the GDI, get coverage in media around the world. Rankings over time may be used (or abused) in future decisions about "good faith" national efforts. Pieces of data can have multiplier effects in various settings.

Let us take just one example of multiplier effects close to the United States. The University of Texas Mexican Center/Lyndon B. Johnson School of Public Affairs co-hosted two meetings at which women from major political parties and NGOs in Mexico could discuss in politically neutral space (Austin, Texas!) strategies to generate more gender balance in political representation. UNDP/HDR data were presented there and at the Latin American Studies Association meetings in English, and will be forthcoming in Spanish when published in Mexico City.[24]

At a time of exhilarating post-Beijing energy surges in the outside world, the United Nations itself operates in budgetary crisis. Member countries are in arrears, not the least of which is the United States. Succession crisis also loomed over the Secretary-General position in late 1996. Never in U.N. history have members aligned with a woman Secretary-General, much less a Secretary-General with a strong track record of action on gender equality. Not until the first race that Boutros Boutros Ghali won, were the names of female candidates ever floated seriously for the job. Of course, single women never work miracles, which is why there is so much talk about critical mass. Some have agreed that 30 percent is the minimum needed to prevent backsliding in women's access and influence. The 1995 *Human Development Report* reports that 30 percent of professionals in U.N. bureaucracies are women. This critical mass has also helped propel more women into decision-making positions, but that figure rests at 17.6 percent. The Secretary-General's target for women at decision-making levels is 35 percent by the year 2000.

Yet advances have clearly occurred in the procedural foundation for U.N. action to involve women and transform development agendas in the process. The distinguished diplomat from Mexico, Rosario Green, with a track record in women's issues as well as in other areas, was appointed as special advisor on gender issues to the U.N. Secretary-General on top of her other duties as Assistant Secretary-General in the Secretary-General's immediate cabinet. She expected to work closely with the ever-expanding number of NGOs with a stake in gender.[25] Yet that responsibility has been added to her many other duties, raising questions about just how much attention is possible. Moreover, how much new action is possible without extra money (due in large part to U.S. arrears)? UNICEF, now under female leadership, produces and publicizes startling reports ("gender apartheid") and striking statistics on maternal mortality and insufficient education for girls that have captured media attention. UNICEF only recently adopted a clear policy on gender, including a focus on women's and children's human rights.

Policy action or inaction on women has rarely informed negotiations over loans and grants. But in another first, the Secretary-General on October 7, 1996, issued a strong statement reiterating U.N. policy on gender equality in response to concerns about the status of women in Afghanistan, where unilateral action was taken to outlaw women in the labor force, including professionals and thousands of war widows who support their families. Indicative of progress in mainstreaming gender in the human rights area, the Secretary-General stressed the importance attached by the U.N. to designing and delivering activities within an internationally accepted legal framework.

Other efforts have established the intellectual, rational, and moral foundation to connect women's experiences to basic human rights. As one of us has elsewhere stated: "The real battlefield in the fight for women's equality is still back at home in the context of the cultural, religious and traditional norms that govern our societies. Only by exposing the real situation of women everywhere to public scrutiny can change occur."[26] Women's engagement with national governments, as well as in homes and workplaces, has begun to move them out of the mire.

Conclusions

Virtually all contributors in this volume would contend that we cannot write off bureaucracy if we seek women's empowerment in our lifetimes. At the very least, attention to bureaucracy can reduce some of the damage it has done to women; at the best, it can channel resources to women and revalue their contributions in ways that augment women's collective ability to transform society.

In working with bureaucracy, however, we cannot buy into its agenda. Contributor after contributor agonizes over the ethical dilemmas activists found themselves in. Not the least of these dilemmas for internationalists is the obscene difference between the so-called rich northern and poor southern countries. Without redistribution of the values, resources, and political wherewithal to make and carry out claims in our international order, the few crumbs of new program resources to women in a given state will do little. The goal we cannot lose site of is female empowerment—an empowerment that is not territorially bounded in the world of states that men have made.

Notes

1. Rounaq Jahan, *The Elusive Agenda: Mainstreaming Women in Development* (London: Zed Press, 1995), p. 26. More analysis is now available on the discourse of development, including Anne Marie Goetz, "From Feminist Knowledge to Data for Development: The Bureaucratic Management of Information on Women in Development," *IDS Bulletin* 25 (1994); Peggy Antrobus, ed., "Alternative Economic Frameworks from a Gender Perspective," *Development: Journal of the Society for International Development* (1995); and Shahra Razavi and Carol Miller, *Gender Mainstreaming: A Study of Efforts by the UNDP, the World Bank and the ILO to Institutionalize Gender Issues* (Geneva: UNRISD 1995). Catherine V. Scott critiques the mainstream discourse in *Gender and Development: Rethinking Modernization and Dependency Theory* (Boulder: Lynne Rienner, 1995). Thanks to Kathy Ferguson for her early work on these issues, including the first of two closing chapters in the first edition of this volume.

2. Catherine Overholt et al., eds., *Gender Roles in Development Projects* (West Hartford, CT: Kumarian Press, 1985). This approach is sometimes referred to as the Harvard Model. The Canadian International Development Agency (CIDA) used this approach.

3. Caroline Moser, *Gender Planning and Development: Theory, Practice and Training* (London: Routledge, 1993). The Swedish International Development Authority (SIDA) adopted this model.

4. Aruna Rao, Hilary Feldstein, Kate Cloud, and Kathleen Staudt, *Gender Training and Development Planning: Learning from Experience* (Bergen/New York: Chr. Michelson Institute/Population Council 1991), and Aruna Rao et al., *Gender Trainers Workshop Report* (Amsterdam/New York: Royal Tropical Institute and Population Council, 1993).

5. At the 1991 gender training conference, about a quarter of panel and conference time was devoted to the institutionalization process. Both the Harvard and Gender Planning models mute power and politics. In an unpublished paper for the United Nations Research Institute for Social Development, "Bringing Politics Back In: Bilateral Assistance Efforts to Mainstream Women," Kathleen Staudt compares bilateral agencies, including CIDA, which reports in several of its own thorough reflective evaluations that "mandatory" training covered no more than three-fourths of staff and none of its many contractors and consultants.

6. Jahan, *The Elusive Agenda*, p. 13. Even the U.N. Voluntary Fund for Women (UNIFEM), formerly the quintessential women's project agenda, transformed its own support into leverage for mainstreaming in the late 1980s.

7. UNDP puts the texts of speeches on line at gopher and web sites. Director

James Speth also makes these remarks, for example, in the introduction to the *Human Development Report* (New York: Oxford University Press, 1994). Staudt participated in background research on comparative multilateral and bilateral agency actions, as noted in note 5 above; Kathleen Staudt, "Getting Institutions Right: Crossing the Threshold to Mainstreaming Women," UNRISD 1993, unpublished.

8. Papers were prepared and presented September 1989 at a week-long meeting in Vienna, among them Staudt's monograph on the topic. The Inter-Parliamentary Union in Geneva has been a tireless disseminator of data on women in parliaments. Its published and unpublished data bases were useful in Staudt's background paper for the UNDP *Human Development Report* of 1995 on political representation. According to the latest figures, men continue to monopolize parliamentary positions, controlling an average of 90 percent of seats. This and other papers have been published in *Background Papers for the 1995 Human Development Report* (New York: U.N., 1996).

9. James Ferguson, *The Anti-Politics Machine: "Development," Depoliticization, and Bureaucratic Power in Lesotho* (New York: Cambridge University Press, 1990). In the *World Bank Policy and Research Bulletin,* January–March 1996, p. 2, a table documents how the *World Development Report* is the most widely distributed Bank publication (150,000 annually). The World Bank's "moving money" mentality is documented in numerous studies over the years, including its own internal Wapenhans Report of 1992. See Staudt, "Getting Institutions Right," a summary of which is forthcoming in "Bilateral and Multilateral Aid Organizations," in *Encyclopedia of Third World Women,* Nelly Stromquist, ed. (New York: Garland, 1997).

10. Giovanni Andrew Cornia, Richard Jolly, and Frances Stewart, eds., *Adjustment with a Human Face,* vols. I and II (Oxford: Clarendon Press, 1987). On international agencies, see chapter 8 in Kathleen Staudt, *Managing Development: State, Society, and International Contexts* (Newbury Park: Sage 1991). Although women or gender are not in the title, those substantive concerns are threaded throughout in hopefully transformative ways for a mainstream readership.

11. Diane Elson, "From Survival Strategies to Transformation Strategies: Women's Needs and Structural Adjustment," in Lourdes Benería and Shelley Feldman, eds., *Unequal Burden: Economic Crisis, Persistent Poverty, and Women's Work* (Boulder: Westview, 1992), pp. 33, 39.

12. World Bank, *World Development Report* (New York: Oxford University Press, 1995). James Ferguson also warns in chapter 2 of *The Anti-Politics Machine* about guestimates packaged in Bank documents as seemingly precise, objective facts down to the penny or fractions of a percent. The statement actually came from internal interviews on UNDP, the other mega-development institution, the sources of which were part of Staudt, *Getting Institutions Right.*

13. Caroline Moser, *Confronting Crisis: A Comparative Study on Household Responses to Poverty and Vulnerability in Four Poor Urban Communities* (Washington, D.C.: World Bank, 1996).

14. UNDP, *Human Development Report* (New York: Oxford University Press, 1995), p. 1. The document contains a whole chapter on political representation, with gender imbalanced politics informing the GEM index as well.

15. See note 12. Nüket Kardam's book, *Bringing Development In: Women's*

Issues in International Development Programs (Boulder: Lynne Rienner, 1991), also stresses UNDP's organizational culture, which in taking national sovereignty seriously loses its ability to exert leverage on gender-fair and other U.N. policy mandates. Kathleen Staudt interviewed staff at UNDP in March 1994 in connection with the analysis cited in note 18 below.

16. Jahan, *The Elusive Agenda*. Also see Anne Marie Goetz, ed., "Getting Institutions Right for Women in Development," *IDS Bulletin* 26, 3 (1995).

17. Anne Marie Goetz, on the weakness of "women's national machinery" (to use U.N. terminology), *The Politics of Integrating Gender to State Development Processes: Trends, Opportunities, and Constraints in Bangladesh, Chile, Jamaica, Mali, Morocco and Uganda* (Geneva: UNRISD, 1995). But also see Deborah Stienstra, *Women's Movements and International Organizations* (New York: St. Martin's, 1994), and Sandra Whitworth, *Feminism and International Relations: Towards a Political Economy of Gender in Interstate and Non-Governmental Institutions* (New York: St. Martin's 1994).

18. Kathleen Staudt, "Technical Assistance and Women: From Mainstreaming toward Institutional Accountability," paper prepared for the U.N. Division for the Advancement of Women, 1994, coordinated by Kristen Timothy, DAW, and Kei Kawabata in the World Bank.

19. One of the few published cases is found in Jiggins, Maimbo, and Masona's "Breaking New Ground: Reaching Out to Women Farmers in Western Zambia" in *Seeds 2: Supporting Women's Work Around the World,* Anne Leonard, ed. (New York: Feminist Press, 1995), pp. 17–40.

20. Staudt, "Technical Assistance and Women."

21. "Beyond Beijing" was the theme of the 1995 Association for Women in Development (AWID) Conference in Washington, D.C., which 1,200 persons attended. AWID, fostering "trialogue" between academics, policy makers, activists/practitioners, can be reached at 1511 K Street NW, Suite 825, Washington, D.C. 20005.

22. Several relevant listservers include feminists in international relations (fem-isa@csf.colorado.edu), Beijing (beijing-conftristam.edc.org), and gender training (gender-train@igc.apc.org). A Bretton Woods listserver (coc@igc.apc.org) emerged simultaneously with the World Bank's celebration of its fiftieth year, just as its critics organized global campaigns that "50 Years Is Enough."

23. *Proposed System-Wide Medium Term Plan for the Advancement of Women 1996–2001,* Report of the Secretary-General for the Fortieth Session, Commission on the Status of Women, March 1996.

24. Victoria Rodríguez et al., *Memoria of the Bi-National Conference: Women in Contemporary Mexican Politics,* vols. I and II (Austin: University of Texas at Austin, Mexican Center of ILAS, 1995, 1996), and forthcoming, María Luisa Tárres et al., *Las Mujeres y la Política en México* (tentative title) (Mexico City/Pittsburgh: LASA).

25. Rosario Green, "Statement by Ms. Rosario Green at the NGO Symposium prior to 40th Session of the Commission on the Status of Women," 10 March 1996. Journalist Daniel Shepard focused on "Jockeying for Lead Role after Beijing," *Earth Times News Service* (posted on beijing-conftristram.edc.org, 21 Nov. 1995). Kristen

Timothy is quoted as saying that Green's appointment will strengthen an already working decentralized system because a single or lead agency runs the risk of ghettoization. Timothy anticipated no hierarchical "czarina" of implementation, but rather a continuation of the nonhierarchical collaborative process already in place. After Boutros Boutros Ghali came Kofi Annan as Secretary General along with a new Special Advisor on Gender Issues and the Advancement of Women, Angela E. V. King. She continues to head UN/DAW.

    26. Kristen Timony, "Reflecting on Beijing," *AWID News* 9, 5 (November 1995), p. 1.

List of Contributors

Sonia E. Alvarez is Associate Professor of Politics at the University of California, Santa Cruz. She is the author of *Engendering Democracy in Brazil: Women's Movements in Transition Politics* (Princeton 1990) and co-editor of *The Making of Social Movements in Latin America: Identity, Strategy, and Democracy* with Arturo Escobar (Westview 1992) and *Cultures of Politics/Politics of Cultures: Revisioning Latin American Social Movements* with Evelina Dagnino and Arturo Escobar (Westview 1997). Alvarez's current research centers on the challenges to democratic theory and practice posed by the (re)configuration of national and transnational civil society.

Sally Baden is a socio-economist specializing in gender and development issues. She manages a briefing service for development agencies on gender and development (BRIDGE) at the Institute of Development Studies, University of Sussex. She has worked on gender analysis of economic reform policies and processes, with particular reference to sub-Saharan Africa, as well as on gender issues in poverty and employment. She has also prepared a range of country gender profiles, sector reviews, and other reports aimed at the development of gender-sensitive policies and programs and the institutionalization of gender concerns in development agencies.

Alice Carloni lives in Rome and has consulted for various international development agencies. Carloni is a rural sociologist at the Investment Center of the United Nations Food and Agricultural Organization. The center provides technical support to international financing institutions such as the World Bank, the International Fund for Agricultural Development (IFAD), and the regional development banks.

Anne Marie Goetz is a Fellow (*sic*) of the Institute of Development Studies, University of Sussex. She is a feminist political scientist and her research focuses on the politics of gender in development institutions. She has studied the politics of implementing gender and development (GAD) policy at the grassroots level in rural credit programs in Bangladesh and at the state level through "national women's machineries" in a range of developing countries. She has also researched the politics of implementing poverty-reduction policies in Africa. She is currently studying processes of political liberalization in sub-Saharan Africa from a gender perspective.

Judith Helzner was Associate in Women's Programs at the Pathfinder Fund from 1977 to 1982. Now based in New York, she has worked for Private Agencies Collaborating Together (PACT) and the International Women's Health Coalition. Since 1987 she has served as Director of Program Coordination of the International Planned Parenthood Federation/Western Hemisphere Region, Inc.

Karin Himmelstrand has worked on women in development issues in the Swedish International Development Authority (SIDA) in both Stockholm and the regional office in Nairobi. She has traveled extensively, particularly in Africa and Asia. For three years she carried out surveys in Nigeria, interviewing nearly a thousand women. She recently retired from SIDA.

David Hirschmann teaches in the International Development Program of the School of International Service at the American University in Washington, D.C. He was Chairman of the Department of Public Administration at the University of Malawi. Hirschmann carried out research on women and development in Malawi for the United Nations Economic Commission for Africa. Previously he taught at the University of Lesotho.

Rounaq Jahan, whose Ph.D. in Political Science is from Harvard University, teaches at the School of International and Public Affairs at Columbia University, New York. She was previously Professor of Political Science at Dhaka University, Bangladesh (1970-1982), and headed the Women's Program at the U.N. Asia Pacific Development Centre in Malaysia (1982–1984) and the International Labour Office in Geneva, Switzerland (1985–1989). Her most recent book, after publishing books on South Asia, is titled *The Elusive Agenda: Mainstreaming Women in Development* (Zed 1995). She has been involved in the women's movement over the last two decades and participated in the World Women's Conferences in Mexico (1975), Copenhagen (1980), Nairobi (1985), and Beijing (1995). A founder of Women for Women, a pioneering research and study group in Bangladesh, she is on the advisory board of *Human Rights Watch: Asia, Asian Survey,* and *Asian Thought and Society: An International Review.*

Katherine Jensen directs the International Studies Program at the University of Wyoming. Her most recent international experience was teaching a course on women's work and world food production in a graduate program sponsored by the Taiwanese Ministry of Economic Affairs. She and Audie Blevins have just completed a book on domestic economic development called *Gambling Fever: Community Transformation in Four Rocky Mountain Gold Mining Towns.*

Nüket Kardam is Associate Professor and Master of Public Administration Program Head at the Monterey Institute of International Studies. She has written on international development assistance and gender issues, including *Bringing Women In: Women's Issues in International Development Programs* (Lynne Rienner 1991). Her current research focuses on the assessment of the international women's regime and on Islamic women's organizations in Turkey.

Barbara Lewis teaches comparative politics at Rutgers University. Based on her field work in the Ivory Coast and in Cameroon, she has published articles on associational ties among truckers and traders and among market women; urban women's fertility and employment; agricultural policy, gender, and food production; and household labor organization among West African peasant farmers.

The Rural Women's Research Team was part of the Center for the Investigation and Study of Agrarian Reform (CIERA). *Tough Row to Hoe,* from which the chapter in this volume is condensed, was written by Lucía Aguirre and Martha Luz Padilla with the collaboration of Carmen Diana Deere. Also participating in the fieldwork upon which the analysis is based were Nyurka Pérez and Aída Redondo. The original Spanish version of this study was published in Managua in April 1984 by CIERA as "La Mujer en las Cooperativas Agropecuarias en Nicaragua." It was translated by Paola Pérez Alemán and Phil Martínez with the assistance of Nancy Conover, Patricia Flynn, and Elena McCollim Medina. The preparation of the revised English version was carried out by Carmen Diana Deere, Medea Benjamín, and Seemin Qayum under the auspices of the Institute for Food and Development Policy. The research project was financed by a grant from the Ford Foundation, and Carmen Diana Deere's participation was facilitated by a postdoctoral research fellowship of the Social Science Research Council.

Bonnie Shepard has been living in Santiago, Chile, since 1992, and working as a Program Officer in the Andean and Southern Cone office of the Ford

Foundation, where she is in charge of the Sexual and Reproductive Health Program. She has been active in this field since the early 1970's when she lived in Chile for two years. She worked at the Pathfinder Fund (now Pathfinder International) for nine years, from 1981 to 1990.

Cathy Small, Ph.D. is a cultural anthropologist whose work has focused on gender, economic development, and social change. She has been a consultant for the World Health Organization in the Western Pacific and has worked extensively in the non-profit sector, marketing handicrafts from producer cooperatives in 17 countries and on U.S. Indian reservations. Her forthcoming book, *Voyages* (Cornell University Press 1997) looks at the contemporary global diaspora, tracing over two generations the lives of Pacific island migrants to the United States and the people they left behind.

Kathleen Staudt is Professor of Political Science at the University of Texas at El Paso. She has been an observer of and participant in bureaucratic politics in the university, the U.S. Agency for International Development, non-governmental organizations at the Mexico-U.S. border, and various United Nations organizations. She has written about women farmers and women's politics in Africa, gender politics at USAID, and population policy. Staudt's most recent book, *Managing Development* (Sage 1991), is in its fourth printing. Her forthcoming books are *Free Trade? Informal Economies at the U.S.-Mexico Border* (Temple University Press 1997) and *Political Science and Feminisms: Integration or Transformation?* with William Weaver (Twayne/Macmillan 1997).

Kristen Timothy received a graduate degree in Public Administration from the Kennedy School at Harvard University and in African Studies from the University of East Africa in Uganda. She did her undergraduate work at Tufts University in Political Science. Timothy is currently serving as Deputy Director in the United Nations Division for the Advancement of Women, having completed her assignment as Coordinator for the Fourth World Conference on Women in Beijing, China. She is a member of the Council on Foreign Relations and the Society for International Development. She has written extensively on women's issues both inside and outside the United Nations.

Gay Young is Associate Professor of Sociology at American University in Washington, D.C. One of her recent projects involves the use and improvement of international data on women and gender; she presented (with Mona Danner) some of this work at the 1995 NGO Forum on Women in Beijing/

Huairou, China. Her most recent co-edited books are *Women at the Center: Development Issues and Practices for the 1990s* (with Vidyamali Samarasinghe and Ken Kusterer) and *Color, Class and Country: Experiences of Gender* (with Bette J. Dickerson). She is currently preparing a book-length manuscript focused on engendering globalization that draws on field work in Ciudad Juárez (supported by the National Science Foundation) as well as some 15 years of paying attention to women workers in that globalized city.

Sally W. Yudelman has been involved with development assistance programs for many years as a practitioner, donor, and consultant. She has worked for non-governmental organizations as well as for the government. Currently a Senior Fellow at the International Center for Research on Women, she consults, teaches, and writes about poverty, human rights, and women's issues in Latin America and the Caribbean. She serves on the boards of directors and advisory councils of several NGOs and chairs the board of a human rights organization, the Washington Office on Latin America.